M000307179

Footsteps on the Ice

Footsteps on the Ice

The Antarctic Diaries of Stuart D. Paine,
Second Byrd Expedition

Edited with an Introduction by
M. L. Paine

University of Missouri Press
Columbia and London

Library of Congress Cataloging-in-Publication Data

Paine, Stuart D. L.
  Footsteps on the ice : the Antarctic diaries of Stuart D. Paine, second Byrd Expedition /
edited with an introduction by M.L. Paine.
     p. cm.
  Summary: "These are the diaries of Stuart Paine, a dog driver, radio operator, and navigator
on Admiral Richard Byrd's Second Antarctic Expedition (1933–1935). Notably, Paine guided a
three-man geological party up the Ross Ice Shelf and Thorne (Scott) Glacier to explore and
map unknown territory near the South Pole"—Provided by publisher.
  Includes bibliographical references and index.
  ISBN 978-0-8262-1741-7 (alk. paper)
  1. Paine, Stuart D. L.—Diaries. 2. Paine, Stuart D. L.—Travel—Antarctica. 3. Explorers—
Antarctica—Diaries. 4. Antarctica—Discovery and exploration. 5. Byrd Antarctic Expedition
(2nd : 1933–1935) I. Paine, M. L. II. Title.
  G875.P35A3 2007
  919.8'9—dc22
                                                                                                    2007002312

Designer: Stephanie Foley
Typesetter: FoleyDesign.net
Printer and binder: Thomson-Shore, Inc.
Typefaces: New Caledonia

Frontispiece: Stuart D. Paine, dog driver, radio operator, and navigator, in 1933 at Newport News,
Virginia, aboard the *Jacob Ruppert*. "Furs," reindeer-skin parka and pants, were reserved for those who
worked mostly outside—the tractor men and certainly the dogmen who suffered the most exposure.
(Paine Antarctic Collection)

To Caleb and Olin

This work is an act of love and respect for my father and for the rest of my family, including his grandchildren, who may want to know more about this man.

Contents

Illustrations

Maps

Foreword

Stuart Paine, Admiral Richard Byrd, and the Second Byrd Antarctic Expedition

In 1933, when Admiral Byrd's Second Byrd Antarctic Expedition began, Admiral Richard E. Byrd was one of the most famous figures of a star-studded era. The first to claim to have flown across the North Pole in 1926, the handsome Virginian added to his fame by flying across the Atlantic the following year. Although he was third to Charles Lindbergh, Byrd, too, had a ticker tape parade and remained in the public spotlight.

Antarctica became the world stage for his accomplishments from 1928 to the end of his life in 1957. Byrd moved polar exploration into the modern era, one that employed airplanes, radio communication, and motorized transport as well as dogs and sleds to explore the most unknown part of the world. His first privately funded expedition there, the largest and most expensive in the history of Antarctic exploration so far, established a base of operations, Little America, at the Bay of Whales. A high point was the first flight across the South Pole, where Byrd dropped an American flag. Ticker tape parades, promotion to admiral, a Congressional Medal of Honor, and a movie by Paramount, *With Byrd at the South Pole,* followed. Parents named children in his honor; some high schools still bear his name. So famous was Byrd that even his dog, Igloo, merited a biography.[1]

---

1. See Jane Brevoort Walden, *Igloo* (New York: G. P. Putnam's Sons, 1931). The last full biography of Admiral Richard E. Byrd was Edwin P. Hoyt, *The Last Explorer: The Adventures of Admiral Byrd.* Hoyt did not have access to Byrd's more than five hundred cubic feet of papers, which were retained by the family until Ohio State University acquired them in the 1980s. Eugene Rodgers was the first to use the papers, and his book about the first expedition, *Beyond the Barrier: The Story of Byrd's First Expedition to Antarctica* (1990), presents a different view of the explorer. At least two biographies of Byrd are currently in development.

Not resting on his laurels, Byrd's first expedition served to introduce the second. While leaving Antarctica in 1930, Byrd remembered, "When I walked out of Little America, in February 1930, to go down to the ship, it was with the firm resolve to go back." His reasons, as stated in his account of the second expedition, had roots in science and in opportunity:

> My decision to return to Antarctica with a second exploring expedition was not so much a spontaneous thought as a maturing compulsion bred by the work of my first expedition. Problems of large geographical and scientific importance remained to be investigated, and it seemed desirable—more than that, imperative—to attempt to close them while we still had the momentum of one successful effort, the advantage of a more enlightened public interest in Antarctic research, and while there was still available an Antarctic-trained personnel from whom could be drawn the nucleus for a second and stronger expedition.[2]

This expedition, larger than the first, explored Antarctica through the methods of twenty different sciences, including biology, geology, glaciology, astronomy, geophysics, meteorology, and oceanography. In addition, Byrd and his men planned to look more closely at areas such as the Rockefeller Mountains and Marie Byrd Land that were found in the first expedition. Finally, Byrd and his men intended to increase their testing and employment of motorized transports. Even as the first expedition had scientist Larry Gould as the second-in-charge, this one had another scientist, Thomas Poulter, as second-in-command.

Stuart Paine was a foot soldier, a dog driver, in Admiral Byrd's second expedition to Antarctica. His diary, as published here, is a significant contribution to the literature of exploration in Antarctica. Of the second expedition, little has appeared in print from expeditionary members themselves. Byrd's tome *Discovery* serves as the official record of the expedition, but his *Alone* is the highly personal account that achieved international fame. Thomas Poulter also published a book; so, too, did Paul Siple, who was a biologist on the expedition and later headed South Pole station during the International Geophysical Year. Stuart Paine himself, with Jane Brevoort Walden, wrote about the expedition and his experiences in *The Long Whip: The Story of a Great Husky* (1936).

Apart from *Alone*, which stemmed from a diary, diaries of the second

2. Richard E. Byrd, *Discovery: The Story of the Second Byrd Antarctic Expedition*, 1.

expedition have not appeared. Such diaries enable readers to gain new insights into historical events and personalities. Typically, diarists record entries shortly after an event happens, not days or weeks later. As a private document not intended for immediate or full publication, the writer can be more honest about feelings and colleagues than may be possible or desirable in a published work.

As a diary, Paine's writing is much more candid and personal than his published account in *The Long Whip*. At times, Paine stood in awe of his circumstances; on May 1, 1934, he wrote, "To live almost within sight of the unknown is a sensation rarely experienced by the fair inhabitants of this earth. To actually penetrate it remains for even fewer. God grant that I may be allowed this privilege." Yet Paine also expressed despair and bitterness, commenting on April 1, 1934, "As far as I can see, our whole trip was futile and in vain. We are merely tools for the Admiral's ambitions."

During and after the expedition, others have questioned whether Byrd worked for science or fed his own appetite for fame and recognition. Both were correct. Byrd's was one of the last privately financed expeditions from the United States to Antarctica. Typically, explorers like Byrd promoted themselves and their expeditions to private foundations, to science organizations, and especially to wealthy benefactors. Byrd was extraordinarily successful in attracting funding from private donations, especially the wealthy, from newspapers that invested in explorers as a source of stories, and from lectures and books after the expedition returned. This was the business model that Byrd followed—zealously so. Charles Murphy, Byrd's publicist whom Paine befriended, played a key role in the expedition, seeding stories that fed the appetite of the media and the imagination of the public.

In raising money for a second expedition to Antarctica, Byrd did so amid the Great Depression, which began in 1929. Despite fiscal hardship, companies and universities helped by granting supplies and scientific equipment. A wealthy few—Edsel Ford, William Horlick, Jacob Ruppert, Thomas Watson, and the National Geographic Society—gave significantly. These benefactors aside, most cash contributions came in small amounts. Byrd and the expedition earned some revenue from stamping postal covers for a fee at an authorized post office in Antarctica. However, such support from private individuals amounted to only about $150,000 of an expedition that would cost more than a million dollars.

Major investment came from the Columbia Broadcasting System (CBS) and General Foods. In an era when the radio was the center for home entertainment, Columbia and Byrd arranged for broadcasts to the living rooms of

Americans from his base at Antarctica, Little America. General Foods paid $100,000 for the opportunity to air commercials during the broadcasts, the first from Antarctica. Charles Murphy was to make certain that CBS had entertaining stories to broadcast.

Financing scientific expeditions with money raised from the news media blended scientific observation with spectacle. In the first expedition, the principal attraction for the public was the flight across the South Pole. For the second, the spectacle was placing an observation hut in the interior of Antarctica during the winter months to record weather and auroral activity. This was both a scientific project—as no one had ever done this before—and an adventure because it placed men alone and in potential jeopardy.

Letters between Byrd and Paramount Studios show how science and publicity mixed in the expedition. Paramount Studios, which had filmed the first expedition, shied away from putting money into what it viewed as a remake of the first expedition. Byrd pleaded with Paramount by offering more flights and more drama: "The point that I want to make clear with you is that I will go to infinite pains to get the proper kind of a movie. It is one of the ways that I can keep from being a bankrupt. When I went down before I did not understand the importance of giving the movie men more of a chance than I did. . . . You will find plenty of drama this time . . . from the fact that two men will spend the winter night at the foot of the mountains only 300 miles from the Pole, where the temperature will be, as I have said, as low as 90 degrees [below zero]."[3]

The story had even more controversy and drama than Byrd had promised. Instead of two men in the hut, Byrd chose to go alone and separated himself from his expedition. Friends, investors who feared for their "star" performer, and members of the expedition questioned this decision, but Byrd was firm. He commanded his men not to rescue him or risk their own lives attempting to do so. As it turned out, Byrd nearly died of carbon monoxide poisoning, probably caused by a faulty generator, and arranged, although subtly, for his own rescue. In fact, one of the enduring works of this expedition was Byrd's diary and account of his solitary experience, which was published in *Alone* (1938), a gripping tale of polar adventure that holds one's imagination in suspense even today.

Paine's own diary stands out for its literary as well as historical qualities.

---

3. Richard E. Byrd to Emanuel Cohen, June 1, 1933, Papers of Admiral Richard E. Byrd, box 59, folder 2673, Byrd Polar Research Center Archival Program, Ohio State University (hereinafter referred to as Byrd Papers).

A graduate of Yale and experienced in advertising, Paine wrote well. In fact, Paine periodically filled in for Charles Murphy, the paid publicist of the expedition, and so impressed Murphy that he promised to find Paine employment as a writer after the expedition.

Paine's diary describes both the physical and the human environment. It records frankly his feelings about the expedition, the hardships of life while traversing Antarctica, and his observations of other expedition members. His sometimes negative comments about others is good evidence of the pressures on men living stressfully in uncomfortable and confined spaces that deprived them of both comfort and privacy. At one point, Paine even speculates that some of the men in the expedition may have been social misfits who saw the expedition as an escape from conventional society.

According to Byrd's official account, this expedition was to "throw a geographical network over the unknown areas to the east and southeast of Little America. In scope and range it promised to be the broadest attack ever launched in the south Polar Regions."[4] One four-member party, under geologist and geophysicist Charles Morgan and physicist Erwin Bramhall, was planned to lead a seismic and magnetic survey across the Ross Ice Barrier to the Queen Maud Mountains and then up to the Polar Plateau.

Meanwhile, Paul Siple, a biologist and future winner of the National Geographical Society's Hubbard medal for contributions to science, commanded a group of four who would explore on the ground the coastal mountains of Marie Byrd Land that the first expedition had sighted from the air only. They were to study the geology, look for biological and botanical specimens, collect snow and rock dust samples, record prominent landmarks, and take magnetic and meteorological observations.

At the same time, a third party of three—geologist Quin Blackburn and drivers Richard Russell and Stuart Paine—would undertake the longest trip, a 517-mile journey across the Ross Ice Barrier to the foot of the Queen Maud Mountains and move up a glacier of at least one hundred miles. Their objectives were to study the geological structure of the Queen Maud Mountains and to look for fossil-bearing strata that would explain the climatological history of Antarctica. In addition, they had to map new mountains discovered and to keep a daily meteorological record in high southern latitudes.

Paine had charge of a team of dogs and served as the field party's radio operator and navigator. Much of Paine's diary documents his adventures and hardships on this scientific fieldwork. Paine had to learn how to handle dogs as well

4. Byrd, *Discovery*, 206.

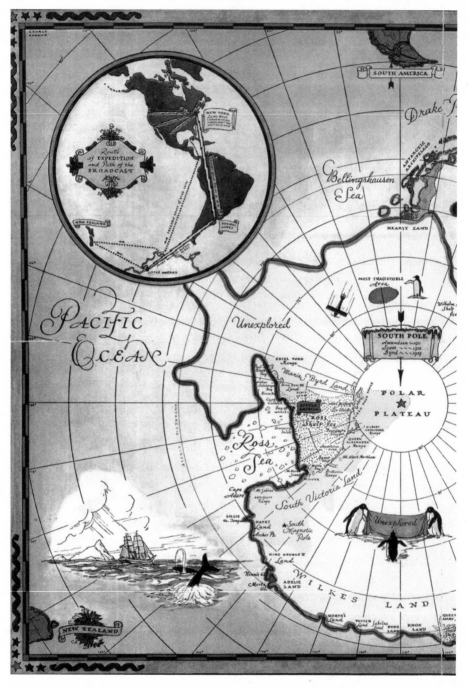

The Authorized Map of the Second Byrd Expedition was published by General Foods Corporation, one of the primary sponsors of the expedition. The continent at the time was almost completely unexplored. (Map constructed by George Annand, General Foods, 1934

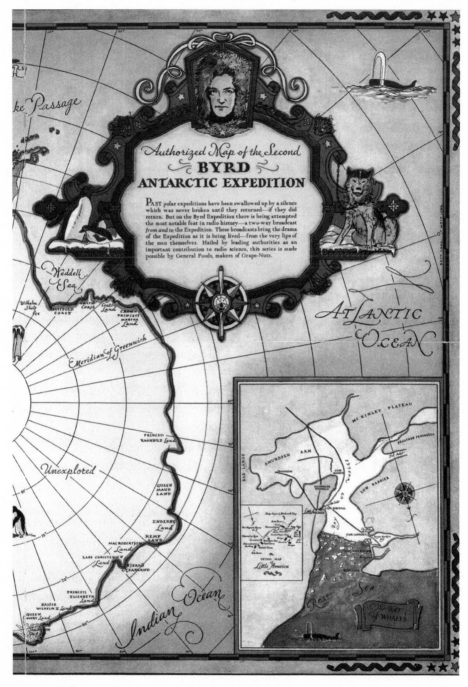

[Kraft Foods], archived at Ohio State University Byrd Polar Archival Program, Papers of Admiral Richard E. Byrd [BPRCAP] image 9260 and General Foods, 1934 [Kraft Foods])

as how to navigate. Pages of the diary point to the hardships and hunger the party suffered; on November 30, 1934, Paine commented, "We are hungry most of time now. Rations inadequate, particularly the fat cereal. Not enough protein."

Each of the field parties overcame life-threatening challenges. They made their way across uncharted lands of snow and ice in temperatures of extreme cold and blizzards, rationed their supplies and foods against the calories they expended, and crossed crevasses that hid under blankets of snow. The tractors were difficult to start in cold weather, a process that sometimes required preheating with a blowtorch, and mechanical breakdowns happened frequently. Morgan and Bramhall's geophysical party used tractors as well as dogs to haul seismic equipment weighing 850 pounds in temperatures below zero. Each magnetic reading took about four hours, while a seismic sounding could take from eight to fifteen hours. Although logistical difficulties, terrain, and bad weather prevented them from reaching the Queen Maud Mountains, they did accomplish nineteen magnetic stations and made seismic soundings at eighty points.[5]

In the end, Byrd's second expedition may have been the most successful of any in reaching its scientific and technological goals. It used motorized transport successfully to move people and supplies into the interior for scientific investigation. Improvements enabled the expedition to use vehicles when temperatures were too cold for animals, but dogs would remain basic to exploration for another two decades or so. For the first time, scientists succeeded in using seismic equipment to measure the thickness of ice of the Ross Ice Shelf and on the Rockefeller Plateau, a technique used thereafter in Antarctica. In addition, the group compiled extensive meteorological data and observations of magnetism and the aurora.

The expedition added significantly to the geographical knowledge of the continent by exploring some 450,000 square miles. Byrd's men discovered that no strait existed between the Ross and Weddell seas and found new peaks of the Queen Maud Mountains, of the Rockefeller Mountains, and on the Rockefeller Plateau. Meanwhile, their ships and planes successfully sketched the eastern edge of the Ross Ice Shelf. Geologists on motorized expeditions garnered evidence that the Ford Ranges had geological likenesses with the mountains of the Antarctic Peninsula.

In other ways, too, Byrd's Second Antarctic Expedition was noteworthy. It discovered five species of moss and nearly one hundred species of lichens on

---

5. The best account of the scientific accomplishments of the expedition is in Kenneth J. Bertrand, *Americans in Antarctica, 1775–1948* (New York: American Geographical Society, 1971), 313–61. For the work of the field parties, see ibid., 341–48.

Scott (Thorne) Glacier and in Marie Byrd Land. At the Bay of Whales, men studied the life history of the Weddell seal and bird life. Meanwhile, David Paige, who accompanied the expedition as Byrd's first artist, captured for posterity the vivid color scenes of Antarctica in his pastel paintings.[6]

For Stuart Paine, this expedition would be his first and his last. He was among the many who left Antarctica with deep memories of the experience but who did not make a career of exploration. For them and for Paine, earning a living and raising a family took precedence over adventure. Nevertheless, Paine always held the awe of untouched nature that he expressed in his diary on August 14, 1934: "I have never come down from the emergency camp without feeling that we do not belong here, are deceitful venturers, perhaps castaways thrown by chance up on this coast. But we do not belong here. Little America, its towers and telegraph poles and wires and smoke stacks and inhabitation are dirty spots on a spotless white prairie. Ugly manifestations of man and his uglier ambitions."

Admiral Richard Byrd returned to Antarctica three more times. In 1939, he led the U.S. Antarctic Service expedition that set up two bases there, but these had to be abandoned when World War II threatened to involve the United States in 1941. In 1947, Byrd was the officer-in-charge of Operation High Jump, an effort to map Antarctica using military ships and airplanes. Byrd was responsible for the limited scientific program, but Rear Admiral Richard Cruzen had command of the 4,700 naval and marine personnel and thirteen ships. Finally, in 1955, Byrd accepted an appointment as officer in charge of U.S. Antarctic Programs in Operation Deep Freeze. The goal was to set up bases in Antarctica that scientists would occupy in the International Geophysical Year, which began in 1957—the year, it turned out, of his death.[7]

As it did for Stuart Paine, the Second Expedition also marked a turning point in Richard Byrd's career, in two ways. Never again would Byrd be able to raise enough money to support an expedition to Antarctica. Such expeditions of multiple ships and aircraft and motorized transport became too expensive for private funding. Governmental support would become the new model for the United States in Antarctica. Second, the carbon monoxide

---

6. See Reinhard A. Krause and Lars U. Scholl, *The Magic of Antarctic Colours: David Abbey Paige, Artist of the Byrd Antarctic Expedition, 1933–1935* (Bremen, Germany: H. M. Hauschild, 2004). See also the digital exhibit at http://library.osu.edu/sites/archives/polar/paige/paige.htm.

7. An excellent account of Operation High Jump is Lisle A. Rose, *Assault on Eternity: Richard E. Byrd and the Exploration of Antarctica, 1946–47* (Annapolis, Md.: Naval Institute Press, 1980). For a history of Operation Deep Freeze based on interviews as well as historical documents, see Dian Olson Belanger, *Deep Freeze: The United States, the International Geophysical Year, and the Origins of Antarctica's Age of Science* (Denver: University Press of Colorado, 2006).

poisoning he had suffered lingered for years. In 1938, three years after returning, Byrd wrote to Thomas Poulter that his health still suffered: "my cardiograph shows that even though three and half years have elapsed since you reached me at Advance Base, I am only two thirds of the way back to normal."[8] In his next visits to Antarctica, Byrd would never live there in the winter.

Raimund E. Goerler

Professor and Chief Archivist
Byrd Polar Research Center
The Ohio State University

8. Richard Byrd to Thomas Poulter, January 12, 1938, Byrd Papers, box 184, folder 6698.

Preface

In the midst of the Great Depression, Stuart Paine found a job in advertising in the New York office of S. H. Kress & Co., a large chain of retail stores. According to the stories his children later heard, Paine took his jacket off on one particularly hot and humid summer day. His boss told him that it was inappropriate for a man in his company to have such a shoddy appearance and ordered him to put his coat back on. Thinking it unreasonable to wear a jacket during such oppressive weather, Paine objected. In a rage, his boss retorted, "Well, if this is too hot for you, why don't you go to the Antarctic where you will be more comfortable!" For Paine, that settled it. With the help of his friend, Kennett Rawson, Paine went to Chinook Kennels at Wonalancet, New Hampshire, where those selected to join the Second Byrd Antarctic Expedition were gathering; he signed on as a dog driver.

Sponsored by the four-year Henry T. Morgan Scholarship, Paine had recently graduated from Yale University and expected to help repair the family finances devastated by the Depression. Instead, the youngest of the five children left behind a close New England family of three brothers, a sister, and a widowed mother in her sixties to explore the most mysterious and hostile environment in the world.

The concept would not have been outlandish to Stuart Paine, as his father, Ralph D. Paine, was an international war correspondent for the William Hearst publishing empire and a prolific author, primarily of daring sea stories and authoritative maritime histories—his father's autobiography was entitled *Roads of Adventure.* Stuart Paine grew up on the family farm in Durham, New Hampshire, not far from Boston and a few miles from the state university. The farm provided a quiet place for R. D. Paine's writing, a large garden, a few cows and chickens, and a wholesome setting for children. The Paine children were reared in a New England tradition that built on its English heritage and culture, where honor, scholarship, and responsibility

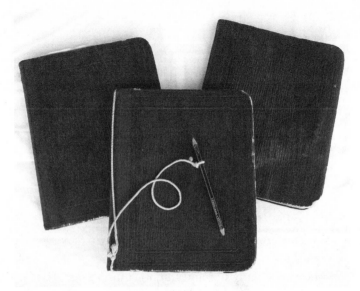

Paine's Antarctic diaries. (Paine Antarctic Collection)

were emphasized. During R. D. Paine's frequent travels and after his death in 1925, his wife, Katherine, affectionately nicknamed "Dearie," maintained the home with a strong hand. But aside from their studies and chores, young Stuart and Phil, his non–identical twin brother, dreamed of their own adventures.

By the time Paine left for the Antarctic, his sister, Barbara, was married and lived nearby with her husband and two children, his brother Phil had temporarily put aside his dream of sailing the South Seas and was working, and his older brothers Lansing and Delahaye had already left for careers in the cities. He would not see them all again for almost two years.

For over sixty-five years, Paine's Antarctic diaries were moved from closets, to damp garages, to storage facilities, and finally to a barren and dry climate when they were reopened. They are in three durable leather-bound books, one with a rough pencil still attached by a string to its binding. Most likely, the diaries had remained unread since their author had put them aside as other responsibilities demanded his attention. Hundreds of expedition photographs, newspaper articles, notes, letters, as well as the diaries themselves were damaged by mildew and insects. Every diary page, letter, and photograph had to be carefully vacuumed before they could even be examined.

The diaries consist of three leather volumes containing four designated chronological segments that are of significantly different lengths; one of the three volumes contains two of the diaries. To aid the reader, chapter headings within the four diaries have been artificially imposed and entitled by the editor; in addition, minor changes in punctuation and spelling were made for readability. Other notations Paine used, such as "+" for *and*, distinctive word spellings, or personal shorthand abbreviations have been retained.

Paine wrote his entries with a blunt pencil, often in temperatures far below zero degrees Fahrenheit and during severe winds from which there was little protection. As seen in the selected pages reproduced as illustrations, Paine's handwriting is sometimes difficult to read, and a few words are illegible. Otherwise, the diaries have been transcribed and published here as Paine wrote them.

To assist the modern reader, this editor has added explanatory annotations and occasional background notes or quotations from other sources. One source is a post-expedition book that Paine and Charles J. V. Murphy, using his wife's name, Jane Brevoort Walden, coauthored, *The Long Whip: The Story of a Great Husky*. The partially fictionalized story uses aspects of Paine's experience but is told from the point of view of Paine's famous lead dog, "Jack the Giant Killer."

Another source that offers important dimensions to *Footsteps on the Ice* are articles selected from the eight issues of the *Barrier Bull*, the magazine that Paine initiated and, with Dick Russell, published during the Antarctic winter night. Like Paine's diaries, the magazine illuminates the context of Paine's world and includes articles written by the men about themselves within Little America and about Admiral Byrd alone at his meteorological station 115 miles to the south. Space considerations have precluded the reproduction of the *Barrier Bull* texts in their entirety. Selections from this periodical have been collected in an appendix to this book; nonetheless, they are of important significance to the central narration.

Also included in the appendixes are selections from Paine's field notes and pertinent subsequent reports of the southern field party. Memorandums, maps, and photographs, most of which have never been published, enliven the narrative itself.

Acknowledgments

My original intent when I first started to transcribe the Antarctic diaries in the mid–1990s was to compile a comprehensive work for my family. But in my research, I met others who encouraged me to distribute it to a wider audience. The following people were turning points in my journey to publication.

Brian Shoemaker, U.S. Navy retired, with extensive experience in both the Arctic and the Antarctic, nearly insisted that I go to the first American Polar Symposium (APS), the theme of which was the "Polar Pioneers"; my attendance at that symposium opened up the world of both historical and current Antarctic knowledge and contacts. Others I met through the APS encouraged or helped me as well; among them were Edith (Jackie) Ronne (Finn Ronne's widow), Bolling Clark (Admiral Byrd's daughter), David Roos (son of the S. Edward Roos, oceanographer on the *Bear of Oakland*), and Norman Vaughan (dog driver on the First Byrd Antarctic Expedition). At the symposium, A. J. (Bert) Rowell, Professor Emeritus at the University of Kansas, the veteran of many seasons of research in Antarctica, reviewed the transcribed diaries and strongly encouraged me to publish the work. Two of his photographs (those of the notes found at Supporting Party Mountain) are in this book.

Raimund E. Goerler, University Archivist and Assistant Director, University Libraries, Ohio State University, consistently guided and supported my efforts on this project, offered potential contacts, and welcomed me to the unique resources at the Byrd Polar Research Center. There, the assistance given by Lynn Lay, Librarian, Goldthwait Polar Library, and particularly by Laura Kissel, Curator of the Ohio State University Byrd Polar Archival Program, has been invaluable to my work.

T. H. Baughman of the University of Central Oklahoma offered enthusiastic support and valuable advice, and Lisle Rose gave me ideas and permission to use his name, which led me to several potential publishers.

Other important people who smoothed the way include Jeffrey M. Kintop, Nevada State Archivist, who adopted the scanning of the photographs in this work as a worthy project and enlisted archives imaging staff Baylen Limasa, program officer, and his assistant, Dan DeMars, who patiently did the finest reproductions possible. Cameron Sutherland willingly tackled constructing new maps for this publication. My special thanks go to Michael Lennie, Esq., my attorney and friend. In the University of Missouri Press, my appreciation goes to Gary Kass, acquisitions editor, for his strong interest in bringing the story to the Press; Beth Chandler, assistant marketing manager and publicist; and the many others who are involved in bringing Stuart Paine's experience to the reader.

The background of the Antarctic diaries could not have been adequately supported without the critical resources and permissions to use excerpts afforded me by copyright holders, including Carleton College, Edythe Holbrook, Island Books, Ohio State University, Richard Byrd III, and the staff of Kraft Foods (General Foods) and National Geographic for their research and images. I thank in particular Thomas Poulter, Jr., for without his father's work, my presentation would have been incomplete. My appreciation also goes to Olin Stancliff's family, who made his memoir available for my perusal through the Byrd Polar Archival Program.

Not least, if my family had not supported publishing this highly personal narrative I never would have completed it. Among the most important in this process have been Stuart Paine's niece, named in the diaries repeatedly, Content (Morse) Richmond, who offered her unreserved endorsement of the project. Active participants in the early planning or research were my cousins Lansie Pearmain and Sally Ford (daughter of Stuart's twin brother) and her husband, Dan Ford. Most importantly, I thank both of my siblings—my sister, Galen Paine, and my brother, Stuart (Doug) Paine—for their generosity and enthusiasm, and I thank my brother specifically for his warm insights into my work. To both of them, I am deeply grateful.

Finally, my husband and personal friends, who have loved me despite my multiyear commitment to research and need for solitude, deserve special and enthusiastic acknowledgment. My friends Ronda Macchello (the first reader) and Lorraine Macchello have both given me their ideas and hearts. My husband, Jim Rhode, has supported my effort from day one with archival research, suggestions, and overall patience and encouragement. In particular, the last year of progress would have been more difficult without his help.

All of those mentioned and surely others who deserve recognition but whom I have mistakenly not included gave me the strength and the spirit to complete this project, and I thank them all.

Footsteps on the Ice

Introduction

The year 1933, and those years leading up to it, are difficult to imagine without reconstructing history. Aviation was in the early stages of development, central air conditioning was rare, and radio was rudimentary. Morse code was the standard mode of field communications, and there were parts of the world yet unexplored, so remote and so forbidding, few humans could even conceive of penetrating those mysteries. The world population was less than two billion souls, Adolf Hitler was elected chancellor of Germany, and Japan and Germany withdrew from the League of Nations. In the United States, Prohibition was repealed and President Franklin Delano Roosevelt launched the New Deal to help combat the effects of the Great Depression. Yet the era that had sponsored Prohibition and terrible upheavals in the American economy also found room to allow a man of Richard E. Byrd's promotional skills, drive, and vision to leave the world problems behind and make a contribution that could never be duplicated—the exploration of the most southern continent. And other men voluntarily risked their lives to explore with him.

The race to reach the South Pole preceded Admiral Byrd's expeditions: both the Englishman Robert F. Scott and the Norwegian Roald Amundsen had already reached the pole. With precise planning and the use of dogs, Amundsen in 1911 first achieved and marked the South Pole; his journey is considered a masterpiece of exploration technique. Scott reached it just twenty-one days later, "man-hauling" his supplies. However, on the return, Scott and his four companions died from hunger and cold within eleven miles of their One Ton Depot, where they had left supplies for the return journey north. Ernest Shackleton, perhaps the most resourceful explorer ever in the southern regions, did not reach the pole at all but is remembered as the central figure in one of the most heroic epics of extended hardship and extraordinary leadership in the twentieth century. These and others like them are the men who provided the background for those on the ice in Richard Byrd's first and second Antarctic expeditions.

Commander Byrd launched his First Expedition in 1928 and set up an American base, called "Little America," near the Bay of Whales in the Ross Sea; he was also the first explorer to fly over the South Pole. The Second Byrd Expedition of 1933–1935, the focus of Stuart Paine's diaries and the last major, privately funded expedition to the Antarctic, bridged the heroic era of Shackleton and Scott and the government-sponsored mechanized age of exploration that began in 1939. In Byrd's words, "dogs still were the infantry of polar exploration."

Building on the work completed on the 1928 expedition, Byrd's Second Expedition sought to explore unknown regions of the southern polar continent, conduct scientific research, test tractor and aviation capabilities, and map and secure American territorial claims as the world set the foundation for World War II. To further justify his expedition to his financial sponsors, Byrd, now an admiral, planned to gather meteorological data not from Little America but from an "Advance Base" proposed south over four hundred miles inland at the foot of the Queen Maud Mountains.

Transported by two ships, the freighter *Jacob Ruppert* and the icebreaking barkentine *Bear of Oakland,* the Second Expedition again set up in Little America. From the ships the men unloaded prefabricated buildings, radio equipment, four aircraft (a twin-engine Curtis-Condor transport, and a tri-motor Fokker, a Kellet autogiro and a single-engine Pilgrim), tractors (a Cletrac, two Ford snowmobiles, and three Citroën tractors), about 150 dogs, dog food, harnesses, tents, sleds, four cattle, various raw materials, and two empty coffins. When the ships left, fifty-six men would stay behind on the ice. Thirteen months would pass before they would again have any physical contact with the outside world. Even personal mail from the States would be read over radio.

After the ships were unloaded, several field teams braved the indescribably brutal fall weather to set trails and supply depots for the summer field season and to construct Advance Base, where Byrd would spend the winter. The winter itself was spent under the snow at Little America for fifty-five of the men while their leader, Admiral Byrd, was in his new station more than one hundred miles away. The leader's absence compounded the stress of the winter night as the dangerous conditions, closeness, and darkness, with no relief for over four months, changed all of the men and brought out the worst in some of them. The issue of whether to chance a trip to Advance Base made the dynamics among the men in Little America even more intense and divisive. The men had not been told that Byrd may have been in trouble. Paine attempted to contribute a lighter note in the underground community by launching a magazine, the *Barrier Bull;* after writing an editorial in which Paine publicly supported Byrd's earlier order to his officers to not go out to Advance Base during the winter night, Paine was then privately told of Byrd's suspected health crisis. Paine finally was able to convince the publicist to inform the men of the truth. The admiral, after a few months, returned to Little America, the sunlight again shone above the horizon and the summer field parties set forth.

During the 1928–1930 expedition, a five-member Geological Party under the leadership of geologist Dr. Larry Gould reached the base of the Queen Maud Mountains. By order of Commander Byrd, they stopped at latitude 85° and turned east into Marie Byrd Land, which Byrd had first seen by plane. At the point of their turning east, Gould named a mountain "Supporting Party Mountain" in honor of the many men who had made their journey possible. As is traditional in exploration, he built a cairn and left a note in an oatmeal can. On the Second Expedition, as the navigator, dog team driver, and radio operator for the Queen Maud Geological Party, Paine took the first American surface party 200 miles south past Supporting Party Mountain to within 207 miles of the South Pole. Stuart Paine and two others skied over 1,410 miles in eighty-eight days to explore and map part of the southernmost continent for the first time.

The Second Expedition achieved ambitious and unanticipated levels of success. While the drama of Admiral Byrd's rescue has distracted some scholars from the greatness of its accomplishments, the Second Byrd Expedition explored and claimed a third of the continent for the first time, made pioneering scientific discoveries, and in 1935 returned to a heroes' welcome by President Franklin D. Roosevelt.

Those responsible for the accomplishments of the expedition—the men who manned the ships, did their jobs at Little America, and who ventured unaided into the interior of the white continent—faced challenges and uncertainty that today can hardly be imagined. Yet in our current world, these extraordinary men are fading from memory. This story reawakens recognition and respect for those who explored the Antarctic for the first time, when survival was not assumed, and each attempt to reach a goal was accompanied, and possibly won, only with great sacrifice and peril.

Nothing is so personal and so bold as one's thoughts. Written down, they may provide a powerful and sometimes startling record. But here they are. From a time, experience, and perhaps societal values far removed from today's, the voice is Stuart Paine's.

Diary One

Personal Diary of Stuart D. Paine

1

Chinook Kennels

September 27–November 2, 1933

September 27, Wednesday, 1933, Durham

Left S. H. Kress & Co., 114 5th Avenue, around August 27 through influence of [Kennett] Rawson. In line for a position as quartermaster aboard *Pacific Fir.* Interviewed Commander Queen at Station Island. Del's Ford broke down on Staten Island Ferry.[1] Unable to make boat which Queen said sailed that Friday afternoon at five. Took train for Boston following morning. Failed to find Ken + came home over weekend, returned to Boston Sunday night. Nothing doing + came back to Durham [New Hampshire]. Returned to Boston following Monday. Nothing doing. Waited here until Labor Day when Rawson called + made me member of Dog Department at Wonalancet, N.H. Capt. Taylor stopped from Boston + took me up. Acted as cook primarily + learned driving. Been there three weeks + a day to date. Fascinating work + I love it. Taylor, Dane, Buckley, Stancliff, Moody + myself constitute dog department at present time.[2]

1. Kennett Rawson and Paine, roommates at Yale University, studied navigation and also earned commissions as officers in the U.S. Naval Reserve. On Admiral Byrd's 1925 Greenland Expedition, Rawson assisted in navigation, and on the Second Byrd Antarctic Expedition, he was the assistant to Admiral Byrd's executive officer, George O. Noville. The *Pacific Fir,* soon renamed the *Jacob Ruppert,* was one of the two ships that Admiral Byrd would take to the Antarctic. W. K. Queen was the chief engineer of the *Pacific Fir.* "Del" was an older brother of Paine's.

2. At Chinook Kennels, run by Milton and Eva "Short" Seeley, dogs were collected and trained for Byrd's expeditions. Norman Vaughan, a dog driver from Byrd's First Expedition, helped collect dogs for the first and initially for the second. The Dog Department was headed by Captain Alan Innes-Taylor, who had been an officer in the Royal Air Force of Great Britain, served five years in

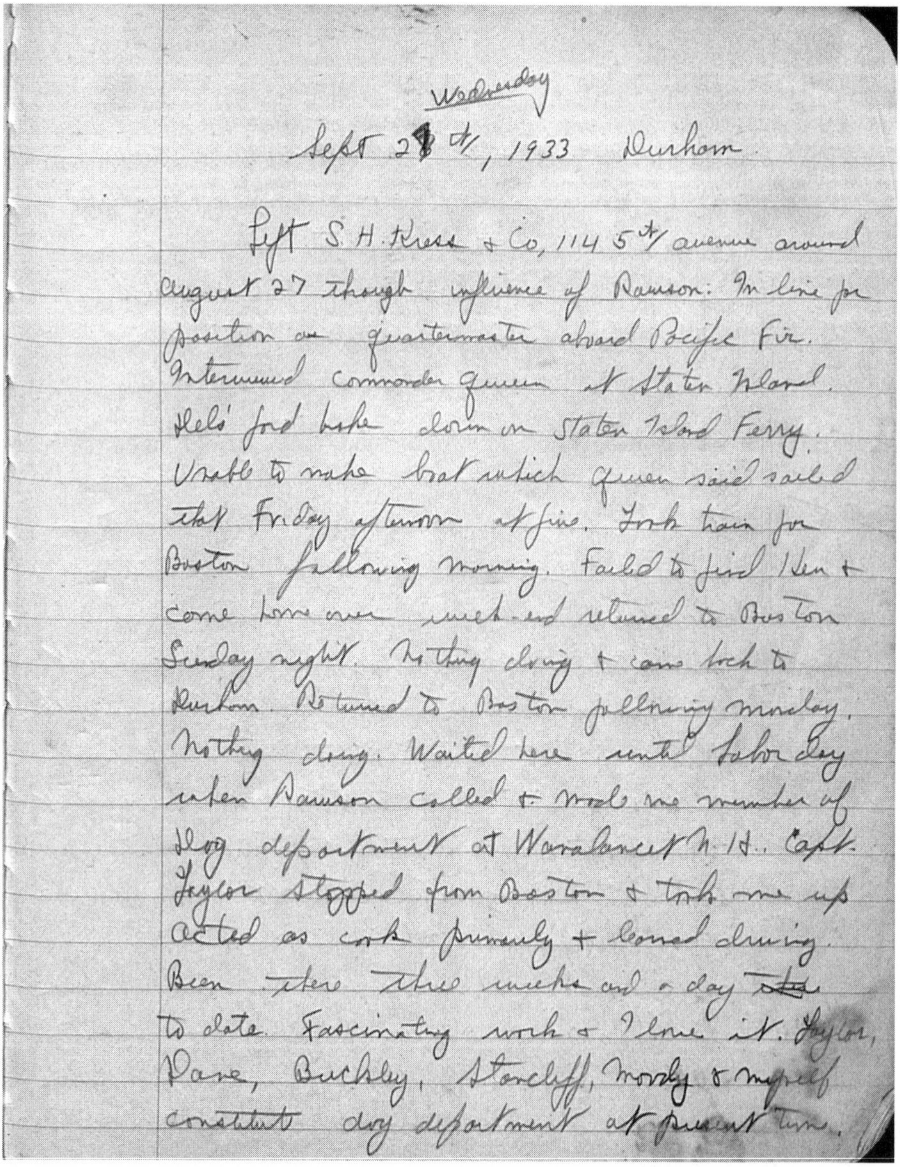

[Handwritten diary page, reproduced as a photograph]

Wednesday

Sept 27th, 1933   Durham.

Left S. H. Kress + Co, 114 5th avenue around
August 27 though influence of Rawson. In line for
position as quartermaster aboard Pacific Fir.
Interviewed commander Queen at Staten Island.
Held food sale down on Staten Island Ferry.
Unable to make boat which Queen said sailed
that Friday afternoon at five. Took train for
Boston following morning. Failed to find Ken +
come home over week-end returned to Boston
Sunday night. Nothing doing + came back to
Durham. Returned to Boston following monday.
Nothing doing. Waited here until Labor day
when Rawson called + made me member of
dog department at Wonalancet N.H. Capt.
Taylor stopped from Boston + took me up
acted as cook primarily + kennel during
Been there three weeks and a day to
date. Fascinating work + I love it. Taylor,
Dane, Buckley, Stancliff, Moody + myself
constitute dog department at present time.

The first page of the diaries, September 27, 1933. Within three leather-bound volumes, with a worn pencil attached, Paine wrote four diaries covering different time segments. (Paine Antarctic Collection)

BYRD ANTARCTIC EXPEDITION II

14 August 1933

OFFICE IN BUILDING 39
STOREROOM IN BUILDING 79
TELEPHONE:
CHARLESTOWN 1400—EXT. 142

ADDRESS
U. S. NAVY YARD
BOSTON, MASS.

IN REPLY PLEASE GIVE DATE
OF OUR LETTER

Mr. Stuart Paine
c/o R. D. Paine
135 East 42nd Street
New York City

Dear Stu:

I am enclosing a card for you for Commander Queen of the expedition ship "Pacific Fir" which is now lying at Staten Island. I think we can start you out as a quartermaster and if you will make good you may be advanced to something more. The pay will be $3.60 a week. Your food, lodging, clothing, etc. are all furnished by the expedition, so you will not need any cash except for your own spending while on leave. I suggest that you take a few weeks' sick leave from Kress and Company and come around to Boston on the Pacific Fir, and see how you like it - that is unless you have enough faith to take the plunge right now.

When you arrive here we can fill out the forms, etc. and we will make a permanent arrangement. If you cannot come around right now on the "Pacific Fir", I suggest that you arrange to run up to Boston to see Dr. Shirey, the Personnel Officer, as soon as you get a spare moment.

I hope this will be satisfactory to you and let me know what you are going to do immediately.

With kindest regards.

Sincerely yours,

Kennett Rawson

KR:HF
Enc.

Kennett Rawson's letter inviting Paine to become a quartermaster on Admiral Byrd's ship, the *Pacific Fir,* which was soon renamed the *Jacob Ruppert.* (Paine Antarctic Collection)

Came down from Wonalancet yesterday, with Moody who was on my way to Topsfield to get Dr. Souther. To date, Noble, Blackie, Snip, Kingmick, Wendy, Wolf, Pete + several others have died from either distemper reaction or form of meningitis. Great consternation. Dr. May consulted + has been up to camp. Returning to Wonalancet tomorrow. Dearie still has severe cold. Very hard to say good-by. Feel as though I were deserting the ship. But she is wonderful + is fatalistic about my going. Phil a brick about his job on bridge + is hauling in $42 a week. His support seems essential to keep us all going. Strange that I should turn out the adventurer + he the capitalist of the family, where it was just a few weeks ago that he was the one going to the South Seas + I was embarking for New York bound upon a career of fame + wealth. But six weeks of Kress + New York was enough. Me for dogs, the expedition + the active life! Sounds dramatic![3]

Thursday, September 28

Returned to Chinook Kennels to-day. Phil drove me up. Got here 1:30, saw dogs + introduced them to old Uncle Philly. He returned about 2:30 after a feast of beets + macaroni. Resumed cooking—rice pudding, hamburg, mashed potatoes + cake which I took credit for. Eleanor Bennett + Janet Palmer here + off with Buck + Moody.[4] Power died to-night. I discovered him in last stages when getting water. Stan + I carried him to autopsy, which was performed by Dr. Souther, the butcher. Some damn ailment, inflammation of stomach + intestines. And I had driven him only 3 days ago. Feel real sad about it.

Left Dearie with cold but with a stout + brave heart. She was wonderful about my going. The Rosary came to her twice when she got my letters about my going + she feels, + I hope it is true, that it is a message from Dad. I am

---

the Royal Canadian Mounted Police, Yukon Territory, and was a member of the First Expedition, on the ship *The City of New York*. At Chinook Kennels, he would initiate Paine (an advertising man), Olin Stancliff (a tree surgeon), Tom Buckley (a lawyer), Ed Moody (a New Hampshire farmer), and Duke Dane (an insurance salesman) into the world of dog driving. All volunteers, the men fed, harnessed, and exercised the dogs and cleaned the premises several times a day. Dr. Souther and Dr. May were veterinarians sometimes called upon for assistance.

3. "Dearie" was Paine's mother; Phil was Paine's nonidentical twin brother. Paine worked as an advertising executive for S. H. Kress & Co., the New York office of a chain of retail stores.

4. Eleanor Bennett was the daughter of Floyd Bennett, Admiral Byrd's pilot on the First Antarctic Expedition, which claimed the first flight over the South Pole in 1929. Janet Palmer was a friend. See Olin Stancliff's memoir, written in 1982, "My Life and Good Times," Byrd Papers, 9.

sure he would approve of my going, in fact he would want to go himself. Very sad leaving Dearie + the winter facing her. I hope to God she will be all right.[5] But what a grand + blessed person she is. Phil gave me $20 out of his wages. I feel 'umble as 'ell.

Friday, September 29

Dane returned from Quebec [from a buying trip] with 10 dogs instead of 30.[6] Everyone peeved—Moody + Buckley out until "after dark" with Janet + Eleanor Bennett. No word from Shorty this time.[7] Stuffed peanut butter into me at 3 this morning + thought it funny. Pooche another casualty. Everyone unanimously worried. Other dogs look ill + no one knows, not even blundering Dr. Souther, what's the matter. Two dogs to be dispatched to Lederle Laboratories in New York to be examined + observed. About time some action was taken. We know about as much as we did two weeks ago when the first dog died. Got word that we sail Wednesday next, Oct. 3rd. Cooked to-night + I am liked. What a hell of a job. And I smell lousy. But it will be good-by to all this only too soon. It has been a swell stay—Sleepy by!!

Saturday, September 30

Six girls arrived + I cook for all squaws. Party last night + I was in very bad shape.

Sunday, October 1st

Recovering from Party. Doris, Phil, Paul, Oscar + friend drove up. Nice to see them. Feel like hell but went to Boston, stopping in Durham on way to leave blankets, etc.

5. Ralph D. Paine, Paine's father, died in 1925. Dearie was left in financial difficulty as a result of the Depression.

6. Of around one hundred and fifty dogs that were chosen for the expedition, forty-five were Alaskans, many of them bred at the Wonalancet Kennels from the dogs from Admiral Byrd's First Expedition. Alaskans were strong, short, and stocky dogs weighing from 65 to 90 pounds and chosen for their speed. Seventy-six or so were Eskimos drawn from the north shore of the St. Lawrence River, all through Quebec Province and Labrador. The Eskimos were heavier, averaging from 70 to 75 pounds and were stronger than the Alaskans. Others included Manitobas from Gimli, Manitoba, which were exceptionally powerful and weighed from 80 to 110 pounds, Siberians, which were small, fast dogs, Newfoundlands, which were powerful and large-boned, and all kinds of mongrels. Captain Taylor emphasized that breed was not important—sledging qualities were. See Jane Brevoort Walden and Stuart D. L. Paine, *The Long Whip: The Story of a Great Husky*, 21–23.

7. This most likely refers to Eva "Short" Seeley of Chinook Kennels.

Monday, October 2

Stayed in Durham Sunday night instead of going thru to Boston. Swell to be home once more before the long trip. Dearie looking + feeling very much better. Phil at work on bridge, so didn't see him. Left early in morning, 6:30 for Boston in Duke's car + got here 8:15. Taylor + I proceeded to *Ruppert* + went aboard.[8] Inoculated the 15 dogs from Manitoba amid much gasps on part of audience + on my part also. Tussle. Have charge of these dogs while Taylor is cavorting around countryside. Knocked down 6 crates.[9] Crew + officers pretty nice but terribly busy + not too friendly. I being a dogman perhaps. Eating in wardroom + bunking way forward, port side, four of us in this cabin, two to be together in another. No lights last night + between the lights + hose for the boat deck, people are getting peeved at me for my insistence. Rawson wishes me to help him with his navigation. Great! He is the good lad + one damn fine friend.

Tuesday, Oct. 3rd

Arose late + got breakfast after Mr. Clark chased me out of the galley.[10] I finished crates + rearranged dogs. Taylor reappeared off + on, not having been to Wonalancet yet, but going tomorrow. Worked in chart house + cleaned it up + sorted out charts—awful mess, like rats' den. Dr. Souther came over at 6:30 after I called him to look at dog's eye. It is ok, an old wound. Studied navigation to-night after going ashore to telephone Lan.[11] No lights in bunk room so worked in chart room. Janet Palmer + Eleanor Bennett were up twice to-day. Nice kids. Janet's apologies accepted many times over.

Wednesday, Oct. 4th

Up too early + have eaten too much of Doris' cooking, but is awfully good + my sweet tooth is being satisfied for once. Dogs in good shape. Hump got bitten through thumb + Mr. Clark very peeved, saying it's our loss if we lose

8. Admiral Byrd used two ships in the expedition, the *Jacob Ruppert* and the *Bear of Oakland*. The *Ruppert,* Byrd's flagship, was a 410-foot, 8,257-ton freighter that had hauled timber along the Pacific Coast. Byrd found the mothballed ship and borrowed it from the U.S. Shipping Board for one dollar per year. Its hull was 7/8-inch steel but was too thin to break ice. The *Bear of Oakland,* a historic barkentine, would act as the icebreaker (Byrd, *Discovery,* 13–14, 48).

9. Crates were to be used, one per dog, as both a transporter on the ship and later as a doghouse inside the ice tunnels in the Antarctic. According to Stancliff's account, he and Paine volunteered to assemble dog crates from precut slats.

10. Leroy Clark was the supply officer and postmaster.

11. Lan was Paine's eldest brother.

Hump.[12] Ba Humbug, they take themselves too seriously. Studied some navigation but didn't get far because of the people who wish to talk to me or ask questions. Tomorrow no one will be allowed on the boat deck if I can help it. I am getting irked. Taylor left for Wonalancet + they [the dogs] are all mine. Duke, with the truck, took up dog feed. Janet + Eleanor down this morning + Eleanor this afternoon. They brought me cigarettes + soap which I highly appreciate. Bill Nelson was down with his wife.[13] She is quite nice.

Thursday, October 5

Up in time this morning. Finished Doris' cooking + eat almost three helpings of everything at table. I am ashamed of my appetite + feel it can only be due to tapeworm or maybe our heleiods, the hookworms. Assisted Perkins + Lindsey transporting food stores from their prospective laboratory to bunkroom.[14] Named dogs. Nero bit Hump [the dog] + he also got a very good bite in his foreleg which I treated with boric acid, licking anything else. Moved into next after bunk room which is larger than the original.[15] Janet + Mrs. Buckley down this morning. Mrs. Buckley sniffed at everything. Tom + Janet down to-night. She is crazy about dogs. Swell letter from Mrs. Brown + one yesterday from the skipper. Find out that he who up to now I thought one of the crew is the captain, Capt. Verleger.[16] I asked him whether he could navigate + whether he was to be the navigator. He pleasantly remarked that he probably would assist in navigation going down. Everyone grumpy at me + curse the dogs. They haven't seen nor heard anything yet. Took bath.

Friday October 6th

Allowed to sleep until 8 this morning. Up three times last night to tie up loose dogs + it made me very mad as I had had a very nice warm bath + my bunk felt so nice + warm. No fights, however, until to-night when there was a good one, much to the horror of the onlookers. Tried to locate six hammocks for Taylor but found Corey has loaded or will load some aboard, so I hope we can get those.[17] But I hate the thought of leaving my Simmons

12. "Hump" was the nickname for A. B. Creagh, who was a cook on the *Jacob Ruppert* and who was also a crew member on the First Expedition. There was also a dog named Hump.

13. Bill Nelson is not listed as a member of the expedition on Admiral Byrd's final roster.

14. E. B. Perkins and Alton Lindsey were biologists.

15. "After cabin" means "aft," or toward the stern of the ship.

16. Mrs. Buckley was Tom's mother; Mrs. Brown was a family friend; Captain W. F. Verleger was the master of the *Jacob Ruppert*.

17. Stevenson Corey was the supply officer.

mattress. Lan down + wished me good luck + gave me three dollars. Good Scaret[?] + three dollars means a lot to him right now. Janet + Eleanor Bennett down this morning + Eleanor + Hilda from Salem down this afternoon. Wonder whether they come down to see the dogs! Supplies being loaded up to all hours of the night + everyone working themselves sick. Captain Verleger didn't like my throwing cigarette butts on the floor of the chart room. I'll have to make my peace with him. Picture in Transcript for past two days.[18] Very silly article. Hope Dearie saw it, for such things don't mean much unless she can enjoy them too. That's one of the things about this whole affair. I'll have all the experiences etc. + I'll have to enjoy them myself. But then, perhaps by my telling them + by whatever publicity there may be, she can enjoy them with me. Stewart Smith of Lederle Laboratories aboard + feels sure it is hookworm which has killed dogs. Recommended they be gotten out of Wonalancet as soon as possible + have dogs + men arrive from there sometime tomorrow morning, early I expect.[19]

October 7th, Saturday

Dogs arrived this morning + no room for them on deck so they sit out there in their crates on the wharf in the rain, though still in their crates. Unloaded them all afternoon, which wasn't an easy job. 15 more arrived to-night via express + Stan + I unloaded them + gave them each 2 fishes. Things are an awful mess + it doesn't seem as though there is a place for a dog in the whole dirty ship.

Supper was bad to-night + Clark sore at what I don't know. Admiral aboard deciding who will go + who will not. I hope for the best. The boys are all here + it is good to be with them again. A swell bunch of lads. Barbara + Tony sent me a check for $25.[20] That means a lot + it was great of them to do it. I love them not for that alone but because they are such great scouts. I almost feel I am a hero between the newspaper men, Janet + Eleanor + the rest of the friends + relations.

18. The *Boston Transcript* was the city's evening newspaper.

19. The dogs were being put in crates, placed on a truck and then shipped to Boston. "Jack the Giant Killer," the dog Paine tentatively selected as his lead dog, was among them. The name "Jack" arose because it was the only name he responded to; he was called "the Giant Killer" because he was both unmanageable and considered vicious. His Eskimo owners in Labrador, who had filed down his teeth to make him less dangerous, sold him for thirty-five dollars to the expedition. The dog was then taken to Wonalancet Kennels. Partially Newfoundland, Jack was five years old, weighed over one hundred pounds, and had slim hind legs, a large head, and powerful shoulders.

20. Barbara and Tony were Paine's sister and her husband.

Olin Stancliff and Ed Moody stand in front of the crates full of dogs waiting to be loaded onto the *Jacob Ruppert*. (Paine Antarctic Collection)

The dog drivers pose at Boston Harbor. From left: Duke Dane, Alan Innes-Taylor, Tom Buckley (rear), Olin Stancliff, (front), Ed Moody, and Stuart Paine (with Power). (Harold I. Orne)

Sunday October 8th

Still aboard *Jacob Ruppert* in Boston. When we will get underway remains a problem but it seems likely now that it will be Tuesday morning. Millions of people on board + asking the most crazy + usually the same questions. I was + am getting fed up with this business + yearn to get to sea + on our way. Loaded, without supper, all the dogs to-night up to ten o'clock. Janet + Eleanor brought down a supper + wine which we now just finished. They have all departed + Dane + I, lacking friends + me, shoes, remain to weight down the good ship. Cow arrived + all kinds of fuss + fumes over the stupid creature. We are to have two on board + it will probably be up to the dog depart. to look after it.[21] Wire from Dearie bidding farewell. But Phil won't get down tomorrow. Boat is filthy + dog manure everywhere. Alas.

Monday October 9th

Moody + Dane came in after dark. Cows hoisted aboard. Girls brought down eats. Phil down from Durham to say good-by. He has been taken on by Crandall Construction Co. + will begin driving soon. Getting $5 + $2 for boat per day + as driver will get $2. It strikes me more + more how extraordinary it is that Phil should be supporting Dearie, Phil the money man of the family + I, who was to salvage the worth of the family fortune, volunteering for a two year job in the most God forsaken land on the globe. Stan + I went to movie + had a bath in Rawson's room. Movie was lousy + it poured cats + dogs on my back. Sailing Wednesday, according to the latest dope. I wonder.

Tues + Wed October 10 + 11, 1933

Missed a day. Last night was too tired to write + fell asleep with pencil in my hand. Day of answering questions, chasing visitors off the boat deck, watering + feeding, + talking to the girls, Janet + Eleanor. Drove up + saw Lan + cashed check for $25. Left good-by for Mr. Hall.[22] Wished I could have seen him to say good-by + so long + a mighty hearty thank you for an education + incidentally for this trip, for it was through my attending Yale I came in contact with Ken + the gang. Several men on board asking for dogs which had died at Wonalancet + it was embarrassing several times but we convinced

---

21. A third cow was later to be procured in New Zealand.

22. Mr. Hall is most likely John Loomer Hall, an 1894 classmate and friend of Ralph D. Paine's at Yale University. Both men were members of the arcane society Skull and Bones. Paine's education was paid for by a full scholarship.

them that they were aboard but were non-findable, the dogs being in their crates.

To-day, 7:30, left Boston at last + got underway for New York + the southern hemisphere. It seems as though we would never get off from Boston, + it was a great relief to leave. Families were there to weep + wave + all tugs + ships gave us a grand tooting on the way out. I got my first feeling of excitement since I arrived at Wonalancet. We were starting upon a voyage 15,000 miles or more long to an unknown continent, practically unknown, + I was a part of it all. It was hard to realize, + I enjoyed the farewell tooting, wishing us bon voyage, good luck, + a safe return. I hope the same.

Middle of afternoon, ship broke down + we drifted for several hours, but trouble repaired + we are at the present moment passing through Nantucket Shoals. The ship does about 8–10 knots + runs fairly smoothly, though there is quite a bit of vibration up here in our living quarters. Dane + Buckley got quite silly to-night + we all had a round of fire water before dinner. New York tomorrow + a trip out to the Pioneer Instrument Co.

Hooray, we are off + on the sea with the bow gently lifting itself + then sinking slowly with the swells. It is grand + I realize that the sea is a very real part of me. Perhaps I got that from Dad.[23]

Thursday October 12, 1933

Late rising after a good sleep on the briny deep. Sea very smooth + the gentle motion of the ship rocked us all to a swell night's sleep. To-day was perfect. Sunny + fairly warm + smooth. A day which, in New York, I yearned to be on the sea. It did my soul good I am sure. Worked this morning cleaning crates until noon. A difficult + nasty job but which has to be done. Helped bosun Voight getting things shipshape + Dane + I washed down decks.[24] Decks actually clean, not like my efforts the other day when practically nothing but oil + tar came out of the hose + the deck was a worse mess than ever before. Succeeded in squirting Taylor with hose instead of Buck who threw a pail of water over me. But all quiet now + all made up. Be damned if they don't appreciate our efforts keep this old tub clean. I sometimes wish we had a navy man skipper. Things would be different. Clark was telling Captain what to do + when to eat. He should be eaten.

23. Ralph D. Paine was an international war correspondent and prolific author, primarily of sea stories and of authoritative maritime histories.
24. Fred C. Voight was the boatswain.

Friday the 13th

Went ashore in Bayonne at 12:30 + got to New York around 2 o'clock. For-tunately Lola + Del had an extra bed + I slept, very briefly to be sure, there. Del was down sick with a cold + remained in bed to-day. They both are fine + very happy + it sometimes makes me jealous to see how happy + contented two people can be. Lola is such an attractive kid + we are all so lucky, most of all Del, to have such a good scout for a sister.[25] Of course Old Delly was same as usual, the old stick in the mud. Though he was very wishful + pup-pyish about my going. I felt rather sorry for him. I seem to have gotten the breaks + he seems stuck in awful New York on Time Magazine when his spirit + ambitions are to wander + experience new sensations, or to be him-self at Shankhassick. If he only knew how much we all thought of him, or even if I may say so, love him, for after all, men, particularly brothers, can love one another with a very true + sincere love. Spent the whole day at the Pioneer Instrument Co. works in Brooklyn adjusting + repairing bubble octants.[26] I learned a great deal about octants + am expected to instruct the rest of the dog mushers in trail navigation. I believe I can help them, though I wonder how much instructing I can do. Del + Lola came down to the boat + said good-by. Oil is all over the decks + the dogs were almost flooded out with oil + all kinds of debris. Sailing to-night, 12 o'clock for Norfolk + so long to New York.

Saturday October 14

Off from Bayonne at 12:30, nearly ramming a pier when the steering engines jammed. In loading oil at Tide Water Oil Refinery, the stupid pumping crew turned pumps on before the hoses were connected + the decks were simply flooded with oil. The poor pooches in the lower crates were standing up to their knees in oil + the duty dog drivers had to wash dogs + crates until three in the morning. The decks + everything about them are a sight + there seems little chance that they will be clean again.[27]

---

25. Barbara, Paine's sister, introduced them.

26. Shankhassick was the farm in New Hampshire. A bubble octant or bubble sextant is used in aviation to find the true horizon and to measure the angle of the sun. Through reference to naviga-tional tables, a geographic position (latitude and longitude) can then be determined.

27. Only four drivers—Moody, Dane, Stancliff, and Innes-Taylor—were aboard with some 150 dogs. To clean off the oil, all the dog drivers later had to wash each dog's footpad first with kerosene and then with warm soapy water. The pads on the dogs' feet were burned and took a long time to heal (Walden and Paine, *Long Whip*, 31–32; Stancliff, "My Life and Good Times," 11).

I cleaned crates most of the day while the others assisted the deck gang in straightening things up. Several more supercargoes came aboard at Bayonne + they do nothing but walk around in their immaculate clothes + curse the food + criticize the conduct of the expedition. Even the members, some of them are criticizing, but not for us, who realize only too well, that we are too lucky to be one of the gang + it is not in our place to criticize something which is benefiting us all. Wade has been transferred from the deck department to the dog department.[28] He is a good scout + deserves it. I was very lucky to have started in as a dog driver instead of having to work up to be one. Wonder whether I would have made it. Thought often of dear old Del to-day, after leaving him in New York, + conclude that I am just getting the breaks now whereas he got them in college. But I feel sorry that he isn't doing what he wants to do + isn't happy like me. Cleaning out crates, strange as it may seem, with dog manure in my hair, ears, eyes + nose, is really fun. Alas! To ever have had the choice to enjoy cleaning up after a collection of wild pooches + to enjoy doing it.

I wonder what it is to lead to, whether this is part of a great plan or, as Dearie so confidently feels, whether it is part of my destiny where I had no choice in the manner or conduct of my life, or whether I am + have been very fortunate in the way things broke for me. I am concerned it is the latter though I would like to believe with Dearie that it was planned + my course is to be steered on one bearing whether I like it or not. I hope it is a favorable one + one that doesn't run me on a reef. Norfolk tomorrow morning + an expected visit from the President of the United States, F.D.R.

Sunday October 15th

At Norfolk tied to Navy Yard Pier One. Constant round of visitors + answering questions + it makes me sick to see how certain members of the crew go after the publicity. No matter how much you like it, there is such a thing as modesty + proper decorum. But perhaps I am as bad as the rest of them, I don't know. Kate Smith on board + got a picture of her.[29] Roosevelt was supposed to have come aboard but he never got here + we were to have been dressed for him all afternoon + evening. Byrd broadcast to-night wishing him + us all bon voyage + good luck including a safe return. I sometimes wonder whether we all will come back. Undoubtedly not, for a thing of this kind

---

28. Alton Wade was originally a geologist.
29. Kate Smith was a popular singer.

involves too much risk for the safe return of every member. His last expedition was very fortunate + lucky. They have loaded two coffins aboard which are a grim reminder of what might happen. I hope for a safe return myself for the sake of the people who are waiting for me, but for myself, I really don't care. Life must end sometime + should it end for me on this expedition, I will not have died for nothing + my name will be remembered, at least for a short time, + I hope + trust with some credit. Enough of this. It is a glorious adventure + the real thing. Moving now to Lambert's Point in Norfolk to take on coal.

Monday October 16th

Ordinary routine of cleaning crates, watering + feeding. Moved up to Lambert's Point to take on a thousand tons of coal + No. 1, 4, + 5 holds are filled. Ship a terrible mess + everything dirty. Lots of niggers on board whom I assured the dogs loved dark meat, at which they all were very particular about how near they came to the pooches. Went off to dinner, the six of us dogmen to a Mrs. Cespinwell, part owners of the Lexaro Co. They were very nice to us, gave us a grand dinner + Buck + I played piano the rest of the evening. Their liquor was simply scrumptious + their hospitality was that of the saint. Later Moody, Buck + I visited a joint + had fun until four in the morning.

Tuesday, October 17

Telegram from Dearie + Phil sending best wishes + happy returns for my birthday. I had forgotten all about it until I got the wire. To-day spent in cleaning holds + I have never been so dirty + grimy in my life. Movie men even took pictures of us heroes we were so grimy. First time I have had my picture taken because my face was dirty. Moody + Buck under the weather but I feel just fit as a fiddle. To-night went to town + saw movie. Move to Navy base from coaling depot at Lambert's Point to-day. Looking across at the Navy skiffs makes me wish I were on one rather than on this one, for it is so dirty + messy + the discipline is so lax, though all of us benefit by it personally, still the ship is not being run properly + in a sound fashion. Sent wire to Phil. It will be a long time before we will spend the 17th together again.

Wednesday October 18

Didn't go ashore but loaded aeroplanes. Up early + cleaned crates, fed, watered early + took rest of the day easy, including reading Gould's "Cold" +

studying Sumner Line. It gives.[30] "Cold" a vivid picture of what we all have to face down at the bottom of the world but I am thirsty to try my hand at it. The old *Corsair*, now the *Oceanographer*, lies on the other side of the pier + went aboard her. What a pleasure to see her + to see how nicely she is kept. Quite a comparison with this sloppy, dirty boat. Too tired to write more. Wrote Dearie.

Thursday October 19th

Cleaned crates + turned to with Bosun in loading. Coffee this afternoon in No. 1 hold until winches gave out + they had to plug holes with wooden plugs which kept blowing out occasionally. Went ashore to see Will Rogers in mime + afterwards played pool with Stan. Plans are to get away Saturday. *Bear of Oakland* lying in nearby pier + she will not go into dry dock until Monday.[31] Looks bad with all this delay. Mrs. and Mr. Aspergren, Swedish Vice Counsel, whom we dined with aboard + gave us card to her daughter in Coco Salo, CZ [Canal Zone]. Lt. + Mrs. Edu. H. Gchelneyer, Fleet Air Base. Wire from Lan wishing us all well.

Friday 20th

Misses Mary Dickson Cooke + Edith Louis came down + had a nice visit + made arrangements for them to come down to get all 7 of us for dinner + after dark party. This was done + all lads enjoyed themselves until 5 in the morning.

Saturday Oct. 21, 1933

Moved from Newport News Shipyard + anchored out in Hampton Roads to take on Condor, which by the way is still dragging at the stern.[32] Dog dept.

---

30. Laurence McKinley Gould, *Cold: The Record of an Antarctic Sledge Journey*. Dr. Gould was the leader of the Geological Party on Byrd's First Expedition of 1928–1930. A Sumner Line is a line passing through the position of the observer, derived from a single astronomical observation. Used with other known factors, it can help establish a location. Paine's sentence was not completed.

31. Built in Scotland in 1874, the *Bear* already had a long and esteemed history. After serving for ten years as a whaler, the *Bear* was purchased by the U.S. Coast Guard, used to rescue the members of the U.S. Arctic Expedition lead by Lieutenant A. W. Greely in 1884, and then patrolled off of the Alaskan coast. It was a 200-foot-long, 703-ton, oaken barkentine reinforced along the waterline with ironbark from Australia to enable it to break ice. In addition to sail power, it had coal-burning engines; the *Ruppert* would carry some of the coal it needed for the long voyage south. The ship had been given to the City of Oakland, California, which auctioned it off (conveniently to a single bidder, Byrd) to use as an icebreaker. In thanks, Byrd named it the *Bear of Oakland* (Byrd, *Discovery*, 13–15).

32. Four aircraft accompanied the expedition: a twin engine Curtis-Wright Condor equipped

Finn Ronne was recruited for the Dog Department: (from left front), Ed Moody, Finn Ronne, and Olin Stancliff; unidentified man (rear). (Paine Antarctic Collection)

Alton Wade also joined as a new dog driver. Drivers Ed Moody (middle) and Alton Wade (right) sit with Joe Hill (left), a tractor driver. (Paine Antarctic Collection)

Another new driver was Dick Russell. (Paine Antarctic Collection)

four constitutionally. Admiral + all personnel aboard to-night preparatory to sail to-night or tomorrow morning. At last we are going. Finn Ronne transferred from *Bear* + is lurking outside in forecastle. Dr. Shirey very drunk + was bitten by Pierrette to-night + didn't know it.[33] All my money gone down to the last cent + had to borrow a dollar to wire Tony not to come to see us off, as they couldn't see me anyway. Wire from girls in the morning in Norfolk sending best wishes.

Sunday Oct. 22nd

Woke up with bad cold + felt like hell all day. Turned to at 4:30 + we left Newport News, VA, around six. Anchored off Cape Henry until goods in holds were secured. I lifted + moved 500 lb. barrels of gasoline all morning until I was stiff + sore. Underway again at 3. One stowaway, Dutch the German engine room boy. Claimed he fell asleep. Admiral came on last night + saw him off + on all day. Dr. Poulter came out [of his quarters] with his governess + 3 kids after pilot boat left us, much to the surprise of all. Pilot boat was the *Gadfly II*, now the *Hampton Roads* + Ken looked very wistfully at her + claimed she was a good boat all right. Russell joined the dog department. Stan + Ed sea sick + I feel like hell with this cold.[34]

Monday, Tuesday, Oct. 23 + 24

I have been put on wheel duty, 4–8 morning + night + I have been too poohed to write at night. We are + have been en route to Panama from Newport News. Last night we were off Brunswick, Georgia + due to sight San Salvador tomorrow. Water in ship is putrid + musty + undrinkable. Something wrong with tanks evidently. Part of dogs moved to after well decks but were soon nearly drowned by the water coming over the side, so

---

with skis and floats, a single engine Fokker, a Kellet autogiro ("gyro"), and a single engine Pilgrim for light hauling and reconnaissance. The Condor itself weighed six tons, had a wingspan of 82 feet, was 48 feet long, and was 22 feet high from the ground to the upper wings. It was to be lashed onto the *Ruppert* deck near the stern. Also to be loaded were five tractors: a six-ton 20–40 Cletrac capable of hauling 20,000 pounds, two Ford snowmobiles, and two Citroën tractors. A third Citroën would later be added (Joe Hill Jr. and Ola Davis Hill, *In Little America with Byrd: Based upon Experiences of the Fifty-six Men of the Second Antarctic Expedition*, 116; Byrd, *Discovery*, 19).

33. Finn Ronne was a dog driver and mechanical engineer. He was also the son of Martin Ronne, who had been on several of Byrd's expeditions, including the First Antarctic Expedition. G. O. Shirey was the expedition doctor and personnel officer.

34. Dr. Thomas C. Poulter was a physicist and the chief scientist of the expedition; Richard S. Russell Jr., originally a banker, was a new dog driver; Olin Stancliff and Ed Moody were dog drivers.

good many of them had to be moved back. Poor JoJo—she hardly reached the surface after one of these deluges + she was howling for dear life. But she doesn't feel the worse for wear to-day. Boys all recovered from their attack of Mal de Mer + I feel a lot better though my cold is still with me. Coal being bagged + at end of day a crew of niggers appear from hold.

Wednesday 25th Oct.

Slept this morning + cleaned, fed + painted this afternoon. Sea calmer + wind dead ahead. Ship much steadier. The 4 hour watches have been discontinued + I go on for 2 hours at 10. Squall this afternoon + we all got soaked. Dogs continually getting loose. It's grand, this sailing the deep blue ocean with the wind almost a half a gale + warm enough to wander around deck without anything on. I expect at home they are sitting before open fires with Jack Frost peering in the window.

Thursday 26th

San Salvador passed about 9 this morning + it looked vaguely familiar + Crooked Island appeared later. The sea was a glorious color, a light blue of the most penetrating + wonderful color. The sea has calmed down + now there isn't even a swell. Everyone has been stripped to the waist + a good many of us are suffering from a newly acquired sunburn. Buckley is blistered with sun + creosote. Dogs were moved out of crates + dunnage was laid on saloon deck + in port side of after well deck. About half are out now + poor pooches are in a much better situation to stand the heat.[35] We have been eating aft with the crew for the last couple of days + we have much more fun than up with the commodore, doctors + other big shots. Vona bit me but not serious. Taylor slinging it all day + tries to dig me with a spoon. Had a hair cut last night almost as short as I have always wanted it but never dared to before.

---

35. While the ship was being secured for sea, the dogs were kept in their crates, however, as soon as possible, the dog drivers used dunnage to build a wooden decking that stood three or four inches above the steel deck. This surface offered more comfort and also allowed each dog to be given a small part of the deck, just out of reach of each other. The dogs were attached by three-foot chains to the decking. The midships, after well, and poop decks all had dogs everywhere, including on top of the hatch covers. Dogs were always getting loose and being attacked from all sides by other dogs. A few dogs at a time would be allowed to run on the open forward well deck for exercise (Walden and Paine, *Long Whip*, 33–34). "For" indicates placement toward the bow of the ship; a "well deck" is a recessed deck between two superstructures, extending the width of the ship.

Friday 27

Very tired to-day. Lack of sleep for the past four days + getting up every night for watches is exhausting to say the least. Day spent in stowing crates + getting dogs out on deck. The Admiral has adopted Carlo + evidently it is my job to feed + water him, the dog. Calm sea all day, like mill pond, + there isn't even a swell. Churning along steadily at 9–10 knots + we should be in Panama Monday. There for 4 days they expect. Radioed Dearie + Del to-day. Time goes so quickly. It is almost impossible to realize this is the 27th. Shirey looks at me in a funny way + I wonder whether I shall be a member of the ice party.[36]

Saturday 28th

Stormy all day, but Corey gave us rubber outfits + the dog department enjoyed itself laying dunnage all day. It really was glorious with the white caps all around, the larger waves slapping against the windward side + sending a sheet of spray over the forward well deck. Occasional rain squalls added to the wetness. All but 25 dogs are out now but those out seem very miserable in the wet. Evening spent in getting hair cuts. Mine was cut last night by Stan. To-night, myself, Moody + Stan were the tonsorial artists on Buckley + Russell, Wade + Healey. Wrote the Browns, Del + Morses. Lewisohn that dumb lubber treated us to Bel Paise [cheese]+ cold beer all around. Sails drunk for last two days + wet bed last night. Eating in Wardroom for a spell + don't enjoy it half as much as back aft with our own department.[37]

Sunday 29th Oct.

Admiral posted a notice announcing a holiday for all hands. So we worked from 3:30 on to eight to-night, at least I did. But at last we have gotten all the dogs out of the crates after their living in those things for two weeks. We have lost 3 dogs largely because of it I believe. Marve is very sick to-night but Taylor thinks he will pull through. Wade + I hosed down at 6 + against orders hosed the after well decks. It is a question of dogs or coal + if I have anything to do with it, it will be dogs. We watered them down several times to-day but

36. Some of the men initially selected for the expedition would not be chosen to stay on the Antarctic continent for the duration of the expedition. Few men dared assume that they would be chosen for the "ice party."

37. J. D. Healey was a *Ruppert* crewmember; W. P. Lewisohn was a radioman; "Sails" refers to L. H. Kennedy, the *Ruppert* sailmaker.

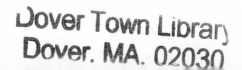

Alan Innes-Taylor, head of the Dog Department and chief of Trail Operations. (Paine Antarctic Collection)

they suffered in this hot weather. Stood a two hour watch to-night, 6–8 p.m. To-night there seemed to be the hope of a full nights sleep, but Taylor started on the fire water + here I am writing up the diary at 11 p.m. He certainly is a great boy + we are all extremely fortunate in having the chief of the dog department none other than Taylor. Efforts have been made to lay the dunnage aft on the poop deck but the awning [shade for the dogs], split at that, was the only result. Crates are all piled on No. 2 hatch + the greater part were stowed below. Moody ok to-day + Stancliff his old plugging self. A beautiful night, a typical tropical night.

Monday Oct. 30th

Day spent in constructing last of wooden platform for dogs, hosing down of dogs, erection of awnings + lastly getting into Cristobal [Panama]. This was done around three this afternoon + we proceeded directly to the coaling dock where the coal was unloaded, 150 tons of it to be picked up by the *Bear*. They had a scoop which handled 2 tons at a time + loaded, raised + dumped

The dogs on the *Jacob Ruppert* lay on steel decks surfaced with wooden planking or dunnage and were protected from the tropical sun by awnings erected overhead. (Paine Antarctic Collection)

in 15 seconds. It was the damnedest sight to see the coal disappear. All dog-men ashore to-night sans Taylor + myself. Taylor on dogwatch until one + myself from then on. Mac sat up drinking beer + now Fred the former Bosun + myself are the only ones holding down the fort.[38] Everyone returning to ship in a very sodden condition.

Tuesday Oct. 31

Admiral's orders to-day that anyone returning to ship in an intoxicated con-dition will be dropped. He was disgusted with the performance last night.[39] Cleaned up after well deck all morning. Such a mess + the same old story, not a person to help us. Perhaps I am getting sour about it. Al [Innes-Taylor] agrees with me. Supper of liver + that's all put me in bad humor + I told Hump [the cook] what I thought. Taylor heard it all + I expect a reprimand

38. "Mac" most likely refers to William or Bill McCormick, the autogiro pilot. "Fred" is Fred Voight.

39. This is the first mention of alcohol being a serious concern; use of alcohol was to become an ongoing and undermining issue throughout the expedition. In Panama, several members of the expedition left the ship for various reasons; all slipped away quietly and unannounced (Stancliff, *My Life and Good Times,* 14).

in the morning. The way I feel now I wouldn't hesitate to take boat back to New York + chuck the whole thing. Mail was sent back to Norfolk by mistake + so no news from home. Came through the Canal to-day, left at 6 + got through around 4 this afternoon. I had seen it all before, but still its marvels impress me very much. What a stupendous task + how many tons of rock + gravel had to be moved before that thing could be made to run! Still there is always something rather sad about it. The French after ruinous efforts gave it up. The remains of their work is still to be seen at the Gatun locks. Staying aboard to-night, first, I'm very tired, second, I haven't a cent of money, not one cent, third, I'm irked at the whole crew + gang. God bless me if I'm right in being irked about some things.

Wednesday + Thursday Nov. 1 + 2nd

Last night was party out in Old Panama in the shadow of the old ruined Cathedral. My girl was very stupid + I called her Standardt after the dog because she was so stupid. Everyone had a grand time. Myself, Dane, Buckley, Moody, being in attendance. Byrd himself we discovered was there too + he joined us for a short while. He certainly is a great scout.

Crowds of people on board, mostly children + they all insist upon patting doggies + it is a wonder none were bitten. It remained for me to be bitten by Phil. He snapped at Collie Penook + got me in the arm. Not serious. Some-one stole my camera + razor. I suspect these soldiers aboard. Hump a continual menace + McKinley says he is slated for the ice. It's just too bad if he is. Slept this morning + to-night had a swim at the YMCA. Later, Wade, Healey + I walked through Panama + ended up by having a steak dinner. It's an interesting city + I saw an awful lot more of it than when I was here in '30 Xmas. Huff drove us all through Old Panama this afternoon + we saw the Cathedral which I so admired last night + the Convent. The walls are still standing in spots, but it makes a most melancholy + desolate impression. Ruins of anything always affect me that way.[40]

A grand letter from Dearie this morning, mailed on October 25. She has decided to put kitchen stove in little dining room with an oil heater in it. That should keep her warm + comfortable. She has such a great spirit + continues to remain plucky + optimistic in spite of the many unfortunate events the past three years. Late watch to-night. Dane + Buckley not showing up. It's a bad example to set at such an early date.

40. It is not clear from the admiral's postexpedition roster who "McKinley" is, nor is it clear who "Huff" is.

2

At Sea

November 3–December 9, 1933

Friday + Saturday Nov. 3rd + 4th

Left Balboa around noon yesterday, the 3rd, for the Antarctic. Crowds on the docks waved + cheered to friends on board + the girls, Kelly Ritz pals, + all were there.[1] Toots 3-long came from passing boats + those at the wharves. We were bound out upon the broad Pacific for sure this time + we face now around 2 months aboard ship without a respite. Watch 8–10 last night + 10–12 to-night. The heat has abated + it is very pleasant now, smooth sea + overcast with nice breeze off the starboard bow. To-day was messman + this afternoon washed all clothes of the DPP's [distinguished personages?]. We have all been put on short water rations, two gallons a day per man. This is rather meager but necessary. Plenty of salt water though. Brutus has enormous hole in side of face + Al + I dig out hundreds of maggots from it this morning. Furious activity on the part of the shellbacks aboard ship for the initiation of neophytes on Monday.

Sunday Nov. 5th

I now have the distinction of being a member of the ancient + honorable order of shellbacks. Neptune came aboard about three this afternoon + took over the ship. For around two hours initiation ceremonies were in order. Charlie Murphy acted as spokesman + read off the charge against each man.

---

1. Kelly Ritz was a public establishment on Central Avenue in Panama.

Shirey was Neptune, Bill Haines his mistress, Verleger as superintendent of the paint pot, Mac as Kitty Charve, little girl.[2] The charge was read off + the punishment pronounced + the sentence carried out. This was a general smearing of the face with a foul + evil smelling slop + then being tipped over backwards into a canvas tank. Fortunately the slop washed off easily + the initiation wasn't as bad as it might have been. The dog drivers' sentence was carried out en masse. Now I feel a man with some yarns to spin about distances traveled + strange places + crossing the line. I'm tired + have to go on watch at 12.

Monday, Tuesday Nov. 6 + 7th

Yesterday spent in tackling harness + measuring dogs. Each dog is being measured + fitted individually. This is the only sure way of having each harness fit. Last night I had all my hair clipped off. Stancliff followed suit + had a friars' hair cut. Buckley looks like a warrior. From volunteer work we progressed to forced haircuts + this morning the crew is certainly a sight. Every man has his own individual haircut, no two alike. I am called Mahatma Gandhi + I can make quite a good one when I put my glasses down on my nose + take my teeth out.[3] To-day was spent on harnesses + sewing all dog equipment. I have learned how to splice + have been working on lead lines. It is the most satisfying thing I have learned yet. Each man now has his own dogs to look after. I have the port side of the after well deck, 23 dogs in all. It makes everything much simpler + easier. Stood watch last night, 2–4, but Taylor has arranged to let us all off sea watches except Dane who continues on for awhile.

Delightfully cool, in fact slept under two blankets last night + wore a sweater on the bridge. All this + we have been across the equator only a day or so. To-night we are only 5 degrees south. What a fortunate break for the

2. Crossing the Equator has traditionally been met with secret ceremonies once practiced to appease Neptune so that storms would not sink the ship. Ceremonies are now conducted with frivolity and each man is awarded a certificate stating their new rank depending on what line has been crossed and the tradition of their maritime service. Bill Haines was the meteorologist. Charles J. V. Murphy, the communications officer, was the only man on the expedition who was on salary, and his pay came from CBS (Thomas C. Poulter, *The Winter Night Trip to Advance Base: Byrd Antarctic Expedition II, 1933–35*, 15). Murphy also accompanied Byrd on his first expedition; on the second, he would prepare the weekly broadcasts from Little America that both entertained mainland America and served as ongoing communications to the financial sponsors.

3. During adolescence, Paine and his brother Phil, who was much bigger, fought, and Paine's front teeth were knocked out; he wore a bridge.

Dog-drivers - Paine, Moody, Stancliffe, Ronne
Dane, Buckley, Wade, Russell

Aha! stand forth, now, you miserable dog-drivers,
handmaidens to bitches, and hear these charges
that the loyal subjects of King Rex have filed
against you:

1 - You have befouled the decks of the Ruppert
with the never ceasing droppings of your
numerous dogs.

2.- You have, in violation of the eternal code of
the sea, shovelled these droppings over the
windward rail. So that no man aboard ship
could tell what next would fly into his eye.

3. You have succeeded, through your diabolical
cunning, in so contriving to crowd the decks
that not even a skilful navigator can move
from fore to aft without befouling himself
in a way that would cause even his own mother
to disown him.

4. You have made the night hideous with the noise
of your beasts, and the days hideous with
their stink.

5. You have required this ship to be equipped with
tattered canvas so that she now resembles a
Portuguese man o' war; and no self-respecting
shellback aboard her can enter port in her except
in shame.

6. You are spendthrifts and idlers; while your
country lies in the grip of poverty, you
squandered money on the fallen women of
Cristobal; from the tallest to the smallest,
you are lecherous and evil. Counsel for the
Crown now has the pleasure of inviting you
to meet King Neptune and tasting the special
delights he has contrived for men of your
stamp . . .. . .

The Neptune Ceremony was tailored for the dog drivers and punished the men for their diabolical ways and for their beasts' hideous sounds and befouling of the ship's decks. (Paine Antarctic Collection)

The men on the *Jacob Ruppert* sported individual haircuts: Olin Stancliff (front left), Paine (hairless in the middle), Bill Haines (front right), Ed Moody (rear left), and Tom Buckley (rear right). (BPRCAP; Papers of Admiral Richard E. Byrd, image 7897-10)

dogs as well as us, this cool weather. Him lost overboard yesterday. Makes four dogs in all that we have lost. Very lucky.[4]

Wednesday + Thursday 8 + 9th

Slipped up in my diary last night for no apparent reason except that I got reading Scott's last expedition. It is a tragic story + slightly alarming in some of its aspects. He had such faith in his ponies + so little in his dogs + in after light we can see the awful mistake he made.[5] Splicing lead lines + to-night adjusting harnesses. Weather continues cool + sea fairly calm. To-night we hear we are to stop at the Easter Islands. That is good news.

4. Byrd stated in his account *Discovery* that he expected significantly more deaths by this point. One of the four casualties was Prince. Innes-Taylor, determined to impress upon his drivers their responsibilities toward the animals, had the men line up along the rail and salute the body as it was buried at sea (Walden and Paine, *Long Whip*, 37–38).

5. Robert Falcon Scott's strategy to be the first to reach the South Pole partially depended on using ponies acclimated to the Arctic. The English Scott and his party reached the South Pole on January 16, 1912, and then died on their return. Using dogs exclusively, Roald Amundsen, a Norwegian, and his party reached the pole on December 14, 1911. Their strategies continue to be debated today.

Friday Nov. 10th

On mess duty to-day. It was not as bad as it was the last time, but oh what a lot of dishes + silver + hungry mouths there are. Orr has been moved to the galley where someone can keep an eye on him.[6] He was caught with Perkins' camera + confessed his various thefts. Too bad that he should have gone wrong for what a great mistake he has made. He will regret it all the rest of his life.

We are now sailing the southern seas, the romantic spot of the globe. Here it is that our dreams have gone to, idyllic seas + skies + enchanted isles. Phil comes to my mind constantly + I become more + more bewildered why I should be doing this rather than he. It is a very strange thing. I awake in the morning sometimes wondering what it is all about + why I am where I am, + bound for the unknown. I recall the days + times I would spend dreaming + building mental images of my going into unknown areas + perhaps being the first man ever to set eyes upon whatever lies thereon. It all seems to be coming true. Now it is the south seas. We are here, oh Philly.

Tomorrow it will be, we are here. Ah Amundsen, Scott, + all the rest of them. But back of all this lies someone whom I know will always be with me + behind me. Dearie is in my mind + what I do or decide to do will depend to a large extent [on] how it would reflect on her + what she would think. I find myself constantly saying to myself, would she laugh, smile, approve or reprove. So we head south to Easter Island, New Zealand + the Antarctic. I get quite excited at times over what the future holds. I thank my stars that my life for a while at least will not be a monotonous routine + drudgery. Something new is around the corner every minute + my soul; praise be if I have one, is completely + thoroughly happy. I can say + have said for the past two months, it is really good to be alive. The members of the dog department + Taylor particularly are a great + thoroughly loyal + cooperating bunch. Rawson leers + sneers + remains aloof. I shall try to avoid all interference with him + let him alone. Perhaps, as Taylor said this afternoon, he has no sense of humor. What a man to go on the trail with!

Saturday Nov. 11th

Armistice Day. In New York I probably would have rushed out of town to get a breath of country air + rushed back to a stuffy stupid office. Thank God such is not the case + I celebrated the holiday by working steadily, first moving dunnage back to its proper place from which it had been moved on

---

6. This man was not listed as on Byrd's final roster of men on the expedition.

account of the lashing of the airplane engines + pumps. Later washed down forward deck, which Cox refused to do,[7] + washed the can forward top to bottom, + that voluntarily. I do not see how the rest can stand the filth. I couldn't + it seems to be I who cleans it out when it is cleaned out. Had test broadcast to New York to-night, the dog mushers supplying music with their songs, Byron Gay accompanying.[8] Later to-night there are hopes of receiving messages from home via W.G.Y.[9] Harnesses almost all completed. 11:30 p.m. Just received wire via WGY from Phil I think it was to wit: "Did you get cablegram from Del in Balboa. All well + love from us all." What a wonderful thing radio is! And that message was one among about 7. Thanks old Phil. I am certainly glad to have heard from you + know everything is well. Bravo!

Sunday Nov. 12th

To-day has been a day of leisure + general recreation. After cleaning + watering dogs, finished Scott's book. It is a tragic book, though all through it is a tale of heroic efforts against almost hopeless odds. But we have learned from his experiences several valuable things + it is very instructive for me + the rest of us who know so little about the Antarctic.[10] One is to provide a greater margin of safety. Second is to put trust in dogs, not ponies. Third to provide sure + certain markers for the depots + caches. They were all heroes + died like "Englishmen." Began shifting dogs around into groups corresponding to teams.[11] Rehearsed for radio program to-night. Took salt water shower with

7. E. F. Cox was a dairyman.

8. In cooperation with CBS, Byrd entered an agreement with General Foods to make weekly national radio broadcasts from Little America. Byrd also enlisted the National Geographic Society as a sponsor, negotiated contracts with news and film media, and contracted with the U.S. Postal Service to raise money by setting up a temporary post office at Little America and selling Second Byrd Expedition commemorative postage (Raimund E. Goerler, ed., *To the Pole: The Diary and Notebook of Richard E. Byrd, 1925–1927*, 121–23). Despite the Depression, Byrd was able to raise $150,000 in cash to fund the Second Expedition—less than half of what he was able to raise for the First Expedition and only a small part of the expedition's true cost. In his never-ending search for supplies, the U.S.-based supply officer, Victor Czegka, only gave up soliciting assistance from a potential donor after he had been refused forty-two times (Byrd, *Discovery*, 2–4). Byron Gay later resigned from the expedition.

9. Messages from home were read over the radio or wired as a radiogram.

10. Innes-Taylor was holding classes on the ship for the dog drivers; they read accounts of former expeditions and discussed problems and solutions. The drivers were also studying photography and more importantly radio, Morse code, and maintenance of F.N. 35 Army-issue generators that were cranked by hand and supplied the power to transmit messages (Stancliff, *My Life and Good Times*, 18).

11. Innes-Taylor and the drivers divided the dogs into tentative nine-dog teams, selected by weight and height, which determined pace or pulling stride, and then for speed, temperament, how

Paine pawned his shirt for his horse so he could explore Easter Island. Duke Dane is on the left, Paine is in the middle, and Alan Innes-Taylor is on the right. (Paine Antarctic Collection)

salt water soap which was a good success. Had talk with Rawson + told him what I thought + what we all thought. He should know better than to act the way he does + everyone from the crew up to the ship's officers either laugh at him or call him a wet ham or worse. I told him plenty + for his own sake I hope he takes it seriously. He wasn't sore + here's hoping he will change his attitude. He has been such a good friend.

Monday, Tuesday, Wednesday, 13, 14, 15th

Monday + Tuesday passed uneventfully. Sighted Easter Island Tuesday night. Cruised around all night + anchored early this morning. First shore party ashore at 7. Easter Island, land I once dreamed of visiting but had wondered whether I was really dreaming or should the dream come true. Made journey to stone faces via horse for which I pawned my shirt. On way back had swim + was joined by Admiral. Matches, shirts, tobacco, etc. got me 10

---

they balanced each other, and the particular aptitudes of the leader. They were then grouped together on the ship's deck. In addition to measuring each dog and constructing individual harnesses (including painting each dog's name in red paint on the wooden cross brace, the "whiffle tree"), during the voyage the dog drivers also assembled fifty sledges, packed rations, cut cloth for thousands of flags for marking trail, split bamboo to make flag standards, and so on (Walden and Paine, *Long Whip*, 38–39).

wooden idols + two devil cones. What a day + I was first on the bridge on watch + now on dog watch. Easter Island impressions I wrote to Dearie + will not repeat them here.[12]

Thursday, Friday, Saturday, Sunday, Monday, Nov. 16–20

I have neglected my diary the last few days. Nothing has happened to me or on board save the customary routine. I was put on duty as messboy in the after mess Sunday + shall continue as such for a week. I was a bit grieved at first, but we all drew lots + as usual I lost. It has not been bad, however, as aside from dishing out food to the men, I have been painting the messroom + generally cleaning it up. For the first time in weeks, the coffee percolator was washed, the dish towels washed etc. To-day I painted a part of it, black. White will go above this + a broad band of orange between. Paige has promised to contribute some pictures + I believe we will have a nice looking place back there.[13]

To-night Paul Siple played some records to us, among which was the 'Nutcracker Suite' of Tchaikovsky.[14] It was thoroughly enjoyed by all hands. Rawson has come around splendidly + I hear favorable comments. What an ass to have carried on the way he did!

My diary tells me we have been underway from Panama 17 days, almost three weeks. It is unbelievable. The weather has been so perfect + calm throughout.

Life aboard ship has become the regular mode of life + I hardly realize that I have ever done anything else. Saturday night we made a broadcast to the states. It was to be rebroadcast but I understand only about 1/2 of it got through.[15] They had me come in feeding the dogs, who immediately set up an awful howl. Then I answered "How" to my name when it was called in the singing glee club. Last night movies in shelter deck, "She Done Him Wrong" with Mae West. There were slight reminiscent flashes of what I + all of us had left behind, but soon came to the conclusion that this was quite superior to night clubs, etc.

---

12. It was customary that diaries be kept so that stories could be told upon a person's return from travel. The final letters would be sent when the last ship left the Antarctic.

13. David Abbey Paige was the artist of the expedition.

14. Paul Siple, in a national Boy Scout competition, won the privilege of accompanying Byrd on his First Antarctic Expedition, 1928–1930. After returning to the United States, Siple continued his education and then came back on Byrd's Second Expedition as a biologist.

15. Broadcasts were relayed through several stations in different countries before finally getting into U.S. airspace.

Byrd's party at Easter Island came on board the following morning. Byrd + a native crew came out first + then we cruised around the lee of the island to pick up the others. On very rough sea + we were lucky to have not been held up.

Friday 24th November

To-day was my sixth day as messboy back aft. I have grown accustomed to it + try to make it quite as painless as possible. I have completed the painting of the room + it looks fairly good. Of course people have put their duty lists on the white paint, so it is not as finished as it could be. The lower half is black, the upper white + on the border we have our orange band about three inches wide. I have caulked the sink board + even cleaned the port holes. It was an awful mess + now I know that it is at last clean + neat. No one comments very much about it + it is a bit discouraging after working all this time, voluntarily + extra hours, to make the thing look well. The men on the boat, particularly the crew aft are not of the highest type + one must use great patience + discretion. The feeding of the crew is similar in all respects to feeding dogs. I am struck with it every time I throw food at them. If one doesn't get as much as the other, there is a squeal + a bellow. If food is one minute late, the place is in an uproar. Food when placed upon the table is gobbled up with all possible dispatch. What a herd! Again the veneer of civilization + gentlemanliness is then very often lacking in a great many cases.

Radio from Dearie to-day + one from the Browns yesterday. All is well + they enjoyed the radio broadcast. Snow + cold at home.

The Pacific is larger than I ever believed. Three weeks from Panama + over a week to go yet. It has been marvelously calm the whole time + cool. How very fortunate we have been.

Friday Nov. 30, 1933 Thanksgiving

A week gone by since my last entry. I have purposely omitted writing because events have been almost exclusively of the routine nature. We have been working on [trail] flags + they are almost completed. I work with Noville off + on. Tuesday we hauled up five tons of sand from No. 5 hold + to-day we poured cement into the forward tanks to strengthen the bow. I worked all morning + came into second mess for dinner. Was a great dinner + does Hump + Carbone credit. Chicken soup, turkey + stuffing, sweet + white potatoes, peas + carrots, cranberry sauce, mince pie, nuts, + a 2 lb. bar of chocolate apiece. I sent a wire yesterday to Dearie + the Morses + I thought of them all to-day.[16] Who would have believed I would be 37° South Latitude 166° W. Longitude for Thanksgiving of 1933. Last week sea gloriously calm + cool. Our run has been astounding, without a single storm to date from Boston. Taylor expects me to act as navigator for supporting party in the event of a relief party being sent out to pick up Byrd should he have a forced landing.[17] I have been working on navigation all afternoon + evening, pouring cement this morning. A rather interesting Thanksgiving. About 4 days from Wellington [New Zealand] + our long voyage will be ended. It has been a long stretch, but we have become so accustomed to the ship I hardly remember any other life. To-night I am on dog watch. Movies to-night— "Tarzan + the Apes." Gay played organ + we had songs in between times. I don't know what Taylor has in mind but he thinks I have been loafing or something + so tomorrow I work just with Czegka + then Noville. I begin to have doubts about my going on the ice in spite of everything. My feelings now are not one way or the other. I'll take what comes. I've gotten this far by God! The Admiral as yet hasn't the slightest idea who I am + I haven't exchanged more than two words with him.

Dec. 5th Tuesday

Yesterday, Sunday, 5:30 p.m., we crossed the 180th meridian + consequently we lost a day. Have been taking sights off + on + am becoming fairly proficient in calculating positions. Last night caught, Paul Siple did, an albatross. Weighed 13 lbs. + had a wingspread of 9 ft. It was a magnificent creature with enormous grey webbed feet.[18] These birds just fly + fly continually, spending the greater part of the time in the air in the relentless search for food. Saturday night movies with "42nd Street" the feature. Sat beside the Admiral, who talked about his visit to Hollywood + the feminine charms who roam its streets. To-day we finished the trail flags, enough to take us to the mountains.[19] They consist of square flags for the trail, large rectangular flags for the depots, burgee flags to run out five miles to the west of each depot at

16. Alphonse Carbone was the expedition cook; the Morses were Barbara, Paine's sister, her husband, Tony, and their daughters, Jananne and Content.

17. Admiral Byrd hoped to use a plane in much of his exploration of the Antarctic. The field of aviation at this time was still in its infancy, and aircraft capabilities were being tested.

18. Admiral Byrd's policy was to avoid impacting wildlife without significant reason.

19. Paine was referring to the Queen Maud Mountain Range, which lies on the edge of the Polar Plateau not far from the South Pole. The First Expedition's geological party skirted the base of the range and then turned east. Plans for the Second Expedition included traveling into the Queen Maud Mountains.

right angles to the trail flags + triangular pennants for the east. These are to ensure the easy picking up of the depots on the return trip.[20] At 3:00 p.m., the shores of New Zealand are in sight + we are following down the coast to Wellington. From here we see nothing but mountains, being 15–20 miles off-shore at the present time.

Sails, otherwise known as Kennedy the sail maker, has at last come out of a weeks drunk. Orr has stolen my pen in addition to what I lost before. Dogs all well with no further losses. All hands are sprucing up for liberty ashore, ironing clothes, trimming off beards, mustaches etc. I shaved mine off last week, concluding I will have enough opportunity to grow whiskers later on. Shirey finishes sewing flags. Paige is messboy aft + is quite distressed by it all. Calm since last entry now for to-day when it has been a bit rough with occasional showers of spray coming over the side.

Friday Dec. 8th Wellington

Tuesday night we anchored in the harbor around 11 o'clock, coming into the pier, Pipatea Wharf, early Wednesday. Our pilot brought her in without tugs, against a tide + a strong wind blow. Approaching the pier with port side to the wharf, he swung her around + out, swinging the ship in a perfect pivot. When she was around, we were only a few feet from the dock. A marvelous piece of seamanship. The Condor was taken off immediately, the Edsel Ford Yacht, the Condor being assembled on the dock. Wednesday I was on dog watch all night. Thursday was spent in sleeping + later going ashore + hav-ing a good time at the Grand Hotel including a dinner which I enjoyed tremendously.[21] Martinis to crème de menthe. Wade + I. Buckley + Russell did not show up 'til three this afternoon very drunk. They are at it again + both are making damn fools of themselves. Coal was unloaded to-day from #4. Thousands of people on board + find them on the whole very nice but the women are not good looking. To-night there was a public reception to Byrd 2nd Expedition men. It was a most boring thing with not very attrac-tive horses thrilling with your dancing with them + older ladies, short, tall +

20. The flags are critical in following a trail by sight. Burgee flags are triangular flags with two tails. The trail itself was to be marked with orange square flags set approximately 1/3 mile apart between supply depots, which are generally twenty-five miles apart. Standard protocol in naviga-tion, "miles" in this account are "geographical" or "nautical miles," which are the equivalent of 1.15 "statute miles." The use of these two different units cause significant confusion in reporting mileage in the Byrd and other accounts.

21. Admiral Byrd sometimes gave the unpaid expedition men a small amount of money to spend when they were able to go ashore.

fat, look at you as though you were Exhibit B. I left early + came back to the ship, buying a pound of candy on the way + which is nearly gone now. New Zealand I am writing Dearie about.

Saturday Dec. 9th

Still in Wellington.[22] Morning devoted to hauling up ton of dog chow + placing guards in front of deck near bridge. I was placed on guard at gangway for several hours + had to be very stern with those wanting to visit the ship. As the Admiral had extended a cordial invitation to all to visit the ship, it was a difficult job. Yesterday Lord + Lady Bledesoe, governor general, were aboard + met us all. He was charming as well as Lady. First lord I have met. A lady Premets or something similar to that name was aboard + she is a native Maori. They are very intelligent + are socially equal to any of the English. Tonight went to Grand Hotel for martinis + out to dinner with Stan + then to movie. Mr. Felton took me for a drive around the bay + I enjoyed seeing everything very much. Anderson has quit so goes the rumor, Ohnen is to stay to have an operation, June threatens to quit + the expedition seems to have developed into a circus.[23]

22. The *Ruppert* was taking on supplies and awaiting the arrival of the icebreaker *Bear,* which left Boston later and traveled more slowly than the *Ruppert.*

23. Harold June, the chief pilot, was associated with Byrd's previous endeavors including Byrd's First Expedition. Neither Anderson, second officer on the *Ruppert,* nor Ohnen are mentioned on the admiral's final expedition roster. Other information about Mr. Felton is not available.

3

The Roaring Forties and South

December 13, 1933–January 16, 1934

Dec. 13th 1933—Wellington—Ross Sea.

45S, 178E at noon[1]

Yesterday around 7:30, we said good-by to Wellington + now we are at last on our way to Little America + our great adventure. It was [a] delightful stay in Wellington + in a way we regretted saying good-by to the cordiality, hospitality + friendliness of Wellington. Dec. 10, Ken + I went up to Judge Blair's house. He is the Chief Justice of New Zealand. Charming including his three daughters. Dec. 11th I stayed aboard + wrote Dearie of New Zealand + my activities, which I won't repeat here. Boat drill yesterday afternoon around four p.m. + three stowaways found in #four life boat. They were Wellingtonites, adventurous souls. It was a serious thing to find them as our clothing + food supplies are not too plentiful. Immediately a check was made to determine whether we should turn back or continue. We continue + the stowaways to-day probably regret the day that they came. Dog crates + then oil barrels, mess duty, lashing, etc. have fallen to their lot. Byrd is peeved with Shirey, as he should be, that so many men were taken aboard here. Shirey has blundered enough with the personnel I wonder he continues on

---

1. Paine was practicing taking readings of latitude and longitude by using a sextant to read the angle of the sun, a highly accurate timepiece called a chronometer to note the exact time using Greenwich Central or Mean Time, and comparing those readings with a nautical almanac to determine the ship's position. This practice is called celestial navigation. This reading means they are 45° latitude south of the equator and 178° longitude east of Greenwich, England.

the job. Sawed up after well deck dunnage this morning + repaired the 40 crates we brought up this afternoon. Movies to-night. "Prosperity" with Dresseler + Moran. Quite amusing. To-night I am dog watch 'til 12. It is very foggy + we are in the ice berg area. Watches are posted at the crows nest + on the forepeak to watch for ice bergs. The dogs are restless because of the fog, the first fog on this trip. Any shadow is reflected on the fog + the dogs cannot understand it. It's almost spooky + I feel as though this is the beginning of that out of the ordinary life which I have always yearned for. Ohnen, because of an operation for stomach ulcers, + Stormy Weather Anderson because he balked at having a new first appointed + consequently went to the American Consul.[2]

At last we are on our way + from now on we are sailing seas seldom sailed. Already it is getting colder, everybody wearing sweaters. It's light up to nine o'clock + it will not be long before it will be continuous daylight.[3] My talk with Ken at the Grand Hotel, at which we both got quite drunk, was enlightening. I am very glad to hear that the Admiral as well as Ken + I agree that there are about 12 men on board who are worth a damn + that the Admiral knows exactly what is what. Ken places great confidence in me, which I hope to justify during the next year + a half. Letter from Dearie, a wire from Barbara. Letter from Aunt Fan in Wellington. How good it was to hear from them. Actually on my own here for the first time, where family is out + your own stuff counts + outside help is impossible, life begins to take on a serious aspect. I am not worried. Far from it, for I feel that I have not been a failure + if what Ken says is true, I may do something yet.

Wednesday Dec. 13th

We crossed the 180th to-day heading East + consequently we made up for the day we lost coming out. Spent morning in finishing flags + afternoon Wade + I cut + brought up bamboos for tents.[4] Sea remains calm with gentle wind but foggy most of the time. The ice berg watch continuous but no bergs yet. Penguins sighted this morning. Getting cooler + we are sleeping under new blankets. Fall sledging journey seems off, the motor transports

2. Part of the sentence was not written. These men left the expedition at this time. See Appendix 1 for a list of the men of the Second Expedition main party and selected men of the U.S.-based staff and ships' crews.

3. Near the poles, the sun does not set in the summer, nor rise in the winter.

4. Bamboo was split into flexible standards for flagging, braces for tents, field radio poles, and so on.

taking our place. We may constitute a supporting party in which case we will get out on the trail.[5] Course continues SE + we are almost out of the roaring forties. Gjertsen is a fair weather skipper if there ever was one.[6]

Friday Dec. 15

Yesterday + to-day were spent in regular routine not the least was getting accustomed to the increasing cold. Last night the thermometer registered around 40 degrees + we all found ourselves rather miserable, having only recently come from the topics + the warm weather in Wellington. The dog department has not as yet been issued their warm clothing + we are rather griped about it. Practically all the others, including the engineering department, the scientists, the mess cooks, etc. have theirs. Now there is little left. Corey has showed his double face, as was expected, + is holding out because of some personal grudge or dislike. We can't figure it out.

Hauled up lumber from No. 2 hold yesterday + transferred it to No. 4. To-day I worked at airplane sledges + dog tethering lines. Sails has at last come out of his drunk which has lasted about three weeks + is now working overtime to catch up on his work + to provide clothing etc. for the Condor, which is scheduled to leave sometime next week on its flight to Little America.[7] Watch, one of the twins, hung himself over the rail + we feel his loss very keenly.[8] Expect to get to the pack ice in another two days. Last night was the last night of complete darkness + from now on we have continuous daylight.

5. Immediately after setting up base in the Antarctic, the fall trail parties were to set supplies for the main field season planned for the following spring and summer. Although they had left the United States in the fall, the expedition would finally arrive on the southern continent in the summer.

6. Commodore Hj. Fr. Gjertsen, who sailed on the designated flagship, was in charge of both expedition ships (the *Jacob Ruppert* and the *Bear of Oakland*), each of which was commanded by a "Master." The commodore was a Norwegian captain and ice pilot with experience in both polar regions. The middle latitudes in the southern hemisphere are known for their prevailing unpredictable and strong westerly winds, thus the area is called the "Roaring Forties."

7. Little America, the Antarctic base Byrd established for his First Expedition, was built a few miles inland from the sea on the thick ice of the Ross Ice Shelf over water one thousand feet deep. The Ross Ice Shelf is part of a gigantic northward-flowing glacier fed from various southern sources, and its four-hundred-mile face continually breaks off into the sea. Admiral Byrd planned to use the Condor to assess the ice conditions for the ships' landings and to see if Little America had gone out to sea since the last expedition. Byrd later wrote that by 1933, Little America had moved to only 3/4 mile from the water's edge (Richard Evelyn Byrd, *Alone*, 24–26).

8. Byrd reported that three men (Dane, Moody, and Innes-Taylor) worked for over an hour to try to resuscitate him. Watch was the seventh dog lost so far out of 153 dogs during the sea voyage; Byrd had expected to lose over 20 percent, or more than thirty dogs, mostly from the heat when coming through the tropics (Byrd, *Discovery*, 34).

At eleven o'clock last night there was still light, enough to see your way about the ship. Shirey continues on the sewing machine. Found to-night that the fall sledging party was to be composed of all dogmen except myself, Dane, who was to be in charge, Russell + Wade. I cannot figure out what is meant by it, whether he [Admiral Byrd] lacks confidence in me + so leaves me behind, or he thinks I can do better work in camp than on the trail. If he would put me in charge I think I could show him, but with Dane, it makes things all the more confusing. I suppose I take the customary place at the rear where I have been in most of my enterprises.

It is thrilling in a way to be sailing seas perhaps never before sailed by men. We are a little east of the Ross Sea just now + steadily making towards the eastward to a point from which the plane can take off + fly to Little America via Graham Land + other unknown parts of the Antarctic. Received yesterday afternoon a letter + money order from Del, which came to me in Wellington but which was evidently carried around in someone's pocket. Nice shipmate somebody is. At present I begin to doubt whether I shall go on the ice as I had expected. It would not surprise me at all to be sent back. The fall sledging party has been called off because it was found the tractors could travel so much faster + carry so much more. The dogs would not be practical, especially if they had to work in conjunction with the tractors. Eh La. Even with such great opportunities like this there are still disappointments. I have been guilty again of "throbbery," as William Sumner terms it, or wishful thinking.[9] It's no use doing that + I must take things as they come without anticipating them.

Dec. 18th, 1933—Monday 63°S.

No ice as yet. It is extraordinary + there seems no accounting for it. We are steadily progressing towards the South East + are traveling uncharted + unknown seas.[10] Father Neptune pounded us a royal welcome yesterday + a bit the day before with the first real storm we have had. Waves up to thirty feet high + a wind of sixty-five miles an hour. It was my first storm at sea + I really enjoyed it, though I continually thanked my fortune I was aboard the

9. William Sumner was an influential Yale professor and Social Darwinist.

10. After a week at Wellington, the ship steamed south toward the Antarctic. However, because of the outgoing ice pack, Admiral Byrd wanted to delay their arrival at Little America by exploring the unknown and unpenetrated seas far to the northeast. In preparation for the southernmost seas, the cows were moved from the forward well deck to the shelter deck, the loose gear was picked up, the hatches were battened down, and the tarpaulins were taken down and stowed in the lockers (Walden and Paine, *Long Whip*, 46–47).

Ruppert rather than the *Bear.* Early in the morning Taylor called us to move dogs off after well deck. We had a heavy following sea + wind + there was danger of a sea breaking over it. Shortly after breakfast, an aileron brace on Condor broke + it was necessary to come up into the wind. It took almost an hour to accomplish this, + when we did get up, one couldn't stay [bow into the wind]. Our propeller was out too much of the time.[11] Waves constantly swept the forward + after parts of the ship. Life lines were rigged + we were warned to take extra precautionary measures. Healey was caught by a wave while lashing some timbers against the rail. He was sent spinning down the deck but fortunately was not hurt badly, only bruised. He had the simplest expression on his face, half humor, half surprise. We were constantly on deck, being thoroughly wet through several times.[12] Driving snow squalls added to the discomfort. Three men were on dog watch all last night, Wade, Buck + I being on the 6–12. Fortunately too the temperature did not drop below freezing.

To-day we resumed our course, the wind having abated as well as the sea. It is light all the time now. At 12:30 this morning it was just dusk, with a visibility I should say of perhaps two hundred yards. I collected chains from well deck this morning + this afternoon I sewed mukluks.[13] Yesterday afternoon we received messages from home. I received messages from Dearie, the second one read, Barbara, Aunt Fan, + the Browns, in fact more than anyone else on the boat. They are all well + still love me, which is all I care about. During last night's cold + lonely watch, I thought how much these messages from home mean. We are in an unknown part of the world, a tiny speck upon a wild + uncertain ocean, beyond all immediate help from our friends, bound upon an adventure of which we do not know the results. To know that someone is thinking of you + loving you even though 16,000 miles away, is extremely gratifying. Particularly so in this huge, impersonal ocean where nature doesn't give a damn + you are just so much drift wood. The winches are turning over continuously now + probably will until we get out

11. Nosing into the wind and taking water over the bow is safer than having a following sea (off the stern), or exposing the boat broadside to the wind and waves, which can cause it to founder. Because of waves tilting the ship, the propeller was often out of the water, so the ship could not be effectively powered. In turn, steering was affected by the lack of consistent forward momentum and by the rudder breaching the water.

12. One wave lifted a dozen dog crates and smashed them against the port rail. Before the second wave could carry them overboard, Paine, Russell, Wade, and Buckley fought their way to the rail and lashed the crates. Herbe, a big Manitoba, was washed overboard but hauled back over the side onto the deck unhurt. Paul Swan, an expedition pilot, was nearly lost (Byrd, *Discovery*, 35).

13. The dogs were fastened to three-foot-long chains bolted to the dunnage.

of freezing weather.[14] We are expecting to run into ice any minute now + the boat is lousy with ice berg watches + look-outs. No heat up forward as yet + with the thermometer at 32 degrees, it is not very comfortable here.

Dec. 19th

To-day, two notable events occurred. We ran into ice at 1:30 this morning, + a cow gave birth to a bull. Both events make news. Herrmann had been up almost all night + all day to take movies of the event for the benefit of the Guernsey Association, but during one of his five minute absences, out popped the calf. A quick + easy delivery.[15]

The ice bergs have been magnificent + truly one of the scenic wonders of the world. All day we have been cruising among these huge tabular bergs, most of them over a hundred feet high, some large a mile long, some mere fragments. The brilliance of this bluish whiteness is dazzling. I have never seen such purity of color. It is the color virginity would be if it had a color. Caves, tunnels etc. were etched into them along the water's edge. Spray sometimes shot clean over them. Whales sighted, gulls about us. Description of these sea borne monsters is left to better writers than me.

Cool to-day but not freezing. Water 31°, winches going. Dogs in crates amidships. Hump quit galley + working on deck force. Steam up forward for first time.[16] It is still chilly.

Thursday Dec. 21st

Yesterday we entered the pack [ice] Lat. about 65°30', Long. 149E.[17] We steamed all day southward until this morning. We turned back several miles to a large open water space to enable the Condor to take off. The ice is very rotten + the *Ruppert* plows right through it at half speed without any trouble

---

14. In cold and rough weather, the winches had to turn continually or they would freeze solid from the sea spray, rendering them unusable when they were needed for launching and retrieving the Condor or unloading supplies at the ice.

15. John Herrmann was an expedition photographer. Klondike, the cow, gave birth to the little bull, which was named Antarctic Iceberg. This event generated a great deal of publicity and became the pride of the American Guernsey Association.

16. The men's living and working areas were steam-heated.

17. "Pack ice" is a large area of floating sea ice. An "ice shelf" is floating ice to 3,600 feet thick. "Barrier ice" is the edge of an ice shelf, generally grounded to land. "Bay ice" is floating ice that may butt up against the barrier ice. A "lead" is open water between floating ice pack. The "Barrier," as it used often in Paine's diaries, is synonymous with what is now called the Ross Ice Shelf as well as the glacier edge where it meets the sea.

at all. This is all new to me + it is a great sight, nothing but these small broken floes of ice with varying sizes of water leads in between. Going in we were careful to follow the leads. Going out we plow right through it all, as the ice is so soft, there is little advantage in zigzagging tortuously from lead to lead. As far as the eye can see, nothing but floating ice pans. Here + there are tabular ice bergs sticking up like huge square blocks above the flat slush ice. Some of these bergs are tremendous. One we passed coming in + going out must be 15 miles long + half as wide. It bumps up in the center + looks all the world like an island. Some bergs have toppled over on one side + remind me of ancient ruins of Europe.

Feverish activity to-day + yesterday to get Condor off. I hurriedly finished mukluks + tent lines + finished up tents for the plane. Plane overboard in very calm water around five this morning + she was off about three hours later. Buckley + I manned the punt + carried supplies + personnel between plane + ship. In the plane were Pelter, June, Bowlin, Petersen + Byrd.[18] They carried provisions for several months with them. Flew southward about two hundred miles + back again. Reported same ice conditions as here. It is possible we might get through here. All area explored to-day is new, absolutely unknown heretofore. We have penetrated farther south in this region than any other ship. It tickles me to think that we are looking at an area of the earth's surface never before seen by man. I can hardly realize that a fantastic dream of my youth has come true. How very lucky I am.

Warm to-day + brilliant sunshine—46°. Water temp 27. An historic day. Weather continues perfect, + the pack is as calm as a lake. Only the grating of the ice on the bow disturbs the silence.

Saturday Dec. 23rd, 1933 66°S, 147°W Long.

I cannot write every day, I don't know why. Too lazy I guess. But then, I am busy. Yesterday + to-day we have been steaming along the edge of the ice pack to the eastward. In + out of ice floes we go. Sometimes we start in only to return to the open sea. Last night storm clouds appeared to the west + it looked like a good blow, but it turned out to be nothing but a blow. To-day, it has been quite warm with a heavy fog. It has been slow speed ahead. The ice here is different from any we have seen. Remnants of ice bergs, thick, heavy ice well undercut by the waves, with the most fantastic shapes sticking

---

18. J. A. Pelter was an aerial photographer and mapmaker; W. H. Bowlin was an airplane mechanic and pilot; and Carl O. Petersen was a photographer and radioman.

Members of Paine's family gathering to pose for a picture. From left, in rear: Phil
(Paine's nonidentical twin), sister Barbara Morse, and Dearie (Paine's mother).
Center: Tony Morse between Paine's nieces, Jananne (left) and Content (right).
Not shown are Paine's brothers Lan and Del. (Paine Antarctic Collection)

above the water. Growlers galore.[19] This afternoon at five we stopped + put
over the punt to go after some rocks + mud seen in a growler. It returned
with a great many samples, + the scientists are very excited naturally.
Broadcast to the states to-night. Sang Holy Night + Come All Ye Faithful. A
good Xmas program. Wire from Dearie, Del, Lola, Lan, Francis, + Phil.
Movie to-night—Zoo in Budapest. Busy writing letters to be postmarked at
Little America.[20] Worked on tent lines to-day + finished them up. My dogs
are in crates in No. 3 hatch. It is quite a bit more work to care for them. This
is a strange silent world we are in now. The ship is stopped + the silence is
tremendous. You can almost hear a person whisper back in the poop. Even
the dogs seem to be silent to-night. It is as if all ye who enter here must keep
silence you.[21]

19. "Growlers" are small icebergs that have tipped upside down. "Tabular icebergs" are huge,
table-topped rectangular-looking bergs, while other bergs are pyramidal in shape or have pinnacles.
Dirt and rocks can be collected on the underside of ice as it scrapes the ground on its way to the
sea. Approximately 90 percent of an iceberg is below the water surface.

20. A U.S. post office would be set up in a tent on the ice; the mail would be stamped with a
Byrd Expedition stamp and then sent back on the final ship to leave Little America in the fall.

21. This is a parody of the inscription at the entrance to hell in Dante's *Inferno.*

Grey to black, icy crater, growlers + ice bergs, some near, some distant, some looming though the fog with misty magnificence. Grey against a grayer background. And the vagueness + obscurity of the fog makes them appear awful + forbidding. Thousands of miles from the nearest human dwelling, yet it is not lonely or depressing. The power, grandeur + beauty of nature is here in all degrees. The bergs with their hugeness + bulk contain the most delicate colors, greens + blues. These pastel shades almost drive you to reach for them to keep + possess them. Taylor remarked before we left that this trip would straighten out many of my ideas. I begin to sense what he meant.

Monday, December 25th, Christmas, 1933

Lat. 66°30′S, Long. 147°W.

A long ways from home + those I love so much. But my heart has been with them + I know theirs have been with mine. It has been a jolly Christmas aboard, even though it is foggy, wet, + cold outside. Last night we sang carols + drank Murphy's brandy. To-day we ate + ate + stuffed + drank Herrmann's whiskey. There has been plenty of Christmas spirit aboard. Everyone shook hands all around this morning + wished one another a merry Christmas. It was a really genuine wish on everybody's part. For dinner we had a feast which was credit to any cook. I have written Dearie about it + shan't repeat here. I trust she is saving my letters.

Yesterday I had about fifteen dogs in the forward well deck. They romped around in great style until Olav deliberately jumped overboard. Dusty went over the side on a rope but the dog didn't see him. Hump, Healey + myself went over in the workboat + rescued him just in time. He was as stiff as a board + his hind quarters numb. We brought him around all right + he is well to-day.[22]

Had short service this morning, Taylor officiating. It was very sincere + appreciated by all. Rough dogmen gathered in divine service was quite a contrast between that + the dogmen of everyday. Have stuffed + eaten until I am almost sick to-night. I've had enough for a while. Hourky is one of the New Zealanders caught stealing clothes + was locked up in the closet of the seamans' forecastle. He is out now, but it was a farce while it lasted. Movie last night, the night before + to-night. A Christmas I shall always remember for its genial happiness + good spirit.

22. Frederick Dustin was a machinist. The incident with Olav/Olaf was written about by several other sources, primarily because of the use of precious whiskey to help revive the hypothermic dog. Olaf had landed a full ten feet from the ship, so most likely he had leapt over the bulwark in a fit of exuberance (Walden and Paine, *Long Whip*, 52–53).

Friday Dec. 29th, 1933 [Thursday, December 28th]

The 26th + 27th were spent in weathering out a fairly severe blow which threatened to destroy the Condor. We have been + still are heading east + southeast towards the 120th Meridian West. For the two days we kept the ship headed into the wind as best we could. High seas + enormous swarms of ice bergs, large + small, continually bore down upon us. Our time was well spent in dodging these.[23] Had our engines stopped, our steering gear failed, we most assuredly would have been smashed against an ice berg with the obvious results. Byrd states none of us realized how close to our maker we were during those two days. There was no anxiety among us + we all were as unconcerned as though we were sailing smooth tropical seas. In fact we were O.K. as long as we had steerage way.[24]

Yesterday the seas calmed + to-day it is very smooth. We are steaming along the edge of the pack + with prospects for a flight tomorrow. Incidentally, before bedtime last night, I counted 85 icebergs off the port bow, all of them a hundred or more feet high + proportionally large. I am on dog watch to-night with little to do. Took bath. We have not as yet been issued our ice clothing. This makes it over two weeks since the others got theirs. Stan tells me Buck has two question marks + Duke one after his name on the ice party list. The reason for the delay in clothing is obviously apparent. The Commodore refused to take the ship through on the 180th Meridian + insists upon going to 174 or thereabouts. I believe he has the ice shivers + is over cautious.[25] Got off feed to-day, lashed canvas to the rails amidship. Dogs in poor shape. Their feet so tender as a baby's face. Oh for some seal meat + some exercise for them. Olav ok. Sun now just dips below horizon + it is broad daylight all twenty-four hours.

23. Thomas Poulter estimated that the ship passed eight thousand full-fledged icebergs on a single day, December 29 (Byrd, *Discovery*, 52).

24. In fact, the ship lost her ability to be steered. In deep fog with fifty-knot winds propelling waves across the forward and after well decks, the ship was caught between pack ice and icebergs with no retreat possible. Above the fog, a berg with spires two hundred feet high was sighted dead ahead and a second berg spotted off the starboard bow. Just as avoidance maneuvers were begun, the ship faltered and word came from the engine room that the fires had gone out, most likely from water contaminating the oil being fed to the burner nozzles. The steam pressure dropped to less than half its normal level—all steerage was lost. By luck, the wind blew the ship narrowly away from the two huge icebergs as the fires were relighted and steam pressure slowly recovered (ibid., 49–50).

25. While Commodore Gjertsen was on the *Ruppert*, the icebreaker *Bear* was still traveling from Boston and would not even reach New Zealand until January 6.

Saturday Dec. 30th 1933

Last entry should have been dated the 28th. 1933 is almost over. For me it has been instead a banner year, Graduation, land a job + now on expedition. Murphy gusted to-night, "1933 is a good year to leave behind you." That is true for most people. I have been singularly fortunate. What ill fortune the depression has brought others seems to have brought me good fortune.

Yesterday we completed our run to the 120th Meridian. It was a calm day + during the journey we kept the pack not more than a hundred yards off our starboard beam. Penguins Adele, + seals were seen on the ice cakes frequently but the soft slush ice which was characteristic of the ice so far is not a favorable place for Antarctic life. To-day we arrived the 116th Meridian + prepared to put over the plane. Snow storm came in + we have been lying to for the last 18 hours. It is doubtful whether we will be able to fly in this area. The weather is so uncertain. Ice bergs continually surround us, but not in the numbers seen previously. Byron Gay stated that if we called the spot where we passed so many bergs The Devil's Graveyard, the name would stick. Modesty! The Admiral has called it that in his radio address to-night.[26] He spoke of the danger we were in. But life on board went on exactly as before + everyone was as unconcerned about it as we are about a dog itch. Like myself, the members as a whole are peculiarly fatalistic about the expedition. To abandon ship would incur no more surprise than the birth of "Antarctic Iceberg." To-day I assisted Taylor in bringing up pemmican + other supplies from No. 2 which we put in the boat deck. These will be used in case of abandon ship. I also began the tedious job of sewing reinforcements on the covers of the tents, a job which should have been done when the tents were constructed. Light snow a.m. on late dog watch, 12–6 a.m. Sleep 8–2 p.m., 7–11 a.m. which gives me about 8 hours of broken sleep. Likes + dislikes are becoming very apparent aboard ship. Among a group of men, I don't believe I've seen so many. It is the close association I suppose, as well as the faults of the persons aboard. But I repeat, a long trip of this kind tells what a man is worth, + a great many have been found woefully lacking. For my part, I have Buckley in mind. He is the only discordant member of the dept. What he wants he takes + to hell with the rest of us. Too much money I guess. Dewclaw just got loose + Caesar tangled his chain.

26. At the time of this publication, the area generally between the 147 and 135 meridians is still known as the "Devil's Graveyard."

Monday January 1st 1934

A new year has come, the old has gone. Never by the greatest strength of the imagination did I conceive a year ago of my being in the southern ice pack this New Year. 1933 has been a desperate year for a great many people, including most of all Dearie, but there have been other rewards, + for one this has been the greatest. For 1933 I can boast of a degree from Yale, a job in New York, + becoming a member of an expedition. Indeed it has been a happy year for me.

New Year's here aboard ship was celebrated by drinks to the New Year, our success, + by the rapid ringing of the ship's bell. Yesterday a seal was procured + to-day the dogs had their first taste of seal meat. How they ravished it! A special program for us from WZXAZ + the mailbag. Letters from the Browns, Uncle Charlie + Dearie + Browns letter addressed to me, "dogman aboard *Ruppert.*" Received Christmas Greetings, all well + send love. Uncle Charlie's, "Best to Byrd, greetings + wishes"—addressed thus—"Please forward to my nephew, S.D.P., dogman aboard *Ruppert.*" Announcer stated he had just received this letter + it was difficult to make out but he would do his best. Lola, Del + Natasha up for Christmas.[27] Phil still has job or has not, I couldn't get it. All well + miss me—God bless you—Dearie. How I welcome such news. Next broadcast Jan 14th 1934, a new year + full of golden opportunities. Our position—69°37'S, 117°32'W. We, hooray, are steaming due south through closed pack with the likelihood of our discovering new land any moment. It is entirely new territory + really thrilling.

Tuesday January 2nd, 1934

Noon—It has been a tiring day. The plane was put over last night about eight. Buck, Wade + myself constituted the workboat crew + we were on duty all night, plying between the ship + plane which was moored astern. About 2 a.m. Harold [June] took it out for a spin on the surface to keep the motors warmed up. He headed into the wind + kept going until we lost sight of the ship. We followed in the motor sailer + it was certainly cold. Both in the work boat + in the sailer, any water coming over spray froze. Our clothes were almost stiff when we came in + my fingers actually were. I thought of poor Shackleton on his trip from the wreck of the *Endurance* to Elephant Island.[28] Snow flurries continued from the time we put the plane in until we

27. Natasha was Lola's sister.
28. Sir Ernest Shackleton's ship, the *Endurance,* was locked in the pack ice for 281 days before

The workboat attends the Condor, which was preparing for a reconnaissance flight to scout ice conditions. It was wet and cold work. (Paine Antarctic Collection)

took it out this a.m. The aviators worked themselves sick as well as the rest of us, only to have our work amount to naught. It was all in the game, however, + we are wrestling the unknown. We must be prepared for anything. Our position now is 116°W, almost 70°S. We attempted to reach what we thought was a barrier looming over to the southeast. Attempts to push the ship through were unsuccessful + we came back to a large open lead where we have been the last twenty hours.

The Admiral has lost patience with the Commodore + we plunged through ice which must have caused his hair to stand on end. It looks now as though we wouldn't be able to find out what the supposed barrier really is. Ship can't get through, so the plane [must be used].[29]

---

the party abandoned the ship in October 1915 and journeyed for months over ice and open water to Elephant Island. With other men, Shackleton then traveled eight hundred miles in an open boat to South Georgia Island in the South Atlantic Ocean to find help. This story is one of the most extraordinary tales of survival and leadership that has ever been told. It happened just eighteen years before this diary entry.

29. Admiral Byrd, at their maximum longitude on their journey to the east of Little America, turned the ship south until it was stopped by the pack ice. There he launched a flight to fly farther south toward Marie Byrd Land.

January 3rd, 1934

I didn't get a chance to write this morning. This week I have been making my entries along about two in morning. Yesterday we put plane over expecting to make a flight but it was hauled aboard again last night. All night the motors were turned over every four hours so as to keep them warmed up. Poor Bill Bowlin hasn't slept for a couple of days. I, with Siple, cut up three seals which were secured in the motor sailer. Dusty + Healey played hooky with motor sailer + came back with three more seals, all crabeaters, + an Emperor penguin, which were cut up this afternoon. I turned in about 7:30 this morning + slept until eleven, meanwhile the plane had been launched + taken off for the unknown.

The motor sailer made another excursion + Taylor back with an Adele + two Emperor penguins, all alone. They must have weighed over 75 lbs. apiece + their dispositions weren't too good. A whack from their flippers could knock you out. The flight resulted in a survey area of 150 miles southward. They saw nothing but ice, heavy ice + ice bergs. No land. It was successful flight, everything running perfectly. The plane was back around two + the plane aboard about four. After a discouraging wait for the light snow to cease + the clouds to lift, we were able at last to make the flight. Now we are to move 75 miles west for another flight. None has had any sleep the last two days. I have had about 7 hours in 48. Movies to-night, "The Greeks Had a Word for It."

Jan 4th

Blubbered two seals this morning + got about two hundred pounds of blubber + I smell like a seal if not worse. For 14 months I shall have to endure it I guess. Seal hamburg to-night for supper. It was excellent. And still they give us salt horse + putrid beef. Sails intoxicated. Sewed tents. Dogs been fed seal meat the last two days. How they go for it. But six seals, each around 600 pounds apiece, only lasted them ten days. Taylor says I am to report the activities of the Dog Dept. in "The Snowshovel."[30]

Jan 5th, 1934.

Buckley has an infected hand + has been laid up to-day. We reverently hope it will go no further + he will be spared the use of his hand. Personally I don't

---

30. The *Snowshovel* was a short-lived shipboard newsletter.

This diary page has two Byrd Expedition stamps pasted at the top. One of Admiral Byrd's fund-raising strategies was to contract with the U.S. Postal Service for a commemorative stamp that would help both the Postal Service and the expedition. (Paine Antarctic Collection)

amusing + everyone is seething with intrigue + politics. The stuff I wrote for it was not printed so I have threatened to go in to the other camp. I really think the "Snowshovel" could be made better + bigger, to reverse the usual order of words.

Tents completed + work on mukluks progress. I cleaned + dried two seal skins. One I shall try to take home with me, the other I shall probably use for something, I don't know. Life continues with continued anticipation of what is to come. The spirits of everyone rise as we approach our destination. The future, I feel sure, holds a great deal in store + I shall play my part.

January 10th

[Pasted at the top of the page are two Byrd Antarctic Expedition II 3-cent postage stamps]

Progress through clear water up to three o'clock. Yesterday our position then was Lat. 69°20', 152°32'W. This was almost as far south as Byrd flew in his first flight + a little to the west of his maximum range of visibility. The ice had all gone out to this point while we were exploring to the eastward. Pushed through sunken floes until 9 when we stopped + prepared to put plane over. Movie "Adorable" was abruptly terminated to make way for this more serious task. Wade, Duke + myself manned the workboat + the plane was put over in short order. A test hop was made with Buck, Dusty, Stancliff as stowaways. 800 gallons gas, provisions for two months, Toby + Pierrette for which special aluminum pens had been built in the plane + four men, Byrd, June, Bowlin + Petersen. The plane was terribly heavy + it seems as though it

Man Food Daily Rations		
Pemmican	9 oz	
Biscuits	10 oz	6 biscuits
Butter	.59 oz	Little more than tablespoon
P. Butter	.29 oz	Heaping teaspoon
Bacon	1.33 oz	2 thick slices
Erbswersts	2.00 oz	1/3 roll
Oatmeal	2.00 oz	1 handfull
Sugar	4.00 oz	quarter cupfull
Klim	4.00 oz	handfull
Cocoa	14 oz	1 per day
Malted Milk	.74 oz	1 teaspoon
Tea	.50 oz	
Salt	.25 oz	
Chocolate	2.00	1 bar per day

On a diary page, Paine carefully recorded "Man Food Daily Rations." Ingredients were carefully measured and packed for one man for one day on the trail. (Paine Antarctic Collection)

could not rise from the water. A short spin up into the wind + the plane taxied back to the ship. The dogs had gone nuts + were taken off. The plane then took the air in 40 seconds + disappeared southward for Little America. 3 hours later they were back—poor visibility + snowstorms. Gas was taken off. We dumped the gas before + plane aboard this afternoon. I got about two hours sleep to-day + must be up all night to-night putting up trail rations. Flight resulted in our going to 178 W + through pack that way rather than through here. Nothing but solid ice + ice bergs seen on flight. Everyone exhausted. Weather wonderful, warm like a May day at home, temperature around 55 + brilliant sunshine.

Jan. 13th

Cruising steadily westward + now we are 69°S + about 158°W. Ice bergs, the large tabular bergs. There is hope of reaching Little America next week, but

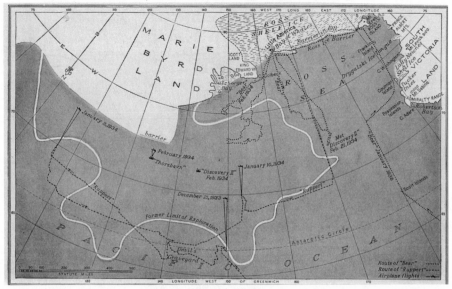

From December 1933 through February 1934, the *Ruppert* explored to the east to allow the ice pack to dissipate and then berthed and unloaded at the Bay of Whales. After the *Bear* arrived and unloaded, Admiral Byrd (in the *Bear*) explored along the coast past Salzberger Bay. After returning, the *Bear* left again to reconnoiter with the British ship *Discovery II* to take on additional supplies and to pick up a new doctor. Both the *Ruppert* and the *Bear* returned to pick up the expedition members in January 1935. (Constructed by R. A. J. English, USN, Herbert E. Eastwood, cartographer, National Geographic Society. Archived at BPRCAP; Papers of Admiral Richard E. Byrd)

it is quite uncertain. Ellsworth plane was wrecked yesterday + there is real sympathy aboard for him in his hard luck.[35] Moody, Taylor + myself were up all last night putting up trail rations. Night before I was on all night dog watch. Movies to-night but no rations. Braking[?] for ice.

January 16th

It was expected yesterday to be at the barrier but last night we had to lie to for six hours on account of heavy seas + snow so we are delayed + consequently expect to get there tomorrow morning. Our arrival at this time is better than we had dared to hope. Our run has been almost entirely through

35. After a test flight, Ellsworth's plane was moved inland, but the continually breaking ice shelf dropped the plane onto a floating ice pan.

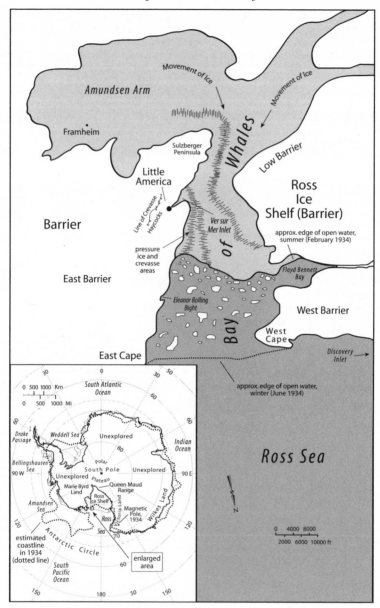

The Bay of Whales was a bay broken out of the Ross Ice Shelf. Shown are the features of the partially frozen bay, the ice flow, and the limits of the winter and summer ice during this 1933–1935 expedition. The pressure ice shown is a synthesis of locations Paine depicted on three different sketches. "Framheim" was Amundsen's base camp years before. Little America, first constructed during the First Expedition, was located next to the crevasses to the left. (Base map information from "The Authorized Map of the Second Byrd Expedition," constructed by George Annand, General Foods, 1934 [Kraft Foods], archived at BPRCAP, image 9260)

open sea. For the last two days, all south of 72°, there has been no ice at all, + one or two ice bergs. During our delay the ice has all gone out + there is no pack where we came through about 172° Longitude. Ellsworth was stuck in the pack three weeks over on 178 E only getting out two weeks ago. His experience was tragic + he is on his way back. His plane was wrecked beyond repair when the bay ice gave way. We passed the *Wyatt Earp* last night at a distance of twenty five miles, but we didn't see her.

We have been putting up trail rations + have finished up all we are going to do. 9 p.m. to 5 a.m. Sleep in morning + work the rest of the day. Not much chance for real rest. To-night I am on dog watch. Everyone on tiptoe in anticipation of our arrival. The trip of 15,000 miles + three months aboard is about to end. Heavy clothing, fur sleeping bags, 10 pairs of stockings to each man, wind-proof pants + parkas etc. for us all. The survey party leaves first.[36] Upon their return we start out. Taylor, Moody + Buckley are on the first party. Our gear is about all packed. We take only our essential heavy clothing on our first trip, the rest follows when we have room or time.

Messages [on] the 14th from Dearie, Barbara + Agnes Lansing. *Bear* still in Dunedin [New Zealand]. Clouds of Antarctic Petrels + Skua gulls about. One more day. I'm set, very soft, a bit tired but ready to go. Took last bath aboard ship.

36. The survey party's mission was to scout Little America and establish a trail. Two sleeping bag styles were used: eiderdown, for use inside a building or as a bag liner, and reindeer skin bags, which also had a second windproof skin made of dense cotton cloth for trail conditions. The heaviest outdoor clothing were "furs," reindeer outer clothing (parkas and pants) that were reserved for those who primarily worked outside—tractor men and especially the dogmen, who endured the most exposure.

4

Misery Trail

January 24–February 28, 1934

Jan 24th 1934 Pressure Ridge Camp.

It has been so long since I have made my entries I hardly know where to begin. I believe, though I'm not sure, we have been in the Bay of Whales a week. It has all been so new + strange + interesting. The first day a survey party was sent out to Little America + they found it intact even to the ringing of the telephones. It was comfortably buried but at present writing it is being dug out. I have made one trip to the base when Wade, Ronne + myself broke out the trail through the pressure area. We stayed there six hours + came back + established Pressure Ridge Camp.[1] Unloading has progressed until 1, 2 + shelter deck cleared. Cletrac, one ford, 12 dog teams + one Citroen haul. One Citroen burned while we were at camp.[2] Ship left last

1. Paine's dog team, with Jack as leader, and Winter, Gav, Pop, Kaiser, Pony, Skookum, Buck and Break-It, was the first team to go to Little America (Walden and Paine, *Long Whip*, 56–57). With untrammeled pressure ice to traverse, the seven-mile journey from the edge of the bay ice to Little America took more than seven hours (Byrd, *Discovery*, 85–89).

2. Unloading proceeded twenty-four hours a day. Byrd originally had intended to use the planes, tractors, and dogs to haul supplies. However, he decided the planes should be reserved, and, of the five tractors, one Citroën immediately burned almost completely, another caught fire, and the crankcases of the two Ford snowmobiles cracked in the cold. Only the monstrous Cletrac was left to work on the unpredictable bay ice. The primary responsibility was thus given to the dog teams, which could not only haul cargo, but also navigate through the pressure ice and avoid the crevasses. But, with only seven trained dog drivers, others (including scientists, mechanics, and crewmen) were recruited as additional drivers. For a time, sixteen teams were in harness. The dogs, however, were in poor condition, with thin coats and feet so tender that blood marked the trail to Little America (Byrd, *Discovery*, 82).

The supplies were unloaded from the *Jacob Ruppert,* which was berthed at the edge of the bay ice. The boxes were picked up by the dog teams and moved at least four times to various caches before they finally arrived at Little America. (BPRCAP, Papers of Admiral Richard E. Byrd, image 7864-10)

At Pressure Ridge Camp, many of the dog drivers slept on the snow, as the two tents were full. (Paine Antarctic Collection)

A sledge loaded with boxes from the ship heading toward the pressure ice in the distance. The nine dogs hauled anywhere from seven hundred to twelve hundred pounds of supplies with each load. The teams sometimes had to leap between floating ice pans on the breaking bay ice. (Paine Antarctic Collection)

night on account of swell + ice breaking.[3] 40 men ashore. Ship still out. All mid-depot moved to-day to here. Worked ten hours out there without a respite. Cold + tired.

Jan. 25th Pressure Ridge Camp.

Ship still cruising in the vicinity of the Bay. Supplies hauled between here + a cache established on the barrier. It is a stiff haul—only about 800 lbs. can be carried on each trip. But it is through a glorious mass of crushed + twisted ice formed by the barrier pushing against the bay ice. It is a magnificent display of the tremendous forces at work in this cold forlorn part of the world.[4]

3. On January 24, the ship's undermined gangway slipped into the water just after the dog drivers who had been sleeping aboard, Innes-Taylor, Russell, Paine, and Healey, jumped clear (ibid., 88–89).

4. Pressure ridges result from moving ice streams or two areas of evolving ice colliding in an eternal shoving match. The pressure area consists of upturned blocks of ice reaching up to thirty feet high, valleys of deep potholes filled with soft snow and both invisible and visible crevasses. At the top of a crest, a dog team had to break the pace momentarily to allow the lead dog to align the team and then rush down into the hollows, where the dogs would often founder as the sledge came down on top of them. Frequently the sledge toppled, requiring the driver to unload, right, and then reload the sledge. "Plainly the dog drivers were in for it; and whatever illusions they may have held

The team rests before a ridge of pressure ice. Supplies were hauled over the steep crests and hollows of the tumultuous surface. In going down a slope, the dogs were often hit from behind by the heavy sledges, or they could hang in the air in their harnesses when the sledges caught on the jagged ice above them. When a sledge toppled or crashed, the men had to unload it, restore it upright, straighten out the team, and then reload before they could proceed. (Paine Antarctic Collection)

With myself, Duke, Dick, Healey + Corey are on the 8 to 8 shift at night. 8 trips to-day. Captain + those of the ships crew on shore still here. Gay + Verleger hiked to Little America + great story sent about their staggering in accompanied by Buckley. Bridges over two crevasses.[5] Buck + I in small tent. Boyd cooking. Ice going out of bay + Kaiser nearly lost. Taylor very sore about it blaming me.[6] Team—Jack, Gav, Winter, Skookum, Pony, Hegaska,

up to that time about the dashing and heroic nature of sledging, they vanished before the sobering realities of Misery Trail" (Walden and Paine, *Long Whip,* 63–67).

5. Two bridges, constructed of telephone poles and hatch covers from the ship, spanned the widest crevasses. The last bridge was over open water and entered at a sharp angle from the trail. A lead dog had to keep the speed, angle, and spacing between the dogs precisely controlled to cross without mishap (ibid., 87–90).

6. Vernon Boyd was a machinist. The bay ice started to break up at an alarming rate. Cracks widened from a few inches to a span of open water several feet wide just in front of an approaching team. Paine and others sometimes found themselves on a moving ice floe, which required quick work to save themselves (ibid., 71).

Dick Black skis at the top of a pressure ridge. The upturned blocks of ice reach thirty feet high. (Paine Antarctic Collection)

Legaska ["Pop"], Buck, Break-it. Most of dogs out here. Wade on ship. Missed coming ashore when ship left day before yesterday. Glorious weather so far.

Jan. 26th

This morning proceeded to ship. It tied up to a sharp edged ice floe which seemed secure. Supplies were unloaded until about three this morning. Cracks were discovered + soon the floe next to it began to move out. Hundreds of tons of ice moved majestically out to sea. It wasn't long before the *Ruppert* followed + we lost only the deadmen we had sunk.[7] Returned here, P.R. Camp + took two loads to top of barrier. Fully half of camp only which were formerly here now aboard ship. Makes our cooking facilities easier.[8] Ice breaking up + the bay is choked with ice. Our situation calls for speed. We

7. "Deadmen" were hatch covers nailed together and buried in the snow and ice; the ship was secured alongside the barrier ice by attaching eight mooring cables to the deadmen (Byrd, *Discovery,* 74).

8. At Pressure Ridge Camp, the exhausted men ate and slept in two crowded tents and overflowed onto the snow to keep behind hay bales, which offered some protection from the wind (ibid., 85–89).

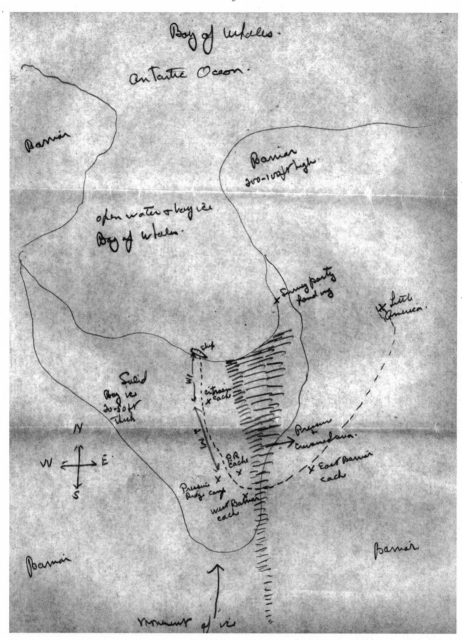

Paine's sketch of Misery Trail shows the direction of haul, the location of the pressure ice and crevasses, Pressure Ridge Camp on the solid bay ice (twenty to fifty feet thick), and the progressive caches from the Bay of Whales to Little America. Little America sits on Barrier ice (two hundred to one thousand feet thick), less than a mile from the water's edge. (Paine Antarctic Collection)

might float off ourselves, who knows? Admiral's last order to June was "Take charge + take Paige with you." Temperature about twenty + has been so except for a day of four below. No wind. Up all night + sleep all day. No difference as far as light goes. Admiral wants ship unloaded in three days. Plenty to eat, lots of exercise + immensely healthy.

Jan. 27th

Day or rather night spent in hauling from cache back of camp to barrier cache.[9] 7 trips in all + from 700 to a thousand lbs. apiece. Dogs pulled like hell. Snowy but cleared later. Ship tried to contact ice this morning but unable to. Bay full of ice. Her fuel is rapidly giving out. Brought in four seals. There is JoJo outside the tent, a trail tent, who has the most delightful howl, a perfect "oooh." How it carries me back to Phil's + my younger days when our hopes + dreams were in a lonely plain, a howl of your dogs, the screech of the coyote + the moan of the wind. Feast this morning of prunes, grapenuts, cocoa, + pancakes dripping with syrup. Have one bag with me, the other on ship. Wish I could write Dearie but I may get a chance either before *Ruppert* goes or before the *Bear* sails. Duke's dogs ran away + nearly wrecked the camp. There goes that howl again. I could squeeze that little bitch.

Jan. 28th

Broadcast from home last night but we failed to get it out here at P. Ridge Camp.[10] The ice continues to go out + all are in haste to get all supplies moved up onto the barrier. This camp will be moved as soon as possible. All but a few sledloads of supplies are either on the barrier itself or about a half a mile back of this camp on a high spot. Ship docking to-day + we will probably haul

9. "The initial loads, until the dogs gained stamina, were about 500 pounds which were then stepped up to 1200 pounds per sledge. Unloaded stores were either momentarily piled on the ice near the ship or loaded from cargo nets directly to waiting dog sledges. As only two tractors were functioning and usually one of those was out of commission, dog teams were used to get supplies to four temporary relay caches between the ship and Pressure Ridge Camp, a distance of 3.4 miles from the ship's berth, Pressure Ridge Camp to Little America was 3.8 miles for a total run of 7.2 miles to Little America, though Little America was only about three miles away as the crow flies.

"West Barrier Cache became the second big cargo dump as it was considered to be a more stable area and for safety, East Barrier Cache was established as well on the opposite heights of the Bay a mile and a half south-southwest of Little America. . . . All night the teams and the tractors nibbled at the caches, inching the stuff south" (ibid., 85–89).

10. Communications from home were read twice a month over shortwave radio from Schenectady, New York (Hill and Hill, *In Little America with Byrd*, 133–34; Byrd, *Discovery*, 10).

The icebreaker the *Bear of Oakland* berths at the bay ice. A dog team waits as the sledge is loaded with supplies. A seal lies in the foreground. The men and dogs utilized the unending sunlight to unload the ships and move supplies, nonstop, twenty-four hours a day, for two months. (Paine Antarctic Collection)

directly from ship to here tomorrow.[11] Made eight hauls to-day. Dogs tired. Collie Penook in place of Kaiser + I tried to kill him three times but his neck is still whole. Night was gorgeous, cold, below zero but warm to us mushers. My team ran away from me twice but I have showed them who is master.[12] Situation about like this.

Very dirty, not having changed clothes or washed for two weeks. What can you do about it? Nothing! Love it.

Feb. 1st, Thursday

Yesterday the *Bear* arrived. It was a grand sight to see her round the promontory at the mouth of the Bay + head in to the *Ruppert*. A visitor in these parts is such a welcome sight. She drew up along side + secured almost immediately. It was quite a contrast to what the *Ruppert* would have done under

11. Maneuvering between the dumps of supplies on the snow without tangling the team or catching and toppling the sledge was difficult. Jack of Paine's team was noted for threading his way through an intricate maze of boxes or past a stalled tractor without fouling the team. He also had a habit of running full speed directly toward the ship and then just before plunging into the Bay of Whales, he would wheel the team into a sharp right-angled turn to bring the sledge to a stop underneath the cargo net (Walden and Paine, *Long Whip,* 78–81).

12. The dogs were controlled by voice. "Yake!" meant go, "Gee!" meant go right, "Haw!" meant go left, and "Whoa!" meant stop. The whip was generally used for attracting the dogs' attention, self-protection, or to separate dogfights. The sled could be stopped and to some degree steered by the "gee pole," which was six feet long and attached to the middle of the sled.

"Jack the Giant Killer," Paine's lead dog, in Dog Town. Jack was four years old and considered vicious when he was bought for the expedition from Eskimos in Canada. He was possibly the largest and strongest dog in the camp. (Paine Antarctic Collection)

similar circumstances. She is moored at the bow of the *Ruppert* + she hardly reaches down to the Bridge. Her crew were all well + happy though without butter or cigarettes. Last two nights spent in mushing supplies between ship + first cache. The new Citroen is ashore + working.[13] The day gang was called out just as they had turned in to help in the construction of the bridge across the tide crevasse. It is now completed + Stan drove a Citroen to Little America. It will be easy I expect from now on. Letters from home + how wonderful + warming they were. I wish I could adequately express my gratitude.

Sat Feb. 3rd

Past two nights, I say nights because I have been up during the nights + asleep during the day, has been spent hauling supplies from first cache to the W. Barrier cache. 4 loads yesterday, 5 to-night. The ships are now entirely unloaded + there remains only the transporting of the supplies to Little

13. The third Citroën was picked up in New Zealand. Total tractors then included three Citroëns, two Ford snowmobiles ("fordsons"), and the Cletrac.

Paine's team, in Dog Town, attached to a tethering line of aircraft cable. Five of the nine are (from front) Kaiser, Pony, Winter, Legaska (Pop), and Jack. (Paine Antarctic Collection)

America.[14] Last night it was 15° below with a twenty mile wind. It was bitterly cold + gave us all a taste of what is coming. I'm game, though at the time I didn't think it much fun. Taylor all in from lack of sleep but complimented me as being the best cook + the best dog driver of the bunch. He says if I don't stay he won't, which I think is a very fine thing to say. Wire from Dearie reporting all well.

Tuesday Feb. 6th

We are here at Little America + are now quartered in the Administration building. Since the ship arrived we had been staying at the Pressure Ridge Camp, sleeping + driving sometimes in 15° below zero weather. It was quite comfortable in spite of everything but it is pleasant to be here with a stove, a table + benches to sit on. The P.R. Camp was broken up last night + moved

14. From the dog teams and especially from the tractors, the trail through the pressure ice was ground down and the equilibrium of the ice was disrupted. Ridges turned into valleys, and huge crevasses opened up. There in the pressure ice, the tractor drivers and the dog drivers began to clash as a few of the tractor drivers, sitting in warm cabs and throwing chocolate wrappers out onto the snow, would refuse to yield to the forty-foot-long trains of harnessed dogs careening precariously while hauling a ton of supplies. The dog drivers never forgave the tractor drivers for their arrogance and lack of courtesy (ibid., 83–85).

up to the West Barrier cache with about twenty men, the tractors drivers except Dusty + Hill, 12 loading men, cook, radio operator. The rest are here at L.A. [Little America]. All told there are about 72 men on the ice. There are not enough bags to go around so we have to take turns. We night dog drivers are being shifted to the day work + to-night we have the time + opportunity to pause + write. Cletrac crossed crevasse.[15] Citroens will haul across crevasse to Cletrac on this side. Dog teams from East Barrier Cache to here. *Ruppert* sailed last night.[16]

Feb. 8th

Mushing supplies between West Barrier to East Barrier. Almost all the food is now over there. I have a team of eleven dogs, adding Mitzi + Panky to my team. They spun round + round most of the time until I put them on wheel + they worked well there. Joe Healey + Duke went into crevasses, Joe this morning + Duke this afternoon when he tried to pass my team.[17] We pulled the dogs out all right + fortunately no dogs or men were hurt. Duke had four dogs go in, Joe seven. One crevasse near top of the barrier was over seventy feet deep. Duke's had a ledge ten feet below the surface + the dogs didn't have far to fall. The west side of the pressure is moving more rapidly, about five feet a day, + it takes continued work to keep the bridges passable.[18] Gorgeous weather, about 26°F + almost melting + brilliant sunshine.

Feb. 10th

Continued sledging between East + West Barrier, making seven trips each day. I have hitched up eleven dogs in my team + can regularly carry a half a

15. The Cletrac was so heavy that it was extremely risky to attempt to cross the telephone-pole-and-hatch-cover bridge. The Citroëns were significantly lighter and of course could not haul as much.

16. In its haste to leave for New Zealand, the *Ruppert* left 200 tons of supplies near the water's edge. Threatened by the ever-breaking ice, these stores were moved inland as quickly as possible (Richard E. Byrd, *Discovery* [film], Moving Images: Admiral Richard E. Byrd Collection, 1926–1935, in Motion Picture, Sound, and Video Records LICON, Special Media Archives Services Division [NWCS-M], National Archives at College Park [ARC id. 89109, 200.382, reels 1–5 and 6–10]). The movement of the ships marked time that otherwise ran together for the men, who were working without respite in the twenty-four hours of daylight. A fresh flood or slowing stream of supplies meant that the *Bear of Oakland* had arrived, the *Ruppert* was steaming back to New Zealand, or the *Bear of Oakland* had taken Admiral Byrd northeastward to explore more of the Ross Sea (Walden and Paine, *Long Whip*, 94).

17. Passing at close range increased the risk of forcing other teams into crevasses, initiating fights among eighteen or more dogs, and losing time and supplies.

18. The ice was moving so actively that the second bridge had to be reseated up to twice a day (Byrd, *Discovery*, 115).

Little America, with six buildings from the 1928 Expedition, was expanded for the Second Expedition. Until a shelter was built for the three cows and one bull calf, they lived in a tent by one of the radio towers. (Paine Antarctic Collection)

ton up on to the barrier, which is some haul. Jack laid up with a lame front foot + I have Kaiser in lead.[19] He is very promising + if I can train him to be as good a leader as Jack, I will consider it the proudest achievement of my whole life. Patience + discretion are constantly needed + above all self control, for his antics certainly are extremely exasperating. Brutus died probably from the after effects of his infection + Wolf dropped stone dead to-day. An autopsy by Moody showed a crushed liver + testicles + general internal injuries. There is no doubt in my mind that he died as a result of a blow or kick by Buckley. Everyone is furious about it + things have reached a point where either Buck goes or we go. He has behaved like a grown up kid all along + utterly selfishly + inconsiderately. The *Bear* is to the Eastward [with the Admiral] + the *Ruppert* is halfway to New Zealand—I can't understand how the Admiral could leave even before his base was established but he did. He never visited the Pressure Camp once during the stay of 42 of his men there though he drove through several times between L.A. + the ship. I have about reached the conclusion he is a publicity seeker + nothing else. Joe

19. A good lead dog had to have a good sense of direction and, on command, be able to travel in the desired direction, control the other dogs on the team including keeping all of them pulling their load, and keep the haul line, the "gangline," taut at all times. Both Byrd and Laurence Gould in their books about the First Expedition mentioned that, like men, one did not know if a dog would be a good leader until tested.

Biologist Earl Perkins in the hatch of the old administration building.
From the surface, one could exit and enter a building through a hatch,
climbing down a ladder into the room. (Paine Antarctic Collection)

Healey talked over the radio which we all are very glad of. Parachute jump
by Skinner yesterday.[20] Taylor going to make history by going over the edge
of the barrier in a barrel or swim nonstop across the Bay of Whales. W.
Barrier about cleared up save for the gas, coal + hay. Cox has a sore back.
Glorious weather. Temperature around zero but no wind + brilliant sunshine. We wear nothing but a shirt + usually no gloves. More perfect weather
for such a length of time I have never seen. Mess hall, radio shack in course
of construction.[21] Mielles[?] House, the cow barn + Mountain House up +
being lived in.[22] The cows in a tent. Working on day shift.

20. Bernard Skinner was a tractor driver and former parachutist.

21. Supplementing the six buildings built for the First Expedition now sitting under snow and
ice, eight new structures were under construction on the surface: the New Mess Hall, Science Hall,
Dr. Poulter's meteor observatory, the cow barn, the radio shack, the Kohler power plant, Dr.
Bramhall's magnetic station, and a shack for Noville and Innes-Taylor ("Dog Heim"). As all the
buildings would soon be covered by drift, hatches were built on the surface to allow entry. Later,
travel between buildings would be through underground snow tunnels. Little America would be
able to generate electricity, receive and broadcast radio transmissions, service tractors and airplanes, house four cattle, observe meteors, record weather, house and feed fifty-six men, shelter
and feed 150 or so dogs, allow research into twenty-two branches of science, provide a combined
library and infirmary, and show motion pictures (ibid., 113). Causing some confusion, different historical accounts use the names "Dog Heim" and "Blubberheim" for more than one building; also,
the terms are sometimes used interchangeably.

22. "Mountain House" was a prefabricated building erected at Little America to house Admiral
Byrd. Later, it was reconstructed as "Bolling Advance Weather Station" or "Base" at the 100 Mile
Depot to use as his winter meteorological station.

Feb. 12, 1934

Yesterday a perfect day, no wind, temperature around zero but such that we wore nothing but our shirts. To-day it was quite the contrary with a twenty five mile wind + drifting. Temp about 10. I sledged from the East Barrier to Little America making four trips + hauling about three tons—all the others save the sealers + myself, worked on huts. Things go very slowly on them due to lack of efficient organization. Poulter is not a good man for coordination of men.[23] Seal steaks for dinner to-night + I had two enormous helpings. I wonder I can eat so much yet not suffer from dyspepsia or cancer or something. *Bear* turned back + due here in two or three days. Shirey has definitely left + does not plan to return. He accompanied Verleger back to N.Z. who had pneumonia.[24] This leaves expedition without a doc!

Feb. 15th 1934

Bear of Oakland arrived early this morning from the eastern trip. It had penetrated to the 150th Meridian + 150 miles farther south than Byrd reached on his flyout. It was a thoroughly successful trip. Wade rode as dogman + super cargo + had a good holiday.[25] It was great to see him again. We took our dogs to ship + loaded personal stuff which came off + hauled to tractors. Came back to East Barrier Cache + made two trips into Little America with scientific stuff. The food is to be transported not to Little America but to a point higher up + further south in the Barrier. The bay ice has broken back beyond the Citroen cache + almost to the pressure ridge camp spot.[26] Several large hunks of barrier have gone out likewise + there is a very real danger of Little

23. To his surprise and dismay, Poulter was named by Admiral Byrd as second-in-charge of the expedition just as they approached the Bay of Whales (Poulter, *Winter Night Trip*, 1, 8).

24. Admiral Byrd convinced Dr. Shirey to resign from the expedition for health reasons. Dr. Shirey accompanied the *Jacob Ruppert* when it left for New Zealand on February 5 (ibid., 1).

25. In his explorations to the northeast, Byrd traveled about 350 miles and reported getting as far as the 152nd meridian west (Byrd, *Discovery*, 112). Wade and a team were taken along in case Byrd had a chance to do some surface exploration (Hoyt, *Last Explorer*, 286). The *Bear* soon left again to meet the English ship *Discovery II* to pick up a new doctor, who had been recruited from New Zealand.

26. "The Bay is crawling with pack ice. From East to West Barrier, in all the small bays, harbors and inlets, along a 20-mile front, the ice is breaking up under the pounding of the gale. . . . At noon a squall hit furiously. The air darkened with flying snow. Half an hour later it cleared. We were appalled to see that the whole ice front between East and West Barrier—a stretch nearly five miles long—had broken out. Gone was the ship's berth. . . . Already open water had crept within a mile of Pressure Camp. For the first time, we could plainly see the dump from the ship. The intermediate relay cache was at the water's edge. Luckily for us, the tractors were now functioning perfectly" (Byrd, *Discovery*, 85–89).

America going. Hence to provide against such an event, the food is to be put in a place of absolute safety.[27] The West Barrier cache is all cleaned up + everything is now east of Pressure Ridge. It is the most colossal feat of moving that has ever been accomplished in the Antarctic. We have the tractors to thank for it. I estimate, approximately 500 tons of supplies have been carried the seven or eight miles from the ship, back three miles across the pressure area + down the barrier to Little America.[28] The Admiral when he came ashore was properly impressed + personally congratulated each one of us. After the chaos + turmoil of the last three weeks it is good to have a bit of encouragement + a man who has the authority to direct things. Poulter has shown himself quite incompetent to direct this end of the expedition + June is the only man who has not lost by this command. He has remained calm + quiet + has accomplished more than all the others put together. Holiday for all hands tomorrow. The East Barrier camp is being broken up to-night + we all will be here. Some will be sleeping in tents + elsewhere. AN ORCHID TO YOU.[29] Will I ever forget that.

Feb. 24th

I lost my diary + now find I merely placed it in my sleeping bag where it belonged. Several days ago Al appointed me leader of the supporting party which is to accompany the Main southern party south about 150 miles. It is a great compliment + I know I can do it successfully. Ronne, Russell + myself are to be on the supporting party. Taylor, Moody, Petersen + Rawson are to be on the main party. The main party will go south for 15 days + return, the purpose of the trip being to blaze a trail for the tractors. We are to carry dog + man food + cache it at various points. Meanwhile I have been breaking my

27. Not only was the fragile bay ice going out to sea but the thick barrier ice as well. The ice was tilting, and cracks several feet wide were threatening to detach Little America. A meeting was called for all members, and it was decided an emergency cache, "Retreat Camp," was to be immediately provisioned with enough rations, coal, and equipment to carry the men through the winter and until the ships could get in the following summer. The cache was located on the high barrier about a mile southeast of Little America and about two miles east of East Barrier Cache (ibid., 70, 118). While the name "Little America" was used again, the Second Expedition was the last to use this base because of its unstable location (Charles F. Passel, *Ice: The Antarctic Diary of Charles F. Passel*, 396).

28. Byrd later estimated that 650 tons of supplies from the two ships were unloaded by the dog teams and tractors. The dog teams alone ran several thousand trips (Byrd, *Discovery*, 115; Byrd, *Alone*, 19).

29. "An Orchid to You" was the only song of many available phonograph records that Carbone the cook was interested in playing.

The "place of absolute safety" is the emergency cache or "Retreat Camp." One-third of all the supplies were deposited away from the unstable ice under Little America. If Little America went out to sea, there were enough supplies here to carry the men over the winter until the ships returned the next year. Little America is visible in the shallow valley behind the pressure ice. (BPRCAP, Papers of Admiral Richard E. Byrd, image 7876–3)

neck to get the dog pemmican ready over in Dog Heim, using oatmeal tins for forms, an airplane torch for heat. Desmond + Healey are helping me.[30] I made a trip out to the sealing camp + blubbered five seals bringing blubber back with me. This we are using with our dog pemmican, 1/3 blubber, 2/3 pemmican. Wade, Dane, Buckley, Perkins + Lindsey out at sealing camp. Food moving up to cache on barrier [emergency cache or "Retreat Camp"].

Feb. 25th

Radio message from Dearie reporting all well, first message in three weeks. Yesterday I spoke over the radio reporting on what the supporting party expects to do + accomplish. I have never been so nervous in my life. But I managed to survive + read my speech. I was as follows: Murphy—"The leader of the Supporting Party—Stuart Paine, son of the famous writer, the late

30. To set supplies for the sledging parties going south the following spring, the plan was to place seven days' rations for four men in depots at 25, 50, 75, 125, and 150 mile points, and 30 days' rations for four men at the 100 Mile Depot. Each sledge would carry the usual camping and trail equipment, navigation and radio gear, medical kits, and dog and man rations as well as the extra supplies; the total load was estimated to be about 950 pounds per team (Byrd, *Discovery*, 133). Pemmican was made of several different ingredients and pressed into hard, dry cakes. One kind of pemmican (made in the United States) was for men, and another kind was made at Little America for the dogs. J. B. Desmond was a *Ruppert* crewman.

Paine stands beside a large seal on his sledge. (Paine Antarctic Collection)

Jack's team waits beside the seal pile. A man works on the roof of a new building in the background. Supplies from the ship are dumped everywhere. (Paine Antarctic Collection)

Paine

You will be in complete charge of the supporting party comprised of Paine, Russell, ~~Wade~~ Ronne.

Your equipment will consist of two dog teams
    18 dogs—two lead + 2 trailer sleds

You will carry man food rations for 15 days (140 lbs.). Safety material—one man 15 day rations—added.

	2 trail tents	50 lbs.
	1 Primus + cooker	17 lbs.
	2—5 gal cans kerosene	70 lbs.
155 lbs. {	Complete clothing equipment for three men (furs to be issued) 3 fur sleeping bags	
3 lbs.	3 small boxes meta—to be issued	
10 lbs.	Repair skii equipment (Ronne looking after this)	
4 lbs. {	Cooking gear— 3 soup plates	
	3 cups	
	3 wood spoons	
	extra cooking pot	

15 lbs. miscellaneous gear
464 lbs.

You will carry 800 lbs. per sled. The balances of your loads to be made up of dog Pemmican of which you will be able to take around 1136 lbs.—

The Pemmican will be bagged— This I will discuss with you at length.

You will require little navigation instruments beyond a compass as you will be following us out + return on a marked trail. This we will discuss with Rawson.

I will issue you a .38 colt and 50 rounds of ammunition. This you will keep with you until you can return it to stores.

Also a small medical kit.

The two teams in your party will be yours and Russell's. Go over both teams and make any replacements you feel should be undertaken.

Come to shack to-night after supper for further discussion + bring this list with you. You will not carry radio for this short trip.

Alan

Memo from Alan Innes-Taylor assigning Paine to lead the three-man Supporting Party to Mile 150 south to help prepare for the next year's field season. Paine was soon transferred instead to the main party as the navigator. (Paine Antarctic Collection)

Ralph D. Paine." Paine—"The Supporting Party will leave simultaneously with the main party. It consists of Russell, Ronne + myself, + two dog teams. With the main party we shall put down depots on the southern trail. One hundred + fifty miles south we shall turn back." Finis.

The *Bear* arrived in the vicinity of the Bay of Whales but found the Bay frozen over + out to a distance of twenty miles. It is a serious situation. The question has been + is—can the *Bear* get in + unload + take aboard the extra men—17 in all. If she doesn't, the expedition will be wrecked—food shortage, housing + clothing. Our oatmeal + soup rolls for the trail are on board. This might mean no trail work should they not be loaded. But at the present time it looks as though she would get in all right + we have orders to stand by to dash to the ship should she make a landing. We have been constructing a seal house back of Dog Heim. The sailmakers are working [making tents, etc.] but not fast enough. We shall not get off anyway before the *Bear* situation is cleared up. It is really a dramatic + serious crisis. An awful lot depends on what happens to the *Bear* to-night or tomorrow. Buckley is going home. 25 below though it felt about twenty above.

Sealers back + got 191 seals.

Feb. 27—

Bear left night before last. I had just turned in after making last entry in my diary when we were called to hurry to *Bear* as she was approaching the ice. We got down there about as she got there. It was only about a half a mile to the ship from the pressure camp instead of three miles. It was about twenty below + the sea smoke was very dense. You couldn't see the ship until you got a hundred yards from it. Then her spans + yards loomed up like a phantom ship. On going closer her hull appeared all sheathed in ice. It was a marvelous sight. With seven dog teams we unloaded about 22 tons of supplies in six hours, hauling it across the bridge by the former site of the pressure ridge. It was the most efficient job yet done by the dogs. 15 men left here bringing the ice party down to 56, a sizeable number at that.

Hardly had we finished unloading than the *Bear* shoved off.[31] Sails Kennedy destroyed all his patterns + threatened to wreck the machines. Sorry to see Joe Healey go. He deserved to stay.

---

31. After Dr. Louis Potaka, the replacement physician, debarked and supplies were unloaded, the *Bear* escaped with rigging already swollen to twice its normal size and its whistle frozen solid. Paine's team tailed the group and brought frozen potatoes—the final fresh vegetables going to the base (Walden and Paine, *Long Whip*, 94–95).

Letter from Dearie reporting all well. Also radio letter.

Rawson taken sick with a throat infection, swollen glands + acute pains in the back. This left the southern party [the main sledging party] without a navigator. Things hung fire until this morning when the Admiral consented to let me be navigator.[32] I don't believe anyone has much confidence in my navigation, which is a bit disconcerting, but I have a great deal of confidence + I think I can do it. It is a great responsibility but I am pleased at their placing it in my hands. The supporting party seems to be left without a leader, consisting now only of Russell + Ronne. Seal house dug to-day. If I ever needed faith in myself + in my work I need it now. Pray for me, Dearie.

Feb. 28th

Day spent in feverish haste to get navigational equipment ready. So much had been left undone that it has been a terrific job. Spent afternoon setting the directional sun compass for Admiral. Made one mistake but he said I did a good job. To-day was the first time I have had any contact with the Admiral. Ken's condition unchanged. Noville feeling ill. Start tomorrow or bust. I believe I can do the job.

---

32. The main party included Black, to break trail, Moody, Paine, and Innes-Taylor, leader. The party planned to put down supply depots for the spring journeys and mark a trail for the fleet of tractors that would soon set forth into the interior to establish a base in which Admiral Byrd would spend the winter night alone. The midnight sun had already set for the first time, and every day the sun set earlier and rose later. The temperature, already dropping as low as 20° below zero, was expected to fall to –60° before the party could return. As the tractors and dog teams during the ships' unloading had dumped their cargo anywhere there was an open place, the piles had to be ransacked to find compasses, medical kits, windproof mittens, and all the other things a sledging party had to have (ibid., 98–99).

5

Journey of "Seven Hells"

March 1–31, 1934

March 1st

sledmeter 10.3
Left Little America for south at 7:15 p.m., going about due south for 10.3 [nautical] miles. Dane + Blackburn had gone over 7 miles to mark trail + find route through pressure area. Steered course magnetic 73. Finn ahead on skis, me next, followed by assortment of teams, sometimes Moody, sometimes Russell. Here at first camp. Taylor in charge, me navigator, Black radioman.[1]

March 2nd

9:00 a.m.—Sky overcast, wind East force 2. Barometer 28.98. Evening 8 p.m. 28.73. Lowest temp last night –25°. Most of us cold all night. Our sleeping bags are faulty + must be fixed before we go out again. Left Camp Buckley 10.3 miles south of Little America around 11 this morning + traveled until around seven to-night. We ran a little less than 15 miles to our first depot 25 miles south.[2] We tried for the first time to establish radio communication

---

1. Quin Blackburn was a geologist. The navigator's team always led the other teams. One man skied ahead to break the trail, and then, in order, followed the navigator and his team and then the other teams. Without the benefit of landmarks on the ice shelf, the navigator steered by watching a boat compass mounted on the sledge and then shouted directions to the man skiing ahead. A magnetic needle in this latitude makes wide erratic swings; a center point must be estimated (Byrd, *Discovery*, 41, 290).
2. At the evening stop, the tethering line and stakes were unloaded and positioned, then the

Led by Paine as navigator of the main party, the teams head south to set trail flags and build supply depots for the following year's field season. White canvas tanks on the sleds protect the supplies from snow and keep the supplies together if the sledge goes down a crevasse. (Paine Antarctic Collection)

with Little America but Black couldn't raise them.[3] What a story it will make if our radio doesn't work at all. We plan to go right ahead, radio or no radio. My watch stopped to-day + the chronometer to-night. This leaves us without GCT [Greenwich Central Time].[4] But we have L.A.T. which is all we need for our sun compass and dead reckoning.[5]

dogs one by one were taken out of harness and led to their places on the line. Each dog was fed a pound and a half of frozen pemmican and ate snow for water. The drivers then put up their orange-topped tents, collected clean snow for the Primus cookers, and shook the snow from the sleeping bags before they carried them into the tents (Walden and Paine, *Long Whip,* 105–10). Useful for identifying geographic locations, each night's camp was named whimsically as they were set up.

3. For the first time in an expedition, all mobile outfits were required to have radios for communication with Little America. Radio transmissions from Little America were in voice broadcasts; messages from the field were in Morse code (Poulter, *Winter Night Trip,* 15). Specifically for the sledging parties, John Dyer built field sets with a five-watt output transmitter and battery-operated receiver all in one 110-pound unit. The transmitter relied on a hand-cranked generator (Byrd, *Discovery,* 211).

4. A line running north and south through Greenwich, England, was established as the "initial meridian," at 0° longitude. GCT is the same as GMT, or Greenwich Mean Time, and acts as the basis of the world time clocks.

5. Dead reckoning is a method of calculating current position by using speed, direction of travel or compass heading, and time elapsed, from a known point. A sun compass is also used to establish

March 3rd

Barometer –28.44 at 8 p.m. 18 above at noon. 19 1/2 miles to-day after a late start around eleven. Black, Ronne + myself ahead on skiis until late this afternoon when Finn + his team went ahead. Made twice as good time. Built depot at 25 mile camp leaving one man's rations for 30 days. Pressure ridge to the west. Sastrugi running from a south easterly direction which are as hard as rocks.[6] Almost foot + a half high on average. Meters continually going on bum + find every one of our kerosene tins are leaking. Leather mittens useless. Hoosh + cocoa excellent. Taylor more than does his part as a cook.[7] Sleeping bags faulty + we sleep in our fur parkas with only our lower regions in the bag. Radio on bum. No communication for last two days. Evidently something very faulty with sending end. Most of the day ascending a slow rise. Blowing thirty miles from south east with heavy drift. Wind moderated as soon as we broke camp + this evening no wind, occasional whiffs from southeast. 5 below 9 p.m. Overcast sky + snow threatens. We are warm + comfortable in spite of the cold + I think we all are experiencing something of a thrill to be out here bound for the south + thanks to a faulty radio out of touch with everything + everybody + living unto ourselves. To think of my going south, navigating a party of six men to the pressure area at least is something I never dreamed of. Such are the breaks.

Mar. 4.

Barometer 28.63. Temp. –7. Beautiful day at time of breaking camp. Got off to an early start around 9.[8] Changed course slightly to the eastward to 71°

---

direction of travel by reading two positions of the sun at given time points and then calculating the course between them. The courses indicated by magnetic heading and the sun compass will be different, as the magnetic poles of the earth distort the magnetic compass readings. Finally, the course is corrected for any deviations and expressed in degrees south. One degree of latitude is 60 nautical miles or 69 statute miles. One minute of latitude is one nautical mile or 1.15 statute miles.

6. Wind speed was always an important factor in traveling conditions. On March 3, the early-day thirty-mile-per-hour wind and ambient temperature of –2°F was equivalent to –29°, according to a 2001 revision of the wind chill chart first developed in 1945 by Charles Passel and Paul Siple for military use. It gauges the amount of skin exposure before frostbite. The current wind chill chart is readily available from the National Weather Service. Sastrugi are rhythmic ridges of snow or ice caused by the action of the wind.

7. Strict rations limited the daily menu on the trail. Only a skilled cook could make the monotany of the ingredients consistently appetizing. Biscuits were brought over on the ships and were formulated to meet nutritional needs. The biscuits and the contents of the trail rations would change over the duration of the expedition.

8. Morning routine rarely varied. After eating breakfast, striking the tents, and loading the sledges, the dogmen harnessed the dogs and lined up the teams. Black, as trail-breaker, skied

Trail Portions of Meals
Fall Southern Trip Feb 26th—
Supporting Party

Breakfast
2 mugs tea with sugar + milk
2 Biscuits
2 mugs oatmeal with sugar + milk

Lunch
1, 2 oz. bar of chocolate
2 biscuits with butter or peanut butter
2 oz. pemmican cold
2 cups tea with sugar or cocoa or
    malted milk.

Supper
6 oz. pemmican made into hoosh (add
    salt)
Erbswersts
4 biscuits with butter, peanut butter
    or bacon fat
2 cups tea, cocoa or malted milk
2 slices thick bacon

On a diary page, Paine copied an example of "Trail Portions of Meals." Rations were adjusted slightly by journey. A one-day ration equaled thirty-seven ounces of dry ingredients, or just over two pounds of dry food per man per day; this amount doubled once melted snow was added as liquid. Dogmen on the trail needed more calories than any-one else on the expedition. (Paine Antarctic Collection)

mag. [magnetic south]. This we did because of a check with the sun compass showed us to be going a little to the westward. At 11:30 arrived at 50 mile mark to establish a depot. Built cairn + ate lunch. Ronne went to the east about a mile putting out pennants [in a line perpendicular to the trail] + I to the west. Overcast sky, light breeze from north + light snowfall. The nature of the light made it impossible to see where to go or what you were travelling

---

ahead, Paine's leader, Jack, would set a steady pace, and the other teams then followed in a column about one hundred yards apart. A sledge meter, an adapted bicycle wheel, was fixed to the naviga-tor's sledge and was connected to an instrument that measured distance. Every third of a mile, Paine shouted, and the last driver plucked a flag from his sledge and jabbed it into the snow as he ran, leaving a wavering line of orange flags marking the trail behind him. Every twenty-five miles, they stopped to make a depot of stacked cut blocks of snow, eight feet high and capped with a big orange flag. Rations were cached inside. Additional raised snow hills, "beacons," were also built as guides between depots. Perpendicular to their north–south direction, the party also planted burgees to the west and pennants to the east at fifty-yard intervals to a distance of several miles out from the depot. These flags served as additional guides if a party missed the beacon in a blizzard (Walden and Paine, *Long Whip,* 111–13).

over. It was like stumbling along blindfolded. I got out about 1/3 mile when something impelled me to stop. I did so + removed my snowglasses, the only time I had done so up to now in the middle of the day. Over to the right lay a large black mound. I thought at first I had doubled back upon the sleds. But my flags were straight. I approached it a few feet + soon the depths of an enormous hole, a crevasse, opened up to me. I was so surprised I was tempted to venture closer, but as I was alone thought it better to wait. I got half way back to the sleds + the blizzard was upon us. It came like the first rush of tide at Mount St. Michel, quick like a mouse. You couldn't see fifteen feet ahead with the driving + drifting snow + a forty mile wind. We made camp immediately + succeeded in doing it in a half an hour. But everything was covered with snow. Our pockets were filled. Snow penetrates everywhere. A small crack anywhere invites a bit of snow to enter. It's almost like gas. Penetrates everywhere + everything. So here we are, fifty miles south of Little America, Lat. 79°24', Long. 163°48'E by DR [dead reckoning] in the midst of a raging blizzard with that big black hole only a third of a mile away. Completely out of touch with all our fellow beings + being a life only onto ourselves + our dogs. It is fairly warm—around 20 above I guess + the snow melts in our clothes making us damp + wet. That makes us cold.[9] It is to be recalled that the last year at this time the party in the Rockefeller Mts. were held up nine days by a blizzard of this kind.[10] Let us hope we shan't have such bad luck. Our mileage for the day was only 5.6. But as the visibility was getting worse + worse + as we were approaching not realizing we were in the crevassed area which Amundsen speaks of, it was just as well the blizzard came when it did.[11] Had Ronne come up to a crevasse similar to the one west of us, he would surely have gone in before he could have seen it. I wonder now about what impelled me to stop + take off my glasses before going on. A little more to the right + a few feet farther would have been too bad for yours truly.

March 5th

8 a.m. Bar. 29.18. Temp. +12. Wind ceased during night + we woke to a

---

9. This was particularly problematic as the water evaporated in the cold dry air and made the men even colder. The small camp stoves were not capable of completely drying anything out (ibid., 127–33).

10. The Geological Party of the First Byrd Expedition was caught in fall of 1929.

11. That day, the texture of the snow became the same as the sky and the line of the horizon melted away. This experience was mentally and physically disorienting. Admiral Byrd likened the sensation to being in a bowl of milk. That night, the winds from the gale reached sixty miles per hour (ibid., 115–19).

heavy snowfall + no wind. Remained here during the day as visibility was extremely uncertain + occasional snow squalls made traveling difficult. Taylor + I shifted our tents around to face north as did Russell + Ronne. 3 p.m. The wind has shifted around to North again + is increasing in strength. With 8 inches of soft snow on the ground the drift will be terrible. Taylor has decided to send Moody, Black + Russell back. Our kerosene supply is rapidly dwindling, in fact every tin leaks except Ronne's. We have lost five gallons in 4 days, which is too much. Hence the necessity for some of us to go back. I am afraid it is a great disappointment to Moody + Black particularly as well as to Russell. But they have taken it with characteristic good humor + are offering us anything + everything from their sleds. We are making one last attempt at establishing communications with L.A. but up to now no luck. We discussed last night the possibility of Little America having gone out [to sea]. If it was to this reason it would have done so last night with the strong south wind. In the event it has, we would immediately return to the emergency cache on the east barrier + hole in for the winter. Our safety would be assured but would those left at Little America be quite so certain? It is a very real possibility + may be only too real when we go back.

March 6th Fall Sledging trip cont.

Awoke around seven to the weirdest sound very much like an automobile horn. A few more minutes showed it to be the Citroen with June, Skinner + Waite, who had come out to find what had happened to us. Up to that time we had had no radio communication with L.A. June tells us Murphy has labeled them the rescue party.[12] They had made the run to the 50 mile cache [50 Mile Depot] in about seven hours running time. They brought with them two tons of supplies man food + gasoline. They also brought two five gallon drums of kerosene, which considerably improved our situation + allowed the supporting party to continue. They were all set to return to Little America.

Taylor, Ronne + myself investigated the big crevasse which I all but fell into last night. It was about 25x50 + over 150 feet deep. It was a magnificent thing to see. We attached alpine ropes to ourselves + each took a look by

12. Late on March 5, Byrd dispatched June and the tractor unit (Skinner, driver, and Waite, radio operator) to carry fourteen thirty-day rations, test the tractor in the snow, and to find out what was wrong; the Southern Sledging Party had not met any of their twice-a-day radio contact schedules since they had left Little America. The tractor met the party at the 50-Mile Depot, fixed their radio transmitter, and transferred to the sledges the 1,280 pounds of rations, giving each dog almost another 100 pounds to haul (Byrd, *Discovery*, 138–40).

At 50 Mile Depot, the tractor crew caught up with the sledging party, which had been out of radio contact since leaving Little America. The crew was sent by Admiral Byrd not only to check on them but also to warn them of a crevasse area that was not on any maps. (Paine Antarctic Collection)

crawling on our hands + knees to the brink + peering down. It seemed to go more or less N + S. There were big blocks of blue ice lying on various ledges but to the westward it went down + down as far as we could see. It was a magnificent cavern open only at the top + colored with light like the deepest bluish green at the bottom. June concluded we were in the western edge of a bunch of crevasses which run east + west for several hundred miles. I had been told nothing of these + that was one of the reasons June was sent out to intercept us. Byrd, it seems, was quite remorseful that he didn't tell me about them. In fact they are not on any maps I have. Took due east course for five miles. 100° to be exact + then south making 16 1/2 miles for the day. The blizzard had made the going difficult with the soft snow + our heavy loads which we took on from the tractors. Seemed to be ascending a slow slope. All afternoon the sun broke through just as we reached the top in a most glorious sunset I have ever seen. Temperature dropped to –36°, but we were not cold, at least I wasn't. Harold had brought us out wool liners for our sleeping bags. Damn those bags.

Paine, with Buck and Break-it, stands at 50 Mile Depot. This photograph was taken at a temperature between –18° and –26°F. (Paine Antarctic Collection)

March 7th Snowmobile Camp

Citroen + party blew in about nine + we gave them the loads we had taken the day before. It was decided I as navigator + Black would travel light with my team + go ahead of the tractors, making thirty-five miles a day if possible. We rearranged loads + Dick + I started off. Taylor + Ronne about two miles back. Russell + Moody had turned back.[13] Five miles Dick spotted what looked like a box on the right, about a half a mile away. We decided to inspect it in spite of our orders to speed quickly as possible. We left team on trail + skiied up. It proved to be the front end of a sledge of the last expedition. About a foot stood above the surface. Not having time to dig it out we skiied back to sledge + prepared to resume course. Wind had changed to north + light snow with decreasing visibility. Decided to wait for Taylor + Ronne, as we had no cooking utensils. They arrived + we all drove up to sledge. It was

13. At Mile 66, the tractors that had surprisingly reappeared took back the extra loads, intending to advance them to Mile 100. Here, supporting team dog drivers Russell and Moody turned back north for Little America, and Innes-Taylor, Black, Paine, and Ronne continued south (ibid., 140–42).

the snowmobile.[14] Hardly had we inspected it then it began to blow + here we are with a fifty mile an hour Antarctic blizzard raging outside. An hour after it first started, the Citroen shows up. June had directed it by means of a flag which he held out of the window to get the wind direction. Dogs + tractors were immobile. They had expected to follow Dick + I closely + when it was time for them to start it had begun, this blizzard. It was singularly fortunate we did stop or we should have been eating cold food + snow to-night. It was a relief to me to find snowmobile, for now I know I'm not off my course. But our progress south is very slow on account of the weather. We are out six days + only a little over seventy miles south of Little America. However, the time of the year makes it impossible to accomplish much.

March 8th

In camp at Camp Snowmobile. Unfortunately when we dug up the sled over what was supposed to be the snowmobile, we found no trace of the snowmobile. The day spent in sleeping, monkeying with radio, repairing harness + general leisure. Wind continues from North with varying visibility. June, myself, Taylor, Waite, Ronne, Skinner + Black in attendance. All eating in our cook tent. Barometer dropping + temperature high around 27° Fahrenheit— I hope for fair weather tomorrow. Admiral questioning why we aren't making better progress.

March 9th—Fall Sledging Party

Left Snowmobile Camp around 9 ahead of tractor. Black putting out flags + I checking compass. Ran for 18 miles due south, variation 112 E., mag. course –68°.[15] June got impatient + for last five miles went ahead + through to 100 mile depot + returned here 5 miles this side of 100 mile depot for supper.

---

14. The Ford snowmobile was abandoned by a party of three men on the First Expedition who were testing it for Antarctic use. It became bogged down in the combination of soft snow and sastrugi, and the rear end gave out at Mile 85. The party was not equipped with a radio and were considered lost; however, the party man-hauled a three-hundred-pound sled back to Little America. Upon learning its fate, Byrd was surprised the snowmobile had gotten even that far but was pleased with potential future mechanical capabilities (Richard E. Byrd, *Little America: Aerial Exploration in the Antarctic, the Flight to the South Pole*, 302–4; Byrd, *Discovery*, 141; Gould, *Cold*, 124–25).

15. Navigation is based on the formula T ± V = M ± D = C. This means True (course or heading) plus or minus the Variation equals the Magnetic (course or heading) plus or minus the Deviation equals the Compass (course or heading). This calculation is based on the compensation needed by the location-specific difference between the geographic pole and the magnetic pole. The distortion specifically at Little America was 107.5° east of true north (Byrd, *Discovery*, 222). In addition, over time, both the north and the south magnetic poles move. In 1934, the magnetic pole

Taylor + Ronne following but failed to reach us to-night. Waite left his living radio set with him + we ought to make easy contact with L.A. Cooked a good hoosh but having only one pot couldn't make any drink. Snowmobile 1/2 mile west of trail. Snowmobile shoved off for L.A. around 9 after hearty hand-shakes all around. Black + I put up [radio] aerial + turned in—Ran 23.4 miles.

March 10th

8 A.M. Bar. 28.81. Taylor + Ronne not in sight yet. Make contact with L.A. Wind turned from S.W. to North around nine + it looks like another blow. Ate chocolate for breakfast + now waiting for Taylor. Running 66° mag.

8 P.M. Bar. 29.01 22 below. Taylor + Ronne arrived at our camp around 12 + we promptly had something to eat. Black + I had had only chocolate for breakfast. They had camped five miles back of us. Made two radio contacts with L.A. Duke is getting no help on his work, which is extremely unfair.[16] Citroen arrived back in L.A. about 12:30. Proceeded to 100 mile depot + built cairn. We had built a beauty but it collapsed when I attempted to climb up on top of it. We rearranged our loads + from here we are taking 12 days rations of dog food, figuring we have to turn back under any circumstances 6 days hence. We will try to get to the pressure, 70 miles hence in that time if we can.[17] If not we come back anyhow. My team in good shape + still complete.

March 11th. 18 1/2 miles. S. 100 M.

Yesterday made about 170° for the five miles to 100 M depot. To-day made about 178° + 18 1/2 miles. Started about 1:30 + ended day at 7 p.m. Dogs pretty well in. S.E. wind + storm threatening. All well + healthy. Ran course 66 during the day.

March 12th

Bar. 28.85—temp. Min –22°—8 a.m. +2

Cloudy with south east wind. Made 6.6 miles 175°. Soft going. Myself out in front. The dogs seem unable to make very great progress + we reached 125 miles depot only after a difficult struggle. Camped to-night give dogs a

---

was almost directly west of Little America in South Victoria Land and over eight hundred miles from the geographic pole. The magnetic pole is currently in the South Pacific Ocean.

16. Duke Dane was caring for all of the dogs left in Little America by himself.

17. The party considered going farther than Mile 150. Here, Paine referred to pressure ice at Mile 170.

Constructing a depot for caching supplies and to act as a beacon to mark the trail on the ice sheet. (Paine Antarctic Collection)

rest. Blizzard threatening. Temp dropped to –14 in an hour but is slowly rising. Visibility is decreasing. We had a shower of snow crystals which formed a beautiful halo around the sun. Yesterday we had high cirrus clouds radiating from a point in the south east. Build snow beacon + cached one man 30 day rations. Pos. [position]—lat. 80°38', 163°36' D.R. Taylor preparing an excellent hoosh not to mention a beaker of anti-scorbutic.[18]

March 13th

Made 20 miles south east of 125 mile depot, my course 20. Surface improved so we were booming along + the dogs seemed to be hauling the sleds easily. Wind from the north west, directly behind us, which was a break for us. It probably blows from that direction only once in the month. It was a day in singular contrast to the day before when we made only a little over 6 miles— 24 when we stopped.

March 14th

Last day on our southern trip. Ran 5 miles south east + established 150 mile

18. As the trail rations were devoid of Vitamin C, a solution made of lemon powder, corn syrup, and water was eaten to prevent scurvy.

Purina Dog Chow checkered bags were used for man food on the trail. One checkered bag plus one white bag of biscuits sufficed three men for ten days. (Paine Antarctic Collection)

depot, one man ration for 30 days. Day overcast but going fine. Minus 47 last night, the coldest yet. Taylor seemed to suffer from the cold because of the faulty zipper on his sleeping bag. Ran 150 south five more miles + established our farthest south.[19] Celebrated occasion by a strong beaker of antiscorbutic, chocolate, chicken bouillon, + an excellent hoosh. Temp about 20 below all day but following wind helped us. Taylor's dogs are bleeding on their feet + all in general seem tired. All dogs had double rations of pemmican. North tomorrow + warmth + a change in diet after being out just two weeks to a day. I judge we shall be back by the 27th. The pressure looms just ahead in mirage all over the southern horizon but owing to the bad visibility we haven't seen it yet. Southern point we have reached is 163°12′W Lat., 81°03′ south. Have formed a club known as D81T.[20] Taylor, myself, Black + Ronne sole members.

March 15th

A.M. Temp. –10,—30 [mile] Wind from North with heavy drift + occasional

---

19. Their mission was complete; they had traveled south to Mile 155, and they had set trail flags and cached supplies for the spring/summer field season as planned.

20. "D-81-T" refers to latitude 81° south. Possibly a joke, it may indicate "Deviation 81 True."

The fall journey's farthest point was at Mile 155, past latitude 81° south. Having set trail flags and supplies for the following summer, Paine, Alan Innes-Taylor, Dick Black, and Finn Ronne turned back north toward Little America. Paine's team is shown. The wind, cold, and closing darkness made for brutal traveling conditions. Photo taken on March 14, 1934, as the ambient temperature reached –47°F. (Paine Antarctic Collection)

snow.[21] Remained in camp during the morning + probably for the afternoon. Had excellent radio contact with Little America + I received message from Dearie saying had received my message + was reassured + still redecorating. Ate five bowls of oatmeal for breakfast + the plan is to sit + eat all day. Had to get up last night about 2 a.m. to chain up a loose dog. I was unconscious most of the time so didn't suffer much. Two primus going in the cook tent + we are having a thorough all around drying. Byrd wires he has flown out to fifty mile depot + cached food. He crashed with Fokker + caught fire but no one hurt.[22] Taylor cut his finger last night slicing bacon. Find bacon fried is

21. According to the current wind chill chart, the combined temperature and wind was equivalent to –40°F, which gives the men less than ten minutes of skin exposure before being frost bitten. See Appendix 3 for Paine's official records, made in his diary, of each day's minimum and maximum temperatures at specific times in both the morning and evening, the barometric pressure at the time of reading, and the wind speed or other conditions in his remarks. The diary narrative includes additional information.

22. In taking off, the Fokker, piloted by Ike Schlossback, with Zuhn, Dustin, and Young, probably lurched into the air off of a ridge of sastrugi and went out of control and crashed irreparably on March 12 at the 50 Mile Depot. They were attempting to assist the tractors in hauling supplies for "Bolling Advance Base" located at the 100 Mile Depot. No one was hurt (Byrd, *Discovery*, 145–46).

better than any other way of serving it. Black has an inexhaustible supply of stories.

Menu for supper—Puree of pea a'ju 81, Pemmican ordinaire, doughnuts en 81, Latmilk with sugar. Slept during afternoon.

March 16th

Turned northward to-day + made 15.6 miles on our northern trek. The going was abominable + we on skiis just plodded along. The surface wouldn't slide in the least bit + the dogs were straining to make headway. Break-it collapsed at 15.6 miles + we made camp. The wind changed to south east + we had it directly behind us. In fact we were quite wet during the day. Temp about –10. To-night it is –30° at 6:30 + it looks like a record low for our trip.[23] We were all a bit tired + discouraged at our poor progress. Expect to meet the tractors tomorrow at 125 mile depot. Byrd plans to put his house ["Mountain House" or "Bolling Advance Base"] there or on 120 mile.

March 17th, Fall Sledge Party

Temp last night –54°, which I believe beats Amundsen's record low. We didn't suffer however, having two primus going in the cook tent until we went to bed. Got off to an early start + made 12.4 miles to 125 mile depot. The going was terrific, soft sandy snow + we + dogs all in at end of day. Gave dogs short rests at intervals, which helped. No tractors here + we fear the worst, down a crevasse or something. 40 below when we made camp.

March 18th

Min. temp. –45° + at 8 a.m. it is 18. Spent comfortable night in our frozen bags. No tractors as yet. Contacted L.A. + find Bowlin made flight yesterday to 100 mile depot with seal meat. All four tractors are snowed in at 50 mile depot. Pilgrim forced down 15 miles from L.A. We are staying here for to-day hoping tractors will catch us here. We have five days dog food left + must make 100 Mile depot before that. Dogs are exhausted + it is well to give them a rest as well as to give us one. That day yesterday was the hardest yet.

---

23. The dogs were in poor condition and the men were severely frostbitten. In addition, the zippers on the sleeping bags, particularly on Innes-Taylor's and Ronne's, would not close, eliminating any possibility of real rest as their bags iced up. Their body heat also melted the ice, so they were not only cold but wet. Break-it and Skookum of Paine's team and Skeelah and Cape Cod in Innes-Taylor's team were very weak (Walden and Paine, *Long Whip,* 124–25).

Were we to go on to-day it is not likely we would get far + then we might have to come back, for it is here REB wants to put his Mountain House.[24]

Meanwhile it is blowing from the east + a storm is not far off it seems. Meanwhile we sit + eat + converse + try not to get on each other's nerves. Our diet will have gotten a bit tiresome after two more weeks of it, but a welcome change awaits us at 100 mile depot. REB wires for us not to lose the trail. That is evidently a word to me. But we had little difficulty in following the trail. Only several times did I go by a flag without sighting the next. Even then with the field glasses I could pick up the next three. Yesterday there was the most curious haze which through the glasses appeared as the edge of an enormous barrier pressing down on us from all sides. Likewise from the surface of the snow there seemed to arise heat waves. The 125 mile depot was visible only when we were around a half a mile from it. Another thing of interest occurred night before last. As we were all sitting in the cooktent, a distant rumble from the north was heard followed a second later by a loud rumble + cracking under us + we settled about three inches. The rumble passed on to the south + that was all. It startled us as we didn't know whether we were going into a crevasse or just what. This has happened twice up to now. It is quite distinct from the frequent settling of the snow crust as we go along. This settling sometimes lets you down several inches + we wonder whether it's going to stop at that.[25] A brief description of us in camp.

We have three tents, two with floors, one without which is the cook tent. These tents are of windproof material with orange material in the top to make them easily visible. Each have two poles at each end coming to a point. Three poles are sewed in so that they are easily erected. Two ropes lead from each end + two from each side. Taylor + I sleep in one tent, Black + Ronne in the other. Black operates the radio in his tent when Ronne gets up. In the cook tent, Taylor sits at the far end on the trail box surrounded by bags + cans + other cooking paraphernalia. The primus is in the center. Ronne sits on the left at the entrance on his duffel bag + Black + I on the navigation case to the right. Suspended from the tent rope at the peak hang all kinds of woolly + wet things, socks, mittens, ski boots, parkas, pants, etc. Hair + sennegrass continually dump from above into the hoosh + tea etc. but our sense of discrimination is becoming nil + we love these gifts as roughage.

---

24. "Mountain House," called "Bolling Advance Base," was manned by Byrd ("REB") alone. Some documentation supports his planning at one time for one to two other men to spend the winter with him. This issue is explored in Goerler, *To the Pole*.

25. Snowquakes are caused when huge stretches of the Barrier's crust, yielding to contraction, suddenly seek a new equilibrium.

March 19th

Temp. rose during night from –34 to around –18. Day overcast with wind from east about 15 miles. Made 15 miles to within ten miles of 100 mile depot. Going was soft but gradually improved during day. Dogs about all in at end of day + we were all tired by the heavy shuffling + pushing. We are concerned that the dog pemmican is not what it should be. Too much fat, 15% in the pemmican + 30 which was added, makes 45% fat in it. Not enough energy builder + too much fat. Tractors unheard from so far but we expect them anytime.[26] If they all stick together they will only make about three miles an hour, as fast as the Cletrac can go. Al nearly froze last night + his bag is sheathed in ice. No wonder he is cold. One of the prime necessities of the trail is to get enough sleep. Without it a man is not what he should be. Attempted to take a longitude sight yesterday around 1 p.m. The damn artificial horizon [in the instrument] wouldn't work because of the low altitude of the sun. It hasn't worked at any time I have tried it. A bubble octant is the only thing, not this contraption + contraptions which Rawson piled into the navigation equipment.

March 20

Blowing from the North about 15 miles, visibility not good but we may be able to travel. Black + Ronne late as usual in getting up.

11:30 a.m. Visibility so bad can't see next flag, even through glasses + stayed in camp. We have about three days dog food + fuel left, but a half day's run will bring us to a plentiful supply of both at the 100 mile depot. No tractors. Evidently, we are getting the storm which delayed them. I favored getting underway + making the depot using the compass but Al preferred waiting since it is not entirely necessary. Spent morning talking, writing + making up a shield for our D81T organization. We sit around the primus occasionally warming our feet + hands over the flame. We are comfortable + warm in spite of its being –14 outside. But I am impatient to get going + get back. We have been living this life, eating the same food + doing the same things for three weeks + the sooner it is over the better for us + particularly for the dogs. Those few mornings of –47, 45, 43, 54, 34, 39 etc. is telling on them. The pemmican I repeat is inadequate.

---

26. The tractors were hauling supplies required to build and provision Advance Base. The Cletrac was hauling the disassembled Mountain House itself. The tractor party was traveling south toward Mile 100 and the sledging party was traveling north toward Mile 100.

I read over some of my back entries, I realized what I did + what happened comes back to me. I like to read of my last days at Shankhassick [the family farm]. When I think of Dearie, her offering to deed the place over to me if I would stay, her farewell, I am ashamed of myself in a way.[27] If I hadn't gone she would have been quite unhappy, for she would have held me back. I think she is happier this way, for things don't seem to go as smoothly when I am home. I can't mind my own business, probably because I feel that Dearie's business is such an important thing to me. My thoughts are often with you, Dearie, out here on this flat, barren, lifeless expanse of snow.

March 23rd. 100 mile depot [actually March 21st]

The 21st dawned cloudy + drifting. 35 below with a twenty mile wind from the N.E. It was impossible to face it more than five minutes without getting nipped [frostbitten] on the cheeks or nose. Made one start in the morning but decided it was too cold to travel so remained in camp until about 2 p.m. Visibility bad. Couldn't see next flag. But wind abated some + we left around two to make the ten miles to 100 mile depot. About 30 below throughout afternoon. Made slow progress from flag to flag. It was impossible to wear ski boots so we ran in mukluks. Black couldn't keep up so rode most of the way.[28] Arrival 100 mile depot 6:30 + found 2 tractors with Mt. House aboard. Camped + turned in after lousy hoosh with Harold June.

March 22

Temp. ranged from –35 to –50°. Constructed hole for Mt. House + erected it working until 11 p.m. to get it finished.[29] Cletrac stuck down around [Mile] 75 with Hill + Pete standing by to repair it. Third Citroen came in + all hands

27. Dearie, despite a potential improvement in her financial situation, did not want to sell the farm. Deeding the farm over to Paine was a significant offer both because of family considerations and because of its excellent location and generous assets.

28. The men were traveling in the equivalent of –65°F. To replace the skier up ahead, Paine decided to recruit his lead dog, Jack, to break the trail, figuring that he was large, strong, and clever enough to figure out what was required. His job would be to go straight ahead without a guide, trample down a path in the snow and respond to Paine's shouted commands to adjust direction. After a few false tries, Jack understood what was desired and responded perfectly. With Jack leading, a human trail breaker was no longer needed.

29. Most of the work had to be done in the dark using pressure lanterns. At 61° below, the kerosene turned to mush, so the men worked by the light of blowtorches. "All of us suffered from frostbite. Stu looked bad. His skin was deadly white, his nose swollen the size of a tennis ball, and his beard crusted with ice" (Captain Finn Ronne, *Antarctica, My Destiny: A Personal History by the Last of the Great Polar Explorers*, 38).

in camp. Taylor, myself, Ronne, Black, Byrd, June, Skinner, Dustin, Hill, Demas, Waite, Tinglof, Siple, Petersen.[30]

March 23.

Temp –47 all day, –60° min. during night. Sun goes down at 6 p.m. Worked with Ronne, Black constructing fuel tunnel for Mt. House. We completed job ourselves all except stretching the tarpaulin over the roof. It was a hard day's job + I know I was very tired + people got on my nerves. Taylor is cook for all twelve men here + he serves us turkey + chicken + buttered corn last night in the Mt. House, we all standing around eating on our feet. Byrd remarked I was very silent + I was. Retired to eat chocolate.[31]

March 24

Awake to a strong wind from NW. Snow + drift. Cleared around eleven + sun came out. Prepared to leave but before we got any of the tents down it began again + by noon a real Antarctic blizzard was raging. We all worked over at the House digging up food boxes etc. which had been left on the snow + carrying them down into the tunnel. Laugh work. Up to to-day Byrd hasn't been feeling well but to-day he was out with us. Temp. –15, 20 mile wind. Dogs feasting on seal meat June had brought out.[32] Ronne made a member of staff, Black doesn't seem to be able to take it + is getting on all our nerves.[33] 6 p.m. worked on food tunnel + completed it to-night. I did the final sealing + now house provisions + supplies are below the surface. Finds his mercurial

30. The Cletrac was stuck at Mile 66; it had been hauling the prefabricated building, but the building parts then were transported by the smaller tractors to Mile 100. Pete Demas was the chief tractor driver; Ivor Tinglof was a carpenter. Brought from Little America on the *Pilgrim,* Byrd had arrived on the twenty-second. When the sledgers arrived, men were already on site constructing Bolling Advance Base. Because the four-man sledging party had already been out for three weeks in extreme temperatures, Byrd pledged to Innes-Taylor to let the men proceed back to Little America as soon as possible (Byrd, *Alone,* 35–38).

31. The dinner was to celebrate Advance Base and to thank the men for their work. Innes-Taylor was elected chef and cooked over five Primus stoves. The sledging party was expected to leave the next morning (ibid., 45–46). Innes-Taylor, Paine, and Ronne retired to their tents set up a few yards from the roof of the underground shack (ibid., 37).

32. The dogs were tethered in the open at –60° with almost no protection from the wind. The weakest dog, Break-it, was put in the cook tent. Skookum, Skeelah, and Cape Cod improved on the seal meat, and seal meat was added to Paine's sled for Break-it for the return home (Walden and Paine, *Long Whip,* 126–27).

33. Ronne was made a member of the "Expedition Staff." The staff could, by a majority vote, set up any rules and regulations for the expedition operations and, with a two-thirds vote, could overrule any order given by an officer (Poulter, *Winter Night Trip,* 2).

After almost a month on the trail, the dogmen were recruited to dig tunnels for Byrd's Advance Base at Mile 100. In the darkness and in temperatures below –60°F, Paine's hands, cheeks, and nose and Innes-Taylor's foot froze. (Paine Antarctic Collection)

barometer broken. That is a serious loss. REB made his first attempt at cooking to-night + made Jello for dessert. Taylor continued as cook for the whole gang + served seal steak. Wind has abated + it looks like a clear day tomorrow. It was fortunate we hadn't started this morning when we planned to. We would have certainly been caught in a tough storm. Trying to dry everything + primus going all day in our tent. One thing about these storms, the temperature always rises. To-day it rose to –15 which made it warm comparatively. I am aching to get back + away from this crowded quarter. To be on the trail is even better than this. Little America is home to us all + we speak of getting home, which it really is. That tractor gang is wild. They haven't the slightest idea about camping or cooking or trail living. I pride myself after looking at their mess that we can have three square meals a day + be fairly comfortable though the temperatures are in the [minus] forties + fifties.

March 25th 87 1/2 S. L.A.

Left 100 mile depot + Mt. House around one this afternoon + made 12 1/2 miles. Weather clear, little wind, temp 30° below. Dogs in good shape after

Admiral Byrd in furs at Bolling Advance Base. (Paine Antarctic Collection)

their feasts of seal meat. Taylor froze his left big toe + caught it none too soon.[34] Black remained behind + is coming through on the tractors which are expected to leave tomorrow. REB was very appreciative of what we had done + came to call me Stu before we left. He was concerned about my nose which is frozen most of the time.[35]

March 26

11 A.M. Looking back at the scrawls of the last two days I wonder I can read any of it. I wrote those entries by the light of a primus, which is hardly any

34. Innes-Taylor cooked dinner on the twenty-third despite a partially frozen foot. "Innes-Taylor remarked casually that he thought one of his feet was frozen. And indeed it was, as we saw as soon as he peeled off his mukluks. I tried warming the foot with my hands and working the flesh gently, but without effect. That superstitious business of massaging the skin with snow isn't done in the Antarctic. At sixty below, snow takes on a hard, crystalline structure; you might as well use sandpaper. What we tried in this case was a method familiar to all polar travelers. Paine, I think it was, unbuttoned his shirt, and let Innes-Taylor slip the foot against the warmth of his stomach. He held it there fifteen or twenty minutes, until the circulation revived with a pounding pain that brought sweat to Innes-Taylor's forehead" (Byrd, *Alone,* 41).

35. "Paine's face and helmet looked like a solid lump of ice" (ibid., 39).

light at all. We are still at last night's camp spot 12 1/2 miles north of 100 mile
depot. We arose expecting to get an early start + make good mileage but soon
after breakfast it began to snow lightly + blow from the northeast + here we
are again weathering out a blizzard or what I feel sure to be a blizzard. A light
snow fall, light wind, thick clouds + visibility, + wind from a northerly direction are pretty sure indicators of a storm. Every blizzard to date has started
in just this way.

Finn + I slept together in one tent while Al slept in the cook tent. He was
not very comfortable nor was I. In fact I spent the most uncomfortable night
yet + I felt like an old man this morning. Strange too that I shivered so when
it was only 15 below this morning. I believe we didn't have a hearty enough
supper last night which incidentally consisted of turkey broth + biscuits +
Latmilk. Had to get up four times during the night. However, we continue
cheerful + optimistic + hope we get in [to Little America] sometime before
the night closes in.[36] Burnt Citroen [rebuilt since the fall fire] went charging
by sometime during the night to work on the Cletrac which is stuck at 66
miles south [of] L.A. They have marked trail every sixth of a mile instead of
every third as we had done, so it is very easy to follow flags. Oh for some
decent weather. Yesterday was fine, good surface + wind on the beam. But
we got such a late start for one reason or another we didn't make as much as
we had hoped.

I wonder now whether REB will make out this winter. He isn't a practical
man at all + hasn't the faintest idea of how to use his hands. He cooked Jello
the other night + it was the first bit of cooking he has ever done. The radio
he doesn't know a thing about, not even the code. Suppose something gets
out of adjustment or breaks. His communications are completely shut off. In
fact, he told Taylor he expected they would be but for us not to worry. He
positively did not want anyone coming out here during the winter, a thing
which would be suicidal to those that attempted it.[37] I rather envy his staying
out there in a way, away from people, cares + worries. He plans to write a
book on philosophy, which will take up much of his time. Everything is below

---

36. Paine was thinking about the onset of the twenty-four hours of darkness. They had more
than one hundred miles yet to Little America.

37. A memo was written March 18 by Admiral Byrd to Dr. Poulter stating that, as he knew little about radio operation and repair, his radio would be nonfunctional much of the time, and not to
worry. Until probably November when the light had returned and the extreme temperatures moderated, in no case was Dr. Poulter to send a rescue party out because of the danger to the men
(Poulter, *Winter Night Trip,* 15). As stated in the diary, Paine learned about the order from Innes-
Taylor. A meeting was also held for the men in Little America when Byrd discussed his winter
absence.

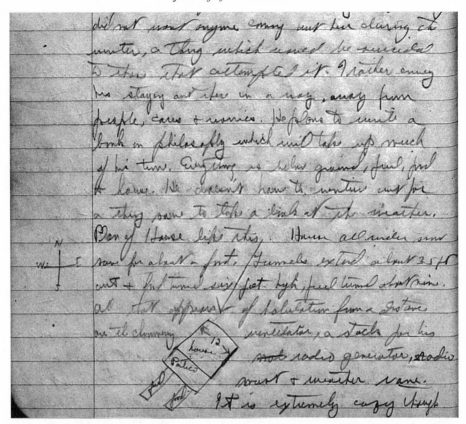

On a diary page, Paine drew a diagram of Advance Base and mused about Admiral Byrd's lack of practical skills, particularly his lack of knowledge regarding fixing radios. The layout of Advance Base is shown. (Paine Antarctic Collection)

ground, fuel, food + house. He doesn't have to winter out for a thing save to take a look at the weather. Plan of House like this. House all under snow save for about a foot. Tunnels extend about 35 ft out + food tunnel six feet high, fuel tunnel about nine. All that appears of habitation from a distance are the chimney ventilator, a stack for his radio generator, radio mast + weather vane. It is extremely cozy though crowded with 14 of us there. 11:30 A.M. Wind picking up. Drying sleeping bag. Taylor reads the *Prophet* by Kahlil Gibran + I read Browning. Ronne talks. 4:30 P.M. This afternoon we placed two sleeping bags on top of each other + one against the tent on top of these which gave us a real chaise lounge. So we dozed. I read Browning's "Columbe's Birthday," which helped pass the time away. It continues to storm with increasing wind velocity but we are snug + comfortable. In fact everyone is in the best of spirits. Temp. just zero, the warmest day in weeks.

```
                                     Little America
                                     18 March 1934

Memo for:

Dr. Poulter:

        It is almost certain that the radio at the advance base will
be out of commission most of the time.

        I have tried to learn something about radio here, but the
interruptions have been too many, and it has not been possible to do
much at night when communication with the States has been going on.

        In case there is no communication at the advance base, it is my
wish that no party come out for me.    I will be all right, and it will be
entirely useless to risk the lives of men unnecessarily.

        I hope that the camp will not be apprehensive because the
chances are all in my favor.

        On looking over these radio sets I find that so many things
can go wrong that it is hardly likely I can keep in communication.
        For many reasons I shall take every precaution.  In this
respect I shall not forget my duty to the members of the Expedition at
Little America.

        There is no necessity for coming out in the spring until it
can be done safely.    I cannot tell now when that will be - perhaps around
the first part of November.

        If it is too cold when you come out for me, I shall probably
remain a while longer.

        What I am trying to say is that I don't want anyone to risk
themselves coming out for me.    Since I have deliberately taken this
chance, it would be entirely wrong for me to cause others to take
unnecessary risks.
```

R. E. Byrd
Commanding Expedition

This March 18 memorandum or a similar message was conveyed in the fall to the men. All of the men were aware of Byrd's orders to Dr. Poulter not to risk men to retrieve him until the ensuing November. (Thomas C. Poulter, Jr. , reprinted from Thomas C. Poulter's *The Winter Night Trip to Advance Base, Byrd Antarctic Expedition II 1933–1935*, 4)

March 27, 75 mile depot

Temp to-day about 35 below + a 30 mile wind from the north west.[38] Enough said. We made 12 1/2 miles to 75 mile depot. It was the toughest day yet, such low temperature + such a wind. The drift was bad + we could only see our way by following in the tracks of the Citroens. Got there around 2 o'clock

38. This is the equivalent of 73°F. below zero. Exposed skin freezes in less than five minutes and breathing the cold air can quickly be fatal (Poulter, *Winter Night Trip;* see also Appendix 2).

after an early start at nine. Lost our first dogs, three all together, one out of each team. Harold in Finn's team dropped stone dead. Taylor had to shoot one in his team + to-night I had to shoot Skookum. He was all in to-night + refused to eat. A little later I found him kicking futilely. He was almost dead when I shot him. But I was determined to see him on his way as he had seen me on my way for the past two months. To have to bring the poor critters down to such conditions, here, then have them pull their hearts out for you + then to shoot them is more than justice allows. Let us hope these poor dogs will not have suffered in vain.[39]

March 28th

Temp. –28. Made 20 miles from 75 mile depot. Beautiful day + hard surface. Could have gone further but Taylor chose to stop. Passed Cletrac + one Citroen at 64 miles. Demas, Hill + Skinner trying to get it going.[40]

March 29th

Temp –52. Made 25 miles over hard surface + with beautiful weather. Ran first 15 1/2 miles in just four hours. Short stop at fifty mile depot + then on to here, 34 miles from L.A. Dogs ran well + mine + Finn's seemed in better shape than Al's. Trying to nurse Break-it through + feed him seal meat + dig holes for him to protect him from wind. Skookum died from the cold + over-work. We will try to protect Break-it from cold. Wind blew in gusts through-out the day. It was curious to observe the drift. There seemed to be small patches here + there. There would be a perfectly straight demarcation between a calm area + a windy one, only a few feet away. Stopped at 25 miles though we could have gone on.

39. Because fuel and food were low, they had to keep going to 75 Mile Depot. The trail flags were invisible in the blowing snow, and Paine relied on Jack for most of the navigating. That day, after Harold in Ronne's team dropped dead, Skeelah of Innes-Taylor's team collapsed. It took ten minutes for Innes-Taylor to thaw the revolver in his mitten before it would fire. Of Paine's team, Break-it, Buck, and Skookum were barely on their feet and were being helped forward by the stronger dogs. After stopping for the night, Paine found Skookum crumpled on the snow with his forelegs already frozen. Paine embraced him, and then he shot him (from personal notes, Paine Antarctic Collection).

40. The dog drivers, especially Innes-Taylor, saw the tractors as the corruption of the world of sledging, which allowed penetration of the unknown quietly and respectfully, a little at a time, and was the most beautiful and lasting side of Antarctic exploration. The dog drivers, and even Byrd, would use the words "limousine explorers" in describing the tractor men, and the tractor men would call the dog drivers "dog catchers." With the conflict partially encouraged over the winter by the cook Carbone, the mutual scorn between the tractor men and the dogmen was shrouded in icy restraint and polite sarcasm (Walden and Paine, *Long Whip*, 135–36; Byrd, *Discovery*, 170–71).

The sight of Little America welcomed the party back. (Paine Antarctic Collection)

March 30th

A.M. Remaining here 34 miles south of L.A. on account of the high wind + drift. Drift about three to four feet high + 30 to 35 mile wind from east. Sun shining in spite of heavy drift but impossible to travel. Can't see flags, nor could the dogs stand in the wind. Temp. around zero I judge. Ate tremendously hearty breakfast + repaired to the chaise lounge in my tent which is made of our three sleeping bags, two to sit on + one at the back, a primus at our feet. Such luxury I don't believe exists this side of New Zealand, not even at L.A.

March 31

Del's birthday but no means of sending many happy returns. This has been a great day for the three of us. We ran the 34 miles into Little America arriving there about 5 p.m., just as it was getting dark. The day was overcast, about 20 below + excellent surface all the way in. We arose at 5 + were off at 8. Averaged about four miles per hour throughout the day. The thrill + I might say ecstasy of looking down upon Little America from the emergency cache was something I will never forget. Taylor stopped us just before we got in + said simply, "Thank you for your effort," which meant the world to Finn + I. Our 30 day trip was over. We had gone 150 miles out + 155 back, suffering temperatures far lower + conditions far worse than any other fall trail party ever suffered. Taylor lost 7 pounds. I gained 4 but blood pressure went

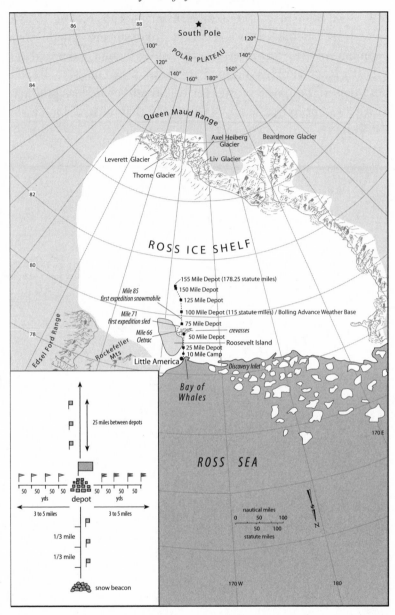

The map shows the route of the Fall Journey South where the teams set supply depots and marked trail as far south as the time, darkness, and weather allowed. The men and dogs suffered exceedingly. Some information for the inset was taken from Laurence M. Gould, *Cold: The Record of an Antarctic Sledge Journey,* and shows the layout for setting trail flags and building depots. Some map information was derived from *National Geographic,* 1935 "Operations Map," by Commander Harold E. Saunders, USN, Rawson and Darley, archived at BPRCAP, Papers of Admiral Richard E. Byrd, image 9267. (M. L. Paine)

up to 180. As we came in everyone came rushing out to greet us, to wring our hands + wish us welcome. It was a very warm + sincere greeting from our fellow members of the expedition. Our first meal, though composed of beans, was the best I have had for months. I ate through two messes. Bread + butter + jam I believe I enjoyed most. Movie, "Street Scene" was put on for our benefit. We all went to bed happy + contented that we had done a good job + done it well.

6

Little America

April 1–22, 1934

April 1st 1934.

Blizzard all day. Easter Sunday. Holiday for all hands. Rawson in bad state with his swollen neck, poor fellow.[1] Feel very tired + fatigued. Couldn't sleep last night. To-day ate well + drank in honor of the occasion.[2] Conversed lengthily with Ken + am a bit, in fact very disappointed + hurt about our whole trip + the expedition as a whole. As far as I can see, our whole trip was futile + in vain. We are merely tools for the Admiral's ambitions. The main sledge trip of next year to the eastward is to be made up of Siple, Stancliff + Corey. We who made the trip + went through what no one will ever know or realize save those who have had to endure day after day of minus forty + fifty weather are completely thrust aside + disregarded. Taylor + I know I am bitterly disappointed. To struggle + work for something worthwhile is one thing, to do that for nothing all too disheartening. If I suffer a breakdown, as I believe I might from the way I feel, it will be nothing unforeseen. My nose frostbitten, both cheeks swollen with bites + my fingers + toes numb from having frozen, I find it has all been rather useless.

April 2nd Little America

Mess duty this morning + only three hours sleep. Clocks set two hours ahead

1. Ken Rawson, unable to go on the Fall Sledging Party because of a streptococcus throat infection, had had throat surgery on March 9, almost a month before (Byrd, *Discovery*, 142).
2. The "occasion" was the completion of the Fall Sledging Party. See Appendix 3 for Paine's meteorological and navigating field records from the trip, March 1–March 30, 1934.

25 Mile Depot	78°58′S	163°48′W
50	79°23′S	163°48′W
75	79°46′S	163°22′W
100	80°13′S	163°10′W
125	80°38′S	162°50′W
150	80°56′S	161°10′W
155	81°02′S	160°51′W

The diary page from April 3 includes notes and summarizes the depot locations from the fall sledging journey. (Paine Antarctic Collection)

to let us enjoy more daylight. I turned in after breakfast + slept all day. Rawson in terrible agony all night + day + it is getting too serious. I wish I could do something but there seems nothing to do. He has had injections of morphine + is at last sleeping. I am frankly tremendously worried + feel terrible that he should be suffering so. Found I made a great mistake in my plotting. I used five meridians of longitude for one + consequently my longitude will be out. I shall replot our trip. Read over Murphy's dispatches + find Byrd, Mt. House, planes + tractors dominate news. We who went through seven hells are scarcely mentioned + it was we who made the whole thing possible.[3]

April 3rd

Blizzard of great intensity from N.E. Routine carried on underground + projected plans to bring in seals + to dig tunnels as well as to bring food down were necessarily put off. For myself I spent the day reading + washing. Ken is better + I believe he is on the road to recovery. Temp. 27 above. Find Sails a most uncongenial, grouchy + childish man I have ever seen. He is worse than Kennedy. Feel rested + entirely normal. Pelter up for first time.[4]

April 4th

Still blowing + blizzarding from North + the north east. It is a blizzard of extra ordinary length + in which feared we would get caught in while on the trail. It would have been disastrous, for our fuel + dog food would have been exhausted yesterday + our only course would have been to conserve fuel as best we could + to start killing off dogs to feed the others. I am very thankful,

3. Paine is referring to Dante's *Inferno,* which describes the nine circles of hell.
4. When Kennedy, sailmaker from the *Ruppert,* left, Linwood Miller, the sailmaker from the *Bear,* remained. Pelter, the aerial photographer, had had surgery for appendicitis.

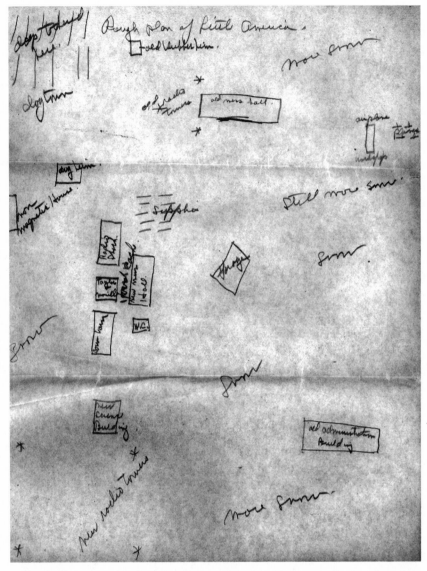

"Rough Plan of Little America." From top left, Paine shows Dog Town with surface tethering lines and underground snow tunnels, old Blubberheim (to which is attached the "Seal Chopping House"), the three old radio towers, and the Old Mess Hall, where the dog drivers and aviators bunked. At far right are the aircraft shop and planes. At midpage left, the scientists' nonmagnetic house and Dog Heim. Grouped, the cow barn, Alan Innes-Taylor and George Noville's shack, the food cache, radio shack (also a bunkhouse), the New Mess Hall, the WC (water closet), and mechanics' garage. Bottom, the new science building, old administration building (a bunkhouse), and the four new radio towers. Unlighted tunnels ran between the main buildings and Dog Town. Snow is everywhere. (Paine Antarctic Collection)

however, that we are here. I replotted our southern trip + found we were a bit more to the eastward than we thought, but our latitude was the same. Spent day in leisurely fashion, feeding dogs, reading, playing phonograph. Had brush with Corey. He is the most childish + intolerant man I have seen in a long time. In fact every time I ask him for something he gets mad + I remain calm. I believe he is suffering from an inferiority complex. Miller, our sailmaker, imagines something wrong with himself + remains in bed. He is hopeless.

It is a pleasant contrast, outside in the strong wind + grinding snow + inside here in the old mess hall which is warm + quiet (from the blizzard) + light. It has been difficult this last few days to get even to the mess hall for lunch so hard has it been snowing + blowing.[5] But unlike our day on the trail, when you stop you find a nice warm room + pleasant atmosphere. Particularly on these days do we enjoy our food, which continues varied + good. Outside an Antarctic blizzard rages. Only the experience of being out in one can fully bring to mind what it really is. Snow particles driven by a forty mile wind sting your face. Wind tears at your pants, your parka + enters up your sleeve. Your clothing, being warm when you come from the warmth inside, causes the snow to stick to your clothing. To face the wind is almost impossible, you can't breathe. Neither can you see. I sometimes wonder nature can be so wild.

April 6th

Yesterday + to-day worked in dog tunnel + have done now all but that for six days. What has been done is a work of art which represents one tremendous amount of labor. I hope to complete tunnels tomorrow.[6] Rawson continues

---

5. The Old Mess Hall was used as barracks for sixteen men. Sleeping quarters were generally separated from other buildings as a fire-control measure. The New Mess Hall was a prefabricated building brought on the *Ruppert* and was used for meetings, movies, cooking, eating, and general projects. The shacks were dug into the snow. As possible, tunnels between them were partially excavated and then topped with wood slats and canvas, which then drifted over. To get into the buildings, one opened a top hatch and descended into a room by a ladder. The tunnels, as well as many of the ice buildings, were not lighted, and the men used lanterns or simply learned to travel the tunnels by feel. Until the tunnels were built, men relied on guide ropes on the surface to help them from one shack to another in the dark or in blizzard conditions.

6. Dog Town, just south of Little America, consisted of ten parallel tunnels, each about thirty yards long and bisected by a tunnel that ran up and joined the main tunnels that passed the meat cache, the coal cache, the cow barn, and "Dog Heim," the residence of Innes-Taylor and Noville. Paine also refers to the building adjacent to the dog tunnels as "Dog Heim" or "Blubberheim," which was attached to the Seal Chopping House and afforded the main entry into the dog tunnels. Digging the tunnels had been delayed as the tractor men discovered that their fuel was running low

A meal in the New Mess Hall. One mess could serve about half of the men. Using a part-time generator for electricity, the kitchen is in the back. The large snow melter that supplied all of the camp's water needs is located in the kitchen. This all-purpose room with its highly utilized chalk board was also used for watching movies, repairing sleds, weighing and packing rations, and so on. (BPRCAP, Papers of Admiral Richard E. Byrd, image 7882-1)

to improve + got up to-day. High drift to-day + light drift yesterday. Temperature around 10 above. Still feel the exertions of our trip in that I lack energy + pep. Probably won't feel really fit for a while yet. Taylor made mention of a trip next year to Discovery Inlet. I doubt if it works out. Rawson, Taylor + myself. We shall see. Yesterday was the 5th + I thought very dearly of Dearie on that date.[7] I didn't wire her, having done so only a couple of days before. L.A. represents chaos + serious prostration after the peace of the trail. Many times I have longed for the peace of mind of the last month. Adieu.

_____

and, in the last light of fall, the dog teams that had just gotten back from the fall journey were sent to retrieve the remaining stores from East Barrier Cache (Walden and Paine, *Long Whip,* 137; Byrd, *Discovery,* 171–73).

7. Paine's mother and father were married on April 5.

LITTLE AMERICA TIMES, SUNDAY, APRIL 29, 1934.   B 4

PERSONNEL OF THE WINTER PARTY, BYRD ANTARCTIC EXPEDITION II
1934 – 1935
Rear Admiral Richard E. Byrd, U.S.N. (Retired) Commanding
Dr. Thomas C. Poulter, Senior Scientist, Second in Command

SCIENTISTS	MEDICAL DEPARTMENT	RADIO DEPARTMENT
William C. Haines, Meteorologist	Dr. Louis H. Potaka, Physician	Charles J.V. Murphy, In Charge
Dr. Charles Gitt Morgan, Geologist	James M. Sterrett, Assistant	John H. Dyer, Chief Engineer
Paul A. Siple, Chief Biologist	AVIATION DEPARTMENT	Clay Bailey, Chief Operator
Dr. Earle B. Perkins, Zoologist	Harold I. June, Chief Pilot	Guy Hutchcson, Engineer
Dr. Ervin H. Bramhall, Physicist	William H. Bowlin, Pilot	Amory Waite Jr., Operator
Alton A. Lindsey, Biologist	Isaac Schlossbach, Pilot	DOG DEPARTMENT
Arthur A. Zuhn, Physicist	Ralph W. Smith, Pilot	Capt. Alan Innes-Taylor, Chief
George Grimminger, Meteorologist	Paul Swan, Pilot	Richard S. Russell, Driver
F. Alton Wade, Geologist	William S. McCormick, Autogiro Pilot	Francis S. Dane Jr., Driver
Walter Lewisohn Jr., Archaeologist	PHOTOGRAPHIC DEPARTMENT	Edward L. Moody, Driver
Quin A. Blackburn, Surveyor	Joseph A. Pelter, Aerial Surveyor	Stuart D. Paine, Driver
David A. Paige, Artist	John L. Herrmann, Motion Pictures	Finn Ronne, Ski Expert, Driver
TRACTOR DEPARTMENT	Carl O. Petersen, Motion Pictures	A.M. Eilifsen, Ski Export, Driver
E. J. Demas, Chief	FUEL ENGINEERS	MACHINISTS
Olin D. Stancliff	George O. Noville, Chief	Vernon D. Boyd
Fred Dustin	Clarence A. Abele, Assistant	Harry R. Young
Joe Hill Jr.	COMMISSARY DEPARTMENT	Kennett L. Rawson, Navigator
Bernard W. Skinner	Leroy Clark, Chief (and U.S.Mail)	Stevenson Corey, Supply Officer
J. H. von der Wall	Alphonso Carbone, Cook	Ivor A. Tingloff, Carpenter
Bernard L. Fleming	Edgar F. Cox (also Carpenter)	Linwood T. Miller, Sailmaker

The men of the Winter Party and their occupations. Lewisohn, a radioman, is listed as an arche-ologist as a joke. One man might have many jobs. See also Appendix 1. This list comes from the U.S.-based *Little America Times* newsletter, which covered the Byrd and Ellsworth expeditions. August Howard, the editor and publisher, was an employee of the National Council of Boy Scouts of America and a longtime Byrd and Antarctic enthusiast. (BPRCAP; Papers of Admiral Richard E. Byrd, image 6474, from *Little America Times,* by August Howard)

April 8th

Blizzard + drift continued yesterday + it was impossible to work out. To-day it moderated so that we could be out but not to dig tunnels. Seals all hauled from the side of the pressure, 152 in number. It represents only about a half of our winter's requirements but with the 191 at the caches on the other side of the pressure we can come through comfortably. Taylor shot Mitzi, Mingo + Collie Penook, all three being worthless. It is again of a question of necessity + concentration of food. If the poor creatures are not fit to perform whatever we train them to do + expect them to do they must go. We all regretted seeing Mingo + Mitzi shot. They were pretty little bitches, but worthless otherwise. Collie Penook was a mess, always has been, + utterly useless. Somehow a dog's life literally comes true down here.

Lanterns or pressure torches were carried into the foggy dog tunnels where the dogs lived in darkness but in temperatures thirty degrees warmer than the outside. (Paine Antarctic Collection)

Had long discussion with Taylor last night. He has been relieved according to him of his appointment as in charge of trail operations + Siple is to take his place. This was done by the Admiral. Henceforth Al is merely head of the dog department.[8] As Al took this step himself by posting a notice to that effect, I argued that such a thing was probably not in the Admiral's mind at all, that making Siple leader of the eastern party was done to appease him for his not staying at the Mt. House.[9] It was a plum which Siple took full advantage of + I can't blame him, though I would not have acted as he has nor as Corey has, both their conducts being inexcusable. Rather than accept the

8. The expedition hierarchy was as follows: the admiral headed the expedition; Thomas Poulter, the chief scientist, was second in command. William Haines, meteorologist, was designated third in charge and Harold June as fourth in charge and as head of the Expedition Staff (fourth in charge would change depending on circumstances). George Noville was the executive officer (and fuel engineer), E. Pete Demas chief tractor driver, Harold June chief airplane pilot, Charlie Murphy communications officer, and Allan Innes-Taylor head of the Dog Department and, as of January, also head of trail operations.

9. Byrd considered having two or even three men to occupy Advance Base. Paul Siple had been considered as one of the men to stay with Byrd and was involved in the planning of Advance Base (Byrd, *Alone*, 16). The Eastern Party (Siple, Wade, Corey, and Stancliff) would be one of three field parties to embark upon specific goals in the spring and summer field season (Byrd, *Discovery*, 208–9).

Paine stands in a primary entrance to the dog tunnels that opened into Blubberheim and the Seal Chopping House. The dogmen dug ten parallel underground tunnels, each about thirty yards long, with dog crates set into the sides. The tunnels were bisected by another tunnel connecting Dog Town to the camp's main tunnel system. (Paine Antarctic Collection)

situation as it is + crab + sputter, I would go directly to Byrd about it. I feel Al is tremendously disappointed + hurt + his actions are being ruled by these two emotions.[10] Al has not been at all the same since he has been back. He seems to take no interest in the dogs, the tunnels or what is going on, leaving it to Ed [Moody] + myself more than anybody else. Ken is better but he sits + stews all the time. If he isn't going to be allowed to go as navigator in the eastern trip he isn't going anywhere at all. Kids, both of them in a way. Of course the whole business is a farce + utterly ridiculous right from the start. No navigator, no geologist, no radio operator, + two nincompoops, the biggest I can't say which. Stan I can't speak too highly of. Naturally we are all disappointed, particularly those of us who went on the trail this fall. We had hoped for some sign of appreciation for our work. But as far as I am concerned, the thing is a closed chapter + I shall carry on just the same though

10. Byrd, however, continued to refer to Innes-Taylor as the "Chief of Trail Operations" throughout his entire book, *Discovery*, his published record of the expedition. Also, Poulter includes numerous memorandums from Innes-Taylor, signed "Head of Trail Operations," in his account of the midwinter effort to rescue Admiral Byrd (*Winter Night Trip*).

Puppies Coniac and Rowdy at a tunnel entrance to the surface. Adult dogs were not tolerated by other adult dogs, but puppies were and thus had significantly more freedom of movement. (Paine Antarctic Collection)

I have lost all respect + confidence in REB as a leader, dubbing him a marvelous promoter, but lacking in the qualities of leadership + justice. What is on the surface is quite different from what is going on in his mind.

Radio letter from Dearie to me, to Al, from Doris + from the Browns— How good to hear + to know all is well.

April 10th

The weather cleared last two days + five men of dog dept. hauled food from emergency cache while I worked here, to-day digging tunnels from Lacooheim to main tunnel which was a considerable job by myself. However it is done. The puppies must weigh almost 12 apiece but what a smell. Tractors hauling seals from far cache. Yesterday twenty men were assigned to help Noville + June build bridge. They have had several humorous! escapes from crevasses but nothing serous. Ken continues to improve. Cox + Corey tried to smoke Noville out by plugging up his chimney. Wild cries + coughs were heard within + Noville burst out quite upset. The broadcast last Saturday was a complete failure, not one word went through.[11] The [fall]

11. While test broadcasts were radioed from the *Ruppert* during the southward journey, the first official weekly broadcast to the United States from Little America was on February 1 while the

Charlie Murphy of CBS, the expedition publicist, was also on Admiral Byrd's First Expedition. He prepared the weekly broadcasts to mainland America and was the voice to the many private sponsors of the expedition. (BPRCAP, Papers of Admiral Richard E. Byrd, image 7890-3)

Southern Party was featured. I spoke as follows: Murphy introduced me thus— "the navigator of the Southern Party—Stuart Paine of Durham, New Hampshire." Paine—"The inspiring thing about polar sledging is the feeling of independence it gives you. You are a mobile, independent unit, carrying your own food, shelter, fuel + clothing. You don't have to worry about money or being nice to people, or worry about what you'll do tomorrow, because tomorrow is always the same. It's a hard thing to express—but there's a beautiful simplicity to life on the trail." I practically dictated it to Charley [Murphy] so feel that it adequately addresses how I feel about it. All dogs

---

ships were being unloaded. Little America generally was able to transmit over ten thousand miles via relays—from Little America, to Buenos Aires, to Honolulu, to Long Island, and finally to San Francisco. The radio men had the lights throughout Little America dimmed at noon every day to signal the men to turn off all unnecessary lights to conserve power so that Little America could tune in to New York. The call sign for Little America II was KFZ (Hill and Hill, *In Little America with Byrd,* 133–34; Byrd, *Discovery,* 10).

underground now, though all are not in crates.[12] Sent messages to Dearie, Browns + Morses.

April 12th

I have been detailed to work in camp, which means finishing tunnels, chopping hard frozen sealmeat for 135 dogs, trailing after Taylor + general dog work.[13] Weather fair, temp. –30. General morale better after Taylor talked to Siple + I believe he has found he was unjust to criticize him the way he did.

Demas claims tractors wearing out so no more seals from the far cache. We have just about enough to get through until the seals come back, but it will mean sealing operations in the spring. All food will have to be hauled by dog teams as well.[14] Even with our clocks set two hours ahead it is almost dark at 7:30 + the sun sets at three o'clock in afternoon. It won't be long now before winter night will be upon us. Tunnels are progressing well with the food from the cache.[15] Pups doing well. Break-It had to be sewed up this morning. Poor dog, his fate is a hard one.[16] On better terms with Corey.

Am plagued by doubts about the purposes + possible results of this immensely expensive expedition but feel that it is worthwhile from my standpoint though not, I believe, in the eyes of the public. Byrd's star is sinking with it. He has made a great mistake in going out to the 100 mile depot on two accounts. His stay out there serves no real scientific purpose + he has deserted his men here at Little America. The latter is the most serious

12. Dog Town, in which the dogs lived for five months, was a black, foggy world twenty to thirty degrees warmer than the outside. Dogs got loose, fought, and sometimes died, usually killed by the nervous and vicious Siberians. After the tunnels were finished, with their kerosene lanterns, the dogmen patrolled the extensive tunnels in the morning to feed the dogs chained to their crates and grouped by team, and toured again in the evening for a final inspection. Paine remarked that the conditions for the men were not much better (Walden and Paine, *Long Whip*, 142–43).

13. The Seal Chopping House was constructed out of ice at the end of February; seals would be slid down a chute from the outside, stored, blubbered, and chopped up. It took five to eight hours of chopping to reduce a seal to meal-sized chunks that could feed Dog Town for one day.

14. All of the outlying caches were being cleared and the supplies being brought back to Little America. As the ice had stopped moving, Retreat Camp was disassembled as well.

15. The inside of the snow tunnels between the buildings were lined with boxes of supplies from the emergency cache.

16. Break-it, on which so much care had been lavished to save him on the fall journey, got loose in the Dog Town tunnels. An adult dog loose in the tunnels set off a usually bloody chain of events. Meanwhile, the dogs had patience and tolerance with the puppies. The puppies were confined while small but soon were allowed to roam Little America. In Little America, the generators were shut off at 10 p.m.; the electric lights died, the stoves were banked down, and the doors to the outside opened to allow for ventilation. The puppies then had free run of Little America, both indoors and out, until the morning.

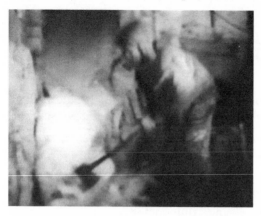

Paine chops up frozen seals for dog food. Frozen seals were slid down the chute from outside (upper left) into the Seal Chopping House, a large ice cave dug into the snow and built up with snow blocks. The frozen seals, weighing up to nine hundred pounds each, were hacked with an axe into edible chunks in five to eight hours of hard work. One seal would feed the dogs for one day. (Richard E. Byrd, III, and National Archives, Moving Images Division, film frame from *Discovery*)

criticism, + one which I felt all along as the most damning. Two coffee cans down Noville's chimney + it almost choked Ken. He continues to improve + sat up all afternoon.

April 15th

Past three days working in camp. To-day Sunday one of leisure. Blizzard on + off all day. Built shelves between my bunk + Russell's + am now pretty well unpacked. Ken sitting up most of time. Taylor + Siple have evidently settled their differences. Stan didn't show up at one meeting + when pressed for an explanation stated he must change attitude. Taylor asked me + I was quite as frank, in fact I talked quite frankly to Taylor for an hour. He says he is disappointed in us all which I feel he has no right to feel for we have more than done our part. Simply because our opinions don't agree with his. But that is settled + things are now going along normally. Still several days of hauling from cache. Gasoline to be brought down for Kohler + coal.[17] Sun rises around 10:30 + sets at 1:30 standard time. Temperatures low—30 to 40 below with varying degrees of wind. Murphy wanted me to sing with the dog drivers yesterday. I backed down. In fact I am getting rather fed up with his song + dance show + ballyhoo.

April 17th

Dogs have been taken off transporting food of which only a day's haul

17. The Kohler shack held three gasoline-driven generators with an output of 2 kW. Some of the coal was stored in the radio shack, which was connected to both the Kohler shack and the machine shop (Byrd, *Discovery*, 189–90).

remains + put on loading tractors. The scientists have no part in this as Poulter feels the scientific program has suffered. Hence this last desperate effort to get everything down here at L.A. is being done by the dogmen, the aviation crew, which has certainly done more than its part, + the tractor men. I have remained in camp on general duty, feeding, digging + to-day made one trip to cache to get tarpaulins for Corey, who was quite affable. Ken now sits up all the time + is very cheerful. The scientific program is being formulated + will be submitted to Taylor soon. I dread to think what they expect + what will be actually carried out. It is found tractor gasoline has been consumed far beyond expectations + the tractor program will have to be seriously curtailed next year as a consequence.

Demas in charge of tractors has very much fallen down as its leader. In fact no one has the slightest confidence in him. This is so true of so many others of the expedition. Those who were expected to do well have turned out miserably. Taylor made a list of them. Fortunately none of the dogmen were on it, nor the aviators, of which enough cannot be said.[18] The key men of the expedition are growing smaller + smaller as time progresses. As had been true up to the time the ship landed + as I have mentioned, the character of a man is brought to the severest test possible. Even more so is this the case now. It is only too plain that those with intelligence, + most of all background, are the ones who are showing up well. I thank God + my good luck + Dad + Dearie for just these things, particularly background. A practical use of my hands, how to do things whether it's cooking, mending harnesses, digging tunnels, or fixing sleds, a sound healthy bringing up in the country means all the difference between knowing how to do it or not knowing.

Cold to-day, –41 at noon. Froze both cheeks + my poor nose on trip to cache. Sun getting lower + lower, rises at ten + sets a few minutes later. In two days it will be gone + our winter night begins. Pups well + must weigh twelve pounds apiece, seven in all. Short + Legaska bred a week ago, April tenth + she should pup June 12th or thereabouts.

It is a bleak, cold lifeless world, this Antarctic continent. Bitterly cold + lifeless save for fifty five men here at the edge of an enormous glacial tongue 450 miles or more from its source held to terra firma only by the constant cold + inexhaustible supply of ice coming down from the mountains. Out 100 miles is REB, alone + now beyond any hope of physical contact until next

---

18. In his account, Poulter referred to Innes-Taylor's list as well, in that no dogmen or aviators are on it *(Winter Night Trip)*.

spring.[19] We then are the sole inhabitants of a continent almost as big as South America. To the east, to the west + to the south lies the unknown, a challenge to us, a mystery to be solved. To-night I stood looking at the stars, brilliant such as I have never seen them before, every star standing out like street lights even down to the horizon + thought that I was the only one on this continent to see it or was at that moment looking at them. It's a childish thought, but how impressive. There is something about it all, the barrenness of it, its mystery, its hardships, its terrible forbidding nature in all her omnipotent magnitude, hard, unsympathetic, powerful, tyrannous. It's grand in a way, land + sea unspoiled by man + safe probably from man's defamations for a good many generations, thank God.

April 18th

Temp averaged between 45 + 50 below with a varying wind from the south. I admit I have done precious little to-day but others did just as little. Efforts to get tractors going almost futile. Around noon, two were going. Hill resigned from tractor division + Skinner threatens to tomorrow, + all on account of Demas. He cannot boss + not work + expect to get away with it. His sour manner + his ignorance will never inspire men to do what he wishes them to do. Tomorrow the last day of sunshine. We had a glorious "sunset" for three hours around noon to-day. A beautiful golden orange sky in the north blending to dark pink in the south, grey cirrus clouds overhead slightly tinged with gold + a black streak of a cloud blocking the rays of the sun itself. Against this background Little America with its numerous smoking chimneys, piles of boxes, telephone poles, airplanes + caches, stood out with the sharpness of a knife. Chopping sealmeat slightly above the general level of the camp I often paused to look at the beauty of it. Al, I think, feels, + I place emphasis on the "feel," the well of spiritual radiance of such colors + setting quite as much as I do. There is an exhilaration, a mental uplifting, a buoyancy which one who either is sensitive or is given an active imagination cannot help feeling. Perhaps it's the stark + naked reality, nature untouched, unchanged, that is so touching. Perhaps it's the feeling of our own weakness + incompetence in dealing with such environment that impresses me down here. Its grip is surely on us, four solid months of night, intense cold +

---

19. Byrd was left alone at Advance Base in the Antarctic fall on March 28. He was expected to be back at Little America late in the spring, which officially began September 21. He told Poulter in his March 18 memorandum not to plan to recover him until sometime in November.

unceasing winds, blizzards + darkness. Perhaps I'm getting sentimental + introspective.

April 20th

Yesterday was the big day of the present half year. The sun went down until the latter part of August. It was cloudy so we couldn't make much of an event of it. To-day it was about as it was the day before, daylight from 8 o'clock to about five. 180th Meridian time, from 6 to 3. I put in four crates to-day, only two to go.[20] I'm tired + besides I had to feed all the dogs, not finishing until about seven. Rest loaded coal + rations from emergency cache, which now is about cleaned up. I can't understand Al's attitude. He doesn't seem to care in the least about the dogs or what goes on in the tunnels. In fact I don't think he has been in them for a week. Yesterday he + I made a storage house for the rations + to-day he helped me stow the sleds + put away the rations. It seems he prefers to sit in his hut most of the time. It is disheartening to say the least as it is next to impossible to dig out the tunnels + put in the crates alone. Jack has a bad eye, a bite or something which punctured his left eye-lid. We have been treating him for the last three days + I have kept him down here in the Old Mess Hall either on my bunk or on the floor. He has behaved perfectly + the eye seems to be on the mend, though I fear he will be blind in that eye. Everyone has been very good natured about my keeping him here. Someone stole my lantern from outside the Mess Hall. I swear if you left your hanging out to dry, you would never see it again. Thief, thief, thief + I'm getting fed up with it.

April 21st

Duke has shifted from driving to helping me. We accomplished very little though the drivers made four trips each between the cache + L.A. Daylight gradually lessens though even now we have still 8 hours of light. Overcast + comparatively warm. Doc. Potaka treating Jack who remains with me here in the Old Mess Hall. I am afraid his eye is going to be blind. The thing is to save his other eye if we can. Treating it with Atropine 1% solution, one dropper a day, + Argyral 10% solution several times a day.[21] Good movie, "State

20. Paine was digging large rectangular holes in the snow wall of the dog tunnels, setting a dog crate in each, and then packing it securely enough to withstand a dog leaping outward against his chain.

21. Paine first consulted with Innes-Taylor, who treated the infected eye with iodine, but the wound festered and a fine, bluish film crept over the eyeball. Dr. Potaka was pleased to help (Walden and Paine, *Long Whip*, 164).

Fair," which was enjoyed by all. The special broadcast to us came through terribly + our program hardly went through. The Kohler stopped just as they were in the middle of it. Ken went to supper + movies, the first for almost two months, poor guy. He was somewhat bewildered by the changes, for when he became ill everything was above ground.

April 22nd

A half holiday. In morning Duke + I cut sealmeat + fed. Afternoon Poulter gave an exhibition in glass manipulation, not blowing as was announced, for he blew only once. Later they showed "Hold 'Em Jail," Woolsey + Wheeler, quite funny. Radio program + messages came in around seven. One from Dearie, the contents of which I didn't get save that all was well, which is all important. Gala supper in honor of the winter night, consisting of lobster salad, fried chicken, corn + fruit dessert. For all the work + effort put into it I would have rather had corn beef hash. Wilcox died of old age + cold. Jack's eye much better but I'm keeping him here until it is quite well. It is too important to keep his eyesight, being the finest + best lead dog in the camp. Plans for next year still unanswered + in the formative state except for the eastern party, who have gone ahead a little too fast + I might say ambitiously.

7

The Old Mess Hall

April 25–June 10, 1934

April 25th

Yesterday my time was spent for the most part in chopping sealmeat, feeding + shoveling snow. Moody helped me. Meeting last night in Al's cabin. The topic of conversation was sex in all its phases. To-day is a day of days. Scandal of the very worst kind has come out. Clark, who claimed he had mailed all the personal letters of the members of the expedition, has been proved a deceitful liar + a cheat. Under Poulter's direction a search has revealed several bags of mail which was posted on the *Ruppert* as well as here, + in several private boxes of his were found more letters, among them some of Taylor's + Wade's, a few of Dane's + most all of Herrmann's. It is a serious affair. Taylor's insurance has lapsed because of it. Boyd lost $800. Herrmann's contacts as well as the friends of the expedition suffered great damage + it bodes no good. There is evil talk from several persons what they will do to Clark. Nothing will be done I'm sure. Those who talk loudest do the least, + I regret to say Taylor appears to be in the category. I'm so sick of wild statements, violent criticism + bitter hatreds that it is a pleasure to come down here to the Old Mess Hall where fortunately we hear nothing of it. We all have had disappointments. But rather than make a public spectacle why not keep them to yourself. Blizzard from north, no outdoor work. Yesterday all hands save the scientists turned to on the Condor.[1] The program of the

---

1. The planes, including the huge Condor, had to be protected from winds and snowdrift by garages built of ice blocks that had to be sawn and stacked by the men. It was grueling physical work.

scientific staff has suffered so, no, they were unable to help. Such as been the situation.

April 30

For the past five days I have been detailed to taking care of the dogs + camp work with Moody helping. One day he + I hauled from [the emergency] cache what was remaining up there, bamboos, vinegar[?], etc. Remainder of time snowing + blowing as it is to-day. Light only about four hours with an additional four hours of twilight. Temp. from 10 to 30 below. Clark remains in bed following his exposé of the mail. Yesterday the 29th was the 9th anniversary of Dad's death. Much time is spent indoors now. Planes not yet dug in but progress is encouraging.

May 1st

May Day, riots, strikes, sabotage + socialism. Here it is quiet + peaceful. A few outbursts of radicalism from several members of the expedition have provoked no enthusiasm whatever. I wired the commandant of the first Naval District, Boston, last night for permission to leave the continental limits of the United States, a belated request to be sure, but better than being caught short in case of a national emergency + so labeled a deserter.[2] Yesterday + to-day Ed + I, Taylor assisting spasmodically, dug out the seal house + remade the roof, raising it about three feet. This greatly facilitates our cutting up the sealmeat. Now we can store as many as thirty seals in it without trouble. Condor now completely dug in, only the top of its upper wing showing level with the surface. To-day –43 + rather cold. Since our return from the trail I have noticed how much more sensitive to low temperature I am than I was out there. Being in warm buildings + sleeping in warm quarters makes me soft I guess. A temperature of –43 on the trail was a splendid day for travelling, particularly if it were calm. No plans announced for next year. I have fallen in to great disfavor I hear with the authorities, for which I may get the rear end of whatever may be planned for next year. However I can only reiterate my very keen disappointment in Al. He criticizes, accomplishes things in such haste that his efforts are far from finished, + seems to prefer sitting in his cabin reading or writing rather than taking an active part in the daily work.

2. Paine was commissioned as an ensign in the U.S. Navy in June of 1933. He was to be available for a call to duty, which was increasingly possible as the tensions in Europe were brewing.

A lovely reply from Dearie to my message of the 19th. I can only thank you, Dearie, for your love + loyalty in my crazy wanderings. Daylight now only from 10 to three, + most light is only little more than twilight. Around noon we have the most gorgeous sunsets lasting for many hours. The clearness of the atmosphere + the intense whiteness of the snow gives the sky a penetrating light green, fading to light purple to the south. Near the northern horizon the green changes to blue, yellow + orange. A cloud, radiantly pink, stretched itself in a line on either side of the sunset. It stood out with startling beauty. Time + again I paused in my work to look at + absorb the beauty that was over + about me. To the south directly opposite was the full moon, which goes round + round, setting only when it passes below the horizon for an extended period. About us lies the barrier, snow, ice + unknown. I look often, as I pass from the Old Mess Hall to the New Mess Hall to the south + south east, to the region of the unknown areas of the earth which human eye has never gazed upon. The near vicinity of this mystery keeps one always awake. To live almost within sight of the unknown is a sensation rarely experienced by these fair inhabitants of this earth. To actually penetrate it remains for even fewer. God grant that I may be allowed this privilege.

May 3rd

Reply from Commandant of 1st Naval District as follows. "Permission to leave continental limits of United States should have been submitted prior to departure. Stop. It is not in the Commandant's authority to grant such permission at this period but your request has been forwarded to Bureau of Navigation for decision." Signed Commo. This looks pretty serious + I may be subject to a general court martial on my return. I guess I am guilty all right. But my excuses are these: I didn't know I was to go until the ship sailed, it had only been mentioned casually to me + I did not realize the seriousness of the offense. I forgot all about it following my departure until the subject was brought up the other night. At the time I did what I thought the best I could do under the circumstances + wired permission. That is how matters stand. I will wait for the decision of the Bureau of Navigation.

May 7th, 1934

I have been transferred to general duties with Noville but I haven't done anything yet. Sat. it blizzarded, Sunday I was house man + to-day blowing.[3] We

---

3. Each man took his turn as night watchman, "house man," to patrol for fires and keep track of the movement of the ice and crevasses that edged Little America.

all have settled down now to the long winter. Little remains to be done from now on. The tunnel to the Old Mess Hall has still to be completed, several days work + the garage, also several days work.[4] That finished + one shall confine ourselves indoors for four months. We have only about four hours of twilight. Moon being bright in the north, gorgeous colors, but dark to the south. Stars visible all day long. I have instituted fudge making, having baked sugar, cocoa + Klim, the proper combination of which makes a good fudge. We also have a whole box of nuts which go well in it.[5] The winter Antarctic University schedule has been announced, courses being given in geology, physics, radio, biology, meteorology + surface transportation. I plan to cover radio, physics, surface transport, which is compulsory incidentally for us dog drivers, + geology. Wade is going to tutor me in geology + I shall try to do more or less work in this. Movies Sat., yesterday + to-night. Sunday was a holiday for some reason. Radio mail log came through swell, having received six letters. Love from Browns, one from Scudders, Doris Dart, Dearie, Phil. Phil has his boat ready to go into water + has formed a real yacht club with constitution + all. Dearie reports one gold fish died but all well otherwise. Hangings up in dining room + garden well underway. What a far cry from this bleak + barren land, or I should say ice. Must wire them all tomorrow.

Life goes on very swiftly + comfortably. I am singularly fortunate to be over here in the Old Mess Hall, for here we have good fellowship, a scrupulous regard for the other fellow's comfort + no disturbing element save Paige or perhaps Fleming. We kid him along so much that even though he does live over me we get along with him quite well. This is the only place in the camp where we don't hear criticism either of the expedition or of its personnel. A finer bunch of men I don't believe you could find. The aviation gang right from the start have ranked first. Always good fellows, always ready to pitch in + help where assistance is needed. The dog drivers, I have commented upon before + a good lot they are. For interest bunks are occupied thus—Eastern wall from south to north——top—Wade, Dane, Stan, Paige, Miller (Sails), Fleming, Moody. Bottom—McCormick, Eilefsen (Boom Boom), Schlossbach, Swan, Smith, myself + Russell. On north wall, top—Bob Young, lower, Bill Bowlin. Every man attempts to herd all his belongings into a space within reach of his bunk. Shelves mostly built of gasoline boxes, run up to the ceiling. Lower bunks have shelves running along the side + all at the front end.

4. The garage for the tractors was built out of stacked ice blocks and the huge boxes used to transport them on the ship.

5. According to Olin Stancliff's account, Paine's example caught on among the other men as a new popular pastime.

Bob Young (upper) and Bill Bowlin (lower) in their bunks. Sixteen men, mostly dog-men and aviators, slept in the Old Mess Hall. They crammed their personal possessions into shelves built into their small bunk area. Light and heat came from various sources. (Paine Antarctic Collection)

Paine sleeps in a lower bunk. Visible are family photographs and pictures of home. A man's bunk space held most of the man's belongings, as well as an amazing amount of other items. (Paine Antarctic Collection)

Every available space is utilized by someone. Near the stairs an enormous quantity of mittens, gloves, stockings, hats, mukluks, Finniskoes, + what not drapes from the rafters + wires + ropes string between them.[6] Near the big stove + stretching toward the north door are wires for our newly washed clothes + these usually are hung sheets, wallies, socks + sweaters. Out a bit from these lines is a rack built by the ingenious Fleming for boots + mukluks, which will not + cannot be stored in any shelves. Toward the door we have a rack for duffel bags, in which are those things we have no immediate need for.

We lately changed the stove from a victrola looking affair to a good old flat topped one which was in the Admiral's quarters in the Ad. Building. A stove pipe runs the whole length of the hall so we get the maximum heat from our fuel. We have been really comfortable for the first time since this was put in, though Corey raised hell about the flagrant + to him unnecessary waste of stovepipe.

May 10th

May 9th was the anniversary of the North Pole Flight 1926, + it was a holiday here for all hands.[7] It was a calm cold day, 40 below, + the activities commenced with a base ball game, Devil's Imps vs. Ad. Building Rats. The game was played three innings + resulted in a 4 to 3 victory for the Ad. Building Rats. It was, I believe, the coldest baseball game ever played anywhere. Even though it was around noon time, it was dark so we could hardly follow the ball much less to catch it. Following this then was an archery contest which Stancliff won, a talk on the North Pole Flight by Demas + a festive dinner at 3. Initiations into the 78 Club followed, which was a rowdy + childish affair.[8] A meeting followed to vote in the members of the expedition on the ships in New Zealand. It ended disastrously with many of the initiates resigning. Bedlam is a mild word for the meeting. So a new meeting will be called later to try to straighten matters out. Movie later on.

Garage is nearing completion. I believe they are erecting the building today. This marks the completion of all outside work for the season. From there on our existence will be largely confined to the tunnels, the buildings + other underground hovels. Taylor is to commence a series of lectures next

6. Finniskoes are reindeer-skin outdoor boots, fur side out, that reach to the top of the calf. Mukluks are also high boots used as lighter footwear for indoors or light outdoor duty.

7. Byrd, then a lieutenant commander, was the first man to fly over the North Pole in a 1926 round-trip flight from Spitzbergen, Norway, to the North Pole, in the trimotor Fokker named the *Josephine Ford*. This claim has been controversial.

8. The "78 Club" derives its name from the latitude 78° south, where Little America was situated.

week. Likewise the Antarctic University commences. I have begun reviewing geology + hope to take this up with Wade more earnestly than the other
courses. I have come to the conclusion "T" is emotionally unbalanced, even
to being slightly neurotic. We are all a bunch of morons, pure + simple, says
he. I wonder whether he has any right to criticize. He has certainly changed.

53 this morning but calm + still. It was colder than this out at the
Mountain House. Ken has been taken ill again with a pain in his shoulder +
arm. Duke says Polooka (Potaka) is all right, but just doesn't understand. He
dumped a whole sledgeload of snow right at the corner of the main thor-
oughfare. So that in hauling snow away from the garage hole you have to go
around it. Everybody is crabby.[9] Duke says "I'm a Sh———." "Make it two,"
says Duke. I'm regusted.[10] Pipes in our big stove burst last night. A job for
Fleming.

May 13th

Last few days I've been feeling rotten. My digestive tract upset + pains in my
back + left arm. I hope to be better shortly. Blizzard raging. Mother's Day to-
day. Expected to say a word over the radio to Dearie but interference made
it impossible. I'm sorry for her sake. Work on geology progressing + I hope to
get into new work within a week under the able tutorship of Yeoman Wade.

Tunnel not yet completed between here + Mess Hall but it won't take long
now. Garage all up save for the runway. My radio technique is improving.
Antarctic University begins tomorrow. I recall the lecture Taylor has given us
about getting along during this so-called trying winter period. To-day he is

9. People, even those highly experienced in the polar regions, can easily be impacted by the
long-term close confinement, lack of natural light, and boredom. Byrd talked about these personality changes frequently in his books. Discussing the option of having two men staff Advance Base,
Byrd posed the argument against it—after the daily tasks were done, each man, Byrd said, would
be left only to take each other's measure: "Not deliberately. Not maliciously. But the time comes
when one has nothing left to reveal to the other; when even his unformed thoughts can be antici-
pated, his pet ideas become a meaningless drool, and the way he blows out a pressure lamp or drops
his boots on the floor or eats his food becomes a rasping annoyance. . . . Even at Little America I
knew of bunkmates who quit speaking because each suspected the other of inching his gear into
the other's allotted space; and I knew of one who could not eat unless he could find a place in the
mess hall out of sight of the Fletcherist who solemnly chewed his food twenty-eight times before
swallowing. In a polar camp little things like that have the power to drive even disciplined men to
the edge of insanity. . . . The ones who survive with a measure of happiness are those who can live
profoundly off their intellectual resources, as hibernating animals live off their fat" (Byrd, *Alone*,
16–17).

10. *Regusted* was a term used in the early radio show *Amos 'n Andy:* "I's regusted!"—meaning
disgusted.

the only one who hasn't gotten along. I wish he would appoint a senior man who could do + take the responsibilities which he should take. I don't believe I've seen such hypocrisy as I have seen in him. He has lost my loyalty + my cooperation but for the sake of the expedition I shan't do anything to prejudice his leadership though God knows he has done that himself. Worked out trip to Mts. of Plateau + geological party. The geological party can be done entirely by dog team. The Plateau party must have assistance either from the tractors or by air. There is no other way possible.

May 18th, 1934

The nights are growing longer + longer. A brief two hours at noontime yields enough light to work outdoors. The garage + machinery pile are about constructed + dug out. In fact they turned the two broken down fordsons around to the garage. One Citroen caught fire but no damage was done save for a broken gas line. The weather has been extremely mild, usually around 20 below, which made it very pleasant outside. We have been expecting a blizzard daily but to-night it's cold + calm + clear. The Antarctic University has been in session a week with each class well attended. Geology, geophysics, biology, meteorology, physics, radio + surface transportation. Navigation also by Herr Dr. Rawson. Haskell looks very pretty beside my bunk—Haskell being a beautiful Saturday Evening Post Girl!

Awoke yesterday morning with the idea of a magazine. Russell agreed that it was all right, + since yesterday we have written + organized it, being known as the "Barrier Bull," + to-night it is with Clark being published.[11] We haven't enough mimeographing paper to permit everyone to have a copy, so will type sufficient copies to place one in each living quarters. I think it is quite good + I believe the first bit of ingenuity displayed in L.A. Received permission to leave U.S. from Como.[12] Ronne + I cutting meat + feeding this week.

May 20th

To-day is notable for Russell + me as it was the first time the Barrier Bull came out. Clark did a good job of typing + we fixed up some good covers of black album paper with the name in white ink + a picture of the autogyro on

---

11. The name was likely a play on words—named both for Iceberg, the newly arrived bull, and for verbal nonsense.

12. Thus Paine, upon his return to the United States, would not face a court martial, go to prison, or face a dishonorable discharge.

The Barrier Bull published not only Paine's articles but also humor, essays, and stories written by the other fifty-four men living underground at Little America. Contributing a regular article, Charles J. V. Murphy summarized interchanges with Admiral Byrd, who was alone at Advance Base. Material regarding the most critical and famous controversy of the winter night, Byrd's unknown fate and its effect on the men was included. Selected articles from each of the eight *Barrier Bulls* are presented in order in Appendix 4.

Barrier Bull, May 19, 1934 (no. 1):

Charles J. V. Murphy reporting Admiral Byrd beginning his second month at Advance Base and receiving a message from President Roosevelt; an editorial introducing the magazine intended for fun; and Skookum, an article exploring the challenges of bathing at Little America.

---

the front with the caption—"Rare specie of McCormick Gull discovered by B.A.E. II." Everyone thought it very good from Murphy + Taylor down. That <u>is</u> a compliment. I am rather proud of it myself. Radio letters to-day from Morses + Dearie—all well there. It is such a long way home + what they are doing is so different from what we are doing it is difficult now to realize it. Flowers, rain, mud, green foliage, etc. I have come to take for granted the intense cold, personalities + politics of Little America. Now for the next issues of the Barrier Bull!

May 23rd

Yesterday a blizzard 40 miles per hour, heavy drift + snow. It is interesting to note that the temperature rose to 17° above zero at noon, May 22nd. May 21st at noon was fifty-four, 54° below zero. During the space of 24 hours the temperature rose 54 + 17° or 71°, quite the biggest rise in temperature I have ever seen. The wind swinging from ~5 mile S.E. to 40 mile North. I took Noville's turn at mess duty, he being ill. Like Rawson's illness I believe somewhat modified. Dr. Potaka stated to-night that any illness here, outside Pelter's case, can be traced to physical unfitness, not necessarily before they came down but since they have been here on the ice. Neither Rawson nor Noville have done any manual labor to speak of, hence no exercise.[13] The

---

13. Aside from manual tasks, the men could walk or take their skis and traverse up pressure hills and ski down them or ski jump off of the crests. Byrd and Dr. Potaka encouraged the men to exercise every day.

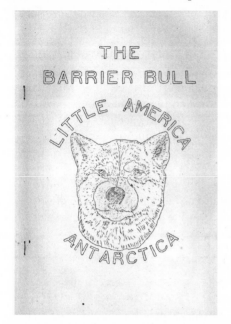

The *Barrier Bull* was launched as a both serious and humorous magazine for the expedition members. Charlie Murphy's news of Admiral Byrd and the first issue's editorial page follow. (Paine Antarctic Collection)

cold, in contrast to that hot stuffy cabin, has done the work, the occupants being physically weak.

May 26th, 1934 Little America

Second issue of Barrier Bull—I believe it was excellent save for one exception, that bedtime story of Dr. Palooka's. It was characteristic of the man becoming simple, childish, gablitive, tending to strain to force humor. Skookum I believe I have never written anything better. Noville's excellent. Warm—17° above last three days. Finished tunnel to Mess Hall, that is so I can get through. Improved in radio to 14 words a minute.[14]

May 30th

My entries seem to be far between. In reality there has been very little to write about. I haven't seen the dogs for a week. I have almost forgotten they

14. They are practicing Morse code, which would be used by the trail parties to communicate with Little America.

1

CHARLES J. V. MURPHY

1.

Admiral Byrd has been invited to reopen the World's Fair at
Chicago May 26. If communication is successful, he will
transmit from Bolling Advance Weather Base a message that
will set off a remarkable fireworks display reading "Greetings from Little America" - even if Admiral Byrd doesn't
spell it quite that way. The affair will be part of the regular Saturday broadcast. The Little America studio will receive
its cue from New York and, shortly after going on the air, will
attempt the switch-over to Advance Base. Preliminary arrangements have already been made. General Dawes and the Governor
of Illinois will speak at Chicago.

2.

Thursday, May 17, Admiral Byrd began his second month of darkness at Bolling Advance Weather Base. He reported all's well.
He now has two weekly radio contacts with KFZ. A message from
President Roosevelt was read to him. The message said, "I
hope all goes well with you and all the other members of the
Expedition. We are thinking of all of you and hoping that the
drifts are not too high, nor winds too strong, for an occassion-
al promenade in the dark. Good luck." As a matter of record,
Admiral Byrd happened to report earlier in the week that he
still manages to walk an hour or so every day, as a rule during
the late afternoon. He reported temperatures fluctuating between 20° and 50° below zero.

3.

Social Notes from Little America . . . The hard riding, hard
drinking, fast set in the Administration Building has opened
the fall social season . . . Dr. Morgan has invited a large
number of guests to the first duck shoot . . . Mr. Grimminger
entertained an orphan from across the railroad tracks, Thursday.
It was just another day in the week for the high flying balloon
runner, but it nearly killed the orphan. "I can't travel that
pace", moaned the orphan, as Mr. Grimminger flung him across
the saddle of his high spirited hunter. "You rich have lived
too close to the cache." . . . The lower classes in the Old
Mess Hall are now clamoring for bread. "Let 'em eat cake and
like it", shouted the Bourbon, Mr. Haines. . . Mr. June has
invited fifty guests to the June levee. Twenty covers will
be set in the cache. . . Our Norwegian colleagues, Messrs.
Eilefson, Ronne and Peterson celebrated Norwegian Independence
Day in bitter isolation. Senor Eilefson, when approached for
a statement on the peculiar significance of the day, rapped
out: "no good - no good - this Norwegian holiday - no whiskey
for Norwegians - Americans all celebrating . . . no good."
He burst into tears, poor thing.

AN INTERVIEW WITH COMMANDER SCHLOSSBACK

     Commander Schlossback, Ike, to his friends, czar of Antarc-
tic railroads, intrepid explorer, capitalist, and friend of the
poor, granted the following interview to a Barrier Bull reporter.
He explicitly stated that he did not wish to be quoted, but
later he capitulated and approved of the following:-

     "Tromso! Ah, that lovely town in the north of Norway.
Years ago I put through a railroad from Tromso to the Greenland
Ice Cap. Quite a fair size undertaking. We had to bridge all
way to Greenland. It cost me a lot of money. But that isn't
why I love it so. Its because its unique. Everybody here has
been to the Arctic Circle. Everybody is an explorer. Its a
town of explorers. And they all take it seriously. People
ordinarily do not go up to the Arctic Circle every day. But here
they do. In fact they go to every continent, the Antarctic, the
Greenland Ice Cap, the Arctic. There isn't any place where they

The *Barrier Bull* column by Charles J. V. Murphy reports on Admiral Byrd and
comments on activities of interest or concern at Little America.

4

THE BARRIER BULL

Published Every Week in Little America, Antartica

EDITORS

Stuart D. Paine - Richard S. Russell

* *

EDITORIALS

In the world of journalism the launching of a magazine, large or small as the case may be, is undoubtedly an anxious moment for its editors. Will it be accepted by the public? Will it be profitable? Will it be accepted by the critics, if the periodical happens to be a literary one? Will it gain sufficient circulation to insure a good price for its paid advertising? Last but not least, will it bring approbation or condemnation upon the aspiring editors?

Such are the questions to be faced by those who foster the usually dizzy career of a magazine in this gullible world. The percentage of failure for newly founded magazines is disastrously high. This, it seems, is the only thing that keeps the total number of monthlies, weeklies, dailies within reasonable limits.

Fortunately here the editors do not have to deal with the problems ordinarily faced by the great majority of editors. We have a public to be sure, but quite small enough to be classed not as a public but as a circle of friends. We know exactly how many readers we have - at least we optimistically claim to - and we likewise know, quite positively, the limits of our circulation. We have no desire for profit. In fact, had we the desire, we could scarcely gratify it. And Mirabile Dictu, we have no critics, the critical critics, we mean, who never say anything nice about anything, but who vie with each other to heap undignified insults upon those so unfortunate as to consider themselves successful. That we do not worry about paid advertisements goes without saying. Of course, we will accept such advertising, but we do not solicit it. Rates will be found elsewhere.

As to what the editors may gain or lose from their undertaking, the answer is very simple. Amusement. We launch the BARRIER BULL purely for fun. It is to be both serious and humorous. Contributions of any sort are cordially invited and earnestly desired. We publish each number once a week or oftener if our material and imagination permits.

Owing to our limited publishing facilities, we are only bringing out six or eight copies at each issue. One will be placed in each of the living quarters and one in the library. There may be several for the editors. Leroy Clark has been kind enough to type these issues. To him the Barrier Bull gives thanks.

The BARRIER BULL is noncontroversial, nonpolitical and nonsensical. Such is the protege of the Editors.

The Antarctic University inaugurated its first winter semester this week. Courses in various subjects are offered. These are being conducted by men experienced in their various fields. We who have no specialized knowledge, particularly in the fields of science, should consider ourselves singularly fortunate in being able to take these courses. Those who are skilled in some branch can profitably look into other branches. Here as in no other sphere of activity are the sciences intimately associated with our lives. We have and will undergo considerable hardships to further the cause of science. Such, in the last analysis, is the reason we are here. It behooves all of us to find out more about what we are here for, and the goal to which we are striving. Though we all have not the same

The *Barrier Bull* editors Stuart Paine and Dick Russell provided the only written community voice of the men of Little America. The editors wrote and collected articles from the other fifty-three men at Little America to make up the magazine.

Barrier Bull, May 26, 1934 (no. 2):

Charles J. V. Murphy reported a temperature of –72° at Advance Base, adjustments needed in Byrd's ventilation system, and his "bum" cooking; Noville's "Antarctic Daze," a satire featuring Robert Falcon Scott; Dr. Potaka's "Bedtime Stories," costarring the "Bear of Soakland" and "Distillery II," which indirectly addresses excess alcohol use; and an editorial citing carelessly broken phonograph records.

existed but next week Finn + I go on again. Short I believe to pup shortly. Mail evidently has reached home or at least some of it. Got a wire from Del about mail + one from Dearie wishing success to Barrier Bull. It's more work + worry than I thought it was going to be. I have been chosen to go on the Geological party next year with Quin + Dick. A couple of good lads. Eastern party to consist of Wade, Corey, Stancliff + Siple. Plateau party is Morgan, who will never get there, Bramhall, Eilefsen, Ronne. Supporting party, Taylor, Dane + Moody.[15] I spent a whole day wiring my bunk to _____ [?] with all Fleming + I found in the old radio shack, three lights + two switches + miles of wiring. But the batteries don't seem to work well + the lights are next to useless. I finally got Noville to fix toilet which had been out of commission for five days. Bob Young has scheme of a 78 Club certificate along the lines of a Neptune Certificate. Came to me + we have Black working on it.

June 2nd

June, month of ideal weather, sunshine, trees, flowers, all that is beautiful + sweet in nature. I can see Shankhassick, resplendent in foliage, iris, weedy lawns growing to beat all, still precious. Phil struggling to keep up with it + act the gentleman at the same time. Dearie is struggling with weeds in the garden, probably quite baffled as to why they don't stay out once they are pulled, perhaps baffled as to the names of three or more new species of Veronica, etc. What a dream all that seems. How far away + long ago such

15. Quin Blackburn, a geologist, would lead the Geological Party; Charles Morgan, chief geologist, and Ervin Bramhall, physicist and meteorologist, would be the experts on the Plateau Party. Three field parties were planned for the summer season: the three-man Geological Party, to which Paine was assigned, would do geological and paleontological reconnaissance of the unexplored eastern reaches of the Queen Maud Range, not far from the South Pole. The others would be the Plateau Party, which would also go south, and the Eastern Party. The Supporting Party planned to set additional supply caches south to assist the Plateau and Geological Parties.

The library with its three thousand volumes and its wind-up record player was used as a retreat and a quiet gathering place. The multipurpose room was also the personal residence of Dr. Potaka, the physician, and was an operating room for dogs and men. (BPRCAP, Papers of Admiral Richard E. Byrd, image 7883-14)

were a part of my every day life. It has been nine months now I left home. What a strange world I have chosen to spend that time away from home. Cold, darkness, ice, snow, lacking everyday utterances with normal people, fighting nature, fighting your fellow expeditioners, fighting yourself. It sounds strange, but true. A clash of ideas now assumes an importance very out of proportion to its relative status.

Barrier Bull came out for the third time to-day. Though it did not have so much humor as the previous week's issue, I believe it was almost as good. Black's article was very good. Rawson's not, Walter's ballad to Morley Bones. Poulter made an unexpected offer of 60 sheets of mimeograph paper for us to print copies for everyone. It is quite a compliment.

I am on dog duty this week with Ronne. All dogs seem well + happy. Pal died a couple of days ago. I cannot believe it was due to a natural cause. Pups

Barrier Bull, June 2, 1934 (no. 3):

Charles J. V. Murphy regarding Byrd's guidelines for the summer field plans; Anon's "Whirl Is King," an essay observing the variety of styles of discordant argument and enthusiastic debate; and an editorial commenting on the plans and cooperation needed for the next field season.

very big + jumping out of their pen.[16] No light at all now except for moon, which circles round + round overhead for two weeks + then sets for two weeks. It doesn't seem so strange, this continual darkness, now that we have become used to it. The University courses on, one class after breakfast, work from ten to qtr. of two + three classes in the afternoon. 4 hours of work. We have begun the repair of harnesses + tents, looking towards next year's operations. Taylor + I on quite good terms now. I am scheduled to go to Mts. next year with Blackburn + Russell, the prospect of which I am looking forward to very much.

June 4th

Warm weather continues. Blowing to-day. Poulter reports, 1. ice tilting because of warm weather. 2. there is only one tide every 24 hours. Had talk with him to-night concerning Black, I frankly told him what I thought, but feel tremendously sorry for him. He is so greatly disappointed. Taylor is an old woman. Puppies continually getting loose. Mentality of majority here is about 9 years, that for Dustin, Dane, Hill, Miller, Young, less. Blow, blow, blow, snow, snow, snow, night, night, night, eat, eat, eat, read, read, read, fight, fight, fight. Such is life in Little America.[17]

16. These were Taku's puppies. In all, fourteen puppies were born at Little America during the expedition.

17. Winning a Pulitzer Prize for his book *South of the Sun,* Russell Owen, a *New York Times* journalist and member of the First Expedition, wrote, "There is a point beyond which a nature unaccustomed to such an environment begins to suffer excruciating mental torture. It wears one mentally and physically, stunts the imagination, distorts whatever of beauty may be within reach, and fills one with a sense of bewilderment and futility." Owen continued, "The hours in bed at night reading are the hours of recuperation from such mental nausea, when often one gives up to black despair, is obsessed by phantoms, and only with an effort and the aid of a good book is able to be free at last, and wake in the morning refreshed and with a new armor against the fresh assaults of the day. But how weary one gets" (Russell Owen, *South of the Sun,* 192–93). Owen also wrote: "To be by yourself, you either crawled into your bunk in the darkness during the daytime, for our

Barrier Bull, June 9, 1934 (no. 4):

Charles J. V. Murphy reporting Admiral Byrd's plans for the summer field parties; an editorial commenting on men's reactions on those chosen for the following field season work; and an exposé, Anon's "All in One Bunk."

Got my light working swell, 24 batteries, one poor bulb. Barrier Bull
becoming a chore. Letters yesterday from Dearie, Browns, Aunt Fan, Duke's
sister.

June 10th

Last week carrying on as usual. Classes, eating, sleeping + editing. We made
a copy for everyone this week + it was a fairly good issue. It was a bigger job
than I thought it was going to be, + being our first experience with the
mimeograph it was naturally slow. We have begun on dog equipment + getting along slowly, too slowly to my mind to get everything done in time.[18] My
editorial was strongly opposed by Taylor but warmly supported by Murphy.
It is like Taylor—he has gone to hell. Warm weather has cont. though last few
days a bit colder. To-day it is blizzarding + I haven't been out to-day. Radio
letter from Morses + Dearie. Sis recommends using a blow torch to thaw out
Klondike's legs. So much for [my] only diary. I wonder whether I'll reread it.

candle supply was getting low, or went for a walk. And so we were seldom alone. We had become
used to vulgarity, and our language was a product of the slums, full of words at which we would have
shuddered a few months before. Our conversations were humorous and diverting but noisy. Some
of us had forgotten how to talk. We argued and laughed or yelled each other down, but we never
talked" (ibid., 192–93).

18. Before the summer field season began, fifty sledges had to be overhauled, all equipment
found, sorted, and packed, and rations manufactured and packed for thirteen men, two tractors,
and eighty-one dogs. About twenty-nine thousand pounds of freight had to be ready (Byrd,
Discovery, 209–10).

Diary Two

Stuart D. Paine

Byrd Antarctic Expedition II
Little America Antarctica
June 10, 1934

8

The Deep Winter Night

June 15–July 17, 1934

June 15th, 1934—Little America

It is symbolic of the past six months for me to begin my second volume of my diary. One book approximately represents one half of the present episode in my life. It is so novel and different I feel that perhaps I shall never undergo an experience quite like this. At the present time it seems only natural to live in continual cold, the temperature ranging anywhere from –65 to 25 and darkness. One gets in a state of mind where he accepts everything as quite an ordinary part of his life. The men here for instance all are an integral part of life. Living in such crowded quarters seems natural. To have a private room, privacy to take a bath etc. is almost beyond the ordinary expectancies of life. In fact it does not matter so much. Money is a mere memory. All our wants are satisfied by issues. You work without pay and in return get the necessities and whatever luxuries there are here. No man has more than the other. It is an ideal communistic society. Of course Corey has his favorites, there are men being paid here but that does not spoil this communistic utopia. Money means nothing here, and goods are shared to a great extent. Russell across the way + Moody, up on top across the way, are swell companions. Fleming, pack-rat that he is, is a decided bore. But I profit by gifts which come raining down to me. I have collected a circular band saw, a sneaker, several packages of cigarettes, etc.[1] He is the constant Friday of Poulter + is thoroughly disgusting.

---

1. A survey of the contents of each man's bunk produced one with a winning collection of enough stuff to fill a small room. Partial contents included one bottle of Worcestershire sauce,

Barrier Bull, June 16, 1934 (no. 5):

Charles J. V. Murphy, regarding Byrd's finding canned food a remedy to his poor cooking skills; an editorial calling off all but necessary field classes at Antarctic University; and reporting of a serious garbage problem in the residence of Innes-Taylor and Noville.

I have been on mess duty this past week with Rawson. Carbone has been cleaning house + instead of having a few hours off each day to ourselves, he has left us there all day. Noville came in and cooked Wednesday + succeeded in dirtying six large pans in cooking the pork and seven twenty-quart pots in cooking beans and potatoes. We washed for four hours straight. To-day we put a pail of garbage in his shack and he seems quite upset about it. Murphy is accused. Russell was supposed to get Bull together this week but contributions are very slow in coming in. Everyone leaves it until the last moments. We received an answer to our wire to Ruppert. None yet from Roosevelt nor Al Smith.[2] I hope to get up a play for the fourth. No one else seems to have any pazazz and if I don't push it, there will be no play. Less than a week to the twenty-first, mid winter. Preparations for next year's operations have hardly commenced. At the present rate of work we will be ready by the last of November.[3] Taylor does not realize the importance of the work and is letting it slide day by day, preferring to sit in his shack and plan on paper.[4] But that will not build tents, put up dog food, repair sleeping bags, sew harnesses.

---

seventy-three boxes of matches, one large box of BAE I pictures, one piece of bread and butter, and one sneaker. The entire contents were printed in the June 9 issue of the *Barrier Bull* (see Appendix 4). The anonymous owner of the bunk, identified by several sources including the *Little America Times,* was Paine.

2. Paine and Russell sent wires to expedition sponsors as well as other well-known people in order to get return communications as material for the *Barrier Bull.*

3. The end of November would be a late start. Spring began on September 21, summer on December 21. The field season should start as soon as light and weather conditions allowed, which was likely to be early to mid-October.

4. By mid-June, the communications from Admiral Byrd were causing serious concern to Thomas Poulter, second in command, Murphy, and the radiomen who were aware of Byrd's erratic schedule and strange content of his transmissions. The other expedition men were not told of any concerns. Poulter had begun thinking of a winter tractor trip to Advance Base and had undoubtedly consulted with Innes-Taylor regarding equipment and supplies needed for potential attempts. Meanwhile, test trips for the tractors were planned, ostensibly to take meteor and auroral observations. After those test trips were completed, Poulter planned to let Byrd know how easily they were able to follow the trail that lead to Advance Base (Poulter, *Winter Night Trip,* 9–12).

QSK	C U later
QRU	I have no traffic
QRK	I receive you well
QRS	Send slower
QSA	1–5 signals
QTC	I have ___ messages
QRV	Send v's
GA	Go ahead
R	OK
HW?	How?
AS	Wait ___ QRX
OSY	Shift your freq. to ____ kc

Schedules—Monday, Wed., Fri.
7:30 AM 180th time
Call W10XCD
W10XCD can break in on schedules
  with Eastern Party on
Tues. Thur. Sat. 7:30 AM.

Radio codes, entered onto a page in Paine's diary. Antarctic University provided a constructive education and a needed diversion for the men living underground. Paine studied radio, physics, surface transport (compulsory for dog drivers), and geology. In the field, the dogs hauled over 110 pounds of radio gear for each field party. Paine was a radio operator. So he could repair the radio, Paine recorded not only codes but also complete radio transmitter, receiver, and antenna circuitry in his diary. (Paine Antarctic Collection)

The same condition is true of all other depts., save perhaps the tractor + aviation. There is no one with authority here and consequently no one to see things are done. It's enough to make you nuts at times.[5]

Had a physical examination yesterday and find my condition excellent. Blood corpuscles 5,400,000, much thicker I understand than normal but quite natural here in the cold, weight 158 stripped, blood pressure 120, a drop from 180 when I returned from the southern trip.

Radio and navigation the most popular courses in the University. The others have gradually faded out. In radio there are two classes, elementary + advanced. I'm advanced though my training has not been any more extensive than the others in the elementary class. It is representative of the general

5. The original command structure was simple: Admiral Byrd, though not present, was the leader, then Poulter, and then Haines and a fourth. The fourth in charge was changed by Poulter during Byrd's absence from Harold June to Charlie Murphy. However, an inherent conflict was created when Byrd invented the additional authoritative body, the Expedition Staff, which, as previously mentioned, could not only overrule, with a two-thirds vote, any order given by an officer but also, by a majority vote, set up any rules and regulations for the expedition operations. Thus, no one could assume the validity of any order or rule. Poulter explained in his later account that to appease Harold June for not being appointed second in command, the admiral invented this new body, headed by June. The staff was generally made up of department heads and men from former expeditions (Poulter, *Winter Night Trip*, 2).

level of intelligence here. Waite, Bud in charge. In navigation, only three or
four will ever be able to understand it. Rawson teaching. It is being recommended by the Bull to call off all classes save those two so that something can
be done.

June 20th, 1934

My entries are far between and few. By the time the day is over and I have
written some Bull for the Barrier Bull I have precious little inclination to write
more. Beside there is not very much to write of.[6] Our existence is very similar from day to day but time flies. I can hardly realize that tomorrow the winter night is half over. Little has been done towards next year's operation in
spite of the press reports. I should say off hand 3/4ths of the work is still to be
done. The dog department is straggling along, doing a bit but lacking entirely
the old spirit of cooperation + loyalty to each other. Gradually but definitely
the camp is splitting into groups, each group working against each other.

This is but natural where there is no dominant personality leading the
groups. The same is true in the departments. Skinner pulls against Demas,
the scientific staff are individually pulling for their own particular interests.
The dog department is not necessarily pulling against each other but it has lost
its unity, and at least mine + Dick's loyalty to Taylor has gone. He wishes to talk
to me tomorrow. I hope he comes out in the open + we have the thing out.
Though I think he has acted extremely foolishly, holding himself aloof, criticizing everything and everybody, acting like a kid, I really feel sorry for him.

This week I'm on dog feeding. Ronne is sick with a crippled back so
Monday Wade helped me, to-day Black + Russell. Dog fatalities seem to be
heavy now-a days. Buzz, Huge, Rattle, Jeff, Olav, etc. I should not say fatalities, but injuries.[7] The dogs are getting restless in the tunnels. Poor things, they
still have a long time to go. I have been trying to enlist some enthusiasm for
a play, July 4th, but the same lackadaisical attitude seems to be in possession

---

6. Admiral Byrd later commented that while British expeditions developed, in response to conditions, a certain sense of tragedy and spiritual enrichment, American expeditions adopted an attitude of indifference: "Nothing outside our own private concerns seemed to strike very deep, nor,
what was even more fascinating, to be very important.

"One way or another a small fire started in the galley. Ashes were smoldering under the stove,
and the place was full of smoke. Rawson and Paine, who were on mess that day, went on washing
dishes, showing no interest whatever in the cook's efforts to beat out the fire, though they were half
suffocated" (Byrd, *Discovery,* 192–93).

7. Innes-Taylor treated injured dogs on a clean burlap cloth spread on the library table, always
attracting an audience of interested spectators. In his hands, the dogs were submissive and stoic no
matter what the treatment (Walden and Paine, *Long Whip,* 153–56).

Barrier Bull, June 23, 1934 (no. 6):

Charles J. V. Murphy announcing that Admiral Byrd will be returning to Little America much earlier than expected for administrative reasons and that Byrd also suffered from carbon monoxide poisoning and got very "rocky," but now all is well. Questionnaire results revealing men voted the most "_____"; an editorial declaiming the nonstop stealing among the men; and "Skookum," about having a tooth pulled by Dr. Potaka.

of everyone. I do not know whether we can put it over or not. Certainly I can't do it alone. Had a tooth out Monday. My jaw is still sore.

Tuesday June 26th

Last week's Bull, I wrote most of it myself. But had unfortunate remark concerning Bill Haines + his work.[8] He was extremely peeved so I went around to everyone + asked them to cut it out. I don't know how many will. It would have been better to let it alone. Talk with Taylor which was unsatisfactory on both sides, apparently. He told me what he thought of me and I told him what I thought of him. He made an effort to please me by coming out of his shack for a time + talking + leveling in the library. To-day we cleaned out some of the dog tunnels + the seal cutting house. He came down, said very little + disappeared. I did it on my own initiative, with help of Duke, Ed and Dick. I am thoroughly poohed out to-night. Tractor complete and newly rejuvenated and burnt one put in. Poulter, Waite + Skinner out now in it to determine whether they can pick up the trail flags in the moonlight. If they can I believe they will go after the Admiral at Bolling Advance Base.[9] The eastern party, Siple, Wade, Stancliff and Corey off this morning for a reconnoiter of the bay + a week's stay. They man hauled their stuff, a task made

8. This remark has been impossible to locate. Because extant *Bull* covers are different than described by Paine and the comment about Bill Haines is not to be found, the available *Barrier Bull* issues must be ones replicated on the ship while going back to the United States.

9. The men at Little America were highly conflicted over the possibility of a trip to Advance Base. The men had not been told that Byrd might be in serious trouble, nor had Byrd been explicit in his communications to those in charge. As mentioned in the *Barrier Bull,* a message by Byrd had earlier been read to the entire assembly stating that because of the danger, no one was to come out to Advance Base before the light and good weather returned. Some of the men also were likely aware of Byrd's March 18 memo that forbade endangering the men who might want to rescue him during the winter. The Expedition Staff, lead by June, became the lightning rod for opposition to the trip. Innes-Taylor and many others as well were vehemently opposed (Poulter, *Winter Night Trip,* 46).

very difficult because they insisted upon taking everything with them that suited their fancy.[10]

The temperature has been fairly high the last few days, –30 to zero. Moon rose several days ago + is now approaching its full. By its light it is easy to see the pressure from here. Not to mention the whole city of L.A.

I've been trying to get Pelter to develop my films but though I've had water ready for him for eight days now he hasn't done a thing. He evidently is like other gales of the Navy. And such quality seems to be characteristic of the men here, with few exceptions. They say they will do a thing + then put it off + and off + off. One thing I try to do above all is be sincere + keep my word. Taylor says I have made enemies both in the dog dept. and elsewhere. To date I have not discovered them, though I have asked many. Sails, of course, is one, but who cares with that hypochondriac.

Last night Dick + I slept out in a tent. We both finished our bags + wished to try them out. Mine seemed to work all right. Classes for last week + a half all called off save for radio + navigation. It was concluded that since precious little work had been accomplished up to the midwinter night, it was time to do something.[11]

June 30th

Jack seems to be the major bone of contention at the present time. I found him with a frozen tail + amputation was the only thing that could save him. Taylor cut his tail off with an axe. He did not seem to feel it very much as the part was pretty well frozen. As it was absolutely essential to keep him in the warmth I brought him down here. He smelled + Alton did not like the smell and he went to Taylor + Taylor to me. I have stuck to my guns + Jack is still here. In fact the first night he slept on my bunk + I stayed in Wade's who was out on Eastern Party trip. What the fellows think this expedition is I don't know. If they can't stand a little smell for the sake of a dog, whose life is at stake—well I haven't much use for them. I haven't much use for many here. Jack is as valuable as a man on the trail because he leads a straight path + breaks his own trail. He will stay here until he gets well or passes on. To lose

---

10. Paul Siple was leading a short trip to the west side of the Bay of Whales.

11. Tasks to be done were many. Ronne and Eilefsen repaired the sledges while the dog drivers Dane, Moody, Russell, Stancliff, Wade, and Paine packed rations with the utmost care. The amounts of each constituent of a man's daily ration was chalked on the New Mess Hall blackboard, and each ingredient was weighed to the ounce or fraction of an ounce and sacked in cotton bags, each one holding one day's ration. This arrangement eliminated mistakes and easily let the men on the trial know exactly how much food they had (Walden and Paine, *Long Whip,* 170).

Bulletin Board notice

Little America
June 30, 1934

NOTICE

The Admiral will likely be back to Little America in about a month, and trail operations will be starting as soon there after as possible.

Nothing to date has caused more inefficiency nor d ne more to cut down the physique of those men who have indulged than liquor.

In vi w of my responsibility in connection with the scientific results of the ex edition, and the w lfare of the men, I am at this time definitely declaring my position in this matter, particularly with respect to those men who are to go on any scientific work away from Little America.

First, that persons contemplating such work are to refrain from the use of all alcoholic bev reges unless specifically order to the contrary by 'r. Potake.

Second, that all persons c ntemplating trail work avail themselves of fre uent opportunities for getting ski practice and other out-of-door exercise.

So strongly do I feel this that if this is not observed, I plan to either re lace them with other men, or even drop the proposed work from the program, regardless of how great its importance.

No single project is worth the undue risk of the men themselves, or their comrades, that might arise by men going into the field in anything other than the very best possible physical condition.

Thos. C. Poulter

Thos. C. Poulter
Senior Scientist.

June 30, 1934, announcement to the men from Dr. Poulter, second in command, addresses both the problematic use of alcohol and lack of physical fitness of many of the men. (Thomas C. Poulter, *The Winter Night Trip to Advance Base: Byrd Antarctic Expedition II 1933–1935*)

Barrier Bull, June 30 1934 (no. 7):

"Extra—Extra—Extra—Extra—Eastern Party Returned from West," reporting on Paul Siple's winter foray to the west side of the Bay of Whales; Charles J. V. Murphy announcing that a tractor party to "lift Admiral Byrd's isolation" will commence during the full moon period of July 23–29. Carl Peterson discovering by listening to San Francisco radio that Byrd narrowly escapes carbon monoxide poisoning!; editorial commenting on the nonstop stealing, and the need in Little America for *one* place among the fourteen buildings, other than a man's bunk, to be set aside for convalescing dogs; and including Morgan's "The Use of Words"; "Jack's Tail"; and "Skookum," on "Crystal Ovens" and the wonders of radio.

him would be calamitous at least to me.[12] Toby [a dog] came back after a week's absence. Stan reports dog tracks on the Bay ice. Dinsy died. Made blubber stove last night in machine shop + had to dig out roof to get it out. Blubbering starts Monday I believe + me in charge for a while. Wade's face very badly frost bitten. Wrote up their story in this week's Bull and it was good I think. In fact the issue as a whole was good. Gorgeous aurora this afternoon. Like a huge snake to the eastward stretching from north to south. Curled and writhed in brilliant display—Gorgeous pinks + greens + yellows—I have never seen anything so magnificent. Movies three times a week. Moody working on flags. Sails hopeless + Ed has his own [sewing] machine in the library. Poulter posted a notice about liquor—no man is to go out who drinks, etc. I have never seen a situation as potent as the drink question handled so badly.

July 1st

Letter from Dearie saying they were celebrating Content's birthday by going on a picnic to the beach. I had another tooth out day before yesterday. My jaw is quite painful. To-day is Sunday, holiday + I spent the day reading the rest of Dostoevski or however you spell it.

I begin to wonder whether my part in the expedition is not all a bad dream. Perhaps its the continuous night + the constant social rubbing with my companions. I haven't had enough to do perhaps. The Bull has kept me busy for a while, but that is not enough. I find that if I don't have something active to do I am not happy. Therefore I plan to do all the dog pemmican perhaps. It will provide active work which I need. Bowlin complains of Jack as usual. But he is still here. His tail is pretty bad. I don't know whether he will get over it or not. To say the least I am pretty concerned. Everyone liked the Bull this week. Next week is the last issue I think.

July 5th

The fourth was celebrated yesterday by a general holiday + a grand supper

---

12. If Paine were to lose his lead dog, it would impact not only Paine but also the success of the summer trail parties. If the tail had been allowed to thaw, gangrene would set in. If they amputated it, the dog, if he survived the subsequent infection, would be subject to continual frostbite on the unprotected wound and also be unable to sleep with his tail wrapped around his nose to warm the bitterly cold air. As it turned out, Jack was hoisted up on the library table, and Innes-Taylor wielded the axe to chop off his tail. After the operation, sores from the infection spread down his hind legs and he became so weak he was hardly able to walk. But with hopes that Jack would recover, Paine made a soft leather covering for the tail stump to protect it from frostbite.

Paine and Jack (the black form on the straw on right behind him) sought peace in the Seal Chopping House. When this picture was taken, the rest of Little America was roiling with conflict over the proposed winter journey to Advance Base; the men had not been told the truth as to why the treacherous trip was being planned. Jack was fighting gangrene after having his frozen tail amputated, and aside from a man's bunk, there was not one warm safe place in all of Little America set aside for convalescing dogs. (Paine Antarctic Collection)

last night. We had a tumbler of brandy which satisfied everyone + no one was drunk. At last they have realized that temperance not abstinence is the best course. I have worked on dog food and so far though I have worked for almost a week we haven't put up any dog food. What we did put up we fed to the dogs because they were underweight. Stancliff is bla- —X!!*-?!!X*. So is Russell + Miller + Pelter + Smith + Taylor + Noville + Murphy + the whole outfit. I'm sick of it + shall probably look back upon it all as a prolonged nightmare. The stink of blubber is all about in my clothes, my skin, hair, etc. Jack was moved back to the tunnel. The garage boys couldn't stand his smell. I've done all I could + if he dies there is no help for it and the blame can be assigned to the supersensitive nostrils of certain expeditionary members. This work is the last issue of the Bull.

Barrier Bull, July 7, 1934 (no. 8): the last of eight issues.

Charles J. V. Murphy announcing that Admiral Byrd is missing radio contacts and is now using the emergency set. Byrd sending that all is well and for the tractor party to take every safeguard in coming out to Advance Base. Murphy complimenting Russell and Paine on the *Barrier Bull* and commenting on the bitterness within Little America; editorial probing the discrepancy in what "the world" versus what "the camp" is being told about Byrd's proposed return. The editors strongly urging an all-camp vote on the hazardous trip proposed for July, recalling Byrd's early message read to the camp forbidding any winter rescue, and, at the very least, calling to delay any attempt to reach Advance Base until the end of August; and "Skookum," "Stink," a story of an expedition member visiting the dogmen and the seal chopping house to experience seal blubbering.

July 6th

Stan + I worked on dog food to-day. We have worked for four days getting things in order + to-day the great wheels began to turn. We put out about 250 lbs. this afternoon. It was a good start. Taylor says only six tons is required so that simplifies everything quite a lot. The smell of cooking and burning blubber has come up into the main tunnels + Walter is complaining as well as others of the radio gang. It is amusing if it weren't so tragic.[13] Pelter is getting nasty about the films + I think I'll get them back + have Perkins develop them. He is just another sailor + acts as such. Jack is now in the seal cutting house nestled in straw on top of the blubber pile. He is better I think. Break-it was killed by Rattle last week—after all the worry and care last fall.

July 11th

My pictures are developed + what a job it was. Stan + I + Wade did the job, but now that we have it done we can't find them all and I suspect someone has helped themselves. Our blubbering + pemmican process is coming along at a pretty good rate, almost seven hundred pounds to-day. Paige was

13. The Seal Chopping House was the largest snow cave—twenty feet long and with a height and width of about fifteen feet. In addition to chopping seals in the room, this was the site of the pemmican factory. For the spring journeys, which would last for as long as three months, estimates called for at least six tons of pemmican for the teams. Using a blubber furnace made out of empty gasoline drums, one acting as a vat fitted inside the other, which acted as the stove, pemmican rations were made from a powdered mix and blubber that was both the fuel for the stove and the fat for the rations (Walden and Paine, *Long Whip,* 166–69).

assigned to help feed this morning but he never showed up + I had to feed this morning myself. Stan + Russell on pemmican.

The Bull is now officially defunct. We signed off after eight issues. I think it was a pretty good success. Murphy complimented us as did many others. In fact to-night Murphy told me I could write real well + urged me to go on with it. Extraordinary! I thought I could get a job on the Herald Tribune if I wanted to. He could do it anyway. Our last editorial I realize now was a mistake. Of course it was justified from many standpoints, but there is more in the situation than most of the men here [know]. He showed me his files, his conversations with REB + now I realize we were in error in opposing the trip. There seems to be something wrong out there. His messages seem to urge haste, haste. What the reason for his impatience is I do not know. But perhaps he feels himself slipping. He has missed his radio contacts for a week. Murphy has been attempting to cover up his retreat by assigning scientific motives to it, which is allowable to protect REB.[14] Things are going along smoothly now. I spend most of my time down in the seal chopping house where it is quiet + peaceful + away from the politics, intrigue + obnoxious prejudices of the group here. It's really extraordinary the state of mind here. Someday I would like to write it up. I was thinking this afternoon what would happen if there was a murder + the assassin undiscovered—

July 14th, 1934, L.A.

Contacted REB to-day + reported all well. What the reason for his ten day silence was not given. Evidently he had some difficulty with his radio set. Poulter + Murphy talked to him about the proposed trip as did Harold. REB approved of it as outlined; so settling for the present an issue which has divided the camp the last two weeks.[15] Since we published the editorial in the Bull I have switched sides. Murphy, as I probably explained before, showed

14. On the evening of July 13, two days after Paine and Murphy's discussion, a meeting of the Expedition Staff was called by Harold June where he issued a statement requiring that it be carefully recorded that he was not to be held responsible for any negative results of any attempt to go to Advance Base; this was granted. Charlie Murphy asked the staff if they wanted to know how the trip idea had arisen; they did. Murphy, reading a transmission dated June 21, stated that Byrd and Poulter had discussed starting field work earlier than usual and that he and Poulter had proposed a meteor observation post at Advance Base to record a predicted meteor shower. Murphy also asserted that contrary to an impression in the camp and to the best of his knowledge, Admiral Byrd was not in distress and even if he were, in no case would he call out the tractors to rescue him (Poulter, *Winter Night Trip*, 41–42).

15. Finn Ronne later stated that the 55 person camp was split 27 to 26 over whether to attempt a winter trip to reach Advance Base (John C. Behrendt, *Innocents on the Ice: A Memoir of Antarctic*

me the files—records of previous radio schedules with the Admiral.[16] Why he does not do the same to the rest of the men here I do not know. To-day's contact clears everyone's mind about it since the Admiral approves.[17]

To-day was Sunday—Dick and I continued with the dog pemmican rather than spend the day in idleness or rather as a holiday. Putting up about five hundred pounds. I think the seal chopping house is the only place where peace, quiet + contentment can be found in the camp. The conflict of personalities is complex enough in civilization but the conflict here in this heterogeneous group forced into intimate daily contact with the depressing continuous darkness, the bitter cold and enforced idleness caused by the two is terrific. Little quarrels + trivialities assume proportions way beyond their true values. The lack of leadership + driving personalities has brought personal animosities and bitter jealousies. What should be a cooperative effort for the expedition as a unit has become as many individual efforts for so many persons. True perspective of situations seem to have been lost. The question—whether to make the forth-coming trip or not—has been a question not of principles, dangers, possible advantages or disadvantages, but that of rivalry and personalities. The reasons I think can be laid to just the caliber of the men here and secondly to the winter night.

Exploration, 1957, 19). The risks of the trip were extreme: there were only a few hours a day of dim light, and finding the trail flags (if they were still present after the numerous blizzards) and keeping to the trail would be difficult. As the ice was always moving, no one could assume that the crevasses of the former season would even have remained in the same position. Temperatures were expected to reach as low as –70°, and blizzards were probable. In addressing these risks, Innes-Taylor would write no less than fourteen memorandums presenting various trail plans, outlining equipment and supply requirements, detailing survival factors, trail conditions, and needs of the proposed tractor parties, and planning backup by the dog teams as a stand-by rescue party for the tractors (Poulter, *Winter Night Trip,* 50–72).

16. As most members of the expedition felt that they were not being informed of something important, some men began using their radio sets, usually listening to U.S. radio stations, to hear radio transmissions between Byrd at Advance Base and Little America. Murphy even tried to discourage the eavesdropping by radioing a totally absurd broadcast to humiliate the listeners. The men were forbidden to tune in and were even checked on during active transmissions; these actions caused only more concern (Poulter, *Winter Night Trip,* 15).

17. Paine mentioned that June, Innes-Taylor, and Rawson were the primary opponents of any rescue attempts before late August. After the meeting of the thirteenth, June and others prepared a memo signed by thirteen members calling for a meeting of the staff to discuss a veto of the proposed trip. Poulter surprised the opposition by then issuing the order that a rescue trip would be made and, to eliminate further power struggles, that he himself would lead it. A chaotic meeting was held on the evening of July 14. Poulter was keenly aware that if June were able to garner a two-thirds majority, he had the power to abort the rescue attempt. The first motion, as Poulter expected, was to forbid a trip to Advanced Base before November. After three hours of heated debate, confusion as to the rules of order and as to the actual motions proposed, the only decision made that night was to adjourn. No minutes were made of this meeting (ibid., 46).

McCormick's brother was instantly killed last week. It was a terrible blow to Mac. He + his brother had always been very close. But he requested everyone to consider him as before and make no mention of the fact to him. So have we done. He has been every brave + courageous about it. Poor kid.

Fleming has evidently been chosen to go out to the Admiral's base along with Peterson. I think to carry on Byrd's scientific records. I do not believe him the best man to do it as he is conceited, dirty, of strong packrat tendencies, deceitful, + careless. Grimminger should be the one, and Pete.

A replotting of our course south this fall reveals we were short one and a fraction miles from reaching latitude eighty one. My ability as a navigator seems to be rather well discredited. However, that is nothing to me. I have repeatedly stated that courses run by dog sled are uncertain and any of my dead reckoning positions may be as much as five miles off.

Radio letter from the Browns, Doris Dart + Dearie. The reception was terrible and I didn't get a thing, only catching my name + the name of the sender. All is well I hope.

Movies usually four times a week, Sat., Sun., Tues., Thurs. They provide interesting entertainment. Wade has almost fully recovered from his frost bites but discovered he has lost 18 lbs. in the last month.[18] Doc. Potaka believes it might be a case of scurvy. If that is the case the blame may be placed squarely upon the careless shoulders of not only Carbone, he doesn't know anything anyway, but also those supposed to be in charge.

July 15th

The picture to-night was "Cyrano." It was beautiful with superb acting. Ronald Coleman + Kay Francis were compelling + charming. A tale of the unfortunate love affair of a respectable man + a shop girl for which neither were to blame. The picture has a haunting melancholiness about it.

To-day we put up about 750 lbs. of dog pemmican, quite the best yet. It is a messy job + unpleasant in itself but compensated for by the quiet of the place. From hauling the boxes into the house, opening the cans, knifing the stuff out of the cans, pounding it up with a mallet, mixing the pemmican with the oil, 20%, mixing + pounding + stirring it, then pouring the sordid mixture upon the makeshift table to mold it into blocks 1 1/2 lbs. each.[19] In addition

18. Wade's face was unrecognizable when he returned from the trip to the west side of the Bay of Whales.

19. A powder made of suet, meat meal, whole wheat, dried milk, cod liver oil, cooked barley groups, and hydrogenated soybean oil was mixed in with the oil (Walden and Paine, *Long Whip*, 168).

"Blubberheim" and the Seal Chopping House are where the dog drivers manufactured pemmican using a blubber furnace made out of gasoline cans. Shown are "The Stinking Trio": Paine (at workbench), Olin Stancliff (in wool cap), and Dick Russell. Paine was making pemmican blocks. The photographer's lighting adds to the light thrown by lantern. A frozen seal head is under the table and a roving puppy is in the upper right. (BPRCAP, Papers of Admiral Richard E. Byrd, image 7863-24)

there is the tending of the blubber pot, which requires filling twice a day. The meat must be cut from the blubber + the blubber sliced so as to let the oil out. The fire must be looked after as well. Puppies scamper underfoot, spilled pemmican + oil gum up your boots, your mittens ooze oil and seal stink, your hair, clothes, eyes, mustache + nose. Not only that but everything stinks + oozes oil. Your presence in the camp is as welcome as a skunk in a parlor. Such are the joys of a dog driver. And Taylor, to be truthful, has been down twice. There's no stink on him. A beer can carefully placed in the pot to thaw out was forgotten by one Olin Stancliff. An enormous explosion, which blew off the top of the pot, blubber + oil rained over everything + the perpetuator of the deed merely laughed. We cooked doughnuts in the blubber

Stancliff mixes ingredients to make pemmican. (Paine Antarctic Collection)

pot this afternoon + they were swell. We peddled our doughnuts around to the camp + most people did not know they were fried in seal oil.

July 17th

To-day we continued with the dog food + turned out over 5 hundred lbs. Stan, Russell + myself. Our supply of blubber has become nearly exhausted + we may have to lay off for a week to allow further accumulations of seal blubber.

To-day marks the six month mark. It was January 17th that we entered the Bay of Whales. The worst is over I believe and the downhill run will be easier + swifter. There will be no unloading thank God. I hope never to go through such an experience again.

I am looking forward more + more to our trip this summer. Our chance of success is far better than any other party. The personnel is better + our program is not too ambitious. We have no theorists, no scientific specialists + we all are good trail men. The tractor trip is scheduled for the end of the week— Let's hope it's successful.

9

The Admiral and Summer Field Preparations

July 20–October 15, 1934

July 20th

The tractor party left this morning for the Advance Base. In the party was Skinner, Poulter, Waite, Fleming + Peterson. The tractor, resembling an awkward moving van, painted an orange color, has just been overhauled + repaired. Over the cab appeared the words "Tractor No. 1, B.A.E. II." With its two headlights glowing in the dark, its motor purring softly, it was reminiscent of a fiery mouthed dragon. Behind was one sled, made by lashing two dog sleds together, side by side. The men going in the tractor were photographed properly + hands shaken. All of them were nervous espec. Waite.[1] They rolled out of here about eleven o'clock + disappeared to the south. We watched the headlights crawl slowly up the barrier to the south of us and disappear. One hour later Waite reported the bundle on the sled had broken but they had repaired it + were going on. I believe it was the most dramatic thing that has happened here.

July 24

The tractor party returned yesterday after reaching fifty four miles. Evidently it was a tough trip but an instructive one for Poulter. In all their mileage was 187 miles. From their stories it was one constant search for

---

1. In his essay included in Appendix 2, Poulter weighed the risk of possibly fatal hazards of weather and darkness to what he felt to be the justification to try to reach the admiral at Advance Base.

The tractor party left on July 20 on the first of three tries to rescue Admiral Byrd from Advance Base, one hundred nautical miles south of Little America. The party was led by second-in-command and lead scientist Thomas C. Poulter. (BPRCAP, Papers of Admiral Richard E. Byrd, image 7902-10)

flags. Byrd's orders before they left were not to leave the trail. Hence the effort to pick up flags. Poulter had rigged up an ingenious searchlight which served them well but in spite of it the flags were not to be picked up beyond the fifty mile depot. They escaped disaster narrowly by coming onto the fifty mile [depot] several hundred yards to the west of it, close to where I almost fell into the big hole [on the fall sledging journey]. Their use of the compass checked with my course pretty well, so they said. I may yet fool them all—the skepticism about my navigation may yet be allayed.

Blizzard blowing to-day. Temp. –35, and a wind as high as fifty miles per hour. Needless to say we all stayed inside. Dick + Stan + I worked at dog pemmican + put up 800 lbs., quite a fair day.

Monotonously rings the "Little Bell," a Columbia record + "The Last Round-up," a Victor record, are melodies I believe shall ever be connected with this expedition. They express perhaps the monotony, the pathos, the struggle, of a group of foolish men gathered here to satisfy an already satiated leader's publicity complex. That's pretty strong but time will test it to find out whether it is true.

The personal relations within the dog department are becoming more +

more difficult + unnatural. Moody, Dane, Wade gravitate to Taylor. He has made puppets of them, destroyed their individuality, particularly Moody's + Dane's. It is almost tragic in a case like his lacking as he does a liberal education, an inquisitive nature, a very high intelligence quota. He daily grows staler + more unoriginal.—Extraordinary.

Dane was put in charge of the dog department in the event of Taylor's going out to the relief of Tractor Number One. A more absurd appointment is difficult to imagine, for with all due respects to Duke who is really a good scout as is Taylor when away from expedition affairs, he is utterly incompetent as an organizer or director. He is a hero worshipper of great intentness and incapable of making a decision. Wade has changed greatly, talks + gabbles like an old woman, but quite as reliable + dependable as always. I should add he never has thought a great deal for himself + the same is true now.

Stan is an independent individual, disappointed as I am in the whole business, but determined to do his duty not necessarily to Taylor but to the expedition. He is ambitious, a swell worker + has changed little since I have known him save for the fact that his determined individualism has come through.

Russell I never knew well before as he lived aft in the *Ruppert,* but the close proximity of our bunks, working with him on the Bull + with the dogs has shown him to be quite intelligent, a satirical sense of humor aggravating at times, of good tastes, + determined to assist the general good cause. Russell, myself + Stan are the rebels of the dog department but I dare say accomplish as much if not a great deal more than the other three. Ronne I need hardly mention save to say he is a regular square head, independent, arrogant + rather childish. So much for the personnel as I see them this day, the 24th of July, 1934, at L.A.

July 28th

The temperature suddenly rose yesterday to 20 above. To-day it is down to 48 below. The warmth was delightful but unfortunately did not last long. Radio contact was reestablished with Byrd. His mercury set was + has been out of commission + he was sending blind. His message was to come now if possible. So the tractor is going out again Monday I believe. He instructed them to navigate new trail around crevasses.

Took bath to-night, Murphy invited me to write a dispatch about dog town, which I did. He says he would send it in under my name, a compliment to be sure + one which will please Dearie should he do it.

Stan, Siple, Dane, Corey went after their tent—out by west cape. They took five dogs + Stan froze his fingers on the way back. Manufacturing plant out of production to-day + will be tomorrow. Five day week under the NRA.[2] Cut Hal Young's hair, Moody's & Wade's. I got better as I went along + did a creditable job on Moody, the last one.

Stan and I have an oscillator rigged between our bunks a key and phones [headphones] on each end. By this means we hope to improve our radio technique.

Black insists he is going to the Mts. with us. We shall see. If he chooses to force himself upon us I shall force myself just as strongly upon him.

The sky in the north to-day was a brilliant red + orange. It was the first time we have seen color in the north for several months. It was like a sunset in Durham a half hour after the sun has sunk in the west, only this was there for an hour or more. How good it was to see it. It means returning sunshine, warmth + home again—Home—how much the pictures of Shankhassick + of the family has meant to me. The sitting room, Dearie in the Wallow before the fire,[3] the Athapit wax on the paneling, the dining room, the big clock, the cupboard, the table + chairs—Oh— another world from which I came + perhaps never leave again.

July 29th—Address—Bunk

To-day was Sunday + a holiday. I fed to-day, having chopped the meat yesterday. Ronne was supposed to have helped me but though we spoke to him yesterday not a sign of him to-day. The goddamn shiftless slacker——A person I cannot tolerate is one who deliberately permits his mate to do his work for him. Such is Finn Ronne——

The glow in the north was even more pronounced + walking back + forth from the Old Mess Hall I was strongly touched by the brilliant colors, reds, oranges, fading to deep purple and black of the sky overhead. It was not light enough to hide the stars + the brighter ones shone through with a pale effort. The surprise of emerging from the hatch + find you do not have to stumble through the dark but can easily pick your way by the natural light. Ah what a feeling of awakening, of relief from the long depressing night. Everyone in camp seemed to reflect the spirit I think + seemed more cheerful.

Radio mailbag—letter from Dearie stating all is well + one from Dr. Richards. I heard Dearie's but none of Dr. Richard's. I shall ask for a repeat perhaps.

2. This may be a reference to imaginary union rules or to existing written instructions for certain camp duties.
3. The "Wallow" was probably the family's name for her chair.

July 30th

No news to-day. Cold, below fifty. Tractor party preparing to shove off but delayed departure until visibility clears. Made a goodly portion of dog food to-day. Grimminger came down + helped. Black insists repeatedly he is going on our party + he has another team, evidently Herrmann's. But I think he has another thought coming.

July 31st

Nuts ————————————————————————————————

As the winter night goes on we strive to wear one another down with a concentrated panning. Probably after living down here for a year we can truly sympathize with the inmates of Sing Sing. Perhaps they just couldn't be put on and take it. We three, the Stinking Trio, seem to be getting the well-known end of the stick. All of us have sore throats from that damnable stench of burning seal blubber. Still some times I am convinced that Stan likes to make those cakes. He really is contented as a child making mud pies. Another peculiar thing about Stan is the way he likes to dig the eyes out of dead seals. I'd hate to die on the trail with him. I'm sure that he would dig out my eyes—the rat. It's about time for a schedule with CC, so I'll leave this mess for some other time. Before I go I might mention that there is no use of the geological party trying to out do or better, their equipment, for the "Great Eastern Party" has it all.[4]

August 4th

Last night + yesterday Stan, Dick + myself made dog food. We were determined to put up at least a ton before we turned in. Consequently we worked until four this morning. Another ton of pemmican completed. Three more such sessions will finish us up.

Ike Schlossbach + Joe Pelter have been cooking for the last four days and have we been eating—Pies, hot biscuits, lots of vegetables, soups + cakes. More delightful perhaps has been the change in atmosphere in the mess hall. Instead of the vulgar chatter of the Great Carbone,[5] uncouth + crude as he

---

4. "CC" may refer to the Columbia Broadcast Corporation. The Eastern Party, with Paul Siple, Wade, Corey, and Stancliff, was just one of three parties planned for the summer field season (the Eastern, the Plateau, and the Geological parties) (Byrd, *Discovery,* 208–9). Siple, because of his affiliation with the Boy Scouts of America, received a great deal of ongoing publicity on both expeditions.

5. In the weekly radio show broadcast to the United States, the cook Alphonse Carbone was known by the title "The Great Carbone."

is, there is some dignity, a pleasant and jovial air + a real effort to make things agreeable. Hats off to Ike + Joe.

The tractor left this morning on its second attempt to get REB. The start had been delayed a week to make sure of the weather + Bill Haines gave the word this morning.[6] The light is more favorable this time, for three hours it is possible to see several miles, though not particularly favorable for picking up trail flags. So much hatred + friction has been aroused about the trip that it is well the thing will be over as a source of political intrigue.

August 5th

To-day is Sunday + I built an igloo. I labored from 9:30 until 5:30 myself. Stan helped me late in the afternoon. It is about 8 feet round inside and about fourteen on the outside. Height about seven feet. When we got all through I read Stefansson's account of building igloos + find mine entirely too heavy.[7] The walls are at least two feet thick instead of four to six inches. No wonder it took so long. I shall build another along the orthodox lines just for practice.

Tractor out nine miles to-night. It took them most of the day to find a way through the pressure. Last night they camped, preferring to wait for daylight rather than waste gasoline cruising around in the dark.

REB wired to-day he is very weak + hardly able to crank the generator. Whether that means he is sick or he was tired of cranking I do not know. Murphy thinks it very grave.

Taylor + Murphy had a quarrel which has been pending a long time. Al is just sour through and through, thoroughly disgusting. If the night has gotten anyone it has gotten him.

The daylight or rather twilight lasted almost four hours to-day. Even with the light an aurora display was plainly visible, in fact the grandest show yet + I was the only one who saw it, evidently. It started with widely spaced curtains of light. Then a long narrow band stretching almost from north to south across the sky came out of the east + gradually rose to the zenith. It was quivering violently, taking about a half minute for a wave to travel from north to south. Overhead it was radiant with colors, rainbow colors. The band passed to the west. A few more curtains of white light hung about + then faded away. The whole display lasted but fifteen minutes. To-night the sky is covered with twitching rays of the aurora but no colors.

6. Haines was third in command of the expedition.
7. Vilhjalmur Stefansson spent much of his life doing research in the Arctic. Among other books, he wrote *My Life with the Eskimo* (1913) and *The Friendly Arctic* (1921).

August 7th

Last night I slept out in my igloo. I used an air mattress + my fur bag with woolen liner. I was a bit cold but only awoke about four times during the night. It was 58 below.

The tractor returned from its 26 mile southing, its fan belt broken, a bearing gone, a gasket blown out + generator broken. It was decided to put [it] in the garage + repair it immediately but later the burnt Citroen, now completely rejuvenated, was selected + the party is scheduled to start out tonight on its third attempt to reach the Admiral. What success they will have is problematical. Noville is organizing a crew to dig out the Pilgrim to stand by, I suppose. I have been assigned to it but I do not know whether I will do it or not. We have been cooking all this week + had planned to put up another ton tomorrow. As Taylor has not even been down in the tunnels the last three weeks while we have been operating, I do not believe he realizes the necessity of haste in this matter. There are enough men here to dig without interrupting the regular work for the trail.

August ninth

Last night, Dick, Stan + I worked through until almost three this morning + finished another ton of dog food. The grand total is now 6 1/2 tons, + 1 1/2 to go. Tractor has made good progress + is now, at 8 o'clock, at [Mile] 52 and going strong. Tractor No. 1 which came back has been repaired and is standing by to dash out should the first tractor need assistance or support. Dane, Skinner + Rawson constitute the personnel of the second. Poulter, Demas + Waite [are on] the one now in the field, the burned one. Slept in igloo + was very comfortable.

August 10th

To-night the tractor is at 81 miles south at 8 o'clock to-night + going like hell. It is very likely that they will reach the Mt. House to-night if their engine keeps going. They reported that their generator was out of commission and their ignition faulty, necessitating frequent stops. I am very glad to see them out there, first because it means relief for the Admiral [who] reports he is in distress and secondly it will effectively silence the opposition of June, Rawson + Taylor, the ignoble opposition.

We meted out to-day. Duke is a tunnel runner—Ed is too + they were quite upset by our accusations. My mustache is really quite slick having about three months' growth to its credit. I soap it to make it look German + its points are of considerable virtue. Russell on mess duty this week with Clark. Reviewing my navigation and assisting Wade in his. Rawson has evidently given up his classes.

August 14th

The returning sun brings a glorious blaze of light to the northern sky every morning + afternoon now, and toward three o'clock to five there is a splendor of reds and oranges + pinks rarely seen. In fact at home only for a fleet minute is such color seen in the sky. Here it lasts for hours, its more brilliant center surging slowly from east to west to the south. The dark grayish rim of the barrier, which is silhouetted against the sky, makes a clear contrast. The barrier, with its vast mass of snow + ice below a sky fairly crying with color and light, is so strange because it is so still and quiet. Such beauty you impulsively believe must ~~have a way to~~ be heard. It's incredible that it should not. Perhaps it is its striking similarity to music, soft low moans of the bases + the chiming ring of the violins on the upper notes. It would seem strange to hear music + not hear it. So is it strange to see this beauty without hearing it. But that is a strange thought. Perhaps it is the purity of the scene, the glistening snow, the softly shaded hummocks and haycocks,[8] the calm grey repose of Ver Sur Mer inlet and the rugged upheavals of the pressure ridge of its front, stand in rows, massive, and pure—All is so smooth + rounded. There are no jagged contours outside the pressure. To the south, west + north, a gentle series of rises + falls, very gentle, soaring at times when there are no shadows + snow, barrier + sky are one, plain + full at other times when the sun is back of them. I have never come down from the emergency camp without feeling that we do not belong here, we are deceitful venturers, perhaps castaways thrown by chance up on this coast. But we do not belong here. Little America, its towers + telegraph poles + wires + smoke stacks + inhabitation are dirty spots on a spotless white prairie. Ugly manifestations of man + his uglier ambitions.

Life, scanty as it is, is clean—there is no evil here, no shadows of fear + hate + envy outside what men reside here. Evil + its associated sins are not a part of Antarctica—all is of virgin purity + peace.

---

8. A haycock is a small, conical ice formation that grows from successive condensations around a small vent hole in a crevasse and grows to over twenty-five feet high. They are hollow inside, filled with ice crystals, form tunnels with others, and are extremely hard to disturb.

Nature, strong + big, has let human ambitions contaminate her realm only at great cost. But it is only for a while——We will return. Other expeditions will come + go, hanging like flies on an edge of a dish, to the edge of Antarctica, here to-day, gone tomorrow. And all the while the blizzards come, the temperature sinks to the seventies + eighties, the seals + penguins + gulls come + go, the overwhelming forces of the ice pressing down from the plateau will go on, tremendous, grand + awful. How few see it—what a pity, a land of inspiration and to most people a land of monotony + terror. As in no other place, peace holds sway, the peace of God perhaps——

Made oil to-day + on pemmican tomorrow.

August 17th

Last night was a big occasion + we making a milestone of the winter night. We finished putting up the dog pemmican. So we took out the oil drum in the stove, inverted it and made of the stove a swell heating unit. Taylor came down with refreshments + I got drunk, as did Taylor, Stan + Russell. Why not. It was enough to celebrate over anyway.

Haines is in command of the camp now that Poulter is away + up to several days ago refrained from liquor. To-day he broke down + now orders Perkins, who has charge of the liquor cache, to deliver so many pints a day to him. Consequently he is enormously plastered. This morning he made everyone go back to bed when he saw them dressing. Everybody did. To-night they fed him a toasted sandwich filled with leather——

August 19th, Sunday

Murphy is sick—bronchitis they think. He has been in bed the last two days. He asked me to write up the highlights for Columbia [Columbia Broadcasting System], which I did. They are to be a part of Wednesday's August 22nd program, that which comes from New York. He also proposes I write a sketch for "Boy's Life" of Joe Hill's life for which, I may be able to get something for—and he wants me to write a dispatch the day the sun comes back.[9] I think that is a break for me + I shall make the most of it. I do not believe it will stand me on too good stead here but what the hell——

9. Joe Hill, a Swedish immigrant to the United States, was a songwriter and labor organizer of the early 1900s during the rise of industrialism. Though there was a national campaign to save him, he was executed in 1915 by the State of Utah for what might have been a framed murder. (A different Joe Hill was one of the tractor drivers on the expedition.) The magazine *Boys' Life* is published by the Boy Scouts of America.

August 21st

The sun has come back. Ike, Dick + I skiied up to the top of the Barrier to watch the brilliant orange disc lift half its head above the Ross Sea. Sea smoke hid the lower part, but still we could see the sun, which was enough to warm our hearts, though no heat comes from the sun. I wrote Joe Hill's story for "Boy's Life" which was sent off. I wrote the "Columbia Highlights" for Charlie as well as the day's press dispatch. I did tomorrow's about the sun coming back but I think I shall rewrite it. He stated he would get me a good job when I get back—Not bad—

August 23

Stan + I put up airplane rations to-day. Why Stan + I were called upon to do it I do not know. Taylor refused to give me my alcohol, which is the remaining gallon which Del gave me, because he feared I would give it to those who cannot hold it including Russell. I said I would not promise such a thing + he refused to give it to me. To-day the assignment was more a test I think than anything else.

Yesterday was a holiday celebration of sun's return. It was 71 below that morning. It was rather a pitiable day with some people drunk, most of the others sober and disgusted + disappointed at the whole business. I know I was. Had long chat with Murphy to-night at which I told him quite frankly the feeling in the camp against him. We discussed it at some length + he finally conceded to post all dispatches concerning the Admiral as soon as received, which would subdue somewhat the criticism of about his being secretive. I tried to point out the group feeling. I hope I wasn't insulting but I do think he had not realized his position. He is up now + writing his own dispatches. I've had enough razzing for a while.

Aug. 27th

To-day the sun remained up for about two hours, hanging just above the horizon to the north. It made a slow march from east to west + finally sank. It was marvelous, exhilarating, invigorating to see it + to see the sunlight in the snow. We saw shadows for the first time in months. Message Sunday from Dearie—all well. Phil enjoying work on bridge—Morses there + happy.

Temperature the last seven days has averaged around –60. Terrifically cold + a light breeze from the west most of the time. The party is still at the Mt. House + their return is uncertain. Barometer to-night 27.54 + 69 below. Something is brewing.

Aug. 28th

The brooding blizzard did not materialize after all. It blew some, . . . what, a maximum of about 35, but soon died down + to-day was fairly calm. The temperature dropped from –68 to –18, a rise of 50 degrees in a few hours. There were no seals in the chopping house + our idea of a blizzard raging above kept us from digging out more. So fed them [the dogs] pemmican. Moved my team into the last tunnel, which was quite a job as every dog passing every crate tried to pick a fight.

Sept. 4th

I tore off another leaf from the calendar to-night—that is one more month gone. September will go fast—then the trail to the south and adventure. It will be good after this long period of inactivity.

The temperature has held pretty low around [minus] 45 to 65 but to-night it rose to zero from a low this morning of –45. Needless to say the wind shifted to the north + a blizzard set in. It is howling out now, flying snow + drift.

The return of the sun has little effect upon the routine. It has been so cold it is not pleasant to be out. I have been working navigational problems, a story + letters. Made a dog whip to-day.

Opened up the end of my tunnel + had all my dogs loose on the surface. I had a fight doing it for everyone prophesied complete annihilation of all dogs. Only a few fights + Gav was bitten in the leg—not serious. Russell's + my teams are in the end tunnel all together. Each man is supposed to look after his own team. How it is going to work out is difficult to say. I fear it will be a bit hard on the dogs.

Made a radio appearance last Wednesday + read a speech—I wonder whether anyone heard me. It went though pretty well.

Had bath to-night. Good. Ate a half pound of chocolate. Talked aeroplanes with Smitty.[10] Herrmann's tent was claimed to be stolen. He had pitched it near the garage. Herrmann got camp quite excited for he said no more movies until his tent was returned. To-day the tent was found wrapped about Bill Haines' anemometer pole. It had blown away. Mac up in gyro [autogyro] every possible day now.

Printed pictures last night + have a good selection. Drilling Yeoman + Duke in art of navigation. All well at Mt. House. Poulter taking metero. observations.

10. Ralph Smith (Smitty) was a pilot.

Sept. 5th

Wrote a story to-day—lousy. The last one I'll write. Who said I could write anyway? Warm to-day but threatening to blow any minute + no work outside. Fed as usual my dogs + Ed + I clipped their toe nails.

Kind of depressed all day. That chocolate did not agree with me I guess + I tasted it when I woke up this morning. Walter on night watch.

Sept 8th, Saturday

Weather too cold to work outside, between –54 to –65, calm at times, otherwise 5 to 10 mile breezes from south. It is quite impossible to work out for any length of time except with furs on + most men here have not furs. Working on the Ford would be dangerous, for a frozen hand or foot would remain frozen for a half hour or more before it would be possible to get the man back in camp. The Ford is a half mile to the east—on top of the rise. Dogs freeze their paws + noses at such low temperatures. In Canada it is forbidden to drive a horse when it is below forty below.

I have been on mess duty the last two days with Quin. It is the most disagreeable job in the camp. Dirty, messy + tiring. We are each up for two days prior to our going out on the trail. Quin was a good mess partner, quite unlike Rawson who was terribly slow + careless. We did practically nothing but eat steaks all day long from a side of beef brought in. I was terribly carnivorous + it did not seem as though I could get enough meat. The diet is insufficient in many respects + I think I needed something that was in the meat. Vitamins perhaps.

The sun has gotten up quite high + shines for 10 hours a day. But there is not any warmth in the sunlight. It hangs in the sky, brilliant + dazzling but no heat. It is an extraordinary phenomenon.

Sept. 9th

Radio letters from WZXAF—one from Lan, Dearie, Bill Chamberlain. All well + Phil has a raise. To-day was Sunday + we slept in. Quite cold. 45 or thereabouts + a blizzard blowing. "Palsy Days" to-night with Eddie Cantor—swell.

REB evidently still unwell + likely to remain out there until the end of the month. Ken may do the navigating in the plane, which would be a good break for him. The plans are still in an indefinite stage.

I'm rather sick of all this. It is over a year since I left New York to join the expedition—And wasn't I glad to leave New York! All was so new + interesting up to about the middle of the winter night. Since then the monotony of our existence has become increasingly trying. Everything to be done here takes so much effort. Brushing teeth or washing has become a trial. It is not really worth the effort. Our personal habits have slipped. To take a bath means washing clothes + to do that requires many times the quantity of snow as water you get.[11] It must be melted, heated + washed in a tub. To dry clothes they must hang over the stove or near it + in everybody's way. When they are done you put them into a sea bag which is probably stowed in the old photo lab—at least mine are, + that is a chore. It is the same with most everything. We have grown soft perhaps. The cold is so intense it is discouraging to stay out any length of time. To hitch up a dog team is a task itself with the dogs in the tunnels. Practically every snap must either be thawed out with the bare hands or handled with the bare hands. Dragging or leading rambunctious dogs up + down tunnels + shafts is not easy with heavy mittens on. For myself the cold has become almost an aversion. I have almost come to prefer sitting or working in the shacks rather than outdoors. This is perhaps natural, for if numbed hands or face or feet, probably frosted at that, is to be endured every time I go out, I naturally like to avoid it. Cold + frost bite are very painful. Fighting the cold is much worse than fighting the grass at Shankhassick. Both are before you constantly but I really believe the grass is not as unpleasant as this.

The blizzard has come again. It is grand and wonderful in a way, blowing from the interior of a barren + frozen continent, where man has but guessed at its features. We are on its fringe only, a frontier settlement, snug, remotely comfortable and more or less precarious. The winds + snow come to us pure, clean + cold. There is no dirt in the Antarctic save what we brought with us. There are no smells or odors. Snow + ice do not smell, nor does pure clean air. There is nothing to give an odor. Even what we strew about does not smell because there is no disintegration, no decay. Anything is perpetually kept intact. It is a continent on which nothing disappears. What is put here stays. It is a strange world.

Sept. 10th

Had medical exam to-day. Blood pressure down to 102 which accounts for, perhaps, my feeling the cold lately. Blizzard blew itself out last night but it was bitter cold to-day –50 + a strong breeze from the south. Wrote a story + stayed in bed until 11 this morning.

---

11. Ten inches of snow equal one inch of water.

The Pilgrim and Condor airplanes had to be dug out of their snow garages. Only two aircraft were left of the original four. After the men sawed, dug, and piled the excavated snow, it still had to be hauled out of the way. (Paine Antarctic Collection)

Sept. 12th

To-day the Pilgrim was dug from its winter hole. We accomplished the job in about six hours of digging. But what a job—I'm just about all in. We hurried that we might finish it to-day + we did. The tractor pulled it out finally. Yesterday we dug out the ramp for the garage. Between the two I am fed up with snow shovelling for a few days.

Sept. 16th

Sunday last we started digging out the Condor. Following the blizzard of yesterday and the day before, the weather turned fair this afternoon + all hands turned to. It was –32 when we started at one o'clock + –52 when we finished at 5. The wind swung into the south and the frigid temperatures of the interior crazed down upon us. A great ice box extremely frigid.

It is due to warm up soon. Not until the sun shines on the plateau + warms it up will we be warmer. And that will be within several weeks.

Soldered, with the help of Cox, five screw caps on five Preston tins. MAS—

Carbone Pres., Cox Chancellor, Tinglof secretary + Pelter something or other. Thinge lunch.[12]

Wrote several stories, not very good. Rereading *Roads of Adventure* + find Dad hoped that his four sons would never hesitate to blame themselves for adversities rather than circumstances.[13] It is a good word to follow. There has been too much of criticizing everything + everyone else rather than themselves. Taylor I believe is the worst. I have never heard himself take responsibility for anything that's gone wrong. Such is that.

Sept. 19th

Tempus fugit—Our preparations for the trail trip are progressing rapidly + successfully + we shall be able to leave within twenty-four hours should the signal be given. However we do not anticipate leaving until the 15th of October at the earliest. The weather will not be mild enough until then. To start with –45 + fifties is to invite dog casualties + we cannot risk losing one.

I made a thorough search of the polar books to find out facts about the use of metal on runners but the only conclusion, which was common to all, was that in cold temperatures metal runs harder than wood + at warm temperatures metal is superior. What they mean by warm + cold is too ambiguous to base any decision upon in respect to our task. So I have made my run tests. At fifty below I hauled a metal shod sled + one not shod around testing + pushing + carefully determining the relation pulling power necessary to move each. The wood was far superior. To-day it was –25 + I tried it again, coasting them down an incline to make very certain. As near as I could tell they were the same. It is a well known fact that at higher temperatures the metal is better + as we shall not travel in weather below 25 or so I feel justified in shoeing the sleds. I believe we will be repaid many times next summer.

Haines slubbering to-day. The Condor has been all but dug out. All hands (30–35)! worked Sunday afternoon, Monday + part of Tuesday digging. Weather threatened + we abandoned our shovels + waited. It came + tonight it is raging from the west. I fear our work will be largely obliterated by tomorrow morning.

A new happiness has come over all of us. The outdoor work + new interests outside ourselves has brightened our outlook considerably. Healthy

12. "MAS" may refer to the mess crew, and "thinge lunch," according to Paine family tradition, means an unidentifiable lunch.

13. *Roads of Adventure,* by Ralph D. Paine (Boston: Houghton Mifflin, 1922), was his father's autobiography.

The dog drivers discuss the upcoming field season: (from left) Paine, Dick Russell, (possibly) Stevenson Corey (supply officer), Alton Wade, Alan Innes-Taylor (at head of table), Albert Eilefsen, Olin Stancliff, and Ed Moody. Finn Ronne and Duke Dane are not shown. (Paine Antarctic Collection)

exercise has done a lot, the sun a great deal + the approaching trips has spurred us to greater efforts + we are happier because of this. I wonder whether the complete absence of ultra violet rays has anything to do with the dispositions. Have had no chance to drive the dogs yet—No, I drove five of them one day for a short run up to Ford. The weather has hardly been over –50 during the month. John Dyer worried about my radio technique. He was very funny, saying he thought I was not the type. I'm afraid I deliberately fostered that impression. I think I am.

Sept 21st

Blizzard continued with heavy fall of snow. I haven't dared look at our Condor hole but imagine it is pretty well filled up. 35 mile wind the last three days from east. Ski jumping this afternoon—Ronne fell down three times. He's one of us nortets after all. Stan complained that his skiis would not go straight—found when he came in he had boots on wrong feet. Made pack board. Looks good.

Paine puts up trail rations in the New Mess Hall for the summer journey. Ingredients are detailed on the bulletin board. Duke Dane is standing to the left. (Paine Antarctic Collection)

Sept 23rd

Sunday. Letters from home—two from Browns, one from Dearie. Phil has sprained back. Tough luck, he's been in bed. Poor old Philadieeeeeeu—— Milton + Short [of Chinook Kennels] sent message + Milton spoke. President + Secretary of National Puzzler's league spoke to Admiral [at Advance Base]. Skiing to-day across bay—4 hours. Jack wore his new tail covering for first time + I think it is going to work all right.[14] Yesterday dug out Condor. 8 a.m. to 10 p.m. Blizzard had filled up hole. Two tractors pulled it out. Quite an undertaking all told but it is accomplished. Everyone worked like hell. Murphy can take it. Every[one] pooped. Warm –18 + gentle snow storm from North. Time is getting short. We are almost ready. Quin doesn't seem to accomplish much, though he has been very busy.[15] Time passes swiftly + we shall be out on the trail soon.

14. Paine made the tail covering of the "softest and finest sheepskin to be found at Little America; it was put together with a fine seam and an outer layer of windproof cloth had been sewn around it." After much experimentation, the covering was attached to the harness and thus held in place (Walden and Paine, *Long Whip*, 190).
15. Quin Blackburn, and Paine and Russell with their teams, were to be the Geological Party.

The mechanics and pilots tested the Condor engines in the now-opened snow garage. Paine photographed the scene looking down into the garage from the former roof level. (Paine Antarctic Collection)

Sept. 27th

To-day + yesterday I drove my dogs for the first time as a team. They are a swell bunch of pooches. They are: Pony & Legaska, Bob + Buck, Winter + Council, Gav + Kaiser + old Jack. I have the best team by far in the camp + I am not the only one to say that. Yesterday they rather got the best of me. I was all in last night. But to-night I think I got the best of them, for they were only too glad to make port. I'm awfully proud of them.

Mac crashed in the Gyro yesterday afternoon. I was below in the Old Mess Hall when Albert Eilefsen hollered down the ventilator that Mac has fallen from the Gyro. I + Taylor rushed out without even stopping to put on a hat. Consequently I froze my ears + I slept little last night. Taylor froze the top of his head.[16] Mac has crashed not far from the Pilgrim. It is a mess. Mac was pinned in the cockpit + we had to cut the fabric + its parachute before we got him out. His left arm was caught between a rotor blade which had folded against the cockpit + the side of the fuselage. Wade realized that. Russell +

16. The ambient temperature was –50°F (Byrd, *Discovery* [film]).

I got a sled + on it we put Mac. His left arm was broken, a clean cut. No other injuries. It was a singularly fortunate freak of God that Mac was not killed. He was a bit shaken up + he did not come to until this morning, that is stop jibbering. He's in REB's bunk in the library + very cheerful.

Got letter from Taylor which stated he did not like my behavior very much during the past winter + was disappointed in me personally. I replied by letter also.[17] I'm sorry the situation ever arose.

Oct. 4th

The time passes swiftly + in a short ten days we hope to be on our way south. There is much to be done yet—the most important I believe is the exercising of the dogs + men, particularly the dogs.[18] The compass must be mounted on the sled, gee poles fixed, my skiis repaired + everything checked. To-day has been a blizzardly one + we were forced to spend a rainy day inside. Every day it blows is a day lost in the outdoor work. The temperatures here moderated + many of the dogs are up on the surface. Dick + I have kept ours below in the reasoning that whatever comfort + warmth we can provide now will help the dogs later. They will get enough outdoor sleeping in a couple of weeks. Bramhall + Morgan's are out. Taylor's + Moody's + most of the Eastern parties'. Each of them have made further efforts to drive them. Bram took from 1 p.m. to four p.m. hitching up, driving a half hour + unhitching his team. Morgan has not even done that. Albert has driven but once. How they expect to get out of here + into the 88th Parallel of latitude is beyond my powers to visualize.[19] Morgan, Black + Ronne went out to take soundings with the seismographic outfit, went two miles stayed a whole day and made one bad shot. They came home because they did not have any tethering lines for their dogs. We, on the contrary, have had our teams out whenever possible + I do not think they are in such tough shape.

17. These letters have disappeared. Whatever Innes-Taylor's thoughts or feelings, he nevertheless chose Paine for the demanding southern journey.
18. The first day the dogs were brought to the surface was relatively warm, –30°. The light, the fresh air, and the temporary freedom made them wild with excitement. Putting the exuberant dogs into harness was nearly impossible (Walden and Paine, *Long Whip,* 178–79).
19. Innes-Taylor had been planning the summer field journeys for much of the winter. The Geological Party and the Plateau Party with dog teams would travel together to the Polar Plateau but on a different mission. The Plateau Party, with physicist Dr. Bramhall and geologist Morgan, would conduct cosmic ray observations, measurements of the earth's magnetic fields, test the depth of the polar ice, and examine rock structure in areas chosen by the Geological Party in the Queen Maud Mountains. Simply to carry their basic supplies and particularly their instruments (850 pounds of specialized equipment) the two men needed four dog teams, thirty-six dogs in all. Experienced drivers Ronne and Eilefsen were therefore assigned to their party (ibid., 177–86).

The tractor party of June, Rawson, Peterson + Von der Wall were reported to be 120 miles out last night + close to three thousand feet high.[20] The four passed around the northern tip of the Rockefellers + should be at Grace McKinley in another day's traveling time. It is a most spectacular trip, justifying great faith in the tractors for Barrier travel. I'm glad Ken got the break to navigate the party. He deserves a break + I wish him all the luck in the world.

REB is standing by waiting for the Pilgrim to go out and pick him up. As far as can be ascertained, the tractor out there is finished, though definite word apparently cannot be had. So we expect the Admiral to be here any day now. And then, things will hum I'll bet.

We have two radio sets rigged, one in the radio shack + one in Blubberheim—We carry on daily schedules with each other which gives us pretty good practice. I feel quite confident of being able to handle the set out there this summer.

The Fairchild has been dug out + found in bad shape.[21] Both struts supporting the wings were bent + the fabric was in poor shape. I do not believe it will be flown this expedition.

God I'll be glad to go——

Oct. 10th

For past week, seven days have had bad weather—overcast, snowing + blowing from the north + east, and two days of 50 mile blizzard, etc. worst wind [we've] had. June, Rawson, Peterson and Von der Wall have been camped just a week. They are at [Mile] 185. George Noville, Hill + Skinner left here three days ago for the Mt. House. First day they made 14 miles, yesterday 38 + still going. To-night they should be at Mountain House with three thousand lbs. of dog food [for the summer field parties].

Dick, Quinn + I drove our teams out nine miles [on the southern trail] + left our trailer sleds.[22] It was overcast + lightly blowing from east. On way home, Winter dropped dead, Winter of all dogs.[23] And we were only a half mile from camp. It was a case of complete exhaustion. The other dogs came through all right. They had a load of only 400 pounds going out + about 50

20. The tractor was heading eastward both to explore and to establish ration depots for the Eastern Party, which would follow them into Marie Byrd Land (ibid., 281–82).

21. The Fairchild airplane was left behind when the First Expedition left in 1930.

22. The sleds dropped off were in preparation for their summer journey, which would begin shortly.

23. Winter had been one of the strongest and most reliable dogs on the fall journey but had gained significant weight over the winter, even when his rations were cut back.

coming back. Thus we felt justified in running the eighteen miles. Poor Winter. I feel like a murderer. He died in harness, perhaps the only honorable death for a husky, whose play has only been pulling + working for heartless drivers. Skookum + Winter—each with tremendous individuality + attraction.

My team ran away from me this morning + ran all the way to the emergency cache before they stopped! David Paige stopped them!!!!

Oct 13th Saturday

REB returned yesterday. Bowlin, Clay + Ike flew out in calm weather + a slightly overcast sky. Byrd so drunk he had to be carried to plane. Rocky when he got here. Came to about supper time. He does not look so bad— perhaps this is the first time he has been sober. Poulter flew back with him. He's fat and has a moustache. Hope to get away Monday. Tending to last minute details. Chief [a dog] will not go but I shall try him again. Friday is to replace Bob, who has a bad rear end.[24] It's discouraging, this last minute mix up of plans. George Skinner + Hill arrived back from Advance Base last night. Royal welcome. Dick + I put out signs from few miles in—"<u>Bunk, three miles ahead</u>," "<u>I died for Byrd, why don't you?</u>," "<u>Welcome Noville, our hero</u>," "<u>Welcome, Little America Garage</u>," "<u>Fan belts a specialty</u>," etc.

Oct. 15th

To-day was the day we had set long ago to be off. But the Plateau Party or rather Morgan of that party was not ready. Even his scientific gear was three miles out on the Barrier somewhere. He had unsuccessfully tried to further its dept. [departure] [on] the Barrier—a tough enough task for the best of us. However Ronne has been put in charge of trail operations for the party + things are now ready. Herrmann persuaded Poulter to hold us so he could get a movie of the combined parties leaving L.A. We are clowns for Paramount all right if a camera man can hold up the departure of field parties! However, we have done much to-day + now I'm at last satisfied that all is in order.

It has taken many months + many hours of labor to prepare for this trip. I feel that this is the eve of the biggest adventure of my life. It is one I am looking forward to with tremendous eagerness. What may happen no one knows.

---

24. Out of the Paine's original team, Winter, Skookum, and Break-it were dead, and replacements had to be found. The most capable dogs had already been recruited by other parties (ibid., 184–86).

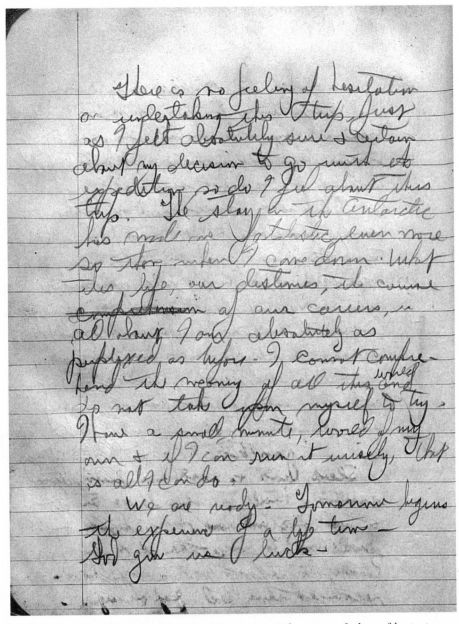

On his diary page of October 15, 1934, Paine wrote, "There is no feeling of hesitation on undertaking this trip . . ." Supported only at the beginning of the journey and with little hope of rescue in case of trouble, his three-man Geological Party would travel over seven hundred miles on skis and by dog team to approach the South Pole. (Paine Antarctic Collection)

We feel confident, however, that it will prove successful in every way. No party has gone into the field in the Antarctic better equipped nor with better men (Amundsen excepted perhaps). The work we are going to do is worthwhile. It is Dick's + my mission to see that Quin has the opportunities + facilities for his scientific work.

There is no feeling of hesitation on undertaking this trip. Just as I felt absolutely sure + certain about my decision to go with the expedition, so do I feel about this trip. The stay in the Antarctic has made me fatalistic even more so than when I came down. What this life, our destinies, the course of our careers, is all about I am absolutely as perplexed as before. I cannot comprehend the meaning of all this world and do not take upon myself to try. I have a small, minute world of my own + if I can run it wisely, that is all I can do.

We are ready. Tomorrow begins the experience of a lifetime. God give us luck——

Diary Three

Summer Sledge Journey

Queen Maud Geological Party

October–January 1934–35

Stuart D. Paine

The Start of the Southern Journey

October 16–November 20, 1934

Oct. 16th 1934

10.7 miles south L.A.

To-day marks the beginning of our southern trip. We left L.A. in the company with the Plateau Party about 11:15 A.M.—I went first, Russell + Ronne following closely. We wound up the barrier slope, seven teams in all, 2 of our party, four of the Plateau party + Herrmann + Moody's team, quite a procession of dogs + men. Bram + Albert caught us when nearing the emergency cache + we traveled with them to this point.[1]

We are 10.7 miles south of L.A. A week previous we had cached our two trailer sleds nine miles out + the run to that point was fast + easy making mt. in three hours. But the addition of the trailers slowed us up terribly. The northerly winds of the past two weeks have showered minute snow crystals down upon the surface so that the unevenness was leveled off. This made stretches of hard surface followed by very soft + sandy stretches. Though averaging around zero all day, 10 below when we camped, the going was as

---

1. The seven teams included two nine-dog teams of the Geological Party (Quin Blackburn, leader and geologist, Dick Russell, driver and in charge of base laying, and Stuart Paine, driver, navigator, and radio operator); four teams of the Plateau Party (Charles Morgan, geologist, Dr. Ervin Bramhall, physicist and navigator, with Finn Ronne and Albert Eilefsen as additional drivers); and one team driven by Ed Moody with John Herrmann, photographer, who would photograph the trip to the first night's camp at Mile 10.7 and then return to Little America. The Supporting Party, with dog drivers Alan Innes-Taylor, Duke Dane, and Ed Moody, was expected to stock the depots to three hundred nautical miles south (Byrd, *Discovery,* 250–51, 258–60).

The Geological Party, consisting of Paine, Dick Russell, and Quin Blackburn, packing their main sledges in preparation for their departure to unexplored areas of the Queen Maud Mountains. The previous week, packed trailer sleds were left on the trail nine miles ahead to be picked up on the outward journey. (BPRCAP, Papers of Admiral Richard E. Byrd, image 7885-10)

On October 16, seven teams left together heading south: Paine, as navigator, led, with Jack, his lead dog, setting the pace; Dick Russell's team; four teams of the Plateau Party; and Ed Moody's team with John Herrmann, the photographer. (BPRCAP, Papers of Admiral Richard E. Byrd, image 7903-8)

bad as the memorable day last March on our way to the 125 miles beacon going north. The dogs simply could not haul the loads. We progress a hundred yards, then a period of rest. Dick's dogs did even worse than mine. Ronne's + Albert's did about the best though Bram rode on the front of his sled most of the time.

To-night we were tired + discouraged. The loads we are hauling are small [compared] to those we must carry leaving 100 miles. The winter night + their [the dogs'] long period of inactivity tells a sad tale as to their strength.

Quin is cooking. He burned a hole in the cook tent floor + burned a small hole in the tent itself. However, it was an accident + I must be tolerant + patient—Tomorrow my birthday. How strange—I'll be 24.

Oct. 17th

Second day out—Made 10 miles exactly to-day, very heavy going, soft sandy snow + our dogs who are quite as soft as they could be, made tough going of it. Ten miles was plenty. We are 20.7 or thereabouts miles from L.A. and quite satisfied with our progress. Still with the Plateau Party. Our progress has been pretty much an independent affair, occasional visits from them or ourselves.[2] John Herrmann + Moody left us this morning after taking some good shots. I was rather peeved at John last night when he made or rather threatened me into rehitching up my dogs. However he has a job to do + I guess we are the tools of his achievements.

To-day warm, −10 to 0 with easterly wind. Excellent day, overcast cirro-stratus + alto-stratus clouds, occasional burst of sunshine.

To-night we celebrated the 17th + drank to the health of Phil—a long ways away. This is probably the most unique birthday I shall ever spend + perhaps the happiest. Had radio contact with John Dyer this morning + he told me to

2. The Geological Party planned to pass the First Expedition's southernmost point at Supporting Party Mountain at the base of the Queen Maud Range and continue south over one hundred miles up Leverett Glacier to the Polar Plateau to do geological and paleontological reconnaissance. The Plateau Party intended to run a seismic and magnetic survey south up the Ross Ice Shelf and then ascend the Thorne Glacier to the Plateau, where the ice was believed to be ten thousand feet deep. (The Marie Byrd Party, the "Eastern Party," left on September 27 to explore eastward to Mount Grace McKinley.)

Some assistance was to be available from the Supporting Party and also from the tractors, each of which would carry a load as well as twelve thousand pounds of fuel. The Fall Southern Party already had set preliminary depots to Mile 155 the previous March, and other supplies were to be picked up from an intermediate depot. Three thousand pounds of just dog food had to be ferried to the Queen Maud Mountains (ibid., 250–51, 258–60). The two functional planes were kept for exploration and backup. A line of food depots from the Bay of Whales to the Queen Maud Range was needed, covering a distance of 517 miles, or 450 nautical miles to Mountain Base (ibid., 206–8).

standby for mes[sage]. Duke + Taylor + several others sang "Happy Birthday to you" + it made the day a real occasion. How similar is human nature. Jananne + Content would be singing it to me were I home to-day. A grand feed of hamburg to-night + anti-scorbutic—the alcohol is about half strength.

Oct. 18th

10 below. –8 at 8 o'clock—the morning calm, completely overcast + snowing lightly. Built beacon + placed birthday bottle atop of it. This camp is to be known as "Camp Bottle." Fed extra half rations last night to dogs. We are eating about 1/3 of man food ration but shall cook the full food ration + feed what we don't eat to the dogs. Each of us wrote notes to Duke, Ed + Al [the supporting party] to be left at 25 mile beacon. Mine was rather sentimental I fear. 12:30—25 mile depot. Mileage in L.A., 306.7—25 mile depot 332.8.[3] Heavy blanket of clouds—5 mile wind from south. Visibility one mile.

Clouds stratus in morning, alto stratus early in afternoon + clear to-night. Sled meter 337.2. Dogs exhausted. Soft surface continues. Re-iced our runners to-night with a piece of cotton + warm water, a smooth thin film of ice. Much dog crap accumulated on all our runners. Finn's + Albert's who have metal on their front sleds were just as bad if not worse than Dick's + mine. Quin went ahead on skiis during the morning but a bad ski boot made him ease up. I went ahead this afternoon + Quin drove my team, which broke trail most of the time. –27 to-night + clear. Light S.E. wind.

Oct. 19th

30 min. but +2 this morning. All slept well save Quin—he is sending for his eiderdown bag. Overcast. Calm with thin line of clear sky to west. Got up once to see whether Jack was all right. He was. Jack can't understand the moaning of the generator. He barks and barks at it.

6 P.M. Camped around 4:30 after a run of 14.3. 351.5 sledmeter. Surface improved as we progressed going from soft light snow to hard sastrugi with flat stretches of soft snow between. We are camped now at 44 mile beacon of last fall's trip. It has taken us four days to make this point + last fall it took three. The surface made the difference in time—last fall it was hard + crusty. On our left is the gentle slope leading, so I'm told, up to a thousand feet. We

---

3. The sled meter, attached to Paine's sled, equated turns of the wheel to a determined unit of mileage. Paine's early notations regarding mileage reflected the sled meter already reading 306.7 miles when the party left Little America. Paine calculated mileage beyond that initial meter reading.

are traversing the slope at roughly three hundred feet. Tomorrow we go down to the fifty mile depot. Dogs pulled better to-day. The icing of runners has helped considerably. But our ski boots troubled us all day and that forced us to stop short of a 15 mile run.[4] Blowing from southeast + clear.

Morgan complains of having hurt his ankle + so he rode a good part of the day. I wonder whether it isn't another case of Black's knee.

Oct. 20th 44 mile beacon

We are held here by a 25 mile S.E. wind + heavy drift + haze. We are glad of the wind for it will make the surface hard + easy to traverse. The delay of a day will not interfere with our trip much for we were allowed ten days to go the first 100 miles. It is just as well, for to date the going has been hard + slow though our loads are light compared to the weights we will have to carry from 100 miles on.

JoJo is still loose + getting wilder. We tried to surround her this morning but she made off as fast as she could. She's wise. Eats scraps which the other dogs leave.

Travel in these temperatures is so much easier + more enjoyable than the cold of the fall. What we underwent last fall will never be realized by those who have not had to put up with such hardships. It is a wonder we got off with what few frostbites we had—and the dogs—they were certainly tough.

Russell is in charge of trail operations to the mtns. Quin explains he knows so much more about trail operation he should be in charge of that end.[5] Quite right—But my experiences seem to count for naught. However, that does not matter.

Quin's cooking is improving; he'll be a first class cook yet. Miss Taylor's chow. Repaired radio this morning. Found loose connection in battery box. Have sleep tent fixed like chaise lounge but something is lacking, the old feeling of comfort + well being. The tent bows + shakes. The floor on which are the sleeping bags shakes.

---

4. The teams were overloaded for the snow conditions and the capabilities of the dogs. Also, the inexperience and inadequate physical condition of the scientists made their progress especially slow. Ronne and Eilefsen, who were to watch over them, were extremely concerned. As the plan developed by Innes-Taylor demanded an average pace of fifteen miles per day, the parties were far behind. Ronne suggested that the drivers add weight from the sledges to their rucksacks and thus relieve the dogs of part of the load (Walden and Paine, *Long Whip*, 185–90). Each man added fifty pounds to his rucksack (Byrd, *Discovery*, 251).

5. Dick Russell was a member of Byrd's 1925 Greenland Expedition.

The teams rested on the trail, usually once for ten minutes after the first five miles were run in the morning, at noon, and then as many times as the dogs seemed to need in the afternoon. The teams traveled up the Ross Ice Shelf toward the mountains to the south. (Paine Antarctic Collection)

Oct. 21st

Made run of 18 miles to 62 mile mark on detour around valley of crevasses. A swell day—the wind of the day before hardened the soft snow + we fairly bowled along, the dogs hauling our sleds at a trot. Made run to fifty mile in an hour + 3/4. Fifty mile beacon almost completely drifted over, only a flag + a little hump marks the spot. Oh, a couple of gasoline tins. Left note for Duke + Al + Ed.

Took radio apart. The receiver wouldn't oscillate. Did not find out the trouble but made it work. Believe the batteries were too cold to function properly. For it was all right when first turned on but soon began to let up on its oscillation until only at the top of the band on coil B moved it [to] oscillate. Finally it quit altogether. To bed at 11 o'clock.

Oct. 22nd

17 miles to 75 mile depot. Swell going as day before, but much of day's run was uphill, our time was not as good. Passed Cletrac. It is not buried any more than it was last fall when we passed it. A high surrounding wall of snow has been built up but the machine itself is still quite uncovered. Passed the

plank sticking from the back of the 1st Expedition Ford + so to here.[6] Had difficulty following trail to the beacon, first because of the scattering of flags + second, those that we saw were not easily distinguishable.

Off to the east appears two islands with a low ridge to the south east. We noticed them last fall. They might be something or they may be only mirage effects.

Temperatures a little below zero, so below to-night. Calm save for occasional puffs from the N.W. Brilliant sunshine. Bram + Albert stayed behind at 62 to take magnetic observations. Came into camp only three hours after we did. Had successful radio contact with John. It's quiet + peaceful here. Our duties are only to ourselves + our dogs—that makes life simple and happy.

Siphoned some gas from Cletrac + took 2 1/2 gals. from 75 mile depot left here by Poulter on his night trip. Have two Primus' going in the sleeping tent + getting things dried out.[7]

Oct. 23rd

16.5 miles to-day. Camped about 3:30 at 91.5 mark. Had planned to make a stop of about three hours, feed the dogs half rations, have something to eat ourselves + move on to Advance Base. However we changed our minds + decided to stay. 25 miles a day is too much for the 8th day out. The dogs are still soft. The Plateau Party however decided to shove on + stayed here two hours. Morgan wanted to sleep in the Admiral's bunk + Albert wanted to be the first to get sinecures.

Picked up a bag of dog food dropped by the tractor. Also a two quart can of figs, which we almost finished to-night. I predict dire circumstances tomorrow.

6. The Cletrac was still stuck at Mile 66; the "Ford" refers to the snowmobile.

7. The Primus stoves were lighted in the morning to boil water for oatmeal and tea, and in the evening to cook and help dry things out. Dishes were cleaned with snow. At scheduled times during the week, the radio receiver and transmitter were set up, the batteries warmed in the sleeping tent, and an interchange with Little America attempted. Then the dogs were harnessed, the leader first so he could hold the gangline in place. The sleeping tent, left until the last minute to offer the men a degree of important comfort, was struck, the men changed from their mukluks into their ski boots, and the trail day started. After glancing back to line the team up with yesterday's tracks, the navigator checked the compass at fifteen-minute intervals on the trail. Once the dogs got into shape, the first five miles were run in about two hours and then there was a ten-minute rest stop. At the lunch stop (after another five miles), the men had a cup of warm tea from the thermos bottle, a small piece of pemmican, and a small bar of chocolate. The afternoon was paced by the level of dogs' fatigue. At the evening stop, the dogs were led to the gangline, leader last, and fed. Camp was quickly pitched, snow collected for water, Primus stoves started, rations unpacked, and wet clothing hung on lines in the tents (Walden and Paine, *Long Whip*, 190–98).

The going was pretty good. Hard crusty sastrugi with intermittent patches of soft snow. I led most of the time but Bram with Whitie was chaffing at my frequent stops. Bram can't stop his team. So he went ahead + did fairly well. Dogs in better shape to-night than they have been since we started. That's encouraging. We will have to load on more than 500 lbs. per sled when we leave Advance Base. Combed beard + hair to-night. Calm overcast + hazy—above zero all day. All together a happy day.

Oct. 24th

Left 91.5 mile camp at 8:30 + reached Advance Base at 11:30. The Plateau gang were up + about + Bram was taking observations. Spent afternoon loading our sleds, eating immensely of jam, peanut butter, grapenuts, pork chops + drying our stuff in the tent. There was no room for any more in the shack. At night a feed of chicken (fried) + cocoa + Jello. Our appetites are already becoming abnormal.[8]

We leave here with over a thousand pounds per sled—a heavy load with which we are scheduled to reach 200 mile depot in seven days—a big order. However we'll try. Filled up with 15 gallons kerosene, 729 lbs. dog food—4 rations + put up 4 rations in checkered bags to be picked up by the tractor + carried to 300.[9]

From now on we will be down to the bare necessities. 3 hours a day on the Primus—all spare clothing cast off, + all extras left behind or eaten.

Oct. 25th

10 A.M. Warm, light cirrus clouds + calm. Breakfast of 6 shredded wheats—an awful mess in the shack. Plan to start early in afternoon + get 10 miles or more if possible. We are one day ahead of schedule. Quin having terrible time about ski boots + wants to take along three pairs. No radio contact yesterday.

---

8. A man on sledging journeys consumed between four and five pounds of food per day, half of which was water. With a water content of less than 3 percent, the pemmican was broken into pieces and added to melted snow to make a meat stew called "hoosh" (Byrd, *Little America,* 33).

9. Each checkered bag, plus one white bag of biscuits, sufficed three men for ten days. The word *rations* was used flexibly. There were "dog rations," "man rations," and a "complete ration," which was usually a thirty-day food supply for one man (Byrd, *Discovery,* 213–14). The two teams of the Geological Party left Little America with 1,584 pounds of supplies. Calculated from a daily use of 7.5 pounds of man food, 27 pounds of dog food, and 1 pound of fuel, the sledges hauling supplies for two teams and three men would reduce the total weight hauled by 35.5 pounds per day. Picking up more weight at Mile 100, they carried 2,049 pounds divided between the two sledges. These figures are from calculations later transcribed by Paine for Admiral Byrd's use (Stuart D. Paine, "Daily Decrease of Weight on 90 Day Journey," Paine Antarctic Collection).

Finn's set went off just as mine did. Believe we should have contacted them for tractors are about to start.

8 P.M. 5 miles south of Advance Base. Left A.B. at 1:30 + camped here, at Camp Hamburger at 5. The going was terrible, soft light snow. Our loads are over a thousand [pounds] per sled + the dogs pulled with great effort. Both Dick + I were pushing most of the time + Quin was out in front on skiis. He carried his pack with the eight pounds of hamburger in it for neither Dick nor myself would carry it. Had the hamburger to-nite.

Plateau Party at Advance Base to-night. Bram wanted to do more work so they stayed their [allotted] ten days. Two days there. Believe they like the warmth too well.

Do not believe we can keep to our schedule as planned before we came by Taylor.[10] Going like this will make us weeks behind skd [schedule], but there is absolutely nothing we can do.

Oct 26th

A.M. Blowing from N.W. about ten miles, temp 28 below—cold. Plateau Party at Adv. Base. Decided to remain here at least for the morning in hopes that it will blow harder + toughen the surface or the Plateau Party will catch up with us. We feel it is too cold for the dogs to make any lengthy distance to-day at the low temperatures + with such heavy loads.

Successful contact with Duke at L.A. this morning. Eastern Party at 180 miles. Tractors left yesterday P.M. and should make Adv. Base to-day.

Supporting Party not going out but will stand by in case of need. Poor Duke + Ed. I + all of us feel tremendously sorry. Their disappointment must be very great. It is a tough break for them, and they alone all of us others should have had a chance to go on the trail. They've worked harder + deserve it more.[11] Quin down to three hours of Primus time but doesn't seem to be able to do it. Taking four or more. Will have to watch that above everything else though we have wired whether it will be possible to bring out five gals. of extra fuel for Mtn. Base. Have to warm radio batteries besides. Must have or curtail cooking or radio.

P.M. 15.3 miles from Adv. Base. Going better, but to make ten miles I had to hitch onto the gangline ahead of Jack + pull. My sled seemed to pull very

---

10. As previously mentioned, progress of 15 miles per day was assumed. This figure not only determined schedules but the amount of supplies that had to be carried to sustain the men and dogs.

11. Innes-Taylor decided that the support function would be better served by the tractors, so the sledgers' support would be unnecessary (ibid., 261).

hard. Dick's on the contrary pulled all right. Plateau Party passed us at 1:30 while we in our bags. Can't burn Primus for heat now though it is 42 below right now. When will it get warm? As Albert says, "it's too cold God Damn it, too cold."

Oct. 27th

14 miles to 4 miles beyond 125 mile beacon. Surface fair but heavy loads + cold made sled pull hard. Stopped three times to clean runners. Plateau Party went on to make fifteen miles but that was more than we could do. They have light loads comparatively speaking though they claim their sleds are weighted down as much as ours. It was planned by Taylor that they would help us out from the 100 mile. They have to the extent of 71 lbs., no more, no less. The old spirit of "let the others hang themselves, I've got mine." We'll see—

Oct. 28th

10 miles exactly to 139 mile mark. Calm, almost, when we left this morning. But almost immediately a 20 mile E.S.E. breeze sprang up + blew all day. Our course lay almost into it. Temperature –36 when we started + –28 when we stopped. It was a bitter day.[12] Could have continued but it would probably have meant a dead dog or two tomorrow. At such temperatures with such winds, animals can do only so much.

The trip to date has been a disappointment. I was led to believe that summer sledging would be somewhat of a pleasure after fall sledging, but to date it has not differed in many respects. The same gritty surface, low temperatures + bitter winds. At least last fall we had plenty of fuel. Now we have only enough to cook with. When our meals are over we either get underway or get back into our sleeping bags. Quin broke a Thermos.

125 mile beacon just as we left it, only drifted up to about a foot + a half. Picked up spare skiis there. Dick's team pulling wonderfully + has taken some of my load from me. I don't know what's the matter with my team. I'll stick by Jack, Pony, Legaska, Buck, Gav + Kaiser. Chief + Friday I do not think do their share.

Plateau Party somewhere up ahead. Cannot see them for the drift. Quin just broke our only thermometer. Eh bien. Without a thermometer much of

12. Considering ambient temperature and wind chill, the temperature was –69° when the party began traveling and was –59° when they stopped.

our work will be inaccurate.[13] It's his party + what he breaks he'll have to suffer for—though it's a bit discouraging for us. He's the clumsiest + most
ungraceful man I've ever seen.

Oct. 29th

A.M. Successful contact with base this morning. Eastern Party 120. Got
mixed up on radio schedule + came in on Finn's time. Reported to Taylor
lack of cooperation on part of Morgan. He says to just plug along until tractors catch us. He expected just such a move.

We are standing by waiting for this infernal wind to abate. It continues
about twenty miles but has shifted to S.E. + South. We hope for a change.
Quin has bite on upper lip which gives him much pain.

The flop flop of tent, the swishing of drift against the windproof, the
smoke from our cigarettes zigzagging upward in the tent as it is pulled one
way then the other as the tent walls flap. Dogs—wads of snow curled up
behind snow blocks to protect them from the icy wind. Jack chained to my
shovel just outside the sleeping tent door.[14] Agony of putting on frozen ski
boots. Quin beating his hands to get them warm. The succulent warmth of
the sleeping bags. God bless the Caribou. Quin's worrying about dirty pants,
his lips, his facial cosmetics. Frost + ice from your breath frozen about the
mouth of our bags—cold feet, cold hands.

P.M. Made 14 miles to 152.2. Broke camp about 1 + camped 7:30. Wind
had made surface very good + our dogs hauled their loads well. Had hoped
to make 155 but Dick's dogs quite tired. Wind died to about 3–5 miles S.W.
throughout the day—clear + cold— –25. The pressure looms ahead but
believe there is a way through a little to the S.E. We'll see. The way must be
secure for the tractors, that's certain, + we'll find it if possible.

Finn came into camp all by himself. He was only 3 miles ahead of the rest
of his party but that made no difference. They are all out for themselves each
+ everyone.

It's rather cruel, it struck me, to-night, to bring animals down here to suffer the way they have to. Outside Jack is shaking in spasms from head to tail
from cold. The same with all the others. They, the dogs, sweat for you, pull

---

13. In order to do their work, they would have to get a replacement thermometer from one of
the other parties.

14. Jack, unnaturally thin, without a tail to wrap around his nose, and still suffering from infection, would sometimes get a little extra pemmican and shelter in the lee of a tent. Despite the care
that Paine had put into constructing a tail covering, Jack refused to wear it.

your loads, work till they drop + if they do not die doing it, you kill them. It's a dog's life. How I pity them.

Oct. 30

15.1 miles from 152.2. Passed furthest southing of last fall + ran mag. course 40, variation 118, true 158 for 4 1/2 miles. Built beacon + ran course 62 mag., variation 118—true 180—for 7.8 miles. Surface excellent + dogs pulled well. Light W. to S.W. breeze 5 miles, temp. 30–40 below. Bram stayed behind with Morgan for observations + Finn + Albert came with us. Picked up 3 bundles of flags at 155, Lat. D.R. 81°6'41" + or –. Drank our healths but found alcohol is half water, a fine bunch of confederates we have back in camp to send us out with stuff like that. Tractors supposed to have left Adv. Base to-day. Expect them tomorrow. No pressure in sight yet though a cliff like mass is miraged to west. I hope we can go through without any trouble. So far so good—

Oct. 31st

Course 180. Var. 118, mag. 62—15.1 miles.
15.1 miles to-day to 182.2. Passed through crevassed area about 3 miles wide. They were in a slight depression of the Barrier. We first came upon some small cracks 6 1/2 miles after we broke camp + later ran into some holes. Further on we came to two large crevasses 30 feet across, for the most part bridged over but in places they were open. We looked down into one + saw no bottom. Light blue ice on vertical walls deepening to dark greenish blue down to black. It certainly made us feel funny. This solid snow surface is not as solid as we surmise + when travelling though crevassed areas one never knows when one is to suddenly drop out of sight down down down to goodness knows where. When crossing these to-day we held our breaths + dashed across. At least I did. Tried to contact L.A. to relay msg. to tractors about crevasses but unsuccessful. Will try tomorrow morning. With great care believe tractors can get through all right. Cold to-day. 35 below. 10–12 mile wind in our faces. All of us were nipped. When will it get warm? There's too much resemblance to last fall to be enjoyable— –42 to-night + wind still blowing.

Nov. 1st

A.M. A strange day. Contacted L.A. on Eastern Party schedule + told them of crevasses—thought it possible for them to get through. Contact at noon. Ordered to return to search for tractor. They should have caught up with us

At Mile 173, Joe Hill's tractor went into a crevasse two feet wide and 120 feet deep. The Geological Party was called back north, backtracking twelve miles through the crevasse field, to help get them out. (Paine Antarctic Collection)

by noon. And as no tractors came back about 14 miles—made it in fast running time. What we took yesterday to be cracks were in reality large crevasses heavily bridged but which would swallow a tractor many times over. Instead of two there were at least eight. It was probably the light yesterday which made us miss seeing the big ones. Tractors seen in the distance. First thought they were moving + so pitched both tents. Keener observation proved they were not, so we packed up + came on. Hill's tractor had gone into a crevasse stern first, one which we had passed over without seeing at all. They had just finished digging it out when we came up, Quin, Dick + I.[15] Plateau Party still at 182.2—185.5 by our wheel. Concluded to stay here, turn back to 160 + strike 10 miles east then south, hoping to find a way around. Plateau Party

15. The crevasse area started around Mile 172, latitude 81° south. As he passed, Russell had marked the most dangerous spots with flagging to warn the tractors, which were supposedly following with part of their dog food and now most of the Plateau Party's instruments. Upon radio contact with Little America, the Geological Party was ordered to backtrack twelve miles to help dig them out (Walden and Paine, *Long Whip*, 202–4).

This loaded trailer sledge with its supplies and tractor fuel did not fall into the crevasse. Survey dog teams were sent out in several directions to examine the terrain before the parties reassessed their options. (Paine Antarctic Collection)

will return here tomorrow bringing our loads. That is the plan at least subject to the approval of R.E.B.

Crevasse [the] tractor went through [is] about 120 ft. deep but only 2 ft. wide—fortunately camped only 10 feet away from it but perfectly safe. Good supper to-night with corn + seal meat— + a Primus in sleeping tent, thanks to Pete [Demas]. Demas, Hill + Waite in tractor party.

Nov. 2nd

Remained by tractors to-day waiting for Plateau Party to return from across crevasses. They arrived about 6—very peeved that we had not come out to help with the loads. They for once had loads somewhere near what they should carry. Slept till 11:30 + ate for two hours. Quin showed me about transit, + took ob. [observation]—161-54-45—81-14. Long. correct I believe but Lat. out—Bummed gasoline from tractors + had luxury of Primus in sleeping tent. Seems we lack fat cereal for return. Never mind—we can get along without it if necessary. We are returning to 55 [155] mile beacon + run S.E. from there till we get through. Shouldn't have turned. My error.

Tractors returned to 159.5 beacon + steered[?] 135 for 12.5 miles from beacon.

Nov. 3rd

D.R. 160°27′, 81 07.4

Stopped by crevasses—Crevassed area lies before us, which through the glasses looks bad. Holes, haycocks + black crevasses. Tractors went through three or four small cracks + we stopped when Legaska fell through. He always goes through if any dog does. It is a bit discouraging. Tomorrow we are to make a last survey of area between here + our last crossing.[16] One party, Quin, myself + Albert, are going S.E. across, S.W. + across again. Pete + Dick + Finn are going back two miles to S.W. for three or four or more + cross—recrossing two or three miles to S.E. Each are carrying radio + taking all safety precautions. I argued to contact L.A. as soon as possible to allow them to formulate plan which could be put into operation immediately—that is as soon as we arrived at the conclusion tractors cannot get through. I do not believe they can, + at the end of two days we decided it cannot be done, the third day to put alternative plan into operation. But all believed it would cause too much confusion + worry. May lose another day because of it. I do not believe tractors can get through.

If we all return tomorrow it will be by the grace of Lady Luck. Feeling around crevasses like these is perhaps more dangerous than war. However I'm game + trust nothing will happen.

Nov. 4th

Camped at 173 as day before. To-day we investigated crevassed area to south. Quin, Albert + myself with Jack + 6 dogs went S.E. 4 miles to the heart of the crevasses, turned N.E. for three miles + return[ed]. We found a mesh of crevasses and cracks + occasional holes running down into the black bowels of the Barrier. It is utterly impossible to get tractors through here. Russell, Demas + Finn went S.W. on this side for 6 miles, turned + ran into crevasses 4 miles + came back. They found a hopeless maze. They came back as discouraged as we were but quite thankful I think for not suffering any accidents—We each of us. Both parties carried a month's rations, sleeping

16. Faced with even worse crevasses known to be farther south, the whole group decided that a less dangerous route farther eastward should be scouted by the dog teams to see if the tractors could get through.

eqpt., tents, radio + dog food for three days besides other emergency equipment.[17] Quin would not take the slightest precautions, no ropes, no stay together, insisted upon running parallel to crevasses for two miles + was not in favor of taking any emergency equipment at all. What a man.

What to do now is the question. Dick + I sent in a suggestion for a five man party, five teams to mts. with supporting party to 300 as planned. Morgan thinks whole party can continue, Pete wants to go east fifty miles + Quin does not approve. Time is precious—something must be decided immediately in order to save the southern program—believe our plan the best.

Nov. 6th

A.M. Ready to leave 173 mile depot.[18] 5 teams, 8 spare dogs; 4 teams of 11 dogs, 1 [team] of 9 [dogs]. Shot along this morning—at beacon there is cached 12 gallons of fuel + two rations to the east of beacon in the snow for supporting party if needed. Ronne putting out side flags. From here steer course 161, var. 115 or mag. course 46 to base at Leverett Glacier. Supporting Party Mtn. I believe is the point—cache 12 cartons of Kools at 173 for return.

P.M. Camped about 7 o'clock only seven miles from 173—but through pressure however. The going was soft + sticky, angular crystals of snow lying on the surface made the going almost more than the dogs could handle. It was go, stop + rest, go a little more + stop. The pressure was easy to pass through here but the number of crevasses was many times those we passed through to west. Our course was S.E. for 2 1/2 miles then south. Albert was ahead + he leaned toward the west so that much of the time we were running almost parallel to crevasses + crossing them at such an angle was not pleasant.

17. Byrd was informed that Paine, Blackburn, Eilefsen, and their teams were roped together in single file with sixty-foot lengths of alpine rope. They searched out the crevasses eight miles to the southeast and east. Demas, Russell, and Ronne went west (Byrd, *Discovery*, 278–79).

18. Byrd later wrote, "Time was pressing. Field schedules called for the arrival of both parties at the foot of the Queen Maud Range 29 days out of Little America. 19 days were gone: only 10 days remained to travel 293 miles. . . . All day November 5th the frosty air was agitated with messages flying between these units and Little America. On one point, . . . agreement instantly crystallized. The Geological Party had to be detached at once, or else its mission would be jeopardized. There was only the problem of its case of borrowing support to lay down food depots to 300 (345 statute) miles. The Plateau Party, on the other hand, was in exactly the box we had feared. . . . The Geological Party remained intact, but Ronne and Eilefsen with their teams, were attached as support, to lay down ration depots between that position and 300 Mile Depot. Morgan's and Bramhall's dogs were absorbed by the Geological Party, Blackburn taking one team and the other being divided all around among the drivers, giving four 11-dog teams and one 10-dog team. The loads per team averaged about a thousand pounds" (ibid., 279–81).

We are faced with problem of what to do. It does not seem possible to carry out plan outlined at 173. Our loads seem excessive. Figured out plan to return with two teams of seven dogs but find loads to average close to 600 lbs. per sled. Too much for seven dogs + make the time. Therefore, if we cannot haul loads must cut dog food + cut time in field. We brought 22 gals. of fuel + we shall cache 5 gals here + I can cache spare batteries but hesitate to do so. Ice[d] runners to-night as did Dick + Quin. Fortunate that Plateau Party program didn't go through for Morgan's + Bram's dogs all shot.[19] Beacon at 2.3 miles from 173 mile depot, and second beacon approximately 4 miles from there. Flags every half mile, beacons every 5 miles to mts.— save weight in flags. Started with 800 flags.

Sent following wire Nov. 6th:

> "To Byrd, Poulter, Taylor—
>
> We suggest 5 dog teams 5 men continue from here with supporting party from L.A. as planned. Two teams killed on arrival at mts. 3 teams stay in field 25 days allowing 20 days for trip from here to mt. base. We figure total load from here 4500 lbs. less sleds. If tractors get through to east they could meet party at mts. Further investigation here futile. Think we should push on. This plan eliminates seismograph instruments. Feel program can be carried through in this way—
>
> signed Paine + Russell."

To get Bram south for his magnetic observations it seemed as though I should go to east with tractors. Bud [Waite] would go south—so sent wire Nov. 5th as follows:

---

19. Early Antarctic explorers used dogs as a multiple resource. Dr. Gould, a geologist from Byrd's First Expedition and leader of the Geological Party of 1929, wrote, "When one plans a long sledge journey entirely with dog power, there are two main ways in which he can make use of the dogs. First he can plan to gauge his travelling and field work with the expectation of bringing all of the dogs back alive." To do this, he explained, one must lay advance supplies, which requires at least three trips over the same route. This necessitates large quantities of food and supplies for both men and dogs, and significant time, already scarce in the short field season. "The second plan for using dogs exclusively on a journey as long was we hoped to make is one that no one can contemplate with any cheer. It is making good one's journey by sacrificing the weakest dogs as one proceeds. The dogs become pawns in a game and the fittest survive the longest." As dog food would be significantly reduced, this plan allows decreased load weights and increased travel speed. Augmenting the prepared dog food, the plan also requires the use of dog carcasses to feed other dogs; while usually reluctant at first, the dogs soon adapt to this food. With the lurking hope that Admiral Byrd might be able to drop dog food to the party by plane along the route, Dr. Gould wrote, "We had no alternative except to make our plans according to the second method" (Gould, *Cold*, 71–73).

"Byrd, Poulter, Taylor

Dick + I have hurriedly figured out weights for 3 man + 4 man party to south. Just with 3 teams, second with 4. Weights per team are about same. To make it possible for Bram to go south + tractors to go east believe it would be best for Waite to go on southern party as radioman + I go with tractors as radioman + navigator. Southern party consists of Quin, Dick, Bram + Bud. Supporting party will make two trips to 300 from here which is feasible. We believe this is a best plan.

Regards—Paine"

I was sent south + Bram with tractors—why I do not know.[20]
173 mile depot 161°05' 81°09.6'
Base of Leverett [Glacier] 148°—85°30'
Course by Mercator 161° from 173 mile depot.

Nov. 7

A.M. Depoted 1 man ration here 180 miles. Good contact with L.A. All well.
D.R. 81°29.2 160°21'
14.1 miles to-day from 7 mile camp 7 miles from 173 mile depot. We are now 194 miles on our southern trail. The surface was soft + sticky + for our skiis almost agony to push along. We all including Finn iced our runners both last night + at noon—overcast all day + we traveled in a murk of haze + snow. No objects distinguishable. Albert ahead with his team + I gave bearings—steered 161, 146 mag. to-day. At noon pitched Finn's tent + lit Primus for comfort. Shot Smiler—Dick did. His shoulders were a mass of abscesses, carelessness more than anything else of Morgan. His collar was too big. Anti-scorbutic to-night. An encouraging day all told after yesterday.

Nov. 8th

12.5 miles course 46 mag., var. 115. D.R. 81°41.1' 159°51'
Ran from 194.1, 5.5 miles + established 200 mile beacon at 199.6. Ronne cached 22 cakes of dog food for return of 11 dogs + for geo. pty. [geological

---

20. Byrd, Innes-Taylor, and Poulter decided to keep the Geological Party intact. The seismic field program would be rerouted to the east, where no seismic and magnetic research had been done and where the tractors could haul the equipment (Byrd, *Discovery*, 281). Numerous sets of calculations were done to test scenarios. The final figures for proceeding from this point are contained as part of Appendix 5.

party] were cached 18 cakes or 27 lbs.—one day's food for 2 teams. Beacon at 204.6, + camped 206.6 miles or 2 miles from last beacon.

D.R. 81°41.1', 159°51'. Jack led for 10 miles then got obstinate + Albert with Pete went ahead. Ice more off [not sticking to] runners toward the end of day.

Started not until 1:30 or so. A thirty mile wind from S.E. made it impossible to get underway, so stayed in our bags until 11:30.

Nov. 9th

225 mile beacon after run of 18.5 miles. Excellent surface—iced runners again at noon. Cloudy with small band of clear sky to south. Comparatively warm with very light breeze from S.E. Jack acted up soon after getting underway so I put him back in the line and Kaiser on lead. Jack fought with every dog in the team. Kaiser went around in circles + it was a pretty mess for a half hour. Finally after the whole team piling on Jack, I put him back in lead + he went straight + hard all day. Not a trace of stubbornness left in him.

Brushed teeth + combed beard. My beard makes me look fat. Perhaps I am getting fat I eat enough.

Nov. 10th

A.M. 225 mile depot. D.R. 81°58.2', 159°11'. Lat. by ob. 82°00'30''. Find my watch has gone haywire so ob. this morning not worth a damn. Ran 25 miles to-day over excellent surface. Iced runners as usual in morning + at noon. Here at 250 mile depot. D.R. 158°08', 82°22'. Shot Lonne to-night. He wouldn't pull even his food.

Nov 11 A.M.

Fix 250 mile depot. Long. 158°39'
Lat. 82°22'36''
P.M. 25 miles to 275 mile depot. Excellent surface + dogs ran well. Camped at 9:30. Shot Short to-night + will cache him here. Collapsed on trail. Have slight attack of snow blindness + rather tired. Not enough sleep. Course 160 or thereabouts.

Nov. 12

Ran 18 miles, course mag. 38, var. 117, true 155. Excellent surface but got a late start owing to getting to bed late the night before, 12 midnight. Decided to stop at 18 miles rather than go on to 300 to allow us to get to bed early. Camped at 6. Eyes bothered me a little but wore my corrective glasses, Quin's slipons and another pair of dark glasses. It was ok. Iced runners at ob. as usual.

Nov. 13th

DR 275 Depot	82°46′20″
	157°32′
DR 200 Depot	157°06′
	83°09′

A.M. 40 mile S.E. wind with gusts of 50. Got good rest + rose at noon—while it continues to blow like this we will stay put. Believe Supporting Party will turn back from here. We can take on their loads here as well as 300 + take on their extra dogs, killing whatever dogs we have to when we get to 300. Will have to do some figuring—a good day for it.[21]

P.M. Wind has died somewhat but still of 20 miles. Spent day repairing radio battery box. Have cut it in half + made terminals on outside of box for A batteries which I will keep out so as to heat them more easily. Dick fixed his camera + we all had supper together. Sherry for dinner for which Quin fixed up a whole pot of Lemon—evidently to mix with the sherry. We ate it as ice cream.

Nov. 14th

Course 44 mag., true 161 for 9 miles from 300 mile depot. 293 to 300 course 155.

Supporting party left us this morning. Both Finn + Albert were sorry to go back. Finn more so than Albert. Good contact with L.A. No flights yet.[22] Warm to-day, –5 with 10–15 mile south wind—a very pleasant day. Clear +

21. Byrd wrote, "Geological Party reports: '18 miles Monday. Tuesday nerve-racking day with wind from SE up to 50 m.p.h. Taking on Supporting Party loads here and Supporting Party turning back. Will continue with 39 dogs, leave 6 at 300 Mile Depot and continue with 3 11-dog teams for 5 days. Figure 10 days to mountains from here" (ibid., 287). At Mile 293, the Geological Party took on another 1,440 pounds of man food and 450 pounds of dog food (Byrd, ibid., 280–81; see also Appendix 5).

22. Byrd was interested in flying inland to see new territory and to determine the axis of the Edsel Ford Range, to further define a new plateau from the Rockefeller Range and Marie Byrd Land, and to investigate the area between the Queen Maud Mountains and the coast. Dr. Gould of the First Expedition had postulated that the Queen Maud Mountain Range might swing north and connect with the Edsel Ford Range, thus proving that Antarctica was in fact one continent, not two (ibid., 307–8). Upon their return to Little America, Ronne and Eilefsen reported to Byrd that the

warm sunshine. Quin a bit fussed at our accusing him of geepole riding—best to forget it.

D.R. to-night 309 miles—83°17.7', 155°40'. Watch 8 P.M. + 49 seconds. gains 7 sec. per day.

Nov. 15th

154°45', 83°35.8' D.R.

Ran mag. 44, var. 117, true 161, 16 miles to 325 mile beacon. Then 3 miles more on same course + camped. Stiff southerly breeze—15–20 miles but hard surface, no drift, warm, +2 + a pleasant day. We saw the mountains almost due south for the first time. They look huge. At last our goal is in sight.[23] Shot Ellie at 325 + cached him. Dick is getting poor as a marksman. On to 350 tomorrow if possible. Each of us driving 11 dog teams, though Dick has now only ten.

Nov. 16th

10 miles course 160—a 15 mile S.E. wind this morning increasing in force as day went on. Stopped after ten miles for ob. + wind must have almost doubled itself during that time. Waited a half hour + then camped. During afternoon wind from 35–40 miles per hour—drift flying + tent flapping wildly. Ate heartily + had anti-scorbutic in honor of seeing the mountains yesterday. Radio skd. this morning OK. Skd. to-night at 6 for weather report. Skd. at 8 for another wx. [weather] report. Flight contemplated to S.E. of tractors to-night. Looks doubtful to me but they want wx. reports anyway.

P.M. Reported weather at 8–11 above, blowing 30–35 S.E. Heavy drift. John reported plane had left at seven + was on its way. Next skd. at 10 P.M. Meanwhile we are brewing up a pot of milk here by the radio and eating biscuits + butter. The tent flaps + bows as though it would burst asunder. There

---

Geological Party was "one party you won't have to worry about." They also said that Paine commented it was like a midsummer day at 20 below and his leader, Jack, seemed "half-man" and had broken trail for the whole party. Byrd noted that the Geological Party was one day ahead of schedule despite losing 5 1/2 days escorting the tractors (ibid., 321–22).

23. Byrd summarized the mission: "The plan involved a 517-mile journey across the Ross Ice Barrier to the foot of the Queen Mauds, and a glacier ascent of at least 100 miles. If nothing miscarried, the party would have sufficient rations for 38 days' field work past this Mountain Base, and a total of 90 days out. The associated objectives were (1) a geological cross-section of the Queen Mauds . . . ; (2) an intensive search for fossiliferous strata . . . ; (3) confirmation of the trend of the Queen Mauds; (4) the mapping of new mountains discovered during the ascent; and (5) a daily meteorological record in high southern latitudes" (ibid., 206).

This picture was taken from inside a crevasse, looking toward the snow surface from below, at the crevassed area at Mile 350. Blackburn's two sledges were hanging in the crevasse. The men had to go down on ropes to rescue the dogs, supplies, and sledges. An ice knife and fifty pounds of dog food were lost. (Paine Antarctic Collection)

is no heat from Primus in the tent with such a wind. Evidently plane disregards our weather reports but now at this place it would be impossible for plane to land.

11:30 Plane still on its way. Hear Clay Bailey's carrier noise + occasional code message. Dick asleep for two hours until next skd. at 12^{24}—continues to blow like all hell + I wonder about the plane. Would much prefer being where I am than in that flimsy metal flying shell.

Nov. 17

D.R. 83°45.2′, 154°16′. Camped for day. Wind continues blowing from S.E. 15–20 miles—a discouraging obstacle to our progress. Plane returned ok. John did not know what it found + batteries went dead on me + had to change batteries. Slept till 1. Dug for four hours, ate + now to bed. We were well snowed in.

---

24. Dick Russell was needed to crank the radio transmitter for the power to send messages. Batteries could only be used on the radio receiver to receive messages.

Nov. 18th

12 miles [course] 160 to 350 depot. Left 2 gals. fuel, 1 man ration, 81 lbs. dog food. Crevasses found by Quin + myself on putting out side flags. Changed course so as to cut them crosswise to southwest + ran for 4.7 miles. To left of 350 or to east appeared high ground—to S.E. + S. + S.W. appeared pressure + crevasses—decided to strike straight through and we struck them, hole, crack, crevasse, one after another. All of us held our breaths, crossing the shallow bridges. A mile from 350 Russell's trailer jammed crosswise in a crevasse, one end of front perched on edge + the hind end hanging by the protruding runner. Took a half hour to get that out. A mile further Jack went through followed by six other dogs. I went down on a rope + released them one by one. All but Jack were hanging in harness. Proceeded to this point where we could look ahead + see clear starting about a mile beyond when there was a tremendous yank on my sled from the rope connecting me to Quin's lead dog + my sled spun backwards. I reached for a tethering pole + forced it down at back of sled to prevent further sliding backward. I looked back. Quin was on his belly but no sled in slight—both [sleds] had dropped down. Hanging from the gangline—He had the scientific gear, 2 rations, 10 gals. of Kerosene + 4 bags of dog food besides personal effects. Took us from 7:30 till 2:30 A.M. to unload it item by item. Quin going down first + Dick later. I put up cook tent and cooked supper while they worked. Lost 50 lbs. of dog food + ice knife only casualties—fortunately.[25] Decided to camp. The ground is riddled with cracks + crevasses but [we] were too tired to go on. Enough for one day.

Nov. 19th

Lat. sight this A.M. 83°56.8'
DR. 366.8—84°10.8', 154°29'
Ran from camp by crevasses 2.3 miles, making 7 miles at S.W. or thereabouts. Built beacon with 2 flags on top. Crevasses ended about then, seven miles through the toughest seven miles we have gone through. Ran south 9.8 miles to this point.

25. A mile out of the 350 Mile Depot, the party hit very large crevasses running northwest to southeast in a belt seven miles wide. First Russell's trailer sled was caught. Then Jack and six other dogs were swallowed while the remaining dogs backtracked furiously to avoid being dragged in. Paine went down on a rope and, using another rope, passed each dog to the surface. Later, when Blackburn's two sledges went down a sixty-foot-deep crevasse, it took the men seven hours to bring the sledges and their contents, the navigation and geological gear, and much of their food and clothing, back up to the surface (ibid., 364–65).

More details about crevasse—

Camped alongside crevasse + it was with a precious step we tethered out dogs + pitched the other tent. The place was just riddled. Turned to at 7 this morning after 3–4 hrs. sleep + underway at 11. Proceeded cautiously. But no more accidents. Quin estimates we crossed 250 crevasses—believe he's right. Dog teams hitched together—me first, Quin second + Dick third.

Shot Punka, Council, Imp, Dana—cache them here at 366.8—built beacon. All very tired. Successful contact with L.A. to-night.

Nov. 20th

Obs. pos. 366.8 miles from A.M. sights.
154°50', 84°10.5'. 8.5 miles S. to 375. 12.5 miles course 154 var. 119. Mag. 35. D.R. to-night 387.8—84°30' 153°55'. Should run from here course mag. 27, var. 119.

11

In Select Company

November 21–December 5, 1934

Nov. 21st

D.R. Lat. 84°50.2', Long. 151°24'. 412.5 miles. 24.5 miles, mag. 27.

Passed over huge rolls, like giant frozen waves. 1 to 5 miles across + 100 ft. high. They run E + West giving evidence of pressure + movement from south. Crevasses all day to-day, some very large, well bridged though running N.E.–S.W.[1] More crevasses ahead—believe it best to run straight south a bit + get clear of them—have had enough of the dastardly things.

The mts. [the Queen Maud Range] are spread before us like a Maxfield Parrish.[2] Their high peaks glistening in the sun, a deep deep blue sky backing them + their slope purplish with a light haze. They jut from the flat surface of the Ross Shelf ice + rise sharply to 14,000 feet—what a sight + what a grand location for a summer hotel. It is a thrill to see them, so few persons ever have. Nansen looms large + magnificent to the west with the Gades, BAE 1st Mts. Vaughan, Crockett, Goodale, besides many peaks unnamed.[3]

1. Paine transmitted to Byrd that from Mile 350 south, their course crossed roll after roll with crests from two to ten miles apart (Byrd, *Discovery*, 308).

2. Maxfield Parrish was a renowned artist who painted grand, romantic landscapes in addition to dreamlike figures in fantastical settings.

3. The 2,740-meter-high Mount Nansen was named by Captain Scott for the Norwegian arctic explorer Fridtjof Nansen. The Gades are the Alice and Ruth Gade Mountains. Thorne Glacier and Mounts Vaughan, Crockett, and Goodale were named in 1929 by the Geological Party of Byrd's First Expedition, for members of their party. Approximately twenty years before, both Scott and Shackleton ascended Beardmore Glacier, and Amundsen traveled up Axel Heiberg Glacier to the Polar Plateau.

Mountain Base, in front of the foothills of the Queen Maud Range. The Geological Party cached supplies here and prepared to ascend 120 miles up a massive, unexplored glacier. (Paine Antarctic Collection)

We are yet too far from them to see the glaciers distinctly but their positions are evident by the gaps between.

Glorious day, like yesterday, temp about zero, 3 mile wind from S.E. Wax runners now + it improves going 100%. 3 dog teams—my team as follows: Jack, Gav, Nip, Buck, Boss, Tuck, Stupid, Pricie + Pete. Pete worn out, Kaiser Quin has for a leader + he makes a good one. Pop + Pony Dick have + they are the same good workers with him as they were with me.[4] Jack is underfed. He goes ahead all day long straight as a die + hesitates only when he gets very tired. I have steered a pretty good compass course with him + he has learned how to cross crevasses. Coming to one he looks up + down it + if the course crosses it at an angle other than 90°, he makes a sharp turn if necessary + races across dragging the others after him. What a wonderful dog.[5] Flight contemplated to-night. Swell weather for it. Radio contacts

4. At Mile 300, dogs in the teams were shuffled, and Pop and Pony were given to Russell to balance his team.

5. Jack would run parallel to a crevasse until he found a crossing he deemed safe, then shoot across it at full speed at a perpendicular. He'd then backtrack on the other side until he returned to the point where he had originally left the line of the trail and resume his old course (Walden and Paine, *Long Whip*, 216–18).

every two hours.[6] Probably mean being up for good many more hours—at least this standby will not be the nightmare the other was. Fix. 84°46′, 150°45′.

Nov. 23rd

Course 47 mag., var. 115, run 33 miles. Crevasses from a mile from fix for next 5—bad large ones running N to S.

We are at Mt. Base.[7] Following night of flight we slept during the day, now 22nd + traveled the night until 11 A.M. this morning, making 33 miles. We were pretty well played out when we got here as were the dogs.[8] We are roughly 10 miles from base of the Sup. Party Mt., which is a small peak, 1200 ft. high at western end of range joining N.E. wall of Leverett. The glacier looks huge from here, descending with a noticeable slope from the S.E. + merging gradually with Barrier. Killed 9 dogs to-night, Buzz, Cole, Pete, Catsan, Duke, Jack jr. ——————— + fed them.[9] We ate fresh liver + heart which were excellent.

Nov. 24th

Blowing all day. We stayed in our bags until about 2 this P.M., then a hearty breakfast + a dinner at 11 of hoosh with hamburger, liver + fat cereal. Dick cooking now—built beacon, put new batteries in radio + did odd jobs. Wind last night must have reached 60 miles an hour. Only the snow walls we built to windward saved the tents I believe. Tomorrow hope to make trip to Sup. Party Mt. + return here. Let's hope for good weather. Changed underwear + shirt to-night + broke out package of Luckies.[10]

6. Byrd relied on the field parties for weather reports so that flights could be planned.

7. As their mission and their lives depended on it, logistical planning for time and supplies was an ongoing task; a major set of calculations were again made at Mountain Base. See Appendix 5 for Paine's calculations from November 5–7 at Mile 173, from November 13 at Mile 293, and from November 23 at Mountain Base at Mile 445.5. His calculations completed at Mile 293 were used by Blackburn when, through Ronne, he reported that he had aboard his sledges enough man and dog food, supplemented with the surplus dogs, to provision them for 33 days' field work beyond the mountain base (Byrd, *Discovery*, 321–22).

8. They ran through the night to outrun a blizzard that then hit them in camp. The season was approaching the longest day of complete daylight.

9. The "9" was written backwards, with the names of the dogs trailing into very faint pencil and then stopping altogether with a long blank space left after.

10. Taking a bath was impossible and changing into any clean clothes was an event. "Luckies" are Lucky Strike cigarettes. Kools, mentioned previously, are also cigarettes.

Paine, dog driver, radio operator, and navigator, in a tent by the Queen Maud Mountains. (Paine Antarctic Collection)

Dick Russell, dog driver and in charge of camp supplies. (Paine Antarctic Collection)

Quin Blackburn, geologist and surveyor. The party's mission was to explore and map the geology and topography of an area of the Queen Maud Mountains. (Paine Antarctic Collection)

Nov. 25th Mt. Base

148°43′, 85°14.7′

Another day of blowing, heavy gusts of wind, followed by short lulls + then more wind + drift. The temperature has remained warm, this morning +27 + this afternoon +15, which is summer weather for us. Shot Breaker this A.M. leaving us now 18 dogs. Following is my team: Jack sr.—Gav, Kaiser, Buck, Boss, Nip + Tuck, Pricie + Stupid. Following is Dick's team: Topsie, Teeka, Rastus, Taggar, Cherrie, Milton, Moody, Pop + Pony, the latter the heavenly twins. We left tractors at 173 with 53 dogs. Left supporting party with 39 dogs—arrived here with 27 dogs + now 18 remain, surely the chosen few. It has been a heavy sacrifice of dogs, but perhaps death on the trail is a happier death than death inside a box in a dirty dog kennel. Of the nine shot here, 4 have been consumed, some by us, mostly by the other dogs who were a bit choosy at first but who now take to it like dogs after beefsteak. 2 more will be fed to-night, leaving 3, 1 1/2 days dog food in dogs here for our return—that is provided we get away tomorrow. The weather should break by then. We have unmercifully opened up each of the dogs + extracted with not too great care their hearts + livers, which with the hoosh are excellent as I said before. I have never tasted better liver. And fresh meat now is not only good to eat but is good for its anti-scorbutic qualities. This noon we had them boiled, which was good but not as good as fried or in the hoosh.

To the south the mts. tower up from the comparatively meager front hills to peaks many thousand feet high. Their northern slopes are in places bare of snow + the black rock shows purple through the haze. A steep line of mts. just across the Leverett appears to be entirely snow covered save for several bare shoulders. Approaching them day before yesterday with the sun obscured + everything milky about us I thought they were pressure ridges not more than a couple of hundred yards in front. They were 30 miles off. This is an example of how totally lacking in perspective this world is when there are no shadows.

Between us + the higher mts. is the Leverett Glacier, reported to be the largest glacier in the world. From here Supporting Party Mt. + its line of small peaks running to the east appears to hem it in like a levee along the bed of a river. But it is evident [from] some submerged nunataks that this levee is not 100% efficient,[11] for the ice is spilling over it in places, particularly so just to the West. The glacier meets the barrier at somewhat of a steep embankment at this point but to the S.W. its incline merges with the flat barrier + it is there we hope to make our ascent, the gods of this here range grant us some favorable weather. It is a grand sight, ice, snow, glaciers with either a solid front, an icefield or a long sweeping slope, pouring, moving rivers of ice, restless, ponderous + majestic, mountains, small peaks in the foreground backed by higher + higher ones in back, to the east, south + west the same grand panorama of black faces, jagged peaks, bold contours of a continent submerged by the rigors of a glacial climate, and all subdued by a mellow purple haze. Sometimes it is more Maxfield Parrish than the artist himself. But we must get to them, hanging on here only about 11 miles away is getting boring after our efforts to get here. Since Oct. 16th we have been underway, 38 days I believe without counting. Do not believe I shall ever go to such extremes to see some mountains again.

Quin built a beacon this morning + laid out a landing field for the planes. We dismantled his sled + I took the slats from his sled + my trailer tank, which I exchanged for his, it being in better shape, + made 5 tall khaki colored flags as additional markers.[12] Obtained fix this morning, which was

---

11. A nunatak is a hill or a mountain that is completely encircled by a glacier.

12. Plans for flights changed frequently. Byrd did not use the airfield. At Mountain Base, the party left behind most of their loads on the trailer sledges. On their main sledges, they took just enough food and fuel (plus the necessary camping gear, clothing and scientific instruments) to supply them for three and a half weeks during the glacial ascent and return to Mountain Base. Some emergency rations were taken as well (Walden and Paine, *Long Whip*, 219–22).

The mountains to the right of the camp are seven thousand feet high. Those in the left background soar to fourteen thousand feet. The party is en route south from Mountain Base. (Paine Antarctic Collection)

148°46′, 85°16.2′. Find our diet very constipating, a strange thing as our trail diet of last fall was purposely modified to eliminate this.

Nov. 26

Away at last + made 14 miles mag. course 44, var. 113.1.[13] Arrived at foot of Sup. Party Mt. around 4:30. Weather cleared + shortly after camping went over + threw ourselves on the loose rock talus. Good contact with L.A. tonight, all well.

Nov. 27th

Fix for foot of Supporting Party Mt. 147°40′, 85°27′, Gould's, 85°25′17″, 147°55′.[14]

13. They were held in camp by the wind for almost three days. At the top of a tripod of skis, they placed and photographed an American flag at the mountain's base.
14. Supporting Party Mountain was the farthest south Dr. Gould's Geological Party traveled on the First Byrd Expedition. The party was made up of Laurence Gould, Mike Thorne, Norman Vaughan, Freddy Crockett, and Eddie Goodale. The USGS National Mapping Division records Supporting Party Mountain as 560 meters high and located at lat 85°27′S, long 147°33′W.

On Supporting Party Mountain, Paine reads the note left in a cairn by the 1928–1930 Byrd Expedition, while Blackburn writes a note representing the Second Expedition. After this point, the party traveled into unknown territory. (Paine Antarctic Collection)

A very pleasant day. Climbed Supporting Party Mt., collecting as we went. Found Gould's cairn + note inside. Quin has note.[15] Clouds obscured most of horizon to south but what we did see gave evidence of peaks far back + heavily snow covered. We are of the mind to go up the Thorne [Glacier] rather than Leverett in order to get at mts. which are close + which are not hopelessly covered with a mantle of snow + ice. Tomorrow morning plan to go up mt. again to photograph + then be on our way.

Mt. all heavily metamorphosed Precambrian twisted + gnarled like a burnt tree trunk. On top we found glaciated pebbles, giving ample evidence of a once greater age of glaciation—rolled rocks down slope + had the time of our lives.

15. As is traditional in exploration, a note was left in a cairn built by the members of Gould's Geological Party in 1929. The Second Expedition's Geological Party recovered this note on November 27, 1934, made a copy to leave in the cairn, and added their own note. The copy of the 1929 First Expedition note and the original 1934 Second Expedition note were photographed and the originals returned to the cairn on December 3, 1992, by a U.S. Antarctic Program party (S-082) funded by the National Science Foundation. These photographs were made available by A. B. Rowell, Ph.D., emeritus professor, University of Kansas, principal investigator and geologist on the NSF project.

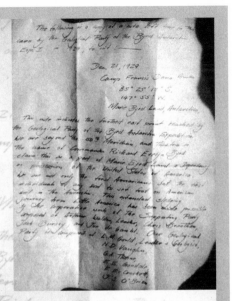

The following is a copy of a note left here in this cairn by the Geological Party of the Byrd Antarctic Exp. I. in 1929, to wit: ———

Dec. 21, 1929
Camp Francis Dane Coman
85°25'17" S.
147°55' W
Marie Byrd Land, Antarctica.

This note indicates the furthest east point reached by the Geological Party of the Byrd Antarctic Expedition. We are beyond the 150th Meridian, and therefore in the name of Commander Richard Evelyn Byrd claim this as part of Marie Byrd Land a dependency or possession of the United States of America. We are not only the first Americans but the first individuals of any sort to set foot on American soil in the Antarctic. This extended sledging journey from Little America has been made possible by the cooperative work of the Supporting Party composed of Arthur Walden, Leader, Chris Braathen, Jack Bursey, and Joe de Ganahl. Our Geological Party is composed of L. M. Gould, Leader and Geologist,

> N. D. Vaughan
> G. A. Thorne
> E. E. Goodale
> F. E. Crockett
> J. S. O'Brian

The First Byrd Expedition note was left by the Geological Party, headed by Dr. Laurence Gould. They then turned east into Marie Byrd Land. On the Second Expedition, Quin Blackburn copied the note and placed his copy into the cairn, taking the original back to Byrd. The Second Expedition Geological Party also wrote a note and left it in the cairn. (Both notes were found and photographed on December 3, 1992, by A. B. Rowell, Ph.D., principal investigator and geologist, U.S. National Science Foundation Geological Party [Project S-082]. Photographs courtesy of Dr. Rowell, emeritus professor, University of Kansas.)

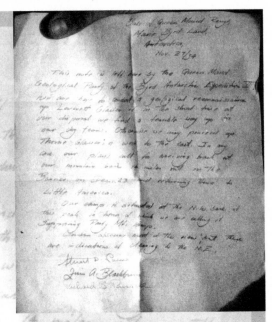

Base of Queen Maud Range
Marie Byrd Land
Antarctica
Nov. 27/34

This note is left here by the Queen Maud Geological Party of the Byrd Antarctic Expedition II. We are here to conduct a geological reconnaissance up Leverett Glacier if the short time at our disposal we find a feasible way up for our dog teams. Otherwise we may proceed up Thorne Glacier or work to the east. In any case our plans call for arriving back at our mountain base 14 miles out on the Barrier on December 23 and returning then to Little America.

Our camp is situated at the N.W. base of this peak in honor of which we are calling it Supporting Party Mt. Camp. Clouds obscuring most of the view but there are indications of clearing to the N.E.

> Stuart D. Paine
> Quin A. Blackburn
> Richard S. Russell

The Second Expedition note bears Paine's, Blackburn's, and Russell's signatures. (Both notes were found and photographed on December 3, 1992, by A. B. Rowell, Ph.D., principal investigator and geologist, U.S. National Science Foundation Geological Party [Project S-082]. Photographs courtesy of Dr. Rowell, emeritus professor, University of Kansas.)

Paine replacing the oatmeal can holding the two notes back into the cairn on Supporting Party Mountain. (Paine Antarctic Collection)

Good to be on rock again. Actually got our boots dirty—little snow on Northern slope. For five miles out Soho blue ice, a frozen lake from run-off from mt. Leverett Glacier almost as high to south of mt. as mt. itself.

Nov. 28th

19.4 miles from Sup. Party Mt. to pt. [point] at junction of Leverett + Thorne.[16] Much of way was over blue ice, particularly to first few miles. It was slightly roughened so dogs could get a hold. Crossed Leverett, struck only a few crevasses. Climbed Supporting Party Mt. before we started. Quin + I did + shot a round of pictures. Dick packed up. No radio contact this evening because receiver would not receive. Everything worked but what stations I did hear were very weak. Believe it influence of mts.

Nov. 29th Thanksgiving 1934

Made run of about mile to point at junction of Leverett + Thorne. We left a

16. Thorne Glacier (now known as Scott Glacier), originating on the Polar Plateau and flowing north to the Ross Ice Shelf, is 120 miles long and fifteen miles wide at its base. The unexplored Leverett and Thorne glaciers were named by Byrd's First Expedition Geological Party.

note + a cairn there + named it Durham Point after Durham N.H.[17] Cairn on very top about 100 feet above level of barrier. From there we made about 12 miles up the Thorne, most of the time clinging close to the east edge— much of the way was over blue ice + we were forced to run. Quin + Dick put hob nails in their boots. Rise in elevation to-day—a little less than a thousand feet. Scenery marvelous. The Crockett Vaughan Goodale Group are almost directly west of us now + this afternoon they were covered with high billowy columnous clouds which rolled away occasionally to reveal their sharp peaks + rugged contours.

All the way up we see little round discs of sand on the ice, granite flung there by the wind + subsequently disintegrated by weathering—perfect round circles of sand. Large erratics too—over to west in further side are crevasses + pressure. We struck crevasses only in one spot where a small tributary glacier came in—but surface is thickly strewn with cracks + veiled crevasses. To-night had hamburger hash, milk, sherry + ice cream. A strange meal in a strange place and Thanksgiving at that.

Nov. 30th

14.9 miles up + increase of over a 1000 ft. in elevation. Hard blue ice all day rippled + crevassed—Some areas were just a patch work of cracks—few large ones thank God. Camped to-night at foot of magnificent peak unnamed as far as we know in the moraine. No snow about so have tied on ice with rocks holding tents down + dogs intermingled with boulders + sand. Some of day Dick + I rode, so easy did the dogs pull the sleds over the ice. They seemed able to keep their feet whereas with us it was with difficulty. Skiis are out of the question here. Crampons necessary to get us over the last roll.[18]

17. Durham was Paine's hometown; current maps show Durham Point and its adjacent peak, Mount Durham.

18. Radio communications were scheduled but interrupted by a freak magnetic storm during the last three days of November. "On the 30th, Waite with the tractor very dimly overhead Paine with the Geological Party trying to get through to Dyer at Little America. He copied the message, which was garbled, but was himself unable to relay it until atmospheric conditions improved on December 1st. The message said: '. . . Have traveled part . . . ice with rippled and crevassed surface for last three days . . . yesterday stopped at . . . we are about 23 miles up Thorne Glacier. Unsatisfied with mantled nature of mountains tributary to Leverett.'" Blackburn had originally planned to ascend Leverett Glacier, not Thorne Glacier. If Byrd had realized earlier that the Geological Party was not following the original plan, he would have directed the party to the unknown lands eastward to help establish the relationships between the new mountain group, the Horlick Mountains, the Rockefeller plateau and mountains, and the trend of the Queen Mauds. However, the six-day radio silence precluded any discussion (Byrd, *Discovery*, 322).

Across Thorne arises a splendor of mt. scenery. The Vaughan Crockett Goodale group are now to the south west of us + across the glacier is a grand mass of unnamed we believe. Ahead to the S.W. the same magnificence—worthy of Maxfield Parrish again.

We are hungry most of time now. Rations inadequate, particularly the fat cereal. Not enough protein. And our biscuits seem to be short. Dogs getting sick on pemmican—that is not right either. We'll have same, then dogs when we get back if we get them all back.

Dec. 1st

13.5 miles up clinging to east side of glacier—several steep climbs—total rise to-day close to 1000 ft. making us roughly 3000 feet up. Dogs very tired. Passed through several miles of crevasses. Quin would not put on skiis—any one of the many crevasses would have swallowed him. Should he drop through it will be no fault of Dick's + mine. Three miles from morning's camp passed onto snow after many miles of blue ice—mts. all around.

Dec. 2nd

A.M. Built beacon + laid flags to mt. side + down to pressure. Here we are caching 120 lbs. of dog food—one man ration, 1 gal. fuel [at 40 Mile depot]. Beautiful day—wind having died somewhat.

P.M. Struck out hoping to follow east wall of glacier but forced to turn south westward out into center—ran through a brief line of crevasses + then climbed a slope. From there on, 5 miles from 40 mile depot, ran into the most frightful + chaotic maze of crevasses + pits I have ever seen. I do not believe any other Antarctic wanderer ever beheld a more magnificent chaos. Here is where the enormous crevasses form which we see so much of down farther—there snow filled. There was mass after mass just broken away + absent, leaving holes + great trenches 200–500 feet deep, a hundred yards across + perhaps 300 yards long.

There was pit after pit, some with snow forming a floor—others with no bottom as far as we dared determine. Blue vertical walls. Jagged broken blocks thrown up into a patchwork of patterns rivaling the best of John Bunyan.[19] Some of these "cracks" would easily swallow a New York sky-scraper + plenty of room for a 25 story office building—what a grand spec-tacle. We tracked our way between them some times over ice, other times

19. John Bunyan was the writer of *Pilgrim's Progress*, a religious classic. Most likely Paine meant Paul Bunyan, the legendary French Canadian lumberjack of mythic proportions.

over sloping snow surface. Quin went ahead picking the way. But we were stopped only a half mile from firm snow on the other side by impossible jumble. We skiied out, each trying to find a route, but they ended in a great pit.[20]

A grander evidence of the overwhelming natural forces at work in this region is nowhere to be seen. It makes our petty cares + ceremonies + don'ts seem pretty trivial to the powers in motion here.

Dec. 3rd, 1934 D.R. 86°26'

3 P.M. About 10 miles made good to south—rose 800 ft.—short run on good surface for about two miles, then crevasses, crevasses + blue ice. It seems we would never get clear of them. Had hoped to make a short run of 4 or five miles, camp on high ground + do triangulation—main purpose however was to let dogs rest. But ice + crevasses forced us to continue to this point. Wind 20–25 from S.E. + about 0°. Picked up considerably since we camped. Would have been forced to camp anyway. Many new mts. + a glacier which surges to the S.E. Ahead are flat topped mts. forming what seems to be a dividing point between new glacier + the Thorne which continues to the south, a link west perhaps. The long line of pressure + crevasses reaching all the way down + the mouth of the Thorne may be due to entrance of glacier on the left.

Dogs are getting gradually but surely thinner + weaker. However they respond magnificently to emergencies such as when a sled gets jammed traversing crevasses + ice or riding over steep ridges. Jack leads behind Quin + follows direction like a human being. He went down once this morning + hung in harness for 10 minutes before we got him out. He was excited + panting very hard.

The cold after the warmth of the Barrier has been very noticeable—we are now about 5000 ft. up + the wind swirling down from the Plateau is cold and bitter.

We are in pretty select company now—Byrd, June, McKinley, Balchen are only Americans ever gone further south than we.[21] But we are the first Americans to set foot on land this far South. That's quite a feather in our hat. No radio since Supporting Party Mt. Have heard them twice + they have heard me but no more messages transmitted. Signals weak + indistinct—at Durham Point presence of mt. cut out all signals. To-day we are well out on

20. Faced with huge pits, crevasses, and ice, the party backtracked down the slope and finally found passage up along the eastern wall (Walden and Paine, *Long Whip*, 226).

21. The group Paine mentions were on the 1929 First Expedition flight over the South Pole.

glacier + hope for good reception to-night.

    Fix for to-night
    86°24.1′
    149°15′

Dec. 4th

Blew cats + dogs so stayed in bags till 11:30 then decided to push on. Away at one + made 13 miles straight for a large tabular mt. stretching across our way. On left rose small mts. not far away looking like so many heaps of black coal. Passed from snow to blue ice heavily cracked—worse going is difficult to imagine—the snow + some ice again. We stopped at first moraine + I walked almost to mt. to determine whether dogs could get to the snow there, but no, so after camped over on moraine, dogs + boulders + rocks still mixed up, ice our beds + more rocks holding down tents. Hoping a storm does not come up—even now it's blowing about 20 but all safe.[22]

    Ahead is an ice fall which appears to block our way. Quin + I will work up there tomorrow to see if we can get through. In the west are huge pits + crevasses. We may be blocked. –50 dogs [50 dogs killed] + still on our outward way!

Dec. 5th

Quin + I went forward to investigate ice falls + discovered way around—at least all well so far. Got underway about two after Quin + I had already done about twelve miles. Wind—that God damn wind we left behind. Overcast + threatening but calm now. Ahead are the falls but to the west they appear to peter out. The mt. of our destination is roughly 20 miles to the SW + we hope to do that to-morrow—long skd. with L.A. Noville still trying to persuade us to go east, quoting Isaiah Bowman + Griffith Taylor, etc. It's too absurd—75 miles up [the glacier], almost in the plateau. Our goal in sight, nine days in the field gone + he wants us to give it all up—bunk directing.[23]

22. The party hugged the eastern wall of the glacier for the first forty miles, fighting the wind. At times all nine dogs were bowled off their feet and thrown one on top of the other, all scrabbling for footholds where none existed. The sledges, despite all of the weight on them, would heave around on the wind and start skidding back, dragging the dogs with them (ibid., 222–26). "'We fell on our faces trying to make headway,' Paine said" (Byrd, *Discovery,* 367).

23. Finally radio contact was restored. Isaiah Bowman was an esteemed geographer and academic who worked extensively in South America; Griffith Taylor wrote *Antarctic Adventure and Research,* published in 1930; both emphasized exploring the unknown. From Mountain Base, where the party might have easily turned east, they were now nine days into their ascent of the Thorne Glacier.

12

Mount Weaver

December 6, 1934–January 11, 1935

Dec. 6th

At least we are here, or all about here—across the small glacier; three miles is a mt. of horizontal strata running from the very base to the summit—tomorrow we go there—19 miles to-day—must be near 87°S.[1] Camped on long drift on snow slope.

Dec. 9th Mt. Weaver

Missed two days—the 7th Dick + I started across glacier, Boyd Glacier. I went half way + perceiving there was snow practically to foot of mt. went back to pack up + Dick went over to find a lee. He returned in about two hours with a large hunk of coal + news that there was a good camp spot—over we came, the wind blowing down Boyd Glacier at 40 miles an hour, almost blew dogs off their feet.[2] Spot we camped at is 100 ft. from the most westerly moraine in the lee of the south shoulder somewhat + enough snow

1. The Geological Party named the summit after Charles E. Weaver, professor of paleontology at the University of Washington. Mount Weaver is located at lat 86°58'S, long 153°50'W, with an elevation of 2,780 meters at the head of Scott Glacier (USGS National Mapping Division, 2000).

2. Boyd Glacier was the name given by the party for the glacier at the base of Mount Weaver. In relocating the camp to the snow slope, where they could better secure the tethering lines, the party fought the winds for two hours simply to cross the glacier. A benefit of the wind, however, was that it had swept away the snow on Mount Weaver, particularly on the northwesterly face near the camp, which exposed its sedimentary layers (Stuart D. Paine, "The Ascent of Mount Weaver," Paine Antarctic Collection, 7–8).

After fifty-three days, and at 728 statute miles from Little America, the Geological Party reached the base of the massive mountain at the head of Thorne Glacier. Mount Weaver (rear left) was named after a colleague of Quin Blackburn's. (Paine Antarctic Collection)

on top of ice to permit our pegging tents + dogs.[3] Made camp + then searched moraines for specimens + fossils. Found many. Ate supper of hamburg, hoosh, sherry, ice cream, biscuits.

The 8th spent all morning in moraines finding many good specimens of leaves. What I thought were fossil shells were mud blocks. Coal litters the place. In afternoon came down with the most frightful stomach ache which continued till this A.M. OK now—I do not know what caused it—even Cascara did not relieve it—and to be sick out here is no joke.[4] Wind has prevented us from doing any climbing. Ever since we've been here it's been raging from S.E. 20 to 40 miles an hour + temperature around zero. It's cold as hell + to be in the wind itself really is hell.

Dec. 10th

A.M. Bar before ascent 7520 feet—all set to climb mt. Wind continues about 20 miles but clear + visibility excellent. To-day + this ascent is primary object of our trip + here's hoping for success.

3. The party ceremoniously placed an American flag at the top of propped-up skis to commemorate the most southerly point achieved by an American sledging party.
4. Cascara is a strong laxative.

The party discovered coal and fossils of leaves, twigs, and tree trunks, supporting the theory that the Antarctic once had a temperate climate. This tree trunk, with an ice axe placed on it for scale, had a diameter of eighteen inches. (Paine Antarctic Collection)

The dogs curled behind snow blocks to shield themselves from the wind. (Paine Antarctic Collection)

P.M. Made start about 12:15 and arrived at summit about 3:15. A good climb. Mt. rises 2300 ft. above us, Bar at top 9880. Quin took round of pictures with the usual difficulty. Ate some chocolate + started down noting each of the strata + taking a sample from each—taking also Bar readings. The strata were thin + so frequent it was 8 o'clock before we decided to make for camp, getting here at 8:30. We examined all strata + took samples down the front 1200 ft. + the few we omitted were similar to those above. Below talus covers the rock.

For the climb we wore ski boots with crampons (excellent articles), each an ice ax, knapsack with tent, two cans sterno, rations for a day (pemmican + chocolate), rope + emergency medical gear besides Bar, compass, geo bags, therm., etc. Built cairn at top + left can containing note. We have climbed our mt. + obtained the desired cross sections—bravo.

We are most southern mt. climbers in the world having climbed mt. further south—Looked to South + all but saw the pole—only three small mts. to south of us.[5]

Dec. 11th

Last day we expect at Mt. Weaver. Spent day bragging + marking specimens.[6] Temperature continues at zero + below with incessant 20–30 mile wind. Glad to leave this spot. Camp Poulter—peace we hope tomorrow night.

Dec. 12th

Camp Poulter again + peace + calm. Such a relief to have no wind after five days of incessant 20–30 mile cold S. Easterly ones—made 21 1/2 miles from

5. If the Geological Party had continued south, they would have been the first Americans and only the third land party after the Amundsen and Scott expeditions to set foot on the pole. In fifty-three days from Little America, including ten days just climbing Thorne Glacier, the Geological Party traveled 633 nautical miles or 728 statute miles to almost exactly latitude 87° south and were within 180 nautical miles (207 statute miles) of the South Pole (Walden and Paine, *Long Whip*, 228–30). Byrd would write, "Well knit, well manned, not too heavily burdened, [the Geological Party] was capable, no matter what happened to the tractors, of detaching itself and pushing ahead on its geological reconnaissance of the Queen Maud Range with just a moderate amount of support. It was as fine a sledging party as ever hit a trail. Had it cared to sacrifice its scientific mission the Geological Party might have made the Pole with a machine-like precision that would have astonished the world" (Byrd, *Discovery*, 261).

6. In the five days on the edge of the Polar Plateau, the party gathered 450 pounds of specimens, including coal and fossiliferous fragments. They noted 15 seams of coal, interbedded with shales and limestones and fossils of plant leaves, plant stems, and fossilized tree trunks up to eighteen inches in diameter, attesting to the tropical climate that had once been present at that latitude (Walden and Paine, *Long Whip*, 233–37; Byrd, *Discovery*, 361).

The party climbs to the summit: Quin Blackburn leads, then Paine, and then Dick Russell (who is taking the photograph). (Richard S. Russell, Jr., and Paine Antarctic Collection)

Mount Weaver rises twenty-three hundred feet above the valley floor, reaching over nine thousand feet in elevation. Quin Blackburn, Dick Russell, and Stuart Paine climbed to the top in three hours and looked south toward the South Pole, only 180 nautical miles away. The members of the Geological Party were the first Americans and only the fourth land party to ever approach the pole. (Paine Antarctic Collection)

Mt. Weaver to-day, getting underway about 9 o'clock, stopping for a couple of hours for observations + arrived here about 7 to-night.[7] Came down a thousand feet + the dogs trotting most of way. They were peppy after their rest + no doubt relieved to get out of cold + wind.

I do not feel we have taken full advantage of our opportunity, particularly on the part of Quin. He is inclined to let everything go, put it off—he has not

7. Observations, beginning with Mount Weaver, were being taken on their return down the glacier to establish their positions and distances between observation points to aid in developing maps. Each position is noted as a "station" ("St. #1," etc.). Each station is shown on the map of the Thorne Glacier. Paine's navigation report to Admiral Byrd is included in Appendix 6.

Paine and Quin Blackburn celebrated reaching their goal by having a bowl of Grape-Nuts for breakfast. Pop from Paine's team is interested. (Photograph by Richard S. Russell, Jr.; Paine Antarctic Collection)

even written up his geo notes yet. I am getting terribly fed up with his sloven-liness. He has got to do his best or I will refuse to do mine.

Dec. 13th

Camp Poulter to-day with Quin adjusting transit + taking new round of shots. Obsv. pos. this station 86°38.9′, 150°05′. Beautiful day + calm. Such a relief after Mt. Weaver. Dogs + ourselves just sported in sunshine. Dick + I cut each other's hair + we look funny. Terrible night last night with Quin snorting + bel-lowing + keeping us awake. I'm sleeping in little black tent + Dick in cook tent to-night—Quin is a hard man to live with.

Dec. 14th

From Camp Poulter, Station No. 4
Ran mag. 28° 7.3 miles true 43°. Changed course + ran 6.7 miles course 13° true. Stopped for round of shots + a Long. sight. Then ran 4.6 miles course true south.

Dec. 15th Camp Dyer

About 14 miles down glacier to camp of 50 miles, 10 miles from [40 Mile] depot, which is almost visible. Most of the run was over ice + crevasses both of which we successfully crossed without incident. My wheel came off but I fortuitously noticed it a hundred yds. after it happened. Dogs went like hell down the grade. Most of way I let Jack pick his own route + what a swell job he did.

It seems I can put every confidence in him + as confidently have them fulfilled. What a fine dog + how proud of him I am. His tail has not completely healed yet but does not bother him.

Took prime vertical shot this morning 3:45 and a noon shot for our position at St. #5. Quin triangulated all morning + I recorded. Believe we'll have a good map to show when we get through.[8]

Passed by Mt. Content and Mt. Jananne Morse + to-night Jananne is about S.E. from us at 5 miles.[9] Content stands on the east corner of Thorne, the northern edge of the conflux of glaciers. It joins with Mt. Jessie in a spur, but the peak itself is very distinct. It is sharply pointed with deep indentation on its sides + of light brown rock. On the Thorne Glacier side it has an ice-fall of goodly proportions + we were forced to keep 4 or 5 miles out from it. For that reason I could not get good rock samples of it but I did pick up some wind blown rock from it on our way down.

Mt. Jananne Morse is about same height as Content but further down glacier. It is twin peaked, peaks N. + S. of each other. It is also igneous but chocolate colored. In other respects it is similar to Content. I have samples of it also which I picked up on the glacier + which I will present to the girls when I get back.

We were fortunate at Station #5 to have little wind—on our ascent our camp which we passed three miles from our station it blew like hell + blew

---

8. Triangulation consists of taking readings on two or more distant sites, and then using angles and known distances to establish the observer's position. Blackburn used a theodolite to take bearings used for making maps. An example from the thirty-page triangulation report for Thorne Glacier is included in Appendix 6.

9. Paine named these mountains for his nieces, Jananne and Content Morse, and for brother Philbrook Paine. Mountains were also named for other family members, and one peak was named "Jack's Peak." However, to be permanently adopted, names had to be approved by Admiral Byrd and also by the U.S. Board of Geographic Names. The southernmost mountain Paine named was for his mother; "Mount Katherine Paine" was permanently adopted, but then the name was later changed by Admiral Byrd and the U.S. Board on Geographic Names to commemorate Stuart Paine, the explorer himself. Mount Paine is "a massive, flat-topped mountain, 3,330 m, forming a buttress-type projection of the western part of the La Gorce Mountains, in the Queen Maud Mountains . . . named by Byrd for Stuart D. L. Paine, navigator and radio operator of that party. . . . Variant Name: Mount Katherine Paine. It is located at lat 86°46′S and long 147°32′W′′". (USGS National Mapping Division). Mount Jessie O'Keefe was later called Mount Blackburn for Quin Blackburn. A Mount Russell was named for both Richard Russell and his father of the same name. The party named many other features that can be identified on current maps.

Geologist Quin Blackburn, with navigator Paine assisting, triangulated positions and angles from fourteen stations to establish points to generate a map of Thorne Glacier. The wheel is the sled meter used for calculating mileage. (Paine Antarctic Collection)

Paine named a mountain group visible from Station 4 for his mother, Katherine Paine. Paine (wearing a leather helmet) momentarily halted before the group for this picture. Mount Paine is a massive mountain almost ten thousand feet high and is located on the western part of the La Gorce Mountains in the Queen Maud Range. (Paine Antarctic Collection)

all the time until we got back to Camp Poulter at foot of Mt. Philbrook Paine. In black tent again. I like it + sleep much better. All well to day—warmer to-night + light wind from south. Cloudy though + it may mean a blow—a storm I mean. Have not had real storm since we left Mt. Base. Nearer we get to barrier the warmer + more pleasant it will be. How we look forward to it, though being in mts. is more interesting.

Dec. 17th Camp Bruce Harkness

Ran 5 miles course 20° true—this is a very rough estimate.

Worked till after midnight on navigational problems trying to effectively locate the 8 depots or stations we have established to this point. Several of them are mere dead reckoning points and I am afraid not very accurate ones at that. If we were on the Barrier, it would be different, for there one can choose a course and maintain it rather accurately. However we are pressed for time + a bad station I believe is better than no station at all.

To-night is Station #9, the most magnificent one of them all. It is in a basin, an amphitheater running back east ward on the north side of depot mt. We have come up into it about three miles and are now approximately at its center. Looking back, when the clouds are more or less dispersed, we behold the Thorne Glacier and the mts. apparent in a sweep 60 miles long. To our north and south are granitic peaks with nearly vertical cleavage, making them stand up like walls or pinnacles like organ pipes. To N.E. five miles away is a row of these gothic pinnacles perhaps 800 feet high—above us, standing like immense gothic towers all in a row. We have named them all, which includes Stancliff, Murphy, Corey, Siple + Perkins. A more spectacular setting nor a more beautiful one I have never seen. It is almost as though we are among friends—friends of radical different personalities, some big, some small, some fat, some lean, but friendly all the same. With the view out from this basin + the soaring masses on the other three sides, we feel truly like gods squatting among the works of their own lords. At least that is the way I feel— very content.

The past three days have been marked by up glacier winds bringing with it fog + low clouds. This morning we had a goodly sprinkle of snow flakes. And on account of it most of the peaks have been obscured, making triangulation difficult.

Passed through [a] mile wide area of heavy crevasses this morning. Quin out front probing + found a path through. All ok. Picked up cached food + fuel at the 40 mile glacier depot + came up here.

Strange out here, the three most isolated human beings on earth, to pick up the earphones of the receiver and listen to messages, news, code + time ticks as well as musical programs from all over the world. Last night for instance we listened to the semi-weekly news letters from WZYAF to L.A. + heard ourselves being referred to as the "coal miners." We heard Rudy Vallee also. Every night during our field work here we get time ticks + our watches out here a lick over two hundred miles from the south pole click to the half second with the observatory watches at Washington.[10] States often come in louder than [at] L.A. If we are camped in the immediate proximity of a mt. radio reception is poor or not at all. At Durham Point no signals audible at all though receiver functioning perfectly.

Our field work is almost over. We have at the present time with us + on our trailers a mile down the Bruce Harkness amphitheater (for such is it named) about 18 days man food and six days dog food—at the end of that time we must be back at the Mt. Base where we pick up more dog food for our return. It might be surmised that we would be anxious because of limited food + the knowledge that at the end of that time if we do not cover so many hundreds of miles + arrive at a certain exact spot we would be forced to extreme measures to keep alive. Not at all—we all feel marvelously self-sufficient, contented + I believe truly happy. There is no peace like the peace brought by complete separation from other people. We are nature worshipers, perhaps pantheists.

Dick has been a swell companion in every sense of the word. Do not believe any man at L.A. better for a trail man. We have worked together splendidly + believe have put our tip across—Quin seems to have come to + realized that a few more days would put these mts. behind him forever + he's been doing his best to make the most of it. I feel to-night that though we came out without the faith of most of our fellows in L.A., we have accomplished as much if not more than any party in the field.

Dec. 18th Camp Bruce Harkness

This is second night in this most attractive of all spots the world over. This morning triangulated + worked sights. Dick + I this afternoon went up to Mt. Scudder + the Organ Pipes + found lichens among other things, the furthest

10. Rudy Vallee was a popular singer. Beginning in 1924 and by agreement with the British Broadcasting Corporation and the Royal Observatory, a time tick or pip using Greenwich Mean Time was broadcast by the BBC to the public to signal world time. Fifteen-minute, half-hour, or hour marks were signified through sequences of pips on the second. Useful for Paine as a check to his chronometer, the ticks he was hearing came via the U.S. Naval Observatory, Washington, D.C.

Stuart Paine in Harkness Amphitheater. The party camped below Mount Bruce Harkness in the Harkness Amphitheater, named for a friend of Dick Russell's. It was perhaps the most beautiful and serene place any of them had ever been. (Paine Antarctic Collection)

south life has ever been found.[11] There was a magnificent snow slope down which we went about three times, roughly a quarter of a mile, very steep + a speed of 40–50 miles an hour. What a sport! Quin stayed in camp + wrote notes, having made a trip up there last night. To-night we are 40 miles from Durham Point, about 55 miles from Mt. Base— + we have about 6 days dog food which could be stretched to seven easily. This being Tuesday we have until Monday, Tuesday at the latest to be at Mt. Base. Sunday is preferable + we are aiming at that, giving us a little leeway.

Fog on surface of glacier all day—up here about 400 feet above main Thorne Glacier on the Franklin Amphitheater we have been almost entirely free of it. The winds from Barrier are creeping up glacier, condensing + forming fog. No wind—fog, no fog—wind—which is worse?

Dec. 19th

Temp. on A.M. From line St. #9 +01 F—4600′ [elevation]

11. Byrd later reported that the surprised party found living green, white, and blackish lichens (Byrd, *Discovery,* 361).

Jack the Giant Killer, Paine's lead dog, in Harkness Amphitheater. (Photo by Richard S. Russell, Jr., Paine Antarctic Collection and with permission from Edythe Holbrook)

About 18 miles to-day, 3 miles beyond Granite Camp + mt.—speedometer became disengaged + did not register for the latter three or four hours. Came down about 1500 feet + the going was swell. Kept closer to the east wall + avoided most of crevasses. The light snow of the past two days has covered ice enough to allow dogs to get a footing yet not enough to keep sled runners from sliding on the ice. Established three stations to-day, No. 10, 11 + this one #12—midway or a little less between the lower group of mts. on the west mouth of Thorne + Granite Mt. group.[12] Here also we are farther to the west + not only have snow to camp on but have avoided the terribly rough ice we traversed on way up. Made swell collection of rocks from moraine at Granite Mt. Flags however showed no appreciable movement. Radio this morning—Ellsworth Mts. have [been] flown.

Dec. 20th

A.M. Another beautiful day—only about 24 miles to go to Durham Point

12. Fourteen triangulation stations were set by the Geological Party for mapping the Thorne Glacier.

Paine and Dick Russell skied to the Organ Pipes and Mount Scudder, where Russell dug in a crevice of the rocks and found the most southerly living organisms ever found—green, white, and black lichens. (Paine Antarctic Collection)

but at rate Quin is getting his work done do not believe we will make it to-day. The camera gadget of Fleming's is not practical in the field—too complicated.

Quin just called me + four Skua gulls are flying round the camp. They are now sitting about 100 yds. to the south looking at us. The first life outside lichens we have seen. Strange beasts so far from their natural habitat.[13]

P.M. 10 miles from Durham Pt. Stopped for triangulation Sta. #13. Beautiful day—calm + warmer. Collected rks. [rocks] from Mt. Farley to-night. Beautiful specimens.

Dec. 21st Sled here—1032.2

Durham Point this afternoon about one. Climbed mt. to-night + feel Leverett is not a glacier but just a big sheet broken by nunataks. Full of ice worms—Mt. Base tomorrow. Our work is done.[14]

13. "That these birds could have traveled four hundred and fifty miles from the sea, over a land which offered them absolutely nothing in the way of food, seemed past believing" (Walden and Paine, *Long Whip*, 236–37).

14. Leverett Glacier is currently known as a glacier fifty miles long and three to four miles wide. It runs from the Watson Escarpment to terminate at the head of the Ross Ice Shelf, east of Scott Glacier (Thorne Glacier). Ice worms are nematodes, 2–3 centimeters long, that live in the top snow layer of some glaciers. They feed on bacteria.

Thorne Glacier sweeps around the western base of this mountain halfway up the glacier. Blackburn is triangulating while Jack sits in the foreground on a tethering line. Hundreds of miles away from any food source, four skua gulls landed at this camp. (Paine Antarctic Collection and with permission from Edythe Holbrook)

Paine operating the radio at the edge of the Thorne Glacier. Clothing was hung to dry, the harnesses were hung on the gee pole, and the 110-pound radio unit was unwrapped from its canvas cover and set up on the sledge. (Paine Antarctic Collection)

Dec. 22nd Sled meter—1054.7

Mt. Base again after a fast run of 22.5 miles from Durham Point. Hit the Beacon right on the nose—good D.R. again. Dogs ate Peteru[?] to-night besides their ration of pemmican. Found beacon almost eroded away. What a relief almost to be here again unpleasant as was our last stay here. The wind is still blowing here however + the sooner we get out the better. Our work is done + all we must do now is to get back safely with our results. 445.5 nautical miles to go. Changed underwear to-night. Everything but absolute essentials now discarded. I have only what I have on, my furs + several pairs of extra socks + mits. No souvenirs now. The Queen Mauds we are leaving—after a brief sojourn here of 26 days. Probably now we will [not] visit them again for a good many years—we three have been fortunate—we have ascended one of the largest glaciers in the world, practically attained the Great Antarctic Plateau, accomplished much scientifically + returned to our mt. base safely. The Queen Mauds, the most remote and inaccessible mt. range in the world, we leave to the next comer. As good luck to them as we had.

At Durham Point left Dick's + my ice ax, one + a half pair crampons, stadia rod, tripod + a stake, beside beacon.

Dec. 23rd 1934

26.8 miles from Mt. Base in an easy run of about seven hours. We trotted the whole way. This afternoon after ob., rigged black tent to serve as a sail, which proved very satisfactory in a 12 mile wind from ESE. I again have a touch of snowblindness from too much sun in the face. I thank some ~~undistinguished~~ scientist who discovered cocaine—for it relieves the very intense pain almost instantly. If it is not cloudy tomorrow believe it best to shift to night skd. then or else will have a severe case.

Weather warm, about 20 above, which is delicious. At Mt. Base 445.5 we left a great deal of rubbish, all that was not absolutely essential to our getting back, and included in that is about four gals. kerosene which we did not need—As Dick remarked we had too much of everything save food.

Letters to-night which we heard in part from WZXAF—one from Dearie saying Phil in Pittsfield + none of family home, God bless me + Merry Xmas. Bless her heart. Also one from Sis saying all well + best wishes. Here we are at about Lat. 85° + to get messages from our families is truly wonderfully dramatic. How much a word from home means here in a world without sentiment.

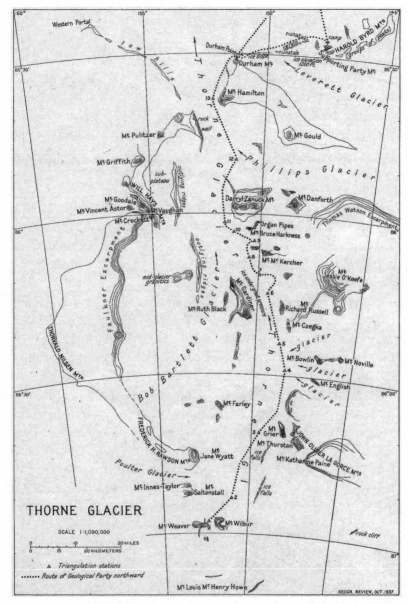

Map of Thorne Glacier, 1937. The glacier (now called Scott Glacier) was explored for the first time by the Second Expedition Geological Party in 1934. The party's fourteen triangulation stations established on the return trip are shown. Mount Weaver is at the southernmost point, and Mount Katherine Paine anchors one end of the La Gorce Mountains. (The latter mountain was later renamed Mount Paine by Admiral Byrd to commemorate the explorer himself.) Durham Point and Mount Durham at the base of the glacier are named for Paine's hometown. (American Geographical Society, *Geographical Review*, and BPRCAP, Papers of Admiral Richard E. Byrd, OSU 9269)

Dec. 24th 1934 Christmas Eve

Sledmeter 1107.2

394 mile beacon after run of 25.7 miles to-day. Wind from S.E. 15 miles boosted us along with the black tent rigged as sails. Dick cut it up this morning + he has half + I have half. We are tough looking ships of the barrier but we are making good time.[15]

Passed through that tough crevassed area from 415 to about the 400 mile depot. A stretch of about two miles was very bad, with crevasses 50 yds. apart + the bridges much weakened by warmth. Passed over one + Dick, who was roped behind, broke through it with his trailer. Quin, who was touring behind his trailer, let go just in time. He was so fascinated by the 40 feet of bridging which let go that he went over to the edge of the still standing bridge to look down + then fell down in it. Stupid thing to do under any circumstances. However they are behind us now + they did not catch us—clear sailing now to 353——then . . .

Jack was very nervous to-day. For the most part the sky was thickly overcast + hazy, making the surface almost invisible. Hence he would very suddenly happen upon a crevasse usually filled with 6 inches to a foot of loose soft snow. He would plunge straight across sort of swimming + leading team behind him. Time after time when we were heading for a flag off in the distance Jack would suddenly veer to the left, hesitate a moment then plunge forward. I knew what to expect + veered sled to follow him. Invariably he crossed them at a right angle. This has happened so often I believe he is even more crevasse conscious than we are. My faith in him is as great as in a human being, a very competent + trustworthy one at that.

Picked up 54 lbs. dog food at 400 mile + fed 2 rations to-night brought from the Mt. Base, leaving us two days food to get to 350—a one day safety margin of dog food in addition to 4 dogs at 367, which we plan to be at tomorrow night.

My snow blindness seems to be about the same, but frequent applications of cocaine + Borafax helps considerably.

To-night is Christmas eve—Never will I spend a whiter Xmas. Had ice cream + chocolate to-night + extra biscuits. We have no presents + we hope for none other than a safe passage thru the crevassed area at 84°. Dearie is all alone to-night, the first Xmas Eve I believe she has ever spent alone. How

15. Called "barrier sailing," the black emergency tent was halved and raised to catch the wind now at their backs, providing the equivalent strength of two more dogs per team (Walden and Paine, *Long Whip*, 237–40).

Barrier Sailing. By December 24, the southern mountains were behind the party. On Christmas Eve, Dick Russell and Paine took advantage of the incessant wind from the south-east, split the black emergency tent in half, and fastened the pieces to the bamboo radio poles. Speeding the sledges along, the wind provided power equivalent to four extra dogs and allowed the party to go an astounding thirty to forty miles per day between the crevasse belts. (Paine Antarctic Collection)

I feel for her + wish I were with her. Next Xmas perhaps. Her message which I heard last night certainly went to my heart—

Dec. 25th Christmas day

392 miles

Awake this morning where we went to bed the night before at the 394 mile mark—wind blowing from S.E. 20–30 miles with heavy drift 10 feet high. After breakfast, decided to have Xmas dinner about three which we did + try to push on to 366.7 mile mark—afterwards—which we tried to. It was much against my judgment but Dick + Quin steadily stated they wanted to go + off we went, snow flying to beat hell. Picked up one flag, passed three + then camped—here we are at 392 much wetter than we were + off the trail. However do not believe we are far from the flag.

For Xmas dinner had chicken which I had stolen + boned before coming. It was a rare old fowl, very tough—Following is dinner prepared by Dick—

Cream of Pope's Nose soup with Noodles (biscuits), Fried Southern Chicken Barrier Style, Corn off the Cob. Coffee ice cream, sweet + strong, tea (ditto). Fresh dog biscuits—Chocolate—Butter.[16]

The cook wishes you "Merry Christmas + hopes he will never have the pleasure of serving you another Christmas dinner on ice (no sherry)." We left sherry at Mt. Base—forgot all about it!

Dec. 27th

3:30 A.M. The 26th, yesterday now we traveled leaving 392 mile past about 4 in the afternoon + traveled 29.7 miles, getting to 362.3 mile mark about 1:30 this morning. We are now on a night schedule + find the light less tiring with sun at our backs. Believe it is going to be more satisfactory in every way.

Oh at 375 beacon, stopped at 366.8 mile beacon + picked up 3 dogs of the four cached there on the way out + fed them to-night. The dogs are literally gorged and putting on weight.

15–20 mile S.E. wind gave us a good boost throughout the day. With the black tent, half on my sled, "Argo," + half on Dick's, we use our old friend to give us a lift. We look like fishing boats with our black sails bobbing up + down as we pass over the sastrugi. Quin back on cooking again, relieving Dick who has been on since arriving at Mt. Base. Quin will also sleep in cook tent, a satisfactory solution to a vexing problem.

Dec. 28th

A.M. Slept 24 hours + want more. The night schedule is confusing. Wind still blows + we are still at 362.3. Visibility continues at about a hundred yards making travelling impossible. Had radio contact this morning—good. Eastern party got back last Saturday the 22nd of December. Their plans called for 90 or at the maximum of 120 days in the field. We cannot understand what made them return so soon.

12 miles separates us from the 300 mile depot and 7 of which are crevasses. To get through them safely is all we ask, but with such poor visibility we would have difficulty picking up flags. Dogs had big feed of dogs which we picked up at 366.7 yesterday morning. Have one feed left, which we will

---

16. There were two kinds of biscuits on the expedition; one was liked more than the other. The expedition ran out of the tasty, formulated biscuits brought from the United States, so over the winter, Carbone, the cook, made trail biscuits from available supplies of flour, oatmeal, sugar, dried beef, powdered milk and lard, and small amounts of bovril, soda, bio-vetetin, and milk of magnesia (Byrd, *Discovery*, 214).

use to-night. Then should we be forced to it can give them fat cereal of which we have an extra quantity of. By that time wind should have died. Plenty of man food, however not so much fuel. 4th day of 20–30 mile SE wind. Temperature remains high, +20 F and sky clear. Now for a break in wx. + we will be on our long way in—362 miles to go—nautical miles.

Dec. 29th A.M.

We are through crevasses of 84° Lat., passed 350 mile beacon + depot + camped to-night at 336. It has been a good day, not that the weather or travelling has been especially fine but the fact that the crevasses are behind us, so that mile post to which we looked forward so long getting to, the 350 mile depot, has been reached + passed. Now we have plain sailing to L.A. save for a brief five miles of troubled surface south of 173. That is not bad however, nothing to these at 84 [degrees latitude].

Started about 4 in afternoon, that is of the 28th, with wind S.E. 20–30 miles. Quin went ahead on skiis to the 357 beacon + in to the 350 because it was easier for him to follow the old trail than it was for me with Jack leading. Drift made flags visible only at about 200 yds. Had only one slip in crevasses + my lead sled tipped over one runner in a crevasse + my skiis bridging it + holding sled up. I nearly went in myself but fortunately got out OK. Split one ski however—now for 25 miles per day and home . . .

Dec. 30 A.M.

Last night best run to date 36.7 miles to the 300 mile depot. Another milestone reached, the mark supposed to have been reached last fall by the so called main Southern Party + goal of this year's Supporting Party. We are only ones to have reached it + here we are again.

Wind continued all day 20–25 miles occasionally dropping to 15 but drift all day. With our sails making us like Arabian fishing smacks we fairly bobbed along. Each flag passed is another half mile passed. Travelling on this ice barrier on Ross Shelf ice is much like traveling at sea in a small boat, particularly the homeward stage. Each flag stands as a buoy, the beacons + depots as harbors, lightships or refueling ships, the sastrugi are the waves + it is truly remarkable how similar in sound is the plunge + wild cavortings of the lead sled and that of a small boat in a choppy sea. The flatness of the surface is like the ocean + haycocks + crevasses correspond to reefs—

We saw no mts. to-day + they are gone now for good. Those magnificent mts. so inaccessible + seen by so few. Yet one of the grandest ranges in the world.

Fed dogs to-night, two of them of those cached here on way out. They stunk to heaven though they had been completely buried for more than a month. The heart of one dog was still unfrozen. As bad as they smelled the dogs relished them.

Wind, wind. That is to be the tale of our account of this trip—ah for a day of calm + sunshine.[17] Everything, tents, bags, clothing + sled tanks, is wet. Every bit of drift driven against them melts + soaks in only to freeze later as ice. Temp. +28 this A.M. Warmest yet. Have superfluity of food + eat double rations of sugar, oatmeal, milk + chocolate. We'll be fat when we get in.

Dec. 31st A.M.

25 miles from 300 to 275 about 8 1/2 hours travelling. Wind let up to about 10 miles + slowed our progress consequently. No radio contact to-night or this morning. The fault is at the other end, for our receiver was working ok. Feeding dogs fat cereal as well as biscuits now as part of their regular ration. Warm and snow soft.

January 1, 1935 A.M.

25 miles to 250 mile depot, made run in 8 1/2 hours—cloudless night with gentle S. wind. Surface soft + dogs sank to their knees in spots yet in spite of it made good time. Quin ahead on skiis most of night.

Have much too much food + feeding dogs biscuits + fat cereal in addition to their regular ration. Better too much than too little. Drink this morning in honor of the New Year—1935.

Jan. 2nd A.M.

25 miles to 225—tiring day, soft snow. Fog overwhelmed us once but cleared in 15 minutes. Radio skd. this P.M. + sent in upon request brief summary of work. Wind from North now + cloudy. Old trail almost entirely obliterated.

Jan. 3rd A.M.

25 1/2 miles to 200 mile beacon. 8 P.M. to 5 A.M., which has been our time

---

17. Byrd later wrote, "From the time [the Geological Party] cast off from the tractors at Lat. 81°09′S. they sledged into steady down-drafts from the polar plateau, blowing across the barrier with the persistence of the trade-winds—all southeasterly winds, with a velocity of from 20 to 60 miles per hour, perhaps more. . . . Up the glacier, the mountain walls of which made a funnel, the wind was even worse. It buffeted them like a solid force. It never blew less than 20–40 miles per hour, and at times approached hurricane force. Men and dogs suffered exceedingly" (ibid., 363).

for the past 25 mile runs, 15 miles before ob. + 10 miles after. Skua gull circled round at 210. He stayed with us for about a half hour—then disappeared. Everyone rather tired after a week of constant running. Plan to spend day at 173 to rest ourselves + dogs——night overcast till late + then cleared off to be beautiful. Light south wind.

Jan. 4th A.M.

27 miles to 173 mile depot. Made run in fast time + got here at 4:30. Passed crevasses OK but lost Nip when he strangled in his harness in a crevasse which broke beneath him. One end of him was held by his collar + lead line the other by his trace line. On top of him was Tuck, Stupid + Buck. I released his neck line after getting other dogs out + Dick pulled him up by his trace line. He was gone then. We hurled him into his crevasse + never heard him land. Poor old Nip, he was a good dog. This leaves me with 8 dogs but quite enough to get us in all right. We have food in abundance now, 600 lbs. of dog food + 4 rations to get us the next 25 miles. Feeding biscuits + milk + pemmican to dogs. There is not the most remote chance of it ever being utilized + we are using it as fast as we can and to the best advantage.

Jan. 5th 2 A.M.

After delicious sleep of 12 hours got up + ate till we groaned. Cut Quin's hair + Dick manufactured an elephant whip. Fed dogs again + they consumed the pemmican as tho they hadn't had anything to eat for a week.

Wind blowing 10 miles from S.W. + sky overcast. We have a grand let down feeling now for the trail is marked every sixth of a mile from here in, we have more dog + man food than one will ever use, the difficulties are practically over, no more crevasses etc. We have had enough trouble with them to last us for some time. Nip's death seems such a tragedy when he was only two miles from all the food + rest he could want. Such a good worker. Feel now the old feeling of satiation + well-being. More sleep now, more to eat + then be on our way the last lap—

Jan. 5th 9 A.M.

A short sleep, 4 biscuits fried in butter with peanut butter + sugar + now for more nap. Wind S.W. 10 miles + are now waiting for sun to get around to west. On night skd. as before. Dogs enjoying full stomach + sunshine. Quin has shaved beard leaving a Hitler moustache + he looks extraordinarily ludicrous. Another week + we'll be in. Oh boy, more chocolate—

Jan. 6th A.M.

23 miles to 150 mile depot. Picked up note at 155 left by Fall Sledging Party March 14, 1934 + the flag.[18] Snow damnably soft + the going last ten miles slow. Jack had a bad day, not having the inclination or desire to pull anything. Guess he ate too much. Lat. at 173—10 mile S.W. wind, clear save for scattered clouds. Found no biscuit ration here. Must have slipped last fall. Do not need them however.

Jan 6th noon

Con't [continued] sleep. Wind continues about 10–15 from SW but warm. Brilliant sunshine.

   Thinking of things I can add to my hat—briefly they seem to be—Laid out entire southern trail from L.A. to the top of the Thorne Glacier—what I did not navigate last year, I did this year carrying on this year where I left off last year. I have been almost to 87°S latitude, have looked out over the Antarctic Plateau + have seen the flatness + white bleakness. I have operated the furthest south radio ground station in the world. Furthermore I have done more sledging than any other member of this expedition + have lived on the trail more than two weeks more than anyone else in the expedition. For a lad who expected nothing, who had no promises made him, who hoped only a break now + then, believe I have been extremely fortunate.

Jan. 7th A.M.

25 miles to 125 mile beacon—found three trailer sleds against beacon as left by us last fall. Dick had Jack to-day + followed behind Quin who was out ahead. I had Gav for a while as leader + also Kaiser. Radio contact this morning—tractors at Cletrac + under the leadership of Demas.[19] Adv. Base tomorrow + then the last hundred—

Jan 8th A.M.

25 miles to Advance Base. Could not find seal meat. Tractors not here. Ate shredded wheat, tomatoes, plums + other delicacies. Had a drink. Wind blowing S.W. 20 miles + drifting.

---

18. This point was the farthest south Paine's party had traveled the previous fall to cache supplies for the summer field season.

19. The Cletrac had foundered in March near Mile 66 and had remained there broken. Repair was being attempted so it could be used to move stores to the ships (ibid., 300, 356).

The Condor took off with 450 pounds of rock samples taken from the Queen Maud Range on January 10, seventy-five nautical miles from Little America. (Paine Antarctic Collection)

The Geological Party—(from left) Dick Russell, Quin Blackburn, and Stuart Paine—returned at 7 a.m. on January 11, 1935, after skiing 1,410 statute miles in eighty-eight days, exploring and mapping new territory, completing geological cross-sections, and finding fossils and living organisms the farthest south ever discovered. They were the first Americans and the fourth surface party to ever approach the South Pole. (BPRCAP, Papers of Admiral Richard E. Byrd, image 7882-8)

Jan. 9th A.M.

25 miles to 75 mile depot—good day. Overcast but sun shining now. Tractors, with Waite as radio operator, reached Adv. Base at noon yesterday. Good to see new faces + hear the gossip.[20]

Jan. 10th

Condor with Poulter, Black, Pelter, Peterson, Mac + Harold landed about noon of 9th, took sounding, 500 lbs. of our load + took off. We ate, packed + made 37 miles to 43 mile north—

Jan. 11th

Home at last after run of about 45 miles. Tired but happy to have finished trip.[21] Everyone here seem appreciative of our work. We are sane + sound in excellent health + happy. Finish probably the most enjoyable summer I shall ever have spent——[22]

20. Of the three summer field parties, the Geological Party was the last still in the field.

21. Paine scribbled in his diary notes, "Long walk—1410 statute miles." He calculated that from Little America to Mount Weaver they had traveled 633 nautical miles; on the return, they took a different route and made it back in 593 nautical miles. This totaled 1,226 total nautical miles or 1,410 statute miles for the trip. The return trip from the base of the mountains would be written up as record-breaking speed for surface polar travel. It was reported in the October 1935 issue of *National Geographic* that the party traveled 527 miles in just sixteen traveling days, an average of thirty-three miles per day (Richard E. Byrd, "Exploring the Ice Age in Antarctica," 258).

22. In a subsequent letter home, Paine wrote, "Never have I felt more satisfaction that I had finished a job than I did when we finished that trip. It had been 88 days since we left. During that time we had lived in nothing but a tent, putting up with each other's idiosyncrasies and personal ways with no chance of an outlet or escape, hiked day after day, good days, bad days, cold days, with wind nearly all the time, for the most part against us, traveled close to 1,500 miles, the same company, the same personalities, the same problems, differing but slightly from day to day, the deadly monotonous trail routine. Yet inspite of whatever hardships we put up with and the monotony of it I shall probably never have such peace and true contentment. It is strange, for our way was supposed to be waylaid with danger etc. But life out there is so simple, no complications, and whatever common sense and what we call 'guts.' Not that I am particularly abundant in that quality. Yet the cold and adverse weather calls for something more than the ordinary expenditure of energy and work. Of the six men I have been on the trail with, this summer and last fall, only four had that extra something which is necessary to push across a sledge journey. It may be some satisfaction to you that it has been my lot to do more sledging than anyone else here. That by about 170 miles and close to three weeks. I was the only one of last year's southern party to go on a major sledge journey this summer. So much for that. I should add that it was worthwhile from my standpoint and I believe that our finds were of some value" (Paine to Dearie, Little America, January 23, 1935, Paine Antarctic Collection).

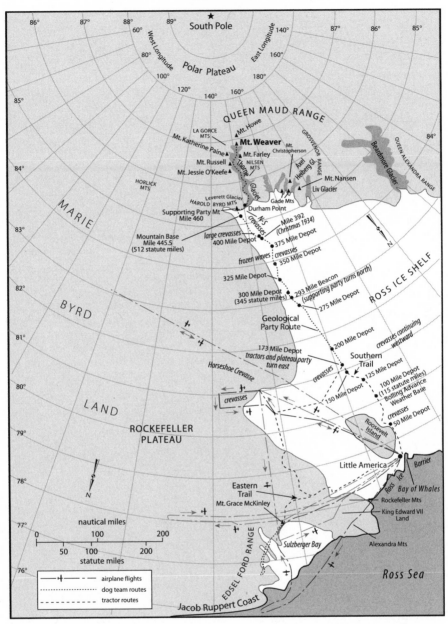

The summer field explorations of 1934 included operations for aircraft and the three main surface parties. To Mile 173, the routes for the tractors and Supporting, Plateau, and Geological parties overlapped; to Mile 293, only the Supporting and Geological parties overlapped. From Mile 293, the Geological Party continued south alone. (Some map information derived from "Operations Map," *National Geographic*, 1935, by Commander Harold E. Saunders, USN, Rawson and Darley, archived at BPRCAP, Papers of Admiral Richard E. Byrd, 9267.) (M. L. Paine)

Diary Four

Stuart D. Paine cont.

Byrd Antarctic Expedition II
Little America Antarctica

13

Homeward

January 13–May 12, 1935

Jan. 13th 1935—Sunday—L.A.

We returned to L.A. 7 A.M. Jan 11th after 88 days in field—traveling 1226 nautical miles, 1440 statute miles + reaching Latitude 87 or a bit short of it—[1]

The trip was successful in every way but mighty glad to have work over with. Can't sleep well since been back because of softness of mattress + the dampness of Old Mess Hall. Change of food has been enjoyable but not as good as we expected because of high living on the way home. Camp here disorganized and scattered into cliques. Everyone well however. Most all sleeping in tents.

Jan. 16th

Sleep, eat + rest has been the routine. Little to do. Have started to type log book but poor progress. Made trip to bay this A.M. with Lindsay to get his tent—dogs have recovered their old pep + vigor.

---

1. Paine quickly wrote "1440" without checking his previous notes. The nautical miles number is the same as that in his notes. For rough calculations in the field, Paine sometimes used the average of 1.2 miles for the accurate conversion factor of 1.15 statute miles to one nautical mile. It was simply faster to multiply and good enough for his needs in translating for statute miles. Nautical miles, however, were the base unit used and were recorded with as much accuracy as possible in the field conditions they faced. These challenges are discussed further in Appendix 6. Naturally, backtracking on a trail, going around crevasses, and so on interfered with developing straight-line mileage from any given point. Paine later reconfirmed the mileage to be 1,226 total nautical miles traveled and 1,410 statute miles.

Quin told Finn he did not cooperate as he should have out on trail + Finn much upset. A stupid statement + a bad blunder. Quin on radio to-day—we were left out.

Jan. 17th

Went penguin hunting to-day with Starrett + got two Adelies—a swell day with dogs + no hurry. Critical situation about landing. Bay ice back about five miles from mouth of bay, a mile north of Eleanor Bolling Bight—must have northerly wind to break up ice. *Bear* due Sunday—*Ruppert* well on way. Commodore aboard after threatening to get west on ship.[2] Dirty work— Paige doing charcoal fire with my side whiskers. Taylor, Duke in tent with door + I'm in Eastern Party tent. No more movies. It won't be long now.

Jan. 20th

The *Bear* arrived yesterday. Duke + I, Herrmann (I was chauffeuring Herrmann about) + Skinner arrived on East Cape just as she rounded West Cape. It was a thrill to see her though we did not get the kick out of it we expected. John got some shots of her coming in. Pitched tent + ate seal steaks till we nearly exploded + proceeded down to ship. Crew a bit cool + inquisitive—I guess we are strange animals after all. She tied up to ice about seven miles from L.A. about in middle of bay. Ice pretty firm, 7–8 ft. thick. Much of Herrmann's stuff, a little food + mail. Read mail last night till early A.M. Wonderful to get news. Everyone was so kind in remembering me. Hauled food to ship from cache atop barrier 3 miles out from L.A. 2 trips is all we can make to-night. Brought [Lieutenant] English up to-night—swell party.[3]

Jan. 21st Tuesday 1935

Bear in bay, ice breaking out. No dog teams to ships—Digging out Ford with

---

2. Byrd would later write, "Choosing to run down the 177th meridian W., well east of the *Bear*'s track, Commodore Gjertsen stubbed his toe on heavy pack just north of the Ross Sea on the night of the 22nd, and was obliged to steer west before he broke into the clear on the 24th" (Byrd, *Discovery*, 377–78).

3. Lieutenant (J. G.) R. A. J. English, U.S.N., was master of the *Bear of Oakland*. The men were now able to receive confidences on paper instead of via broadcast radio. Byrd noted that men received pictures of their children, a bible, news of a fellow aviator who crashed when the wings of his airplane came off, and a letter announcing that the Depression was finally over (ibid., 375–76). Fresh food and mail and so on were unloaded from the *Bear* and then the directional movement promptly reversed itself. The tractors deposited a cache of equipment and supplies from Little America on the barrier summit, which then was to be relayed by dog team to the ship (ibid., 376).

Herrmann making transparencies. Hope to get her out tomorrow—meeting in dog dept this A.M. but hauled snow this P.M.—5 dog teams—

Reaction to Expedition not very encouraging judging by newspaper reports + letters. World frenzied by too many other important things.

Jan. 24th

Ronne, myself, Duke + Wade burst way through pressure this afternoon at foot of Ver Sur Mer. Made a good job + there is an excellent route through both by dogs + tractors. *Bear* still out in bay—wind continues northerly. *Ruppert* arrives tomorrow morning but will evidently have to stand by till ice + bergs in bay go out. Plan to tie up at Eleanor Bolling Bight.[4] New Yorkers + Time [magazines] I have been devouring—Del + Lola sent them. Little realized till I read them have been much out of contact with world we have been. I want to get back + soon too. The cold + snow + wind is getting on my nerves. I'd go nuts should we be forced to stay here another year.

Jan. 26th Sunday

Wind continues from N + NE about 15 to 25 miles, occasional snow flurries. Bay jammed with ice + three large bergs. *Ruppert* + *Bear* off mouth somewhere, have not seen *Ruppert* yet. Went sealing with Stan this A.M. + P.M.— took three seals + a lot of steaks for galley. Found mess of well-preserved fish in belly of seal which we turned over to Lindsey—like smelts. Delay getting serious—nothing can be done, however.

Jan. 29th

Wind + snow flurries continue with a let up from the North + East. The *Bear* was pushed into Eleanor Bolling Bight to-night + she lay along side the ice about as high as her gunwales. It was decidedly a risky affair, for the ice was badly undercut and several large ice bergs as well as densely packed pack

---

4. Between the nineteenth and the twenty-fourth, the *Bear* was driven five times from her docking by outrushing or windblown ice that threatened the ship (ibid., 376). Even by January, the year-old ice, twelve feet thick and rotten, was fixed in a line due east across the bay from a point just south of West Cape. A year before, the *Ruppert* had been able to steam to within three miles of Little America. On January 8, half a mile of the bay ice went out in a few hours. Potential routes from Ver sur Mer Inlet and a five-mile route over the bay ice were too dangerous for both the tractors and the dog teams, which were already falling into cracks into the sea water below. The only solution was to load from Eleanor Bolling Bight on the barrier, located 4 1/2 miles north of Little America. Innes-Taylor found a gentle descent down the ice foot to the Bay that only required avoidance of a narrow-roofed crevasse at the top and a shallow pool of slush ice at the bottom (ibid., 374).

were gradually closing in from the west. When she pulled out after getting aboard a goodly supply of food, there was less than a hundred yards between barrier and encroaching pack + bergs. Four large tabular bergs were gradually bearing down from the North + in a few hours will be locked up in the bay pack, filling the bay with ice to its very mouth. It is now utterly impossible to load + all we can do is to wait.[5]

I took June down to *Bear* + waited until after midnight for mail from *Ruppert*. Commodore would not put over but [at] last the *Bear* did + took mail from *Ruppert* into the Bight in a dingy.

Plans are now almost final for my going back on the *Bear*. It is my choice. Taylor + Noville + English have consented. I want the change + it will provide work for the passage home. It will be stupid on the *Ruppert*—I like the *Bear*. She is a grand old ship, leaky + perhaps rotten in spots—yet a faithful old ship + I want to sail in her. The other dogmen are a bit gripped at my desertion but who cares. They had the same chance.

Jan. 30th

After getting to bed late last night slept till noon then was aroused to get seals. The others did nothing to-day as usual. Highet, the young New Zealand doctor + I got two young Weddells + made a pretty thorough dissection of each. I enjoyed myself tremendously. Had headache.

Weather clearing + it seems that tomorrow the wind will shift to south + we can commence loading with a rush. We must be getting out of here soon—

Jan. 31st

Took team to ship after breakfast. *Bear* tied up at Bolling Bight last night. Duke, Stan + Al there + I relieved Duke—Taylor came back later.

Ruppert unable to come alongside as yet + we are loading *Bear* + they are transshipping it to *Ruppert*. Tractors, Cletrac + Citroens on full time—we of dog dept. on 8 hr. shifts at ship—5 miles to Bight from here + make a 12 hr. day for us. Things upset + Taylor staying up for no good reason. Wind still from N + NE. Much of ice has gone out of bay but still unsafe to *Ruppert*. When will we get a break in wx?

5. Bergs were encroaching from the sea and breaking off the barrier at the same time: "The *Bear* was nosed against the Barrier when 50 feet of the Barrier broke out alongside the ship. Men on the gangplank were thrown and the ship heeled over and then slowly righted herself. Lieut. English steamed backward away from the edge to let the ice go out and then took a new position at the edge nearby" (ibid., 379–80).

The *Bear of Oakland* briefly came alongside the undercut ice at the Barrier, where four large bergs were closing in. Because of the rotten and breaking ice, berthing by the bay ice was impossible. In this image, the dog teams are loading the *Bear* at Eleanor Bolling Bight. (Paine Antarctic Collection)

Stan fell + cut his neck on a box—in bed on *Bear*. Didn't get a chance to see him this morning. Settled about my going on *Bear*—at least Grimminger says so. Better to keep mum about it.

Feb. 1st

Wind still North—The most astounding break I have ever seen—We are looked upon with great disfavor by the gods I believe. Albert + I worked all day at Eleanor Bolling Bight + the two of us loaded her completely from 10 A.M. to 4 P.M. this afternoon. Of course we had to haul only a little over two hundred yards. Still all but a few loads were loaded + handled ourselves. We worked like hell + without suitable cooperation from this end. The ship seems to be in only during our watch. Many people have rumored I am to be third mate in the *Bear.* There is nothing in it + I believe I shall be just a coal heaver. That's all right with me.

It is all but over now. Wade and Ronne are going aboard the *Ruppert* tonight with their dogs. Another loading of *Bear* will clear up about all that is to go back. Except of course planes, tractors + dogs. I have not moved anything yet for I am not sure where I am to go. Leave that for last load. To be actually going home seems too good to be true. There are times that I get home sick all of a sudden + yearn to be home + my own family again with Dearie + Phil + Del + Sis all whom I know love me + take me regardless of my idiosyncrasies + failures. I have changed the last year and a half I know. I have grown more cynical—Contrary to what I express I have had great disappointments, not in opportunity but in personalities. I expected too much I know + not one lived up to expectations. Never again will I idealize men. I shall take every man as a mortal each with a weakness which I hope to be able to see soon. I have learned to put little faith in anyone's word. Their motives are under suspicion in almost every case. It is lack of sincerity more than anything else I guess. Of course it is to be remembered that those in the expedition are here for reasons not adventurous necessarily but because they are misfits at home—Hence they are not normal. The same is probably true of me—Eh bien?

Feb. 6th 1935

We are away at last—I am writing this on the *Bear of Oakland,* to which I am assigned and to which I wanted to come. The expedition is over as far as its activities go and we are enroute home. Left Bay of Whales about 3:30 this afternoon and are heading for Discovery Inlet, accompanied by the *Ruppert,* to pick up Adele Penguins. My quarters are aft with Starrett in the sickbay, an excellent location, though wet in heavy weather they say. Still it is in the middle of the boat + very nice otherwise. There is even a wash stand in it which is quite a luxury.

I am eating aft with the officers and am temporarily an oiler in the engine room, a new experience and one which I shall stay on only for a short time. Then I go on deck, a good break.

Last few days rather hectic. *Ruppert* tied up at Eleanor Bolling Bight only for about 10 hours—all planes put aboard. *Bear* picked up one Citroen, leaving Cletrac, another Citroen and the Fords besides a small quantity of gear,

The *Jacob Ruppert* was only able to berth beside the Barrier for seventeen hours, during which time the cows and the planes were loaded. The rest of the supplies and equipment were transshipped from the stronger-hulled *Bear* to the thinner-hulled *Ruppert,* which was waiting in safer waters. In this photo, Paine's team, led by Jack, waits for the next task. (Paine Antarctic Collection)

largely rubbish.[6] I came down from Little America with Murphy's gear three days ago + stayed up driving + assisting loading for two days + finally turned in last night after *Ruppert* put to sea. *Bear* unloaded [to *Ruppert*] this A.M. + I came on board. So here we are after a year on the ice, safe + sound in better health than I ever have been. I have had a priceless experience + one which I do not believe I shall ever regret. I feel I did my share in the accomplishments but am tremendously happy to be going home.

Feb. 6th

Aboard S.S. *Bear.* Stood 4–8 watch as oiler morning + to-night. Fog lifted early this P.M. + we steamed into Discovery Inlet leaving *Ruppert* outside. Must have come in 15 miles or more, the last three through a cut about as wide as the Panama Canal. On each side the barrier towered, a magnificent sight reaching almost to the topmast.

6. The rest of the equipment and supplies to be taken by the *Ruppert* were loaded first onto the *Bear,* and then reloaded onto the *Ruppert* a safe distance from the calving barrier and the outrushing ice. The *Ruppert* was only able to berth at the ice for 17 hours. During that time, the planes (the Condor, the Ford, the Pilgrim, and the Fairchild) and the three cattle still living were precariously loaded (the cow Klondike had succumbed as a result of frostbite) (ibid., 379–82).

Landed at end at 6 P.M. + most everyone went ashore to either get penguins or kill + skin seals. Have 20 old Adeles + about five Emperors + about 20 small seals. The ships' crews enjoyed themselves immensely + will spend next few days cleaning the blood from their clothes.

Hope I get on deck soon. The engines make me ga-ga—round + round, heavy moving black to slowly revolving steel, up down back + forth rods bright + shining unceasing—

Friday Feb. 8th

Steaming with sails hoisted and making about 7 knots—an oiler still but find job boring. Crew here dissatisfied + bitter. Don't blame them. *Bear* has had precious little recognition for its part in the expedition. 11 days to go to Dunedin if all goes well. Not seasick yet. Sea fairly smooth though quite rocky to the *Ruppert*.

Sunday Feb. 10th

Skipped Saturday when we crossed from West long. to East long. Seas picking up + ship rolling + pitching a good deal. Several of ice party ill + I do not feel too well myself. Making 9 knots however, an excellent clip for the old *Bear*. All sails up. Every hour brings us closer to N.Z. thank God + then the smooth placid Pacific, Panama, Norfolk + finally New York, a long ways off.

Monday, Feb. 11th

Lat. 68°27'. Still going strong. A fair breeze from the port beam sending us along at about 8 knots—Oiling getting boring + stupid—wish I were on deck. But I asked for it + it's not firing, which is much worse. English doesn't seem very warm to me, in fact very cool. Letters from Browns + Sis to-day saying all well + glad I am out of Antarctic—I am glad in a way but I know right now I shall not sit still until I get back there again. There is something appealing about it which I hope someday will bring me back. I have a feeling I'll be here again——

Feb. 12th Tuesday

We are past 66° and are now running into ice bergs but no pack. *Ruppert* a 120 miles ahead of us + all going well. Fresh westerly wind + all sails set. Making about 7 1/2 knots I believe. We are on the fringe of the Ross Sea + tomorrow will say good-by to it. What a change awaits us the other end of it.

The *Bear* wends its way out of the ice pack and north to New Zealand. Paine is on a spar off the foremast. (Paine Antarctic Collection)

The *Ruppert* seen from the deck of the *Bear*, as the Second Expedition leaves the Antarctic continent. (Paine Antarctic Collection)

Waves from a storm break over the rails of the *Bear* and crash in through the scuppers at deck level before draining back out to the sea. Paine was assigned a bunk in the sick bay, which sloshed with seawater during storms. (Paine Antarctic Collection)

Ship rolling and pitching quite a bit but it does not affect me at least now. Several have been sick but I have fortunately escaped any great discomfort.

Hat blew overboard.

Feb. 23rd 1935 Dunedin

Diary was missing for a week or more having gone adrift during one of the heavy blows aboard the *Bear*. Finally found it beneath my bunk sloshing around in the water which continually poured in from the deck above. It is undamaged however.

The *Bear* got in here the morning of the 20th, two days behind the *Ruppert*. We had a very rough passage, several days during which it was almost impossible to eat aft in the wardroom. Racks of course were rigged but though each plate + cup was surrounded by a square two or more inches high, yet that did not prevent cups + dishes from toppling to the deck or a plate of soup from hopping unexpectedly to the lap of the hungry owner.

The sick bay was continually wet + soaking. Both Starrett and I were on watch in the engine room + our clothes were dirty and filthy. This, combined with the cramped quarters and the wetness, made it rather unpleasant.

Night before we got in, a hot night for us just from the ice and hotter still in the engine room. I asked English whether he intended to keep me in engine room through tropics + he replied yes. So I came over to *Ruppert* tout de suite upon arrival here. I also told English what I thought of him, my disgust at his conduct as a naval officer, his criticism + malicious remarks of his commanding officer, the ice party + individuals under his command. He said he would give me the works for it but I believe R.E.B. can prevent his going very far. So, after a very rough trip on the *Bear* + enduring many difficult times aboard her, I am now back on the *Ruppert* + very glad of it.

First night ashore resulted in my getting frightfully drunk + a terrible session next morning. However, first night is first night. Herrmann gave a party the second night. I went late after seeing "One Night of Love" with Grace Moore, a beautiful production, one which I shall see again. Last night a reception + dance to which I went only for about ten minutes. I am not the social kind I guess.

The money order sent down last time to me by Del has been cancelled here + I shall be unable to get my money from it until I get back to N.Y. Ken + George have offered to lend me whatever I need so that will take care of me all right.[7]

Getting back here is all very nice in a way. Our reception here as cool as a cold ice box. Not over 6 people on the dock to welcome the *Bear* when she came in. I have made no contacts here + have not made any effort to. Somehow I don't care so much + am not willing to make the effort. To-night am going out with Quin to some professor's house, Prof. Parks I believe, a noted geologist of this region.[8] The girls here are stupider than first grade teachers.

Feb. 25th

Still on board *Ruppert*. Had party last night with Dick + Mac + drank beer until late. Sick in bed to-day. Had "tea" to-night with Doc. Highet at his home. Very nice. Went through hospital + University of Otago with him + Jim Starrett. Admiral back tomorrow.[9]

---

7. This might have been George Noville but was more likely George Grimminger.

8. This man was likely James Park, who, from 1901 to 1931, was the dean of the faculty of Mines and Metallurgy, University of Otago.

9. Marie Byrd, Admiral Byrd's wife, met him in Auckland during the expedition's stay in New Zealand. They would later leave together on a passenger ship to Panama, where the admiral would again join the expedition (Hill and Hill, *In Little America with Byrd*, 252).

From left: Paine, Duke Dane, and Alton Wade. The men toured New Zealand while the condenser on the *Bear of Oakland* was being repaired. Both ships would leave New Zealand together, planning to arrive in the United States at approximately the same time. (Paine Antarctic Collection)

Feb. 26th 1935—Queenstown, N.Z.

Queenstown about 200 miles from Dunedin. At McCarthy's Hotel with Stan + Dick. Came up by bus. Left Dunedin 9 A.M. + arrived here 7 P.M. Most of way through rough rolling bumpy country with the roadway built into the side of the mts., no fences or the like + often times a sheer drop of 500 feet to a boiling river below. Country very dry, almost a desert, but 11 inches a year of rain at mts. a touch over 1000 feet through here. At Queenstown they rise to 3000 or more I believe. Doing trip on a shoe string but hope to stay here tomorrow returning Thursday. In comfortable bed for first time since leaving Shankhassick, October 1933, almost a year + a half ago. More tomorrow.

Feb. 28th Enroute Queenstown—Gore

Yesterday at Queenstown with Dick + Stan. Took walk in morning through park which reaches out into the lake. Lake Wakatipu. The lake is very beautiful itself being 50 miles long + 1–3 miles wide, water of the greatest clarity + depth, entirely surrounded by mts. up to 7000 ft. rising sharply from the banks of the lake. But foliage—almost entirely lacking save in the park. On the mts. sides there is mustard colored grass, tall tufted grass burned brown by the sun + drought. Rocks except at the summits are not very apparent + the mts. are not extremely attractive. The green verdure of our mts. is lacking. Queenstown however is nice because trees have been planted + are cared for. The climate is very dry.

In the park is monument to Scott, Wilson, Evers, Oats, an impressive plaque bearing Scott's last message.[10]

In afternoon hired boat + went rowing. I bought a fishing license + rented tackle but got no fish. Didn't try very hard. Went swimming later + layed in sun a good part of the time.

Stayed at Mountaineer Hotel for 12 shillings a day including meals.[11] Houses here for most part one storied—Country mountains with infertile valley between. Sheep everywhere. Boat from Queenstown to Kingston crowded with sheep, a thousand head at least. They were everywhere save in the first class saloon + we took refuge there.

Left hat at Kingston after two hour ride + boarded train for Gore, a small train, narrow gauge. Four cars, the one train going this way each day—2 classes first + second, each car divided into two sections, forward part the first. Seats are softer there, that's all.

Stop every few minutes at small stations not as large as PresWarren River, a large town up here consists of 500 people + is on maps in large letters. Stopped at Riversdale for lunch + everyone piled out for 23 minutes to a refreshment stand, where we had tea + as many sandwiches + cakes as we could eat for 9 d. [old pence].

Stopped now at Otamita where there is one shed. Across the road is a corral with several hundred sheep—evidently awaiting shipment somewhere—a row of willows borders the stream not far away + fields flat, browned + rough lie all around, with mts. standing in the distance. Now we're underway again.

---

10. Paine took photographs of both the Scott and the Oates memorials. Scott's party had died on their return journey from the South Pole twenty-three years before. In the "Message to the Public" written in his diary, Scott told how the expedition's disaster was not due to anyone's fault or to poor planning, but to bad weather and bad luck, and asked his county to provide for his family: "but for my own sake I do not regret this journey, which has shown that Englishmen can endure hardships, help one another, and meet death with as great a fortitude as ever in the past. We took risks, we knew we took them; things have come out against us, and therefore we have no cause for complaint, but bow to the will of providence, determined still to do our best to the last. . . . Had we lived, I should have had a tale to tell of the hardihood, endurance, and courage of my companions which would have stirred the heart of every Englishman."

11. New Zealand was using the English imperial currency system.

Sheep dogs are wonderful—small dogs black + white—with brown, very nervous + weighing perhaps 40 lbs. They obey their master's commands like human beings + when driving sheep harass them by barking + nipping the backward ones. Coming up by here day before yesterday passed a half dozen herds, some well over a hundred, being driven down the road by one man + two or three dogs.

Country very sparsely settled + very poor save for the sheep industry + cattle. This section of N.Z. is the desert section + not indicative of the county as a whole. People, what few there are of them, seem well off however. Though wool, their bread + butter, is but half 1930 price. Day is hot, very clear + stuffy in the car. Stop at Gore for 20 minutes for refreshments. We change trains. This goes to Invercargill, the capital of the South Island.

March 8th

Still in Dunedin, with poor prospects for getting away before another four days. A man sent down by Anderson cashed Del's money order + have sufficient money.[12] In addition we are paid 15 shillings a week while we are here. Most of time I remain aboard ship, taking my turn at dog duty + one night as night watch. We are all terribly fed up with our stay here + want to get busy. But the *Bear* is holding us. The condenser is giving trouble + there does not seem to be enough initiative or push to put it together again in a hurry. R.E.B. woke me early yesterday morning + wanted my opinion of English, which I frankly gave as I had as frankly told him [English] to his face. To-day on dog watch.

What a life!!

March 13th 1935

Aboard *Ruppert* en route to Panama. Got underway 11:30, followed by *Bear* shortly afterwards. Many people down to see us off, which was surprising. Quartered with Highet in Potaka's Cabin, a swell cabin + a great change after the airy passage way bunk up forward. Had fight with Wade about going below but finally drew lots + Stan lost. I felt sorry for him. Went out last night to Highet's + had a lovely homey evening. Met Pat later.[13]

---

12. Charles F. Anderson, a U.S. postal inspector, had been sent down on the *Bear* to handle the Little America cancellations on outgoing mail.

13. Paine took a picture of a well-dressed and attractive woman leaning against a ship's rail with the caption, "The girl I left behind." She may have been "Pat."

Paine poses with Standardt as they were going home on the *Jacob Ruppert*. (Paine Antarctic Collection)

Going home at last— + still have three pounds, a triumph over temptation. Dunedin an awfully nice city + the people extremely hospitable + cordial. I shall look forward to seeing it again—

March 14th 1935

Midnight. 132 miles since midnight last night. *Bear* to port about 3 miles. Stood 4 hour morning watch. 2 look out + 2 on wheel + was supposed to stand 4 hours to-night but refused and stood 2 hour wheel watch. Am quite excited about the watch list + had talk with Poulter this A.M. Unless it is changed will refuse to go on watch + Russell + Ronne + Highet are of same opinion. Insist upon 4 hour watch per day + not 8, more men taking watches + not the willing horses. Another man below to permit Stan to have 4 on + 12 off instead of 4 on 8 off + one or two men fill in dog dept. to care for dogs.

No care respite to-day but Dane did them. I have an issue + am going to see it through or I'll refuse to work.[14] Now about 200 miles out. Running slowly to keep back with *Bear.*

March 15th

No action on new list as yet and shall stand one more watch before refusing duty. It is the only way to get action here. Day windy from N.E.—slow speed only about 6 knots. Very bad—*Bear* to starboard + astern. John Dyer put radio in for me + so get news + everything. Reading Pearl Buck's *A House Divided*—excellent.

March 17th

Close to 800 miles on our way in a rough sea with rather unpleasant rolling. *Bear* making better time + now doing close to 7 knots.

Crossed name off watch list + now refuse to stand wheel watches as well as look out, refusing because Poulter went back on his word + this is the only way I can make him see I am sincere. Dick went back on his word as I expected + now was around gloating that I am a quitter, etc. I waited four days for Poulter to put up new watch list + then rebelled. I do not think he ever intended to make out a new one. And I will not stand for the old list with the willing horses being made suckers of. Noville drunk since we left N.Z.

Real happiness has been left behind + I shall not probably find it again till I get out on the trail again somewhere, sometime. I know now I have no friends on the expedition, ones I can really depend upon + it is rather disheartening. So it has been + probably will be. Friendship is a priceless thing, something I have not yet found. I had hoped for Dick for we had so much in common but he is crude in many ways, subtle + not reliable. I have learned my lesson now—never will I expect real friendship from anyone outside Dearie + she will always be mine. I have grown much harder than I was + perhaps it is a good thing. But not less sensitive really.

March 21st

Now a few miles north of Dunedin's latitude + well over a thousand miles on our way. No storms— + with a south wind with long slow rolls—cold to-night with south wind. Built a table for cabin + it looks well. Radio going swell.

14. This issue was of significant controversy and prompted numerous men to hold signs and form protest lines on the ship's deck.

Movies three times a week. Finished copying Quin's trail diary + Dick is starting on summary notes. Am standing no watches but take regular turn at dog
duty. Finn stands no dog duty but stands watches. So we are all mixed up.

Pace the forepeak in the moon-light + it is really exhilarating. Jack comes
in now + then—gets fed cake + candy. Trying to make a house dog of him.
He certainly is huge slothing around inside here.

March 23rd

170 miles out from Dunedin at noon to-day + a little over 2000 to go to
Easter Island. Cloudy, + light south breeze, fairly calm sea + rather chilly.
Finished Joe's story to-day. Movies to-night not good—. A long trip + tomor-
row ought to be half way to Easter Island.

March 29th 1935 *Aboard* Ruppert

All well, ship's plowing through rather heavy swells with a 4 Beaufort wind
from the north west.[15] Quite warm + damp needing only sheets to sleep under.
Been tremendously busy printing photographs + we now have many hundreds.

Read Russell Owen's *South of the Sun* + contrary to the opinion of others
find it very interesting + more personal + intimate than any other articles or
books about polar expedition. What occurred in the first expedition I believe
occurred in the second. For Owen writes of the vulgarity + profanity, the
deadly monotony, conflicting personalities, atrophied mentalities, the harsh-
ness + beauty of Antarctica + all the thousand + one things we went through
+ saw. He asks one night in July whether all polar expeditions were similar to
the one [of which] he was a member. At least he hoped not. I can say yes.
The same sordidness, general lowering of moral + intellectual standards, the
same difficult task of molding temperaments of many different hues into a
whole + directing that whole to a profitable end rather than turning upon
itself + devouring itself in a spasm of hate, envy + jealousy.

Life here on board is very comfortable + soothing. The return voyage
lacks the interest + kick the outward voyage had, but that is only natural.
Now our work is done, our future uncertain. We are still together, those who
have already spent too much time together + probably know entirely too much
about each other to really enjoy one another. This afternoon while watering
the dogs I went to draw water from the galley. Carbone, Cox, Pelter + several

---

15. The Beaufort Scale is a system for measuring the force of a wind specifically on land or sea;
a 4 rating indicates a moderate wind of 13–18 miles per hour.

others were talking + boasting with their customary vigor + profanity + I was almost sick. I felt like throwing a red hot brick at all of them, their materialism, greediness, their lack of all that makes a person attractive: manners, dignity + poise. Their ways are that of brazen beasts with due apologies to the beasts. But this nauseating line of thought + talk is most repelling, + I longed to quit them, the expedition + all this for good, to be alone + with someone who cares for something other than themselves, women, sex + egotistical effrontery.

Took a sun bath this A.M. The usual gentle rise + fall of the forepeak as the bow rides the length of the long swells is very peaceful + comforting. Even in the cabin the motion is like being safely in a cradle. To compensate for antagonistic personalities there is this fact of being on shipboard + living the life the sea calls for. The slow rolling + the slower pitching of the *Ruppert* is perhaps _____[?] with all the unpleasantness aboard. When I dreamed at L.A. strange as it may seem it was of the very thing of riding the long swells to the crest, down the passing slide into the trough, up, up the oncoming swell, a hesitating pause + down again. I stand no watches.

April 6th

Enroute from Easter Island to Panama. Arrived at Easter Island night before last, the evening of the 4th. Left *Bear* about 50 miles before arriving + steamed ahead of her. Approached on the side across from the settlement. The natives built fire for us. The morning of the 5th *Bear* came along side + we unloaded 50 tons coal from No. 1 and about 40 from after well deck port side. Finished after supper. I was on dog duty + did not handle coal. No natives till this morning when the *Bear* came along side again to take on the coal from the starboard side. Two boatfull of natives loaded as usual with images, stone + wood + odds + ends. They wanted terrific prices for them but more with an idea of philanthropy than hard business. We gave them their price, a shirt for an image—shirt + pants for a good one, etc. etc. Got them to sing several songs for us + later Poulter showed them one reel of a movie. They were dumbstruck + gazed open-mouthed at the spectacle, particularly at the women. They were all as cheerful as usual. They made a better impression on me than the first visit. I noticed particularly their excellent teeth + fine physique. It was amusing to barter with them. They enjoyed it + were in no hurry to close a deal. They asked exorbitant prices + laughed when you said no-no. It was a day of days for them, last boat until ten or eleven months from now. Mellon's boat it seems was here last week + several expeditions have been here during the past year. We recognized many of our former friends + they remembered us. One had fancied my glasses + he offered several nice images for them but unfortunately I did not want to part with them. Now for the last stop.

April 7th 1935

Waska whelped this morning, giving birth to 6 pups. They are Jack's pups, all with the characteristic markings of Jack—I feel like a father of sextuplets—

April 15th 1935, 50 miles S.W. Galapagos Islands

Last night Dick + I gave a talk on our trip, both of us making very poor talks. Boring, inarticulate + non-humorous. To-night Eastern Party gave talk.

Weather has been depressingly warm + humid the past week—I have been reading a good deal + now am working on *Life of Woodrow Wilson* by Ray Stannard Baker.[16] It's an unusual + personal insight into the life + letters of Wilson, extremely well done, interesting + complete. What strikes me particularly at this time is the reliance Wilson placed on friendship. Wilson's life was for ideals + doctrines. That was his career. Politics was secondary. Yet his emotional side, as hard as he tried to suppress it, blossomed into idealistic friendships which seemed now + then to become hopelessly wrecked, causing immense grief to Wilson. The faith of friends + their love + kindness seemed to almost overwhelm him at times. Yet when a friend proved unfaithful, nothing caused him greater misery. Just at the present time, such is the state I am in + have been in for the past year + a half. Those on the expedition I believed to be real friends are in reality mere passing acquaintances, none of whom will go out of their way one step to do a favor. Now I have adapted the same attitude, instead of trying to cultivate friendships. I discourage them, for they never turned turn out to be sincere + real—hence causing me misery, the intensity of which no one will ever know. In fact the only unhappiness of my life has been the superficiality of friendships which I believed to be deep + lasting. If I can only bring myself around to believing wholeheartedly that I have no friends then I shall be happier—many times happier + my sentiments + energies can be directed to some thing other than fretting about mistaken confidences + trusts. There is nothing more elating nor more ecstatic than a real friend + nothing worse than to have friends false. I have no friends here + the sooner I get it through my head the better. It is not self-pity but merely a statement of fact, a fact which may be of great value later when analyzing

16. Ray Stannard Baker, *Woodrow Wilson: Life and Letters* (New York: Doubleday, 1927–1939).

the past two years + what occurred. How I long to be home, where I <u>know</u>, never doubt, have real confidence in knowing that no matter what I do or say Dearie will love me + I will love her. The knowledge of this is priceless. It is one of the few rocks upon which I live.

April 18th 1935, Galapagos Islands

Yesterday made landfall early in morning + scientific party went ashore on Albamora or Ishabella [Isabela] Island for penguins. Excursions largely (piscary). Thunder shower to-day, got wet. To-day went ashore in A.M. + Wade + Lindsey + Brown etc. went ashore for scientific work. Siple + Poulter stayed in motor sailer along with myself among others to fish. Poulter + Siple for penguins, of which they secured five. Fishing was grand. We caught close to a ton of fish, mostly black sea bass up to 25 lbs. per fish. It was a great day + I enjoyed it thoroughly. I caught I should say 30 to 40 lbs. fish myself. Was ashore for a full half hour but all to be seen was lava + eroded craters. Sea lions, turtles, penguins, iguanas + cats—a desolate island—but a swell day. Cleaned 40 fish to-night.

April 26th, Cristobal, P.C.

Arrived day after Easter, April 22nd, at Balboa. Docked that night + had one night ashore. The 23rd proceeded through canal, leaving 7 A.M. + making Colon by 3 P.M.[17] Hot + sweating—24 + 25 over at Coal Pier though at noon of yesterday moved over to Pier 1, not far from the center of the town. Lost Spot [a dog] through heat prostration. Spent most of time either aboard or ashore drinking beer which is wonderful here. We were given $5 in Balboa but of course that went the first night. I had three pounds from New Zealand, which brought me but $3.40 per pound.

Panama is just as we left it + so is Colon. The same stores, bars, women. Shipping seems to be bustling + boats pass through constantly. Pelter, Zuhn leaving here + Czegka coming aboard. Mrs. Byrd has gone home + R.E.B. here on board the ship; the heat is oppressive + I hope to goodness we get out of it soon. Scheduled to sail tomorrow 9 A.M. Hope so.

April 31st

Off Cape Maysai to-night, the S.E. end of Cuba. Passed Jamaica + Haiti this A.M. Left Colon 10 A.M. April 27th. Time goes very slowly, partly because

17. Colon is a seaport on the Atlantic side of the Panama Canal.

of the warm weather, more because of anticipation of getting home. It is tremendously exciting, the thought of seeing our friends + families. Have decided to take Jack + two of his pups. I can take care of them all right. Am rather distressed about what I am going to do. It worries me more than I say. I don't want to work + I do. I love leisure + the ecstasy of living at Shankhassick, yet it cannot be done without money + Dearie has none. So what!

May 4th

Every day since Easter Island clear + sunny. Not a bad day yet—now cruising at 6 or 7 knots. Admiral made a proposition to a group of us to go to some port within a reasonable distance. We found it possible to go to Nassau + so it was decided. But engine trouble the night of the 2nd + morning of the 3rd delayed us so it made it impossible. He was game to go but we in a written memo released him from his promise, for which he was grateful + to which he replied by a humorous proclamation—

Got sunburned + tanned to-day!

May 12th Quantico VA

Geursig Latham [the officer]
Latham Hotel, Virginia Beach VA
The Washington Festivities are over. We are lying alongside the dock at Quantico + we sail tomorrow A.M. Arrived here the evening of the 9th after spending 3 leisurely days coming up the Potomac. Went ashore at Piney Point, Md. the 8th + here for a bit the 9th. About 9 [on] Friday the 10th we all boarded the *Bear* except for 3 New Zealanders + steamed up to Washington. Marines took charge during our absence + Geursig Latham, the custom officer who boarded ship at Norfolk + who has been living in with me, acted as dog driver extraordinary + Melrose assisted him. We presented him with a testimonial.[18]

18. Cecil Melrose was a crewmember of the *Bear*. The Washington, D.C., ceremonies were held on May 10. As a naval crew disbands at the port from which they sail, final ceremonies were to be held in Boston on May 15 (Hill and Hill, *In Little America with Byrd*, 252–53). Only the *Bear* went to Washington. Days previously, the *Ruppert* and the *Bear* simultaneously entered Quantico, the Marine Corps Base near the mouth of the Potomac River. The ships were greeted by cheering crowds, a marine band, circling airplanes, and ships' whistles. As the *Ruppert* was too large to go up the Potomac River, all the men and Admiral Byrd's flag were transferred to the *Bear*. As the *Bear* headed up the river, the expedition was serenaded by bands and cheered by crowds all along the shore from Alexandria and Mount Vernon up to the Washington Navy Yard. The ceremonies in Washington began at 5 p.m. on May 10, when Admiral Byrd and his men descended the gangplank of the *Bear* to be greeted by President Roosevelt (ibid., 252–57).

At Washington Navy Yard we were greeted by the Navy band, various admirals, officials + committees. Received a 13 gun volley for R.E.B, 19 for [Secretary of the Navy] Swanson, 17 for Asst. Sec. Navy + finally 21 for Roosevelt. We filed off led by R.E.B. + shook hands with the President. Following that we got into official cars + drove to the Willard Hotel. We were not allowed to see our families till then. I looked in vain for a familiar face in the crowd + finally in extreme dejection went aft to get a closer look + suddenly the Morses appeared waving + shrieking wildly.[19] I got the only thrill of the past three days when I saw them. Mrs. Brown's gram + Gertrude came up too, which was very touching. I loved them for it. Had a brief hour with Browns + Morses + then had to leave for banquet in the Willard given us by National Geographic Society. Dr. Grosvenor presided. At 8:30 went to Constitution Hall, where we filed onto the platform + thereon sat.[20] Everyone was feeling pretty well + Dick insisted upon talking the whole time. Afterwards drank + went to bed. Saturday Morses came around + we toured Washington stopping briefly at the Capitol, Lincoln Memorial + Arlington. It is a beautiful, beautiful city, a city of marble + beautiful streets. Came to *Ruppert* at Quantico in P.M. + showed them around. They seemed to enjoy it. Sunday, to-day, took care [of] dogs + spent time idly. Sail tomorrow.[21]

19. Paine's young nieces, Jananne and Content, wore white dresses and stood just right of President Roosevelt's podium at the Washington harbor ceremony. They are clearly apparent in the films of that event, searching for their uncle. However, at that time, Paine did not see them.

20. The men marched onto the platform to the stirring music of the Marine Band and were followed by the admiral and the society dignitaries. As this was happening, a huge American flag was lowered from the ceiling, and the audience stood in respect and appreciation for the Second Expedition men. After society president Grosvenor welcomed the admiral, Admiral Byrd summarized the twenty-two-point scientific program and the expedition accomplishments. Among them were that Antarctica was found not to be two continents but only one; 450,000 square miles were covered by plane or surface parties and, of that, 290,000 square miles were previously unknown; and at sea, another 160,000 square miles were explored and added to the map. The surface triangulations were carried out in the Edsel Ford Mountains by Paul Siple, in the Alexandra and Rockefeller mountains by Dr. Ervin Bramhall of the tractor party, and in the Queen Maud Mountains by Quin Blackburn, leader, and Stuart Paine, navigator. In the Queen Maud Mountains was also found, near latitude 86° south, the southernmost life ever discovered. In a special comment, the admiral lauded the dogmen and stated, "Dogs still are the infantry of the polar regions." Afterward, the executive officer, Lieutenant Commander George Noville, now named the second in command, presented each man of the expedition to the audience. The proceedings of the entire ceremony were broadcast over sixty-seven CBS stations and twenty NBC stations to the United States, Canada, and Central America ("The Society Honors Byrd Antarctic Expedition," 107–15; Byrd, *Discovery*, 385–93).

21. The men would sail again on May 13 back to Boston for the final ceremonies to be held on May 15. This time, the *Ruppert*, which had been anchored off of Governor's Island, would enter the harbor and be met with booming cannon, sirens, circling planes, and the cheers of "hundreds of thousands of people." For the second time, guns fired thirteen times in salute and then the

On May 10, 1935, Admiral Byrd, with his men waiting behind him, descends from the *Bear of Oakland* at Washington Harbor to a personal welcome from President Franklin D. Roosevelt. Also receiving the expedition members were the secretary of the navy, a congressional committee, and the governor of Virginia. (BPRCAP, Papers of Admiral Richard E. Byrd, image 7855-1)

President Roosevelt greeted and shook the hand of every member of the Second Expedition. (Paine Antarctic Collection)

The great day is over. It did not seem so great. I got twice as great a kick out of seeing the Browns + Morses as pumping the paw of Roosevelt—I long to get to Shankhassick + home + Dearie + Phil——

---

admiral, the Massachusetts governor, and the mayor were paraded through the streets from Boston Harbor to Boston Common in the first of many celebrations given in their honor (Hill and Hill, *In Little America with Byrd*, 252–57).

On May 10, 1935, at Constitution Hall in Washington, D.C., the National Geographic Society welcomed Admiral Byrd and the men of the Second Antarctic Expedition, shown sitting on the stage. Admiral Byrd presented the expedition's accomplishments to the audience of four thousand members of the National Geographic Society as well as to millions of radio listeners in the United States, Canada, and South America. Each man was introduced to the assembly by Lieutenant Commander George O. Noville, the executive officer of the expedition. (Willard Culver/National Geographic Image Collection)

The last page of Paine's personal diary, May 12, 1935. (Paine Antarctic Collection)

Afterword

S tuart Paine was twenty-two years old when he joined the Second Antarctic Expedition. By the time he was twenty-five, he had experienced challenge and intensity that might have sufficed for a lifetime. No one else on the expedition was in the field, exposed to the weather and dependent on his own mental and physical resources, longer than Paine.

Leading the first American surface party to within 207 statute miles of the South Pole, Paine and two others skied over 1,410 miles in eighty-eight days to explore and map part of the southernmost continent for the first time. Paine credited their success to those who had forged the way ahead—Amundsen, Scott and Shackleton: "The forerunners of ourselves, the men who showed us how. And it is to them the explorer in the Antarctic today owes an incalculable gratitude. Just as Byrd pioneered the way in polar flying, so did these men blaze the trail in surface travel."[1]

Whatever the Geological Party learned from their predecessors, they achieved their hard-won goal at 87° South. If the Geological Party had continued, they would have been the first Americans and only the third land party after the Amundsen and Scott Expeditions to set foot on the Pole. With little or no external mechanical assistance, these three parties achieved their farthest point under their own power. And, as Admiral Byrd wished, the Geological Party focussed not on accomplishing a "first"—but on forwarding science and on exploration of new lands.

1. Paine, "Ascent of Mt. Weaver," 18.

The Second Expedition was over. After his pioneering achievement in the Antarctic, Paine, the explorer, viewed everyday life in the United States from a fresh viewpoint.

> But how does it seem to be back? That is the question which is put to me.
>
> I like the warmth of a temperate climate, the soothing love of friends and family, the comforts which man has long endeavored to surround himself and to make his life easy and conservative. I like the regularity of everyday living, the routine into which all of us fall when we settle down to try to make good. I like the diversified amusements, the autumn walk beneath the burnished colors of oak trees, the opportunity to indulge in urban festivities, the smell and caress of green grass and waving branches . . .
>
> But still there is something lacking. There are the crowds, the talk, the chatter which all does not accomplish anything. The life is full of trifles and petty cares and more petty woes. We are bound up in the intricacies for which we have worked so hard that we cannot see the goal to happiness through the maze of laborious detail. Our joy seems to be the accumulation of many things, and once gained they lose their gift of satisfying the craving from which we seemed to have suffered. There is a constant succession of little woes, little quarrels, little irritations which sum up to a grave dissatisfaction with life as a whole. . . .
>
> My answer is— . . . Let me go back to . . . where I contributed to the knowledge of the earth, where my work is of lasting value to science, to the only place where I enjoyed complete happiness and inward contentment. Even should I never do this, still I shall live, happy to a certain extent that I had done my part, as small as it was, to further the knowledge of mankind.[2]

After his return, the complexities of daily living commanded his energies. The postexpedition excitement included command performances at ceremonies and parades, and Paine, with Jack and his team, were cheered by three hundred thousand people at the June 1935 Shriners Parade in New York. Paine went back to New England and worked in advertising and sales at Wolcott and Murray, an advertising consultant, and then at Johns-Manville Corporation, manufacturer of building materials, until he became involved with the New England Council in regional economic development.

Jack, Paine's lead dog, earned acclaim that followed him back to North

2. Paine, personal essay, 1935 (1936?), Paine Antarctic Collection.

Paine and Jack on the farm in New Hampshire. (Paine Antarctic Collection)

America. After the expedition, both Paine and Admiral Byrd wrote glowing tributes to Jack, establishing him among the greatest of all sledging dogs. As Byrd explained, "The work and plodding of the faithful husky dogs made the trip possible. Paine had a leader, a large black and white Labrador, whose performance was equivalent to that of another man. Never before has a major field party gone south with a dog breaking the trail. Jack the Giant Killer also picked the way through many crevassed areas and followed a compass course without swerving."[3] In 1936, G. P. Putnam published Paine's book, *The Long Whip: The Story of a Great Husky,* which was about Jack. Before Admiral Byrd could finish the foreword, G. P. Putnam hurried the book to press in order to have books in time for the Christmas season. Jack died at age ten and was buried on the Paine farm; his death was covered by a long article distributed by the Associated Press; in it, Admiral Byrd lauded the lead dog as "the only hero of the Expedition."

Over the years, Paine kept in touch with Admiral Byrd and several of the expedition members from the first and second expeditions; he instigated a ceremonial dinner to celebrate Byrd's fiftieth birthday and occasionally got together with Ed Moody to drive dog teams in the New England winters. Upon Byrd's request, Paine collaborated in the staffing and logistics planning for the Third Expedition, which started in 1939. According to Paine family lore, Admiral Byrd asked Paine to go on a later Antarctic Expedition, but by then Paine had a family and he declined. Eventually, the ice on which Little America, Admiral Byrd's original base of operations was located, broke off the Ross Ice Shelf and floated out to sea.

The United States entered World War II, and Paine was called to serve. In 1941, Paine, as a naval ensign, reported to active duty and was sent to Panama, and later to Peru, as an intelligence and liaison officer. From 1943, as a lieutenant, he served as the U.S. naval port officer for London, as harbormaster for Cherbourg, France, and also served in the port offices of New York and San Francisco. By 1944, he was a lieutenant commander. In 1945, he became the port director for Hokkaido, Japan, and then in March 1946, Paine, as a full commander, was released from active duty. In addition to the Special Congressional Medal for service on the Second Byrd Expedition, Paine received letters of commendation and service medals for his exemplary service in South America and in England.

At the end of the war, Stuart Paine married Margaret Sharrah, moved to California, and became a businessman, entrepreneur, and family man. Their

---

3. Byrd, "Exploring the Ice Age in Antarctica," 458–59.

The members of the Second Expedition received a Special Congressional Medal in recognition of their accomplishments. The back of the medal shows ships, antennas, a plane, and a dog team and reads: "Presented to the officers and men of the Second Byrd Antarctic Expedition to express the very high admiration in which the Congress and the American people hold their heroic and undaunted accomplishments for science unequaled in the history of polar exploration." (Paine Antarctic Collection)

children, two girls and a boy, all learned his Antarctic story and deeply integrated his values and reverence for the natural world. In the years that followed, his work and his family were his focus until 1960 when Stuart Paine died from cancer at the age of fifty.

Before he left on the southern journey, Paine wrote in his diary, "There is no feeling of hesitation on undertaking this trip. Just as I felt absolutely sure + certain about my decision to go with the expedition, so do I feel about this trip." Paine met the ice unreservedly—and, as his diaries reveal, the white continent provided him a measure of living far beyond the cruelties and discomforts it exacted.

After leaving the Antarctic, life went on for Stuart Paine. But his yearning for the omnipotent purity that had enriched his spirit never abated. And the scars on his face from frostbite never went away.

Appendix 1

The Men of the Second Byrd Antarctic Expedition

The Ice Party of the Second Antarctic Expedition is listed below; other expedition members mentioned in the diaries are also included. Eighteen of the men on this expedition, including personnel based in the U.S. mainland, on ships, and on the ice, had been with Byrd on his previous polar expeditions. Several of the men were enlisted men or officers in the U.S. Navy.

The members of the Second Expedition had primary responsibilities but also were assigned to other duties as needed. Information for the list below came primarily from Byrd's final roster as published in his account of the expedition, *Discovery.* Additional information regarding the men's responsibilities and nicknames has been derived from additional sources as available.

ICE PARTY

Clarence. A. Abele, Jr.	*Assistant fuel engineer*
Clay Bailey	*Chief radio operator*
Richard B. Black	*Surveyor*
Quin A. Blackburn	*Geologist; member of the First Antarctic Expedition*
W. H. Bowlin	*Second pilot and airplane mechanic*
Vernon Boyd	*Machinist*
Dr. Ervin H. Bramhall	*Physicist and meteorologist*
Admiral Richard E. Byrd (R.E.B.)	*Leader of the Second Expedition*
Alphonse Carbone	*Cook*
Leroy Clark	*Supply officer and postmaster*
Stevenson Corey	*Supply officer*

Edger F. Cox	*Dairyman*
Francis (Duke) S. Dane	*Dog driver*
E. J. (Pete) Demas	*Chief tractor driver; member of three other Byrd expeditions*
Frederick G. Dustin (Dusty)	*Machinist*
John N. Dyer	*Chief radio engineer*
Albert Eilefsen	*Dog driver*
Bernard Fleming	*Machinist; member of previous expedition*
George Grimminger	*Meteorologist*
William C. Haines	*Meteorologist; member of the First Expedition*
John Herrmann	*Photographer*
Joe Hill, Jr.	*Tractor driver*
Guy Hutcheson	*Radio engineer*
Captain Alan Innes-Taylor	*Head of dog department and chief of trail operations; member of First Expedition*
Harold I. June	*Chief airplane pilot; member of the first and other previous expeditions*
Walter P. Lewisohn	*Radio operator*
Alton A. Lindsey	*Biologist*
William S. McCormick	*Autogiro pilot*
Linwood T. Miller	*Sailmaker*
E. L. (Ed) Moody	*Dog driver*
Dr. Charles G. Morgan	*Chief geologist*
Charles J. V. Murphy	*Communications officer; member of First Expedition*
George O. Noville	*Executive officer and fuel engineer; member of two other Byrd expeditions*
David Paige	*Artist*
Stuart D. L. Paine	*Dog driver*
Joe A. Pelter	*Aerial photographer and mapmaker*
Dr. Earl B. Perkins	*Biologist*
Carl O. Petersen	*Radioman, movie cameraman; member of the First Expedition*
Dr. Louis H. Potaka, M.D.	*Physician*
Dr. Thomas C. Poulter	*Chief scientist and second in command*
Kennett L. Rawson	*Navigator and assistant to Executive Officer Noville; member of 1925 Greenland Expedition*
Finn Ronne	*Dog driver*
Richard S. Russell, Jr.	*Dog driver; member of the 1925 Greenland Expedition*

Isaac (Ike) Schlossback — *Airplane pilot*

Paul A. Siple — *Biologist, dog driver; member of the First Expedition*

Bernard W. Skinner — *Tractor driver*

Ralph W. Smith (Smitty) — *Airplane pilot*

Olin D. Stancliff (Stan) — *Dog driver and tractor driver*

J. M. Sterrett — *Biologist and physician assistant*

Paul Swan — *Airplane pilot*

Ivor Tinglof — *Carpenter*

John H. Von der Wall — *Tractor driver*

F. Alton Wade — *Dog driver*

Amory H. (Bud) Waite, Jr. — *Radio operator*

H. R. Young (Hal, Bob) — *Machinist*

Dr. Arthur A. Zuhn — *Physicist and meteorologist*

ADDITIONAL EXPEDITION PERSONNEL[1]

Victor Czegka — *Supply manager, on primary duty U.S.A.; member of the First Expedition*

Thomas C. T. Buckley (Buck) — *(Resigned February 1934)*

Byron Gay — "

S. D. Pierce — "

G. O. Shirey, M.D. — "

SELECTED OFFICERS AND CREW, *JACOB RUPPERT*, FIRST TRIP TO BAY OF WHALES, 1933

Commodore Hj. Fr. Gjertsen — *Ice pilot and captain for numerous Antarctic expeditions*

W. F. Verleger — *Master*

H. Bayne — *First officer*

W. K. Queen — *Chief engineer*

L. W. Cox — *Crewman*

A. B. (Hump) Creagh — *Crewman*

H. L. Fleming — "

J. D. Healey — "

L. H. (Sails) Kennedy — "

F. C. (Fred) Voight — "

---

1. Men mentioned in Paine's account are included.

SELECTED OFFICERS AND CREW, *BEAR OF OAKLAND*,
FIRST TRIP TO BAY OF WHALES, 1933

Lieutenant (J. G.) R. A. J. English, U.S.N.	*Master*
B. Johansen	*Sailing master and ice pilot*
W. B. Highet, M.D.	*Physician*

SELECTED OFFICERS AND CREW, *JACOB RUPPERT*,
SECOND TRIP TO BAY OF WHALES, 1935

Commodore Hj. Fr. Gjertsen	
S. D. Rose	*Master*
J. J. Muir	*First officer*
Joseph D. Healey	*Third officer*

SELECTED OFFICERS AND CREW, *BEAR OF OAKLAND*,
SECOND TRIP TO BAY OF WHALES, 1935

Lieutenant (J. G.) R. A. J. English, U.S.N.	*Master*
B. Johansen	*Sailing master and acting first officer*
W. B. Highet, M.D.	*Physician*
Cecil Melrose	*Crewman*
F. C. (Fred) Voight	"

"What Is It Like to Travel at Seventy-five below Zero?"
by Dr. Thomas C. Poulter

In the following essay, Dr. Poulter, who led the trip to rescue Admiral Byrd, carefully described what happens to lungs in cold weather. This document is an appendix to his work justifying the trip (Thomas C. Poulter, *The Winter Night Trip to Advance Base, Byrd Antarctic Expedition II 1933–1935*, 85–86).

What Is It Like to Travel at Seventy-five below Zero?

If a person goes from a warm room out into a temperature of 75 below zero, he has to breathe very shallow for a time until his lungs become accustomed to the cold air. One of the greatest dangers in traveling at those low temperatures is freezing the lungs.

Pups will play around in temperatures of minus seventy-five and enjoy themselves but you cannot use a dog team on the trail at more than about sixty below. If they are pulling a heavy load and breathing heavily, they will freeze their lungs. If this starts to happen the dog will start to breathe faster since a part of the lungs are ineffective. He will increase his breathing rate and that causes it to freeze even faster.

If there is only one person with the dog team, there isn't much that the driver can do, particularly with the large dogs we had in the Antarctic with weights up to 140 pounds. Once a dog starts to breathe fast, he will be dead in a matter of minutes. If, however, there are two or more people so that the dog can be immediately held down and his nose placed in a person's clothing so that it will breathe warm air, it will quickly recover. My dog team averaged 125 pounds and one person cannot safely put them down and get its nose into warm air.

After a trip in these low temperatures for a day or more, our lungs would be painful for several days and we took every precaution so as not to come down with pneumonia.

As the temperature goes from a minus sixty to a minus seventy-five, one notices a marked difference in his breathing. At a minus seventy-five and with a high moisture content of the breath, the carbon dioxide changes to a solid. This causes a large change of volume and produces a distinct hissing noise as you breathe.

It is necessary to wear a face mask of some kind and it is impossible to wear glasses. We used face masks made of sheepskin and contoured to fit our faces with small openings for the eyes and a triangular opening for the nose and mouth. Over this triangular opening we placed a piece of windproof cloth in the form of a large nose to protect the nose and lips from the direct wind.

Ice would then collect on the inside surface of this windshield so that it would be completely filled within forty-five minutes. One could easily tell when the ice had completely filled it as your breath would start coming out of the eye openings. By tapping this windshield with something, the ice would be broken loose and could be removed and you were good for another forty-five minutes. This shield also serves another very important purpose. As the exhausted breath passes this a layer of moisture collects on its surface. Then when you inhale this moisture is frozen. The heat of fusion that had to be given up by the moisture as it freezes goes into the air being inhaled thereby causing it to be warmed appreciably. The ice that is thus formed is at a temperature of 32° above zero which is more than 100° warmer than the incoming air. Thus the ice warms the air up some more.

This heat exchanger effect is the primary purpose for putting wolverine around the face on the hood of a parka. It provides even more surface on which water can collect.

Wolverine is also used because the collected ice brushes out of it much more easily that it does out of most furs.

Skiing on a hard snow surface at 75° below zero is about like trying to ski on sand. At the warmer temperatures there is enough melting to cause the skiis to slide easily over the snow but this does not occur at 75° below.

One cannot use metal sled runners at these low temperatures. They pull very much harder than wooden runners do. If a person is han [?] hauling it is advisable, if you have the means of melting a little snow to turn the sled over and pour a little water on the sled runners. This will very quickly freeze becoming a layer of ice on the runner and will make it pull much easier. This thin layer of ice will last most of the day.

Being aware of all this as I was, would have been reason enough to dissuade me from making the trip to Advance Base had I not been certain in my mind that Admiral Byrd was in trouble.

Appendix 3

Fall Southern Trip Meteorological and Navigating Records

The following three diary pages are the complete meteorological record from Paine's Fall Southern Trip. On each day, he recorded the minimum and maximum readings in the morning and evening and made additional comments in the far right column. March weather was blustery, cold, and unpredictable as the winter was closing in. The fourth page depicts a diary page labeled "Navigating Record of Fall Sledge Trip, March 1–30, 1934. These are the notes from the first half of the journey. (Paine Antarctic Collection)

Fall southern Trip
metrological record

	Bar. Reading	Temp. max.	min.	Remarks
March 2 A.M.	28.98	-10	-25	N.E wind cloudy. no diff
P.M	28.73	-2	-4	E. 70 m cloudy diff
11 3. A.M	28.44	+8	-2	S.E. 3 m. cloudy snow
P.M	28.79	-2	-5	cleared toward noon S.E 3 m
4 A.M	28.63	-12	-18	Partly cloudy
P.M	28.98	+8	+6	Blizzard 5 miles. snow
5 A.M	29.18	+22	+13	Blizzard. 10 m clear at 12:15 snow 6". W to S.E wind
P.M	29.12	+30	+8	no wind. cloudy
6 A.M	29.10	+4	+2	no wind. clear in A.M. cloudy P.M.
P.M	28.97	-26	-18	Beautiful sunset
7 A.M	29.10	-28	-36	cold clear. S.W wind 1 mile
P.M	29.01	+12	-2	Blizzard. N wind 40 mile Cloudy
8. A.M	28.87	+20	+18	Snow. N wind 25. cloudy
P.M	28.73	+16	+14	
9. A.M	28.78	+8	+6	Cloudy colder. S.E. P.m.
P.M	28.80	-12	-4	Cloudy S.E wind 12 m.
10 A.M	28.81	-12	-22	Clear in noon
P.M	29.01	-10	-8	Cloudy
11. A.M	29.19	-8	-22	Clear. very high cirrus cloud
P.M	29.08	-6	-12	cloudy in south
12 A.M	28.86	+2	-22	Cloudy. south 6
P.M	28.69	-10	-18	Partly cloudy. S. 4 mile

		Bar.	Temp. max.	min.	Remarks
March 13	A m	28.61	-18	-24	Visibility good N.W
	P m	28.87	-22	-12	" " cloudy *average temp to date - 6.2*
14	A m	28.89	-33	-47	Clear N.W 4 miles *vis sugar*
	P m	29.01	-12	-32	Cloudy N. wind
15	A m	28.92	-14½	-20½	Blizzard
	P m	28.80	-9	-13	N wind 10 m. clearing
16	A m	28.82	-13	-21	S.E wind. Cloudy
	P m	28.98	-10	-30	" " 4 m. Partly Cloudy
17	A m	29.11	-30	-54	Clear No wind
	P m	29.27	-28	-43	Clear No wind
18	A m	29.30	-18	-45	Cloudy E wind 6 m.
	P m	29.29	-16	-35	Clear. Clouds to N.
19	A m	29.28	-18	-36	Cloudy S E 12
	P m	29.18	-10	-14	Broken clouds snow N 15
20	A m	29.02	-12	-14	Blizzard 20 m.
	P m	29.00	-9	-13	Cleared for 3 hrs. N wind
21	A m	28.78	-19	-28	N wind 15 shift. Clear
	P m	28.76	-25	-32	NW 15 m. Cloudy Snow air.
22	A m	28.78	-46	-52	Clear & cold Hazy to N
	P m	28.70	-44	51	Vis good
23	A m	28.92	-54	-60	Clear & cold. S.E 1 m.
	P m	29.01	-49	-50	Partly Cloudy S E 2

March 24.	A.m	28.90	−15	−30	Cloudy wind 35m
	P.m.	28·91	−12	−28	Drift.
25	A.m.	29.34	−42	−48	Clear SW 10m
	P.m.	Bar to 14.17	−28	−32½	Clouds breaking n.w.
26.	A.m.	—	−13	−24	NE 10 increasing,
	P.m.	—	0	−4	Blizzard. Snow
27.	A.m.	—	−38	−43	Clear & N.W. wind K?
	P.m	—	−40	−33	Vis ¾ mile & increased
28.	9.m.	—	−27	−34	Clear no wind
	P.m.	—	−13	−18	Clear
29.	A.m	—	−41	−52	Clear. N.E 6 m.
	P.m.	—	−20	−18	Clear E P.m.
30	A.m.	—	−10	−25	E wind 40 m. Heavy drift. clear. 30 mi/hr

Navigating Record of Fall Sledge trip.
March, 1st March 30th/1934.

	Mag. Course.	True Course.	Variation	Distance
March 1	93	180	107 E	10.3
2	92	180	108 E	14.7
3	72	180	106 E	19.5
4	71	180	109 F	5.6
5	at 60 mile depot			
6	35.1	100	109 E	5.0
	70	180	110 E	11.5
7	68	180	112 E	5.1
8	Camp Sled			
9	66	180	114 E	18.0
	56	170	114 E	5.4
10	56	170	114 E	5.6 100M
11	66	128	114 F	7.0 100 at 7 P.0
12	61	175	114 E	6.6 125
13	20	135	115 E	20.0
14	70	135	115 E	5.0 150
	35	150	115 E	5.0

Appendix 4

Barrier Bull *Selections*

The *Barrier Bull* was the only internal magazine compiled within Little America during the expedition. The following selections from each of the eight issues are representative of the environment in which the men lived during the long winter night spent in buildings and tunnels under the snow. The tension and conflict among the men over Admiral Byrd's fate are undercurrents that emerge.

The *Little America Times,* by August Howard, was reporting on the expedition from the United States; using versions of expedition events carefully crafted by Charlie Murphy and others working with him or Admiral Byrd, the newsletter was intended for the interested public and published amusing and dramatic expedition events. Created as onboard diversions for the men on the *Jacob Ruppert* on its way to Antarctica, the other two and mutually rivaling newsletters mentioned by Paine (the *Snowshovel* and the *Stormy Petrel*) were extremely short-lived.

As a pleasurable distraction during the winter night, Paine initiated the *Barrier Bull.* Editors Paine and Dick Russell, in addition to publishing their own pieces, solicited articles from the other fifty-three members of the ice party at Little America. The column by Charlie Murphy both supplied information regarding his communications with Admiral Byrd, who was alone at Advance Base, and made wry comments about the internal dynamics of Little America. More straightforward were the editorials about the summer field plans, the conditions, problems, and possible solutions within the men's society, and a strong commentary on leadership and the issue of whether to rescue Admiral Byrd before spring. In addition, selected articles written by Paine vividly describe the world of the radiomen, the dog drivers, the solution to dental problems, and the story of an ill-conceived winter field trip across the Bay of Whales. (Paine Antarctic Collection)

THE BARRIER BULL
Published Every Week in Little America, Antarctica
EDITORS

| Stuart D. Paine | Richard S. Russell |
| Publisher—Leroy Clark | Staff Photographer—Joe Pelter |

• • •

THE BARRIER BULL
May 19, 1934 Issue #1

CHARLES J. V. MURPHY

1.

Admiral Byrd has been invited to reopen the World's Fair at the Chicago May 26th. If communication is successful, he will transmit from Bolling Advance Weather Base a message that will set off a remarkable fireworks display reading "Greetings from Little America"—even if Admiral Byrd doesn't spell it quite that way. The affair will be part of the regular Saturday broadcast. The Little America studio will receive its cue from New York and, shortly after going on the air, will attempt the switch-over to Advance Base. Preliminary arrangements have already been made. General Dawes and the Governor of Illinois will speak at Chicago.

2.

Thursday, May 17, Admiral Byrd began his second month of darkness at Bolling Advance Weather Base. He reported all's well. He now has two weekly radio contacts with KFZ. A message from President Roosevelt was read to him. The message said, "I hope all goes well with you and all the other members of the Expedition. We are thinking of all of you and hoping that the drifts are not too high, nor winds too strong, for an occasional promenade in the dark. Good luck." As a matter of record, Admiral Byrd happened to report earlier in the week that he still manages to walk an hour or so every day, as a rule during the late afternoon. He reported temperatures fluctuating between 20° and 50° below zero.

EDITORIALS
In the world of journalism the launching of a magazine, large or small as

the case may be, is undoubtedly an anxious moment for its editors. Will it be accepted by the public? Will it be profitable? Will it be accepted by the critics, if the periodical happens to be a literary one? Will it gain sufficient circulation to insure a good price for its paid advertising? Last but not least, will it bring approbation or condemnation upon the aspiring editors?

Such are the questions to be faced by those who foster the usually dizzy career of a magazine in this gullible world. The percentage of failure for newly founded magazines is disastrously high. This, it seems, is the only thing that keeps the total number of monthlies, weeklies, dailies within reasonable limits.

Fortunately here the editors do not have to deal with the problems ordinarily faced by the great majority of editors. We have a public to be sure, but quite small enough to be classed not as a public but as a circle of friends. We know exactly how many readers we have—at least we optimistically claim to—and we likewise know, quite positive, the limits of our circulation. We have no desire for profit. In fact, had we the desire, we could scarcely gratify it. And Mirabile Dictu, we have no critics, the critical critics, we mean, who never say anything nice about anything, but who vie with each other to heap undignified insults upon those so unfortunate as to consider themselves successful. That we do not worry about paid advertisements goes without saying. Of course, we will accept such advertising, but we do not solicit it. Rates will be found elsewhere.

As to what the editors may gain or lose from their undertaking, the answer is very simple. Amusement. We launch the BARRIER BULL purely for fun. It is to be both serious and humorous. Contributions of any sort are cordially invited and earnestly desired. We publish each number once a week or oftener if our material and imagination permits.

Owing to our limited publishing facilities, we are only bringing out six or eight copies at each issue. One will be placed in each of the living quarters and one in the library. There may be several for the editors. Leroy Clark has been kind enough to type these issues. To him the Barrier Bull gives thanks.

The BARRIER BULL is noncontroversial, nonpolitical and nonsensical. Such is the protege of the Editors.

RATES FOR ADVERTISING

One 2-ounce bar of chocolate for each insertion of not over five lines.

Additional lines at the rate of one suit of underwear washed per line. Underwear must be those of the editors.

NOTICE:—If any of those who are taking the various courses of study wish to have their lecture notes typewritten in the smooth so that they can be permanently bound, I will be glad to do this typewriting as I have spare time, if the notes are passed to me.

Clark

SKOOKUM [edited]

Back home baths are more or less of an everyday affair for most of us. It consists of completely disrobing, and either stepping into a closet sort of gadget where the water drips down onto you from a spigot, or gingerly leaping into a rectangular tub filled with water . . .

Now what is so compellingly attractive about taking a bath? Is it the warm, tingling feeling you get when you first dip into the water? This does not seem to be the answer, for people say they love to take cold baths, showers or plunges into lakes before breakfast. No one really likes to do this though he swears by all that is holy and sacred that he would rather do it than eat, drink or love. Perhaps it is something that we are taught in childhood; that cleanliness is next to godliness, and as we all like to get close to the Saviour as we can without being godly, we submit to cleanliness.

The cold tub enthusiasts enlist no support from me. No matter how virtuous or energetic I feel I cannot enjoy a cold bath. Scent it with the most exotic of rare bath salts and I still would shudder before testing it with my big toe. The very thought even now causes my big toe to contract.

However, the hot water advocates have my entire sympathy. I like to be hot as well as anyone else. To feel the warm caressing flow of hot water as well as anyone else, not too hot but just right, you know, slipping over my shoulders and down the middle of my back, is truly a sublime experience. Those who take hot baths are no fools, unlike the cold tubbers. They are not imbued with such stuff as cleanliness, virtue and godliness. Their motive is honest and sincere. Just to feel the warm water running down onto my tummy or to be in a rectangular tubful of hot water and sort of float, suspended as it were, with only my head resting on the sloping end of the tub, is nearer being godlike than scrubbing yourself with a vulgar scrubbing brush in a cold shower. I have floated thus many times. So have you. . . . Baths in the Antarctic are of a hybrid variety. They are both hot and cold. A paradox perhaps. The pleasant with the bad. Sitting on the edge of a cold iron tub in a temperature sometimes above freezing is the unpleasant. Your feet are in hot water. That's the pleasant. But that is all you can get in—your feet. You positively cannot get all pleasant. But to get all unpleasant is the easiest thing in the Antarctic. I'm not defending those who do not bathe here. But knowing how I feel about cold baths, cold even though the water is hot, you certainly will not condemn me when I say to you who have not taken a bath since you have been here, "I don't blame you."

THE BARRIER BULL
May 26, 1934 Issue #2

CHARLES J.V. MURPHY

Two radio schedules were held this week with Admiral Byrd at the Advance Base. The Leader reported a minimum temperature of 72.5 below zero, Sunday May 20th. This surpasses the record low of 72.4 on the first Expedition. This surpasses the record thus far on the Antarctic Continent is 76 below zero. The coldest period is yet to come, and in the opinion of Mr. Haines, Admiral Byrd will probably not only surpass this latter temperature but may even record temperature as low as 80 or 90 below. He likewise reported a terrific temperature swing early in the week that followed in the wake of strong northerly winds. Here at Little America the temperature rose 79 degrees in a period of 42 hours. On the Ross Barrier the swing was 82 degrees over approximately the same period. Admiral Byrd reported "all's well." He has been obliged to change his ventilation system in his shack to get a freer circulation of air. Tuesday's blizzard apparently carried away his antenna and he was obliged to make a hurried splice. In the course of a conversation with the Base he reported that he was losing weight, having already taken two notches in his belt, which might be due, he explained, to the increased exercise, or "my bum cooking." He is much interested in affairs at Little America, and asked to be informed if we were having any trouble with the diet.

ANTARCTIC DAZE

The farflung Antarctic vista was enthralling in its beauty—the southern trail wandered ahead dotted with its little flags. This was a panorama for the artist—for David Paige—a perfect #6 moon pressing a #11 sly—with a #9 aurora stabbing the universe. The small patch of mist ahead seemed to be changing shape—fascinated I gazed until with sudden and astonishing clarity it assumed human form. My blood chilled—I wanted to run—my knees however seemed to have developed universal joints—they bent in all directions. The figure approached—my terror increased until a courteous voice inquired, "Are you from Little America?" This was too much— I gasped—I choked and finally blurted out "Who—who—are you?"

"Captain Scott—sir—at your service."[1]

"What can I do for your Captain—could I show you Little America." (I'm like that—I don't like to get rough with ghosts.)

---

1. The reference is to Robert Falcon Scott, the English explorer, whose party had perished on its return trip from the South Pole; his last diary entry was on March 29, 1912.

We turned back—

"No—no Captain this is not a picket fence—those are trail flags marking the southern trail *** yes I know you used to navigate *** but this is so much easier. We entered the tunnel—"This is quarters for Captain Innes-Taylor and myself—come in. We try to make ourselves comfortable—Captain will you please turn off the loud speaker while I answer the telephone *** some one wants to know what time we have motion pictures tonight *** oh yes we have pictures three times a week *** excuse me Captain *** thank you Bailey *** m—m—m—no *** no—no nothing serious, just a radio from New Zealand, a couple of our men found something where it wasn't lost and the authorities have locked them up for safekeeping *** No—the huge structure in the corner is Capt. Taylor's desk ** *** ha—ha—no—no that isn't the kitchen that is my desk *** underneath those cups, plates and condensed milk tins you can see my typewriter. Would you like to see the old mess hall—fine—the men are just being called. Here we are—that isn't a football scrimmage—merely calling Paige for breakfast **** this is the Norwegian House *** no the roof isn't falling in—I think they built it like that. Did you know we had cows? You must see those *** This is the cowbarn **** why did we bring cows *** well you see, we had some kittens *** be careful don't step on them—Cox loves those kittens *** No that is not a permanent wave machine—that is a mechanical milker—Down here we have the mess hall—we keep it locked so the cook can't get out *** this is Carbone our chef *** will you have a doughnut *** yes we keep those shelves full of canned food **** sometimes the boys get hungry and is very handy **** yes, we leave out a quarter of beef every night so the boys can cut a steak and grill it *** it's all very convenient and homelike. Across here is the Science Building and Library **** would you like to hear a good phonograph record **** you didn't like that ** no—no popular music in here—horrors no—this is the science building you know—that is, this side is—the other side is the artist's studio. Shall we go to the Ad building **** be careful this shaft is deep **** this is the sick bay *** no, those are not surgical instruments—those are the tools Dr. Potaka uses in his daily carpenter work on June's bunk **** I'm afraid you must excuse me now Captain—I must go and rehearse with the quartette for next Saturday's broadcast *** out this way **** those figures in parkas and trail gear? *** no that isn't a trail party, that a searching party from the L.A. Country Club **** no—no one has been lost **** they are looking for the alcohol cache **** be careful you don't stumble over that wire mooring hawser *** what did we bring that for *** well—you see *** Captain I must go—won't you come and see me again?"

Rex Noville

BEDTIME STORIES

Tonight children I am going to tell you a story about the meeting of two ships, and what I am going to tell you happened long, long ago.

One of the ships was named the "BEAR OF SOAKLAND" and it was built of wood. The other ship was named "DISTILLERY II," and it was built of steel.[2] From more than one thousand miles apart these two ships, in order to find each other, traveled as fast as they could. They met such a long way from land and such a long way from any other ship. Where they met there were tremendous pieces of ice floating upon the sea, there were huge fishes called whales swimming about in the water, and pretty little white birds flitted about the ships.

Very soon after the two ships met, you would have seen them being tied together side by side by great ropes. Then all the men worked as hard as hard could be. They rolled hundreds of barrels from DISTILLERY II and placed them upon BEAR OF SOAKLAND. It was not until every barrel and every bottle had been taken from one ship and put upon the other ship that the two ships separated, each to go its own way.

Children, you must be wondering what it was that was in all those barrels and in all those bottles.

The BEAR OF SOAKLAND had left more than one hundred strong men upon a great sheet of ice. This sheet of ice was floating upon the sea in some places, and in other places it rested upon the bottom of the sea.

All the men upon the ice were so brave that they were called heroes. It was their intention to battle against fierce things that were called the elements of nature. It promised to be a very even battle, for the heroes were going to give the elements of nature a sporting chance.

Each hero was very busy writing a book about himself as well as separate books about each of his fellow heroes. Every day, besides writing up his diary, each one wrote radio messages to be sent to all of his relatives and friends to let them know that he was well. Each one wrote newspaper articles and poetry daily and hours and hours were spent practicing signature writing.

Of course, you can see that there was lots and lots of writing to do.

2. The use of alcohol was a troublesome and sometimes crippling issue during the expedition. Poulter not only retrieved a cache of liquor waylaid by an aviator during the initial unloading of the ships but secretly dumped what he thought was the entire official supply of liquor. He then buried the five hundred empty bottles in the snow and burned the boxes. Men still desiring liquor either resorted to private supplies or drank the flavored extracts from the kitchen. Poulter then found and dumped thirteen quarts of vanilla extract. Another man found and dumped even more. Later it was found that numerous compasses were opened and the alcohol removed (Poulter, *Winter Night Trip*, 1–16).

There was plenty of paper to write upon, there were plenty of pens to write with, there was plenty of ink to put in the pens, but it was impossible to do any of the writing because the ink was frozen solid.

They had brought a great quantity of alcohol with them, and if they had put alcohol into the ink, the ink would not have become frozen. However, all the alcohol had become mislaid and though many of the heroes kept on searching for it they could not find it.

Now children, can anyone of you tell me what was in all those barrels and in all those bottles that were put upon the BEAR OF SOAKLAND? That is right, Georgie, those barrels and those bottles had alcohol in them, and it was needed by the heroes to stop their ink from freezing.

Hush! Wally and Charlie have fallen asleep, so Georgie do be a good little boy. I must turn your light off. It is 10 o'clock . . . So you must go to sleep.[3]

UNCLE PETER[4]

EDITORIALS [edited]

This expedition is a self-contained unit. It is composed of fifty five men at Little America, and one man at the Bolling Advance Base. Most of us here have precious little in common outside similar motives for being here, and certain experiences shared together. Every man has a definite job to perform, and certain responsibilities to uphold; first to the Expedition as a whole, its work and its program; secondly, to the other members of the Expedition, his companions with whom he shall live for the next ten months; thirdly, to himself, his name and his family.

I believe every man here feels his responsibilities to the Expedition and to himself. But the second—responsibility to the other men here—seems to be lacking in certain individuals. Carelessness is perhaps a bad quality in most of us. But when that carelessness on the part of one or two persons causes discomfort and hardship to the other men here, it becomes not a bad quality, but a black evil. That man is selfish beyond any standard of the civilized world. Even though things go wrong and we are put to some inconveniences,

---

3. The Little America generators were shut down and lights went out at 10 p.m. every night. The power would be brought up again in the early morning. All men were expected to rise by 7:30 a.m.

4. Dr. Louis Potaka, the doctor who would replace Dr. Shirey, left New Zealand with the *Discovery II* and transferred to the *Bear of Oakland,* which then proceeded to the Bay of Whales to drop him off (Byrd, *Discovery,* 104). Though Dr. Poulter had done a great deal to destroy the liquor supplies in the middle of February, it is implied by Dr. Potaka's story that significantly more liquor was obtained at the end of February when the *Bear* met the *Discovery II* to pick up Dr. Potaka. According to Poulter's account, continuing and severe liquor problems occurred during April and May.

5. According to several sources, these were the contents of Paine's bunk.

that fact should be no excuse for letting ourselves take advantage of other men simply because it is the easiest course of action. I have in mind carelessness in the use of the toilet and the mishandling of Victrola records in the library. I need not say more about the toilet.

The large records in the library belong in the albums provided for that purpose. If they are not put back after they are played, they are certain to be broken. Four have been broken in the last two weeks because of their being left out on top instead of being replaced in the albums. Continued carelessness in this matter means more broken records and that much less enjoyment for all of us. Can't we all stop, when we are inclined to be careless, and think of the other fellow? It will do more to make the Expedition a success than all the ballyhoo in the world.

❊ ❊ ❊

Are you walking around in a daze? Do you need fourteen hours sleep? Can you conquer your inferiority complex? What makes people laugh when you sit down? For answers to these questions apply to David Paige, address Bunk.

THE BARRIER BULL
June 2, 1934 Issue #3

CHARLES J. V. MURPHY

There was but one radio contact this week with Admiral Byrd, the usual Sunday schedule having been cancelled because of the special schedule in connection with the reopening of the World's Fair, May 26. Admiral Byrd is carefully guarding his fuel supply. Thursday's contact was in the main a review of spring plans. Admiral Byrd asked Dr. Poulter to present an outline of the programme drafted by the officers of the camp. This for the most part followed specifications laid down by the Leader. Admiral Byrd said he was pleased by the way in which the camp was pointing for spring operations. He made the following recommendations.

1. Owing to the difficulties of finding Advance Base, he recommended that a tractor, rather than an airplane, be sent to relieve him in the spring.

2. The first exploratory flight shall carry between the Edsel Ford Range and the Queen Maude Range. A base shall be put down in the vicinity of Grace McKinley Mountain.

3. He does not believe it feasible to attempt to navigate Thorne Glacier with a tractor. The plateau party should plan to make the ascent by dog team, and shape its plans accordingly.

4. Radio equipment is of the greatest importance, and must be made efficient. An expert radio operator should be dispatched with every field party.

5. "We must be absolutely certain that the expedition does not attempt more than it is humanly possible to accomplish."

Admiral Byrd reported that the warm spell holding at Little America pervaded the Barrier. Unfortunately, the failing gasoline supply in his generator made it impossible for him to broadcast the temperatures. Admiral Byrd cheerfully signed off—"so long"—and returned to his isolation.

WHIRL IS KING

One of the most baffling manifestations of Antarctic life is the ease with which it gives root to argument. To be sure, argument is one of the most ancient of human afflictions. Quite likely it had its origin in the pourparlers of elderly Neanderthals, huddled over a bed of glowing embers, with the day's work done and nothing else to occupy their minds. A warm fire does that to men. A pleasant glow coasts along toasted shins, rising up through the veins, stimulating the spleen. The ensuing mental activity is as varied as the nomenclature. It is called "gassing," "shooting the breeze," "picking the bones of contention"; it is almost never logical; being so much venom from contented rattlesnakes.

The Antarctic argument, or at any rate the Little America species, exists in all the finer grades of venom. There are the mild, gentlemanly dialectics of Doctors Perkins and Bramhall; the hair-splitting sophistries of Mr. Sterrett and Commander Schlossback; the Launcelot-like disputations of Mr. Lindsey; the pertinacious, unyielding empiricism of Ensign Rawson; the wandering anecdotal contentions of Messrs. Bailey and Pelter, and unusually mellow sample of which was permanently recorded by Mr. Dyer: the proletarian unrest whose massed contentions seek the sympathetic intervention of Mr. June; and, finally, the homicidal controversies in which Messrs. Fleming and Paige are usually to be found defending a crumbling bastion. This latter form of argument is especially peculiar to Little America. These two gentlemen are two against the Gods, anyway, and the particular controversies in which they engage, while very lively and full of fine clean fun, follow a certain monotonous pattern, with the former usually explaining why he did it, and the latter why he didn't do it.

It has been recalled that the leader, on the eve of his departure for Advance Base, solemnly assured us, with a frank and open countenance, that the winter night would be a period of tranquility and repose. Only the other day Commander Schlossback asked where this tranquility was, and wasn't it time we had an issue? It can't be that we are running short of that, too. There is far more reason to suspect that the supply officer is saving it for the trail parties in the spring. There's nothing like a good shot of tranquility to dispel the gloom of the winter night—just a ration per man per week, that's all. There is no reason why the Mercitan and Mapleine addicts should have all the tranquilly: not the trail parties, either.

It is the opinion of certain gentlemen in the camp, who have given deep thought to the matter, that a certain measure of tranquility can be achieved by directing arguments along more scientific lines. The present policy of "laissez-faire" is all but ruinous. There is not true argument here. What we have is only a conflict of unyielding assertions. Mr. Rawson, for example, coldly insisting that, contrary to the dead appearances of the ashes in Commander Noville's stove, the fire is still alive, is apt to find himself tangling with Capt. Innes-Taylor, who is heatedly discussing the failing of the pemmican formula. Under such conditions, no agreement is possible, and both men retire to their bunks with a feeling of frustration, and a pathetic opinion of his adversary's intelligence.

It has therefore been suggested that, in order to give the hair-splitters a real workout, that regular details be made according to the reserve of man-power in the camp; with one man assigned to deal with Pete Demas in the morning, instead of having everybody try to do it; another to act as "straight" man for Commander Schlossback's homeric epics; a third (he must be a man of great industry) to fabricate straw men for Rawson; a fourth to set up wind-mills for Lindsey's quixotic forays; and still another to provide Paige with mis-information from the highest authorities for incorporation into the theory of relativism. In this manner the major disputants of the camp will not only be properly accommodated; the rest of us can also go our way in ignorance and peace.

EDITORIALS

There are only five copies of the <u>BARRIER BULL</u> for general reading by the men of the Camp. One is placed in the Old Messhall, one in the Administration Building, one in the Radio Shack, one in the Library, and one in Dogheim.

It is only fair that these copies be left where they can [be] found by any-one desiring to read them. If they are taken the day they are issued, obviously someone is going to miss out. What becomes of the copies after they are issued is no concern of the editors. But it seems fair that each copy should be left out at least four days after the date of issue, and the copy in the Library should stay there permanently!

We ask your cooperation in this.

The field program for next year, as outlined at the present, is extensive and ambitious. The various projects must and will be concluded successfully only if there is the closest cooperation of all departments. We all have certain duties to perform and though some may feel theirs to be of little conse-quence, they all count in the final summing up. This expedition is known as a scientific one, the most completely equipped to have ever landed on the Antarctic continent. To be successful the results must be far-reaching and conclusive. We should bear this in mind and realize we are all working toward the same end—not personal recognition and glory.

This applies mainly to the members of the surface transport who will be on the trail next spring. Both the dog and tractor departments will be serving science. It may be difficult for a dog driver to console himself to transporting tractor equipment or vise versa, when he would like to be striking into the unknown only with his own needs. Since the time in the field will be limited and there is so much to be accomplished, equipment will have to be abandoned, many dogs, and perhaps even a tractor, sacrificed. This will detract little from the success, for the scientific results are the real goal.

It must be emphasized that only the closest cooperation on the part of all groups of surface transport will enable the expedition to successfully carry out its scientific program.

THE BARRIER BULL
June 9, 1934 Issue #4

CHARLES J. V. MURPHY

There were two radio contacts this week with Admiral Byrd at Bolling Advance Weather Base—June 2 and June 7. On the first schedule Admiral Byrd reported the following temperature records on the Barrier:

March 25–April 30				May [1]–May 31			
60 deg. or colder— 6 days				70 deg. or colder— 2 days			
50 "	"	13	"	60 "	"	3	"
40 "	"	7	"	50 "	"	6	"
30 "	"	7	"	40 "	"	7	"
20 "	"	2	"	30 "	"	2	"
10 "	"	10	"	20 "	"	3	"
0 "	"	1	"	10 "	"	4	"
				0 "	"	4	"

In the course of the first conversation, the writer read him the outline of the proposed preparations for the southern advance of the Geological and Plateau Party. This outline was based upon the plan drafted by Mr. June and Captain Innes-Taylor to fit the specifications laid down by Dr. Poulter. The plan in the main met with the Leader's approval. He was at first disinclined to accept the feasibility of sending tractors in advance of the dog teams, chiefly because of the danger of blind crevasses. However, Mr. June and Captain Innes-Taylor met his objections. Admiral Byrd advised, however, that Tractor No. 1—the through tractor—should halt at a reasonably safe distance north of the crevasses at the foot of the mountains, and await the arrival of the dog teams before proceeding. "Most operations in the unknown fail because of the taking of unnecessary chances," Admiral Byrd said.

The June 7 contact was brief. Admiral Byrd reported that the warm spell had broken the day before, and the temperature had fallen to 35 degrees below zero. He said "all's well."

EDITORIALS

Through the kindness of Dr. Poulter, THE BARRIER BULL has been given enough mimeograph sheets to enable everyone in camp to have at least four numbers. There seems to be a desire on the part of everyone here to have one of each issue. For this the editors feel complimented. But owing to the scarcity of this special paper, we can only print four. However, upon our return to the land of plenty of mimeograph paper, those numbers which were not printed for everyone can be mimeographed then, thereby permitting all to have a complete set. This the editors hope to do before the good ship JACOB RUPPERT reaches New York.

The men who are to take part in next year's field operations have been tentatively decided upon. Besides these men there are others who have been designated to take the place of any one of the fieldmen should a substitution be necessary or expedient. There has been considerable discussion of the choices as announced. Many feel hurt that they were not included. Others feel favoritism was shown. But it is hoped that the selection was based upon sound qualifications. What these qualifications are, I quote from Sir Douglas Mawson's "The Home of the Blizzard":—

> "Age, and with it the whole question of physical fitness, must ever receive primary regard. Yet these alone in no sense fit a man for polar work. The qualifications of mental ability, acquaintance with the work, and sound moral quality have to be borne essentially in mind."

The men designated to go on the trail next year were supposedly chosen because [they] fulfilled the above qualifications. What, then, of the men left behind?

Fifty five men were picked to stay on the ice because it was felt there were fifty five positions to fill. Every man had a part to play. Whether his job was in the science building, in the dog tunnels, or out shovelling snow, all were essential to the progress of the expedition. Whatever job we find ourselves assigned to now, it is to be remembered that your job is quite as important as the next fellow's whose work may be of an entirely different nature. It is true there may seem to be men here who are more important to the expedition than others. Those that are going on the trail seem to be doing more for the expedition than those who stay at home. But this is not necessarily true. There is absolutely essential work to be done here. The men who maintain the camp during the absence of the trailmen are doing a necessary though perhaps an unpleasant job.

Most everyone here wants to go on the trail. It is unfortunately impossible for all of them to do so. Those remaining are, of course, losing a great experience, but they are not failing in their work. If whatever they do next summer is done well, their work will materially contribute to the success of the expedition. They should feel that the importance of their function is not lessened because they are not going on the trail. The work here will always be of invaluable aid to the expedition as a whole.

ALL IN ONE BUNK
(Anon.)

2 pairs scissors, 2 pairs wristers, 3 pairs gloves, 1 steel clamp, 9 wet electric cells, 1 roll lamp wick, 1 glass of grease, 1 bottle Mistol, 1 bottle Worcestershire sauce, 1 box machine screws, 2 boxes Meta, 6 packs cards, 73 boxes matches, 1 oil can full of canvas mukluks, 6 pairs miscellaneous boots, 1 bag sennegrass, 3 rolls cotton cloth, 1 snowshoe, 8 flashlight batteries, 1 chisel, 1 pair crampons, 2 rolls plaster, 2 large jars cold cream, 3 spools thread, 1 box gum, 1 foreign soap box, 4 B batteries, 1 tube carron oil, 1 box kodak plates, 1 magneto, 1 box deodorant powder, 2 lenses, 1 large spool safety wire, 8 copies Physical Culture, 5 library books, 63 pictures of women posted on wall, 1 large box BAE I pictures, 1 package Telephone Bond, 21 rubber bands, 1 roll old photo film, 1 sheet brass 6x12 inches, 1 electric booster, 15 feet strung wire, 3 blankets, 2 flashlights, 8 pairs holey socks, 1 pair fur liners, 8 feet Ford duraluminum, 1 tube ski wax, 1 electric magnetic light, 1 pair pliers, 1 bottle mouth wash, 2 envelopes 18x27 inches, 1 pair stocking boards, 1 piece bread and butter, 3 tubes toothpaste, 2 blotter pads, 1 book "Suspicious Characters," 750 sheets typewriter paper, 1 oily rag, 1 spark plug, 1 set picket wrenches, 2 carburetor valves, 1 large Stillson wrench, 1 electric plug, 1 Yale key, 1 carpenter's square, 1 pce "Gerlock" packing, 2 electric switches, 1 sneaker.[5]

---

5. According to several sources, these were the contents of Paine's bunk.

THE BARRIER BULL
June 16, 1934 Issue #5

CHARLES J. V. MURPHY

On the basis of recent conversation with Admiral Byrd at Advance Base, it would now appear that his isolation will be celebrated less as a triumph of man over nature than as a glorification of the tin can. This humble metal structure, simple enough in conception and form, is apparently saving the Leader from starvation. Never a cook he has lately confessed he has resigned all hope of ever becoming one. It will be recalled that two weeks ago he reported he had already taken up two notches in his belt, and more slack was appearing. That was at the height of the flapjack crisis, when the full resources of our benefactor, General Foods, Inc., were being frantically mobilized to devise a satisfactory method of keeping his flapjacks from sticking to the griddle. How effective this research was Admiral Byrd has never disclosed; but it may be significant that in the course of Thursday's schedule he referred in awed accents to the merit of canned food, announcing that he no longer was losing weight.

EDITORIALS

Five weeks ago, with the inauguration of the classes in Little America, we wished the sponsors the best of success, and suggested that everyone concentrate in one or two courses. It now seems that radio and navigation are the two courses chosen by the majority, and this is only right. Several new courses have been added so that now twenty three hours each week are consumed by the "university." The attendance at the classes has become haphazard, even among the instructors themselves. The classes have been moved from the messhall to the Science building thereby greatly hindering the work of the scientists.

We have only two months before the outside work begins once more, and in that time everything must be prepared for next year's field activities. This work, which should now be half finished, has hardly been begun. Soon after the sun returns the work of digging out the planes will commence. The trail men will be busy exercising dogs and learning to ski. The scientific department will be wanting to do the work they could not do this winter on account of the classes held in their building, and the sick list will be as large as usual.

For the program in the field to be successful, the various parties must leave Little America with the personnel well rested. The start will probably be made in mid-October. So little is known about the weather here that it might be possible to make even an earlier start. This will mean that everyone in camp will have to do his share of the work. This fall there were far too many attempts made to avoid work by offering trivial excuses.

Everyone is now well rested from the work of "digging in." The "university" has had a fair test and it has been shown that work and extra study cannot be successfully combined in this camp. All classes, save radio and navigation, should be abandoned. An intensive program should be outlined involving every man in camp, and this carried out until the spring program has been launched. It is easy to see from past performance that if this is not done now there will be a tremendous rush at the last moment with the trail men and the aviation department bearing the brunt of the work.

The Stench of putrid garbage stunk up Dogheim, residence of George Noville and Alan Innes-Taylor, one day last week. A large garbage pail chuck full of Carbone's refuse was intentionally left there. For two days and two nights it remained, filled even the outer tunnel with its sour odor. Taylor and Noville could not agree on who was to take it out. It is said Charles J. V. Murphy placed it there. When accused of it he merely grins. There are rumors of a trial.

THE BARRIER BULL
June 23, 1934 Issue #6

CHARLES J. V. MURPHY

It now appears that Admiral Byrd will return to Little America much earlier than was expected. In the course of Thursday's radio schedule he ordered Dr. Poulter to examine the possibility of sending a tractor out to the Advance Base as soon as there is sufficient light to enable the party to make the 123 mile journey without undue hazards and suffering on the part of the crew. The principal reasons persuading him to return are the straightened financial condition of the expedition and his desire to get field operations underway as rapidly as possible. He remarked, in the course of the schedule, that if the present weather continues it may be possible to start the field parties at a much earlier date than has heretofore been considered practicable.

Naturally no date has yet been fixed for the start of the tractor party, nor have the details of the journey been decided upon. Dr. Poulter plans to make a test journey in the tractor at the end of the week, and very likely the results of this test trip will have a large effect upon the planning of the journey. When informed of this trial trip, Admiral Byrd immediately suggested that Dr. Poulter and the crew make a determined effort, if it were possible, to pick up the trail flags in the darkness. It is also expected that the trip to the Advance Base will serve the function originally planned—that is, carry out some 3000 pounds of dog pemmican for the use of the plateau and geological parties. Indeed, even a greater load may be carried for the benefit of the southern party. It is Dr. Poulter's belief that the journey to the Advance Base will be attempted sometime in August when the twilight will be sufficiently prolonged to give the tractor crew some benefit.

Admiral Byrd was advised of the projected trial journey across the bay ice by the eastern party under Mr. Siple. The plan met with his approval, but he suggested that the party remain within the Bay of Whales to avoid danger of being carried out to sea by breaking ice.

The Leader had a narrow escape from carbon monoxide poisoning on Sunday, June 17th. Fumes from the small gasoline generator set powering his radio penetrated his cabin and made him feel, as he expressed it, "quite rocky." This generator is mounted on a shelf in one of his tunnels. Feeling ill, he cut short the June 17th schedule without explanation, and in the course of Thursday's schedule revealed why. He reported no after effects and said all was well.

The following are the final results of the BARRIER BULL questionnaire. After each question are listed the first and second choice:—

Who has the greatest affection for dogs?   Potaka; Moody.
Who is the greatest lover?   Noville; Siple.
 "   "   "   expedition clown?   Murphy; Dane.
 "   "   "   worst radio man?   White; Corey; Dane.
 "   "   "   dogman?   Herrmann; Taylor.
 "   "   "   scientist?   Wade; Rawson.
 "   "   "   tractorman?   Morgan; Swan.
 "   "   "   airplane pilot?   McCormick; Bowlin.
 "   "   "   greatest bullthrower?   Murphy; Carbone.
 "   "   "   your favorite cow?   Southern Girl; Iceberg.
 "   "   "   dog?   Don; Pinook.

Who do you think most representative of BAE II?   Hump; Morgan.
Who is the most likely to end in a penitentiary?   Fleming; Dyer.
Who knows the most about women?   June; Lindsey.
Who is the boss in L.A.?   Paige; Byrd.
Who is the most intelligent?   Poulter; Perkins.
Who is the most helpful?   Paige; Rawson

What do you expect to do on returning to
  civilization?   Drink; drink.
What do you miss most?   Food; elevators.
Who is the worst skiier?   Ronne; Cox.
Who expresses himself most fluently?   Bailey; Carbone.
If L.A. adopted human sacrifice,
  who would be the first sacrificed?   Noville; Grimminger.
Who is the greatest sit-by-the-fire?   Taylor; Miller.

Who is the neatest?   Albert; Young.
 "   "   "   sloppiest?   Ike; White.
 "   "   "   handsomest?   Hutch; Corey.
 "   "   "   most polite?   Perkins; Bramhall.
 "   "   "   biggest grouch?   Taylor; Smith.

Who has the best set of whiskers?   Dane; Miller.
Who is the best dressed?   Corey; Lewisohn.

Worst?	Rawson; Wade.
Who bathes most frequently?	Fleming; Stancliff.
Who has the greatest appetite?	Grimminger; Dane.
Who is the champion bunk director?	Noville; Paige.
Who is the greatest wire puller?	Clark; Swan.
" " " most popular professor?	Rawson; Perkins.
" " " best parachute jumper?	Fleming.
Worst?	Skinner.
" " " most temperamental?	Lewisohn; Taylor.
" " " most likely to succeed?	Paige; Haines.
" " " camp goat?	Young; Dustin.
Who has the rosiest cheeks?	Albert; Hill.
Who has the best chance to succeed in marriage?	McCormick; Bowlin.
Who is the most athletic?	Demas; Abele.
Who is the camp sport?	Zuhn; Bramhall.

EDITORIALS

Of all the disloyal and niggardly acts, stealing is probably the worst. This is particularly so on an expedition where the very existence of the expedition is dependent upon the quantity of goods brought with it, and the conservation of those goods. Should some of these goods be misplaced, lost or stolen, and if those lost are trail goods, without which next year's field plans will be incapable of fulfillment, then it is a serious and damaging fact. Just this has happened here.

Someone, or ones, have broken into boxes in the food and clothing caches and removed eight pairs of heavy woolen socks, four pairs of mittens, two heavy grey shirts, a quantity of innersoles and thirty pounds of chocolate. All these items are trail items. They have been deliberately taken without the consent of Corey.

On an American naval vessel, theft is provided for by a general court-martial, and sentence to a penitentiary, besides dishonorable discharge from the service. But the conditions on a naval ship and our condition here is quite different from the point of value of the goods taken. Something lost on a ship can be replaced in a short time. Here it is quite impossible. And though the objects taken are themselves not worth a great deal in money value, they are immensely valuable from the point of worth to the expedition. The theft of expedition goods, vital to the success of the expedition, is the most traitorous deed that can be done. Such deeds tend to make us look with suspicion upon the other fellow. You will not trust me, and I will not trust you. If such an atmosphere is created, an atmosphere of hostility and suspicion, God help the expedition.

It is time to stop and think.

The Aviation Department wishes to make a request. All five gallon tins which come from the galley, or other sources, are needed for the laying of gasoline depots next year. It is absolutely essential that these be saved if these depots are to be laid.

In all about two hundred will be needed. And the tops are quite as necessary as the tins themselves. Therefore, please do not take the empty tins. They are needed by the aviation gang.

SKOOKUM

Having a tooth out is ordinarily an affair to be thoroughly considered from many angles. You are losing an integral portion of your body, and once lost it cannot be put back again. It is quite impossible to change our mind afterwards and say, "Oh, I guess I was wrong. Stick it back, Doc. I think I'll keep it, if you don't mind." You can't do that.

Then there is something sentimental about losing a tooth. It signifies the beginning of your physical disintegration—if you are losing your first tooth. The more you have out, the more depressed you become about your declining powers. Still no one give you the right kind of sympathy. They usually laugh when you state "I've had a tooth out."

That is what they did to me. I had to lose a tooth because it is not possible to repair a broken tooth in the Antarctic. So after dinner I breezed down to consult Dr. Potaka about it. "I haven't had dinner yet, but if you will sit here I shall be back in fifteen minutes," he said.

I sat down while he went out. A minute later he dashed back and said, "You sit here, in the light. I have five minutes before second mess."

I thought he might look at it, poke it, inquire whether it hurt, etc. but he did not. He merely grunted and told me to open my mouth. "Wider," he exclaimed, grabbing my jaws with his hands and lifting his knee. Seizing a "hoosis," he jabbed my gums, injecting cocaine. "Did I get the right tooth?" he asked. I assured him I thought so, though I could not be sure because now I could not feel anything there anyway.

"A little wider, please," he said, turning me around so as to get a better footing. I attempted to explain that I really could not do much better. "Hold it, please," he said, lifting his knee again. I tried to see what he was going to do. I still had hopes of his asking me some question, perhaps comment on the weather, or tell me a funny story. But no. He threw one arm around my neck, picked up a pair of forceps with the other, grinned, and pulled the tooth out. I did not have time to even sigh or say, "Begone, lovely tooth, you have served me well." I had only time to be amazed.

"Here," he said, triumphantly thrusting the tooth into my hand. "I've got to eat." And he dashed off. Only myself, the tooth and George Grimminger remained. Since then I have tried to re-enact the scene in my mind, putting in the sentiment which should have been there when the act took place. But it's no use. Dr. Potaka took the tooth, and with it all my sentiments about having a tooth out.

I nominate for oblivion, Dr. Potaka, for deliberately destroying so tender an emotion.

THE BARRIER BULL
June 30, 1934 Issue #7

EXTRA——EXTRA——EXTRA
EASTERN PARTY RETURNS FROM WEST [edited]

The Eastern Party, under the leadership of Paul Siple, boy scout, returned yesterday to the base. They have been out since last Tuesday. One man, Alton Wade, geologist, had to be towed in on the sled by his companions. His face swollen grotesquely from frost bite, one eye completely closed, Wade is in the worst shape. Dr Potaka immediately gave him first aid on his return here, and stated he had never seen a worse case in all his medical practice. That his companions escaped as serous injury from the cold is a singular freak of good fortune. However, Corey and Stancliff, the other two members of the party, both show frostbitten cheeks and blistered hands.

Leaving Little America at eleven thirty, Tuesday, the twenty sixth of June, the Eastern Party, under the leadership of Paul Siple, set out to the westward to observe whatever life there may be living in the Antarctic at this time, to determine, if possible, the currents of the waters under the floating ice, discover, if possible, how far out open water lay. In addition they hoped to take net hauls through the ice. With him were Olin Stancliff, Stevenson Corey and F. Alton Wade. They used no dogs, preferring to manhaul their supplies to their camp on the west side of the Bay of Whales. When they left they were lugging 650 lbs. of trail gear on a dog trailer sled, and an airplane sled loaded with 400 lbs. of additional gear was picked up at the foot of Ver-Sur-Mer inlet. It had been hauled there the day before.

With the two sleds in tow, they struck off across the frozen bay. The surface was of snow and quite hard, Stancliff said. Half way across they decided to relay their loads, as the four men found it difficult to haul the two sleds at once. Leaving one sled, they made for West Cape, their camp site, with the other. It was four and a half miles out . . . [There they camped the night.]

For three miles they footed it along the rolling, cracked surface of the bay to West Cape. To the left of them the steep face of the barrier loomed high and massive. At eleven that night they reached West Cape and headed north out into the Ross Sea. In the distance a dark cloud indicated open water. How far it was they had no way of telling. The wind was almost at their backs, and though the thermometer registered minus 42, they did not suffer.

A half mile from the cape the black cloud changed into a jagged wall of ice. It was an iceberg caught by the sea ice and held prisoner. Corey states they almost walked into it before they realized what it was. Skirting the berg, they turned eastward and followed the rim around until they could once again go north. Now the going became more uncertain. They crossed numerous cracks showing water in them, pot holes from which water seeped up through. Just off the eastern end of the iceberg the ice was smashed, crumbled and broken. There were pressure ridges as high as twenty five feet in places, over which the men had to cross. For a while they followed the trough of one of these pressure ridges. Siple thought that the pressure was caused by the moveable sea ice being forced against the more or less stationary mass of the iceberg.

Farther on the going became worse. The ice appeared as though the Gods had tossed countless tons of ice blocks, the size of small boulders, into this one spot. The sled which they were pulling capsized repeatedly. The camera slipped off, among other things, dislodging the cartridge. That destroyed any chance of taking photographs. They finally reached a point where further progress with the sled was impossible so they abandoned it, and made a dash to more pressure evident in the distance.

Stumbling, sometimes crawling, they approached the pressure. The full moon made it stand out dark and strange and exciting. Scrambling up its side, they looked beyond and saw the silvery reflection of the moon in the black waters of the Ross Sea. Someone shouted, "La Mer, La Mer." It was echoed by shouts from the other three men.

From where they stood the ice sloped to the water like the sand of a beach; high where they stood, and low where it merged with the water. Siple turned and made a short run on skiis to the westward; Wade to the Eastward, in the hopes of sighting some seals on the edge of the ice. Stancliff and Corey remained where they were, their teeth chattering in the frigid wind, their eyes gazing at the dancing beauty of the full moon in the water. At one o'clock Wade and Siple returned and they started back.

Retracing their way over the broken ice, they picked up their sled and made for the eastern end of the iceberg and West Cape. The wind blew ten miles an hour from the southwest, making it agony to face it. Then after time they stopped to adjust their harnesses, cover up some exposed portion of their faces, and to inspect each other for frost-bites. For lunch they stopped in the lee of the iceberg. Here they munched a biscuit and a small bar of chocolate. The full moon shone with its full radiance against the walls of the berg, and upon the huddled figures of the four men. The temperature hovered around minus fifty.

Back along the trail they had marked out by flags, they trod. At six o'clock they reached camp and warmth and hot food. But now Wade's face and hands began to show evidence of freezing. Ten minutes after they got in, Siple said, Wade's face began to swell. A half hour later his left eye was completely closed. He felt weak and exhausted. He ate nothing then, nor did he eat until he arrived back at the base. Siple rubbed his frozen parts with camphorated alcohol, but the best remedy seems to be warmth and rest. They all turned in.

Six o'clock next morning, the twenty ninth, Siple, Stancliff and Corey emerged from their sleeping bags cold, tired and hungry. Stancliff communicated by radio with the base, and he said he was so excited about getting his first message he could hardly write it down.

After breakfast, Corey and Siple went up on top of the barrier to set a precipitation meter and returned in an hour and a half. Picking up Wade, sleeping bag and all, they strapped him upon the airplane sled and left for the base. The three, Siple, Corey and Stancliff, hauled Wade as far as the pressure at the foot of Ver-sur-Mer Inlet. There they gave in to Wade's protests and permitted him to walk the rest of the way to the base.

At eleven yesterday morning, the Eastern Party walked into Little America. Wade's face was swollen beyond recognition. Pelter insisted upon taking a picture of him, as the contour of his face more nearly fitted the title of "The Shadow" than the blond, handsome youth he was before he left. Wade modestly waved him aside.

It is interesting to record that they saw dog tracks on the bay ice. No doubt these were made by the for-long lost Toby, who returned unexpectedly several days ago after a week's absence.

The BARRIER BULL welcomes the Eastern Party back. We feel justified in saying they can take it.

CHARLES J.V. MURPHY

1.

If everything goes according to schedule, the tractor journey that will lift Admiral Byrd's isolation will commence from Little America during the full moon period of July 23rd to July 29th. Weather conditions, of course, will determine the starting time. In the course of Thursday's radio schedule, Admiral Byrd dictated a message to the Second-in-command covering the tractor operations. He is reluctant to expose any man in this camp to the hazards of such a journey unless all possible precautions for their safety are taken. The full moon period late in July is the most propitious time to undertake the journey. During this period the moon will be full in the south at midnight, and the light of the returning sun will be at its maximum at noon, and the party will have the benefit of conditions approaching twilight. The successful trial journey of Tractor No. 1 Monday night encouraged both Admiral Byrd and Dr. Poulter in the conviction that the journey is entirely feasible.

Quite likely two men will be stationed at Bolling Advance Base until the start of the spring operations to continue Admiral Byrd's meteorological and auroral records, and also to observe an important meteor shower early in August. A second observatory cooperating simultaneously with the station at Little America will greatly enhance the value of the meteor record, Dr. Poulter said. The intention now is to dispatch two tractors to Advance Base, one acting as reserve for the other. Tractor No. 3 is to be ready and stand by at Little America to proceed to the relief of the party in case of emergency.

2.

Siple's winter party is now camping on the Bay of Whales at the foot of the south ridge of Floyd Bennett's Harbor. Siple reported by radio Friday morning that they had investigated local conditions and found open water one mile out to sea. Wade's face is badly frostbitten.

On Tuesday night your correspondent, who was skiing with a number of other hardy explorers to the Bay of Whales, encountered Commander Schlossback and Vernon Boyd returning from a ski trip to the base of the winter party. Things were apparently in an appalling condition. According to Commander Schlossback, the indomitable manhaulers had all but collapsed the first day out. They had abandoned one sledge two miles this side of camp, and when the visitors had arrived the four men were vainly trying to start a stove and all but the leader had surrendered to fate. The opinion around camp is that it was a gross breach of etiquette to call upon this party. It was like breaking in upon a bride and groom upon their wedding night. They should have been left alone with their joys.

Carl Peterson, industrious editor of the NEWS, sat one day last week recording news dispatches coming in from San Francisco. Suddenly his eyes lit up. "Admiral Richard E. Byrd narrowly escaped carbon monoxide poisoning . . ."

"Holy smokes!" he exclaimed, "I wonder whether anyone knows anything about this." He rushed off to inform others in the camp. Carl was a little upset. Wagging his tousled head of golden hair, he said, "One hundred million people know what's going on here before I do." And he went back to listen for more news about Little America.

EDITORIALS

The Byrd Antarctic Expedition No. 2 is known the world over as the best equipped expedition to have ever set foot upon the Antarctic continent. Most of us realize this and are well satisfied with the share of the equipment we are allotted. It is quite evident that some are not. The continual crabbing and stealing demonstrates this. Last Sunday Mme. Schurmann Heink paid Admiral Byrd and the members of this expedition a most glorious tribute. Some grasped the full meaning of her words, others merely laughed. Her thoughts were typical of those harbored by thousands of people at home. Daily little instances indicate that very few of us are worthy of such praise.

There is one group here deserving of much praise, who live in no comfort, have the same food day after day, and who are always willing to work until they fall in their tracks. Then an unfriendly whip makes them struggle to their feet again with no chance to run for the messhall and a warm cup of coffee.

We expect to do a great deal in the field this spring with the help of the dogs; in fact the success of the operations depends entirely on them, which means their health must be watched closely.

Contrary to opinion, the slightest cut on a dog almost always becomes infected down here. Then the healing is a very slow process, especially on a dog who must remain in the cold. We have in Little America fourteen buildings for fifty-five men, and in all these there is not the slightest space set aside for sick dogs. It has become necessary for a dog driver to give up his bunk so a sick dog may have a warm place to be treated. One can easily see that the dog is appreciative of what has been done to help him.

When you break or lose your ski bindings, instead of taking the bindings from the pair standing next to yours, you will see Finn Ronne or Albert. They will gladly repair or replace your own faulty piece. It is hardly fair to take somebody else's.

Editors

Strange as fiction was the condition of Jack's tail. Jack is a big black lead dog. His large dark eyes moved swiftly, perplexingly. Something was wrong. He could not move his tail. Only by grasping it with his teeth could he make it move. When he chased it, it wouldn't be chased. It remained straight and stiff. "It's frozen," exclaimed wide-eyed Edward Moody. "Thaw it out," exclaimed enthusiastic Duke Dane. "Cut it off," bawled Alan Innes-Taylor. Jack was placed upon the library table, and Dr. Potaka pretended to play mouse with his ear. Chop—Jack lay on one side of the axe, the tail on the other.

THE USE OF WORDS [edited]

Kipling made use of this title in a series of essays discussing the value of words in human expression. He would have found more than enough uses, misuses and abuses of words in Little America to provide subject matter for several volumes.

Seriously, many of us here have apparently lost our sense of balance in the use of words to express ourselves. The speech and topics of conversation we hear all day would be considered amazing, and to some degree disgusting, anywhere else in the world.

For the individual words themselves, some are indeed a bastard breed of vocal sounds and do not have a place in Kipling's text. Webster would say that they are not in good use in decent society. That, possibly lets us out, so to speak. And, after all, the objection is merely in the words themselves. We may, for the time, overlook the misuse of otherwise accepted words as simply an expression of ignorance or thoughtlessness.

The abuse of words and phrases constitutes the real evil to which any group is subject. And this [is] particularly so in an isolated group such as this where the subject matter for conversation is limited and we abuse the gift of human expression for petty criticism, inconsequential trivialities, gossip, sarcasm and venomous insinuations.

Never was the old saying that "Silence is Golden" proven quite so clearly as it has here. Certainly many talk too much, and, having nothing to say, indulge in spreading rumors or attempting to promote their own distorted impressions. It is peculiar to some persons, usually school boys but occasionally others who have ostensibly reached manhood (or at least claim that status by reason of their years), to amuse themselves by making faces and uttering sounds which are sometimes defined in the dictionary.

Mentality expresses itself in words usually, and it is ordinarily a good policy to think about what we say, or it will be the consensus of opinion that there is nothing in the mind of the speaker to think with.

Charles Gill Morgan

SKOOKUM

You know, there is something mysterious, almost supernatural, about radio, electricity, wireless telephony and other things electrical. It seems that the impossible is done when you can step before a small round disc dangling from a stand and speak into it, knowing as you speak that then thousand miles away there are persons listening to you and hearing you. Sometimes they do not, of course, but that does not decrease the wonder of it. It only increases your admiration for those busy-bodies who wander apparently quite unconcerned amongst the countless switches, tubes, transformers, wires and other strange paraphernalia. And they seem to understand it all. They confidently plug tubes in here, pull a switch there, connect two wires, and the place does not blow up. Looking at the switch board I am tempted— oh how much I am tempted—to pull them all just to see what would happen. Waite tells me nothing would happen, but he will not let me do it. So I do not believe him. Something would happen I am sure. I may sneak in there sometime when all the radio experts are asleep, or eating, or playing with the dogs, and deliberately close all the switches just to satisfy the awful craving.

Bailey was fortunately snoring in his bunk when I went in. Waite was official host. Murphy was thumping the typewriter with determined vigor. Hutch was putting something together in the machine shop and Dyer was fooling with a crystal oven. The scene is set.

"What's that?" I said turning to Waite.

"Oh, that's a connector which leads through the transformer to the grid leak."

I looked at him, but he seemed to be quite serious, so I guess it was true. Pointing to a series of open boxes set on their side and holding all sorts of wires, square chunks of metal, tubes, etc., I asked what they were.

"Receivers, my good man," explained Amory.

"But why so many?" I asked.

"To receive many wave lengths, and also to receive many programs all at once." I said that one ought to be enough at one time, but he did not say anything further, so I guess that was true.

Turning to the switchboard, I peered under a switch to read what was written on the label. Crystal Oven. "What's that?" I asked.

"Here, I'll show you," said Dyer, and he pointed out a square silvery box lying on the table. I stared at it. I had envisaged a large ornate rectangular object, sparkling, brilliant, exotic, perhaps like a soothsayer's crystal sphere. But no. It was just an ordinary silvery box. I was terribly disappointed. "Isn't there something more to it than that?" I asked, trying to hide my disappointment.

"That's all," said Waite, and he took me behind one of the two big black stands which are the broadcasting apparatus.

"Here are some more," he said, pointing the ray of his flashlight through the protecting iron screen. Down on the floor, under masses of wires and black long things and glass bulbs, I saw a black box seemingly divided into six sections. My spirits rose at the sight of them. Here, I thought, was the real thing. Six of them all together and hidden under an array of imposing radio parts. Down there in the dark, half hidden, the Crystal Oven more nearly fulfilled the image of what they were. "Fascinating," I said. Amory laughed. He incidentally knew that they were. He said they were Crystal Ovens and I was only too eager to believe him. Thinking it over afterwards I am afraid he was only trying to please me. My disappointment at the banal shiny box on the table was probably written on my face and he, seeing it, was quick to erase it by showing me those dark hidden things. Whether it would be technically correct or not, I believe they should be called Crystal Ovens, and not the plain shiny boxes which John was working on.

It is really tremendously instructive to go into the radio headquarters. You will find there guides who are only too happy to show and explain what is there. But if you should, and the guides forget, don't fail to ask to see the Crystal Ovens. Fascinating.

THE BARRIER BULL
July 7, 1934 Issue #8

CHARLES J. V. MURPHY

1.

For the first time since he went out to Advance Base, Admiral Byrd, on Thursday, July 5th missed a radio contact. KFZ called Advance Base for an hour and twenty minutes that day without response. However, emergency schedules had been fixed in the event contact should be lost, and KFZ again went on the air the following day at a fixed time in an attempt to make contact. This fortunately was successful. Admiral Byrd reported that the gasoline engine powering his main set was out of commission—from what cause he did not say—and that he was therefore using his emergency set—a regular trail set. The contact was necessarily brief because of the great difficulty in using this set, and the necessity of conserving batteries. Admiral Byrd reported all's well. With Dr. Poulter he briefly discussed the proposed tractor journey to Advance Base, again repeating his dictum that above everything else the party must be surrounded with every possible safeguard. He expressed the hope that all hands here were well, and that he would be eager to rejoin the expedition.

2.

I understand that this will be the last issue of the BARRIER BULL. I am rather sorry to see it end. It was started with a fine purpose, and Russell and Paine have really worked very hard and with real ability to make it a success.

The reason it is now passing out of existence, I think, is due, in large part, to the same conditions that have made our winter existence more unhappy than we might have reason to expect. At various times I have tried to analyze what these conditions are. I must admit that I have not yet penetrated to the root of it. I do think, however, that in large part it is traceable to a strange, baffling lack of solidarity. One would think that the rigorous nature of our existence, the common objectives, the intimacy of our lives would tend to bring us close together; yet it has tended rather to drive us, or many of us farther and farther apart; and this action has brought a certain amount of bitterness and misunderstanding which I think some of us will never forget. Unfortunate as it is, it is not altogether unusual.

William James, one of America's most distinguished philosophers, in an essay on a homely truth, got quite close to the human factors involved. The essay is entitled "On a Certain Blindness in Human Beings." Let me give a few quotations from that essay:—

> "Now the blindness in human beings is a blindness with which we are all afflicted in regard to the feelings of creatures and people different from ourselves. We are practical beings, each of us with limited functions and duties to perform. Each is bound to feel intensely the importance of his own duties and the significance of the situations that call these forth. But this feeling is in each of us a vital secret, for sympathy in which we vainly look to others. The others are too much absorbed in their own vital secrets to take an interest in ours. Hence the stupidity and injustice of our opinions, so far as they deal with the significance of alien lives. Hence the falsity of our judgements, so far as they presume to decide the absolute value of other persons conditions and trials . . . The spectator's judgement is sure to miss the root of the matter and to possess no truth. The subject judged knows a part of the world of reality which the judging spectator fails to see, knows more while the spectator knows less; and wherever there is conflict of opinion and difference of vision, we are bound to believe that the truer side is the side that feels the more and not the side that feels the less."

Now James wrote that essay on the blindness of human beings as they acted in conditions of life far less rigorous and far less intimate than ours, and here these feelings—these human feelings that things arouse in us are intensified because of necessity, and centered in things that are often trifling, and that are often rooted in petty prejudices and ambitions.

Very likely when trail operations are resumed, and we have larger and more important matters to claim our interest, a large part of the cause of this unhappiness will be removed. I hope so anyway. We have all had a certain blindness, and I hope, as I think all of us do, that the time will come, and come soon, when we shall be able to see things more clearly and more steadily, not in the light of personal bias and personal hopes, but in the light of larger meaning and merit of this enterprise.

EDITORIALS

1.

With our Fourth of July dinner each of us was served with two ounces of brandy. Everyone got the same amount and everyone thoroughly enjoyed it. There was no abuse of it, no criticism, and we were all satisfied. Its effects certainly were not harmful. It would be highly desirable if such a quantity of spirits were served out once a week; preferably on Sunday. It is our opinion that the liquor question would be settled, the general discontent in the camp about liquor would be quieted, no harmful effects would result, and it would solve a problem about which more trouble and mischief has been made than perhaps any other issue in the camp.

2.

Admiral Byrd left Little America last March with the fullest intentions of staying at the Advance Base until October. He left behind a message which was read to the assembled camp. In this he stated that absolutely no attempt should be made to reach him during the winter night, even if his radio schedules should cease. It has been announced to the camp that the Admiral would return earlier than expected due to the pressure of business, and the warm weather which augured an early spring start. The trip has now been temporarily set for the end of this month, and will be made by one, or maybe two tractors.

We believe that taking into account the success of the Expedition and the safety of the men, this trip should be delayed at least until the August moon. This would bring the Admiral back to camp in plenty of time for spring operations. In spite of the warm June weather, the average temperature for the month was three degrees lower than during June 1929. This certainly gives no grounds for the assumption that we shall have an early spring. On reading the records of other Antarctic expeditions, one finds that many attempts have been made to commence operations in September, but each time the explorers were forced to retreat because of the cold with the final start not being made until late October or early November.

It has been announced to the world that a tractor trip is being seriously considered to observe the meteor shower during the early part of August; that it is expected this trip will carry the tractor to the Advance Base, and in this case the Admiral might return to Little America; that by observing the meteors from two points, it would be possible to determine the height of the meteors. This is strictly a scientific expedition, and this trip would be serving one branch of science, but we must consider very seriously what would happen if this trip were not to be successful. By that we mean the loss of a tractor, or if two should make the trip, the loss of two tractors. For the field operations, to be successful and swiftly carried out, the use of three tractors is required. The loss of two tractors would mean the complete wiping out of this program and this would mean failure. The loss of one tractor would be serious and probably call for a curtailment of activities. As the spring program has already been announced, this would also call for a good deal of explanation. It does not seem right to serve one branch of science with the risk of curtailing, or even canceling, all field work this spring.

The trial trip made by the tractor last week was not wholly successful. It was practically impossible to pick up the trail flags with speed. As soon as the tractor crossed the last pressure ridge and gained the high barrier, leaving landmarks behind it, travel was very difficult. The trail to the Advance Base is by no means straight, and in spots there are flags leading in many directions, which might cause considerable confusion. The slight twilight existing for a part of the day at the end of July will be of little or no assistance in spotting the trail.

We strongly advocate that the trip should not be made until the end of August. At that time the sun will be back and the light will be improving every day. This would seem to be the logical time to make the trip. And then it must be realized that only the highest degree of perfection in planning and preparing before departure and in executing in the field can give such an operation even a possibility of success. If a July trip is to be made, we feel that first it should be discussed and voted on by the staff. This brings to mind a similar case at the time of the Pilgrim's landing on the Barrier. Before the rescue operations commenced, the Admiral called a meeting to obtain the opinion of the camp as to the best method of procedure. If he were in Little America now and the identical trip were being planned to the Advance Base, we feel he would do the very same thing.

3.

This is the last issue of the BARRIER BULL. Our supply of mimeograph paper has run out, and further issues would necessarily have to be typewritten as were our first three numbers. We feel that a large part of the interest in the BULL has been for its souvenir value. With only five copies a week, the interest would undoubtedly drop; and then the duties of the dog department are becoming increasingly heavy as the winter night advances. So the editors reluctantly say good-by. We thank all those who have contributed to its success, for such do we consider the BULL. Our purpose throughout has been the general enjoyment of the camp, as well as our own. If we have brought laughs, fostered thought, provided entertainment no matter how mild, we feel the effort has been worthwhile. We reiterate our promise to mimeograph the first three numbers as soon as sufficient mimeograph paper becomes available, thus permitting everyone to have a complete set of eight numbers.

Goodby and many thanks for your co-operation.

SKOOKUM

"Stink" is an unpleasant word. It has nasty connotations about it. Its use is usually taboo among the gentle, still, it is applicable, decidedly so, to the odor of melting and burning blubber. Of all unpleasant, nauseating and overwhelming smells, blubber in the burning state is probably the worst. Those who have lived only in the sweet contentment of the radio shack, or the Administration Building, or the Cow Barn, can scarcely realize the overpowering pungence of the stink in the seal chopping house. There, seal blubber is being melted down, and likewise burned, to mix with the dog pemmican for the trail parties next summer. The pemmican in its present form is deficient in fat. Hence the necessity of further addition of fat.

In a stove made from a fifty five gallon gasoline drum and a smaller twenty gallon drum, you who have sufficient interest to take in the smell and incidentally see how it works, will see bubble burning in the bottom and blubber smoking in the top. Oil, you will observe, has spilled over and is slowly running down the sides of the barrel stove and down the stove pipe. You no doubt believe such an occurrence should be avoided at all costs, for the smoke and acrid odor from the slopped oil all but drives your breath away. The unfortunate dog driver tending the stove at the time will laugh at your suggestion and tell you to throw some more blubber into the pot. Sure— Gingerly lifting the lid, the lid handle is smeared as is everything else with oil, you toss a piece in. A fantastic crackling and sputtering from the pot— That's not hard, you say to yourself. Where is the catch?

The interested dogman eyes you, eyes the pot and grins. That smile no doubt provokes you. But Wait. The pot is becoming agitated. The piece of blubber you tossed in does not agree with it somehow. "She's going to vomit," says the dogman. True enough. The seething pot of boiling oil rises high and higher toward the top rim. You, no doubt want to do something. It's going to overflow. "Do something," you yell at the dogman. The dogman heard you but he's out chasing an inquisitive pup. The oil rises high and higher. You seize a stick and stir. That does not help. The oil is now at a crucial level. Can't something be done? The oil oozes over the rim, down into the top of the stove and down the stovepipe. It's done. A putrid, smarting stink crawls up into your nose, into your eyes. You cough. Your eyes water and you duck for the door. The dogman returns and throws another piece in. You have probably had enough. Groping your way through the smoke and steam, falling perhaps over a couple of puppies, you reach the door. Looking back through the fog and steam the dogman is still there. He is throwing more blubber into the pot. Enough—and you dash back to the radio shack, the Administration Building, or the Cowbarn.

Appendix 5

Logistics Planning from Mile 173 to Mile 445.5, *Thorne Glacier, and Return to Little America*

On six diary pages, Paine, in consultation with Dick Russell, calculated the logistics for reorganization of the trail parties. The first four pages were written on November 5 at Mile 173, the last two pages, respectively, on November 13 at Mile 293 and November 23 at Mountain Base, Mile 445.5. Food, dogs, load, and all items needed for their mission and their survival are planned by milepost location. The start point for the plans for the Geological Party and their Supporting Party begin at Mile 173, where the tractors and the Plateau Party turned east instead of continuing south. (For convenience, Paine called Mile 173, "Mile 175" in his notes.)

On pages 1 and 2, Paine detailed the plan for the Geological Party leaving Mile 175 heading south to the base of the Queen Maud Mountains, estimated at Mile 450 (later corrected to Mile 445.5, the site of "Mountain Base"), and then determined the plan for their return from that point back to Little America. Page 3 planned the caches that the Supporting Party would place leaving Mile 175, traveling to Mile 300, and then returning to Little America. Page 4 inventoried the supplies in the possession of the Geological Party leaving Mile 175. Page 5 planned the supply depots and travel times leaving Mile 293 to their trip to Mountain Base. Finally, on page 6, Paine determined the supplies needed for their fieldwork in the Queen Maud Mountains including emergency supplies and the laying of a depot at Mile 40 on the 120-mile long glacier, and including their return to Mountain Base after finding their southernmost point. The times and rations for their seven-hundred-mile journey back to Little America were previously calculated on page 2. Throughout the journey, Paine refers to these calculations in his narration. (Paine Antarctic Collection)

Reorganization of trail parties to south—
Plan for Adv. Party & supporting Party—
Nov. 5th

Quinn Blackburn
C.E. Paine   } Adv Party
R Russell

Finn Ronne   } supporting Party—
albert Californ

Leaving 135 mile depot, 193 to be exact—
Main Adv Party—
30 days to mts—3 teams — 810 lbs dog food.
25 days in field—2teams   675 lbs dog food
8 days return to 3 00—2 teams—216 lbs. dy food
                                    1701 lbs dog food—

Two dog teams killed— one at 3 00, one at
mts— 9 dop at mts cached for return—
equivalent of 110 lbs — leaving 1591 lbs
dog food to carry out program—

Russell carries   868 lbs dog food.
Paine   carries   469
Blackburn carries 366.

Supporting Party carries to be carried intact to 300,
521 lbs dog food — a total of 1724 lbs of

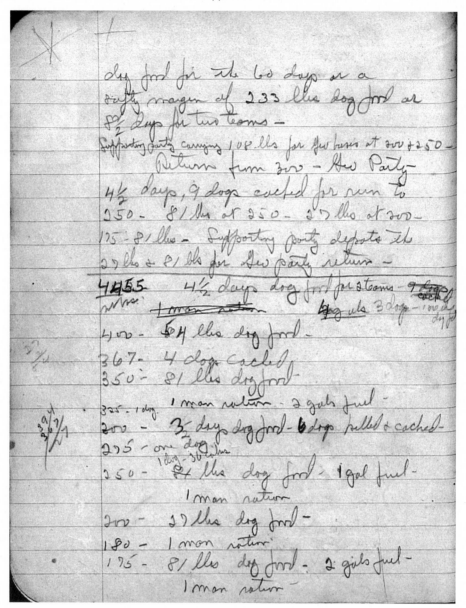

dog food for the 60 days or a
safety margin of 233 lbs dog food or
8½ days for two teams –
Supporting party carrying 108 lbs for few turns at 300 ÷ 250 –
        Return from 300 – few Party –
4½ days, 9 dogs cached for run to
250 – 81 lbs at 250 – 27 lbs at 300 –
175 – 81 lbs – Supporting party deposits the
27 lbs & 81 lbs for few party return –
_____
4155   4½ days dog food for 3 teams – 9 dogs
                                                       cached
                            big als 3 dogs – 100 als
                                                       dog food
400 – 54 lbs dog food –
367 – 4 dogs cached
350 – 81 lbs dog food
325 – 1 dog 1 man return – 2 gals fuel –
300 – 3 day dog food – 6 dogs pulled & cached –
275 – one dog
250 – 1 dog – 36 lbs 81 lbs dog food – 1 gal fuel –
            1 man return
300 – 27 lbs dog food –
180 – 1 man return
175 – 81 lbs dog food – 2 gals fuel –
            1 man return –

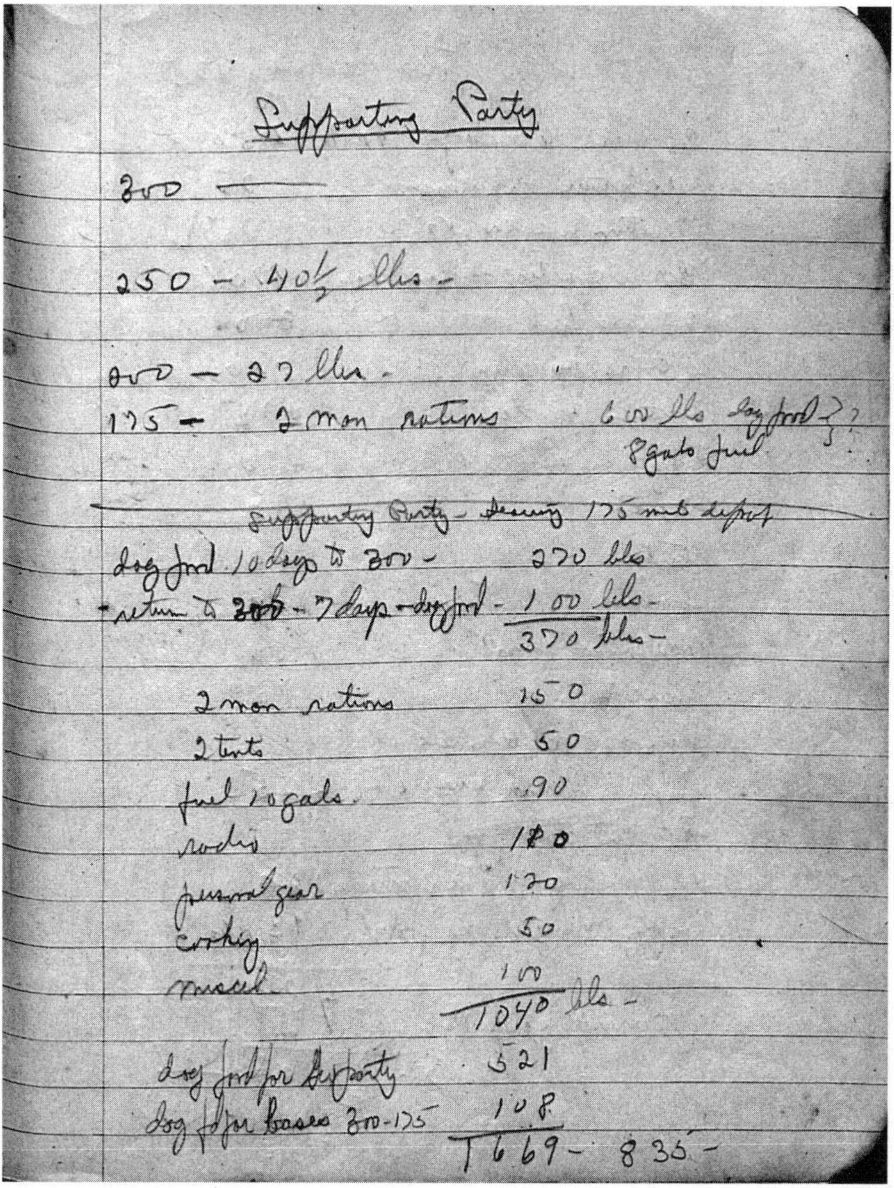

<u>Supporting Party</u>

300 ――――

250 – 40½ lbs –

800 – 87 lbs –
175 –   2 man rations   6 00 lbs dog food ? ?
                                          8 gals fuel

――――――   Supporting Party – leaving 175 mile depot

dog food 10 days to 300 –   270 lbs
– return to 300 – 7 days – dog food – 1 00 lbs –
                                     370 lbs –

    2 man rations   15 0
    2 tents   50
    fuel 10 gals.   90
    radio   180
    personal gear   120
    cooking   50
    rescue   100
                          1040 lbs –

dog food for Sup party   521
dog f for bases 300-125 108
                    T 6 69 – 8 35 –

22
8
7/6   Geo Ply leaving 125

3 men   60 days   brats   450

1 ration emergency   75

1 ration to cache at 3550   25

3 men clothes, sleeping bag   175

22 gals fuel.   200

3 teams 30 days   810

2 teams 25 days   675

2 dog teams 4 wks 125   270

radio   110

tents   60

cooking   50

navigation & nav   100

misc   75

flags 8 oz, 6 panels -

~~days~~   Pens + hinges - 225

~~8 days extra food~~

10 days dog food for 8 extra dp 180

safety margin dog food   13 lbs.

carried by sup Pty.
      3483
      521
3) 29 62) 987
      27
      26
      24
      22

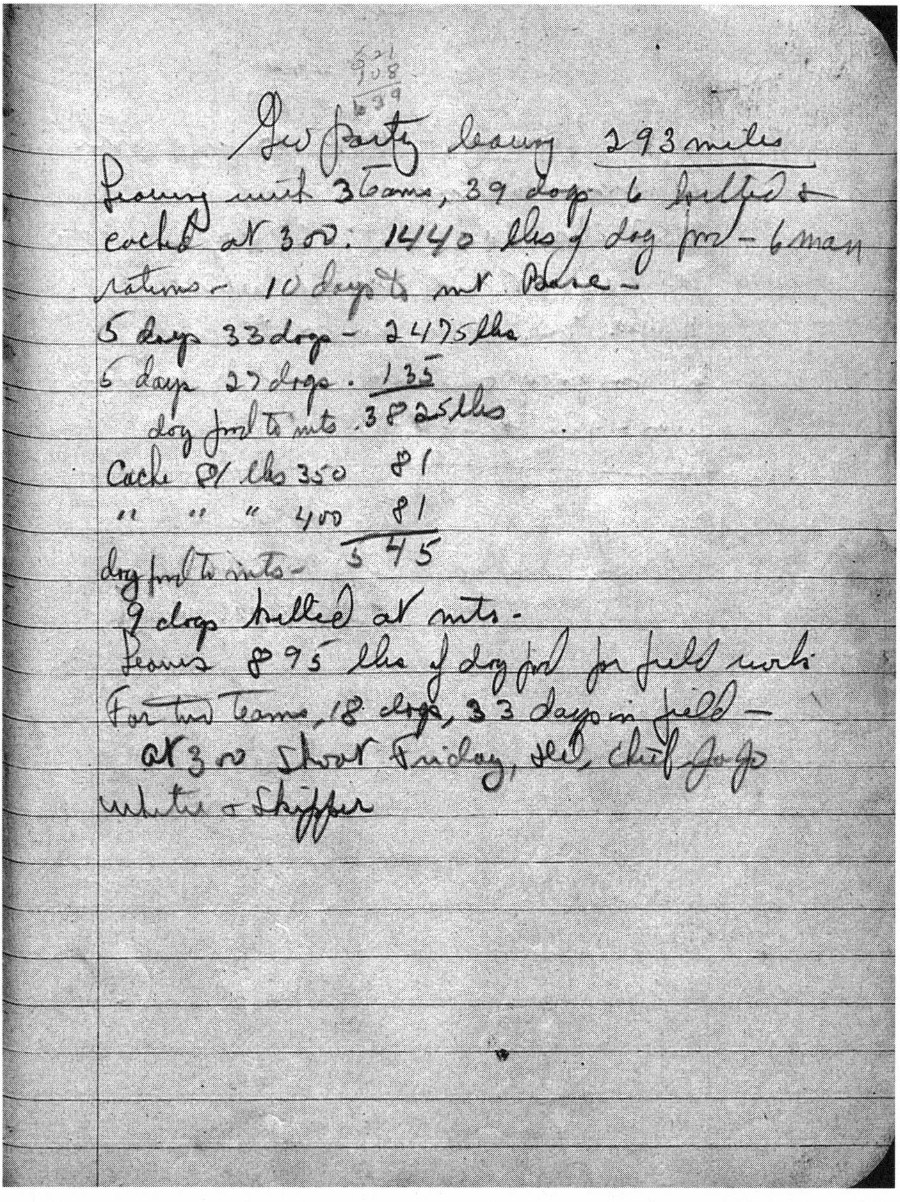

521
908
699

Geo party leaving 293 miles
Leaving with 3 teams, 39 dogs 6 pulled &
cached at 3.0: 1440 lbs of dog food — 6 man
rations — 10 days to mt. Base —
5 days 33 dogs — 2475 lbs
6 days 27 dogs · 135
      dog food to mts 3825 lbs
Cache 81 lbs 350   81
  "   "   " 400   81
                    5 75
dog food to mts — 5 75
9 dogs killed at mts.
Leaves 895 lbs of dog food for field work
For two teams, 18 dogs, 33 days in field —
   at 3.0 shoot Friday, etc, chief dogs
white & Skipper

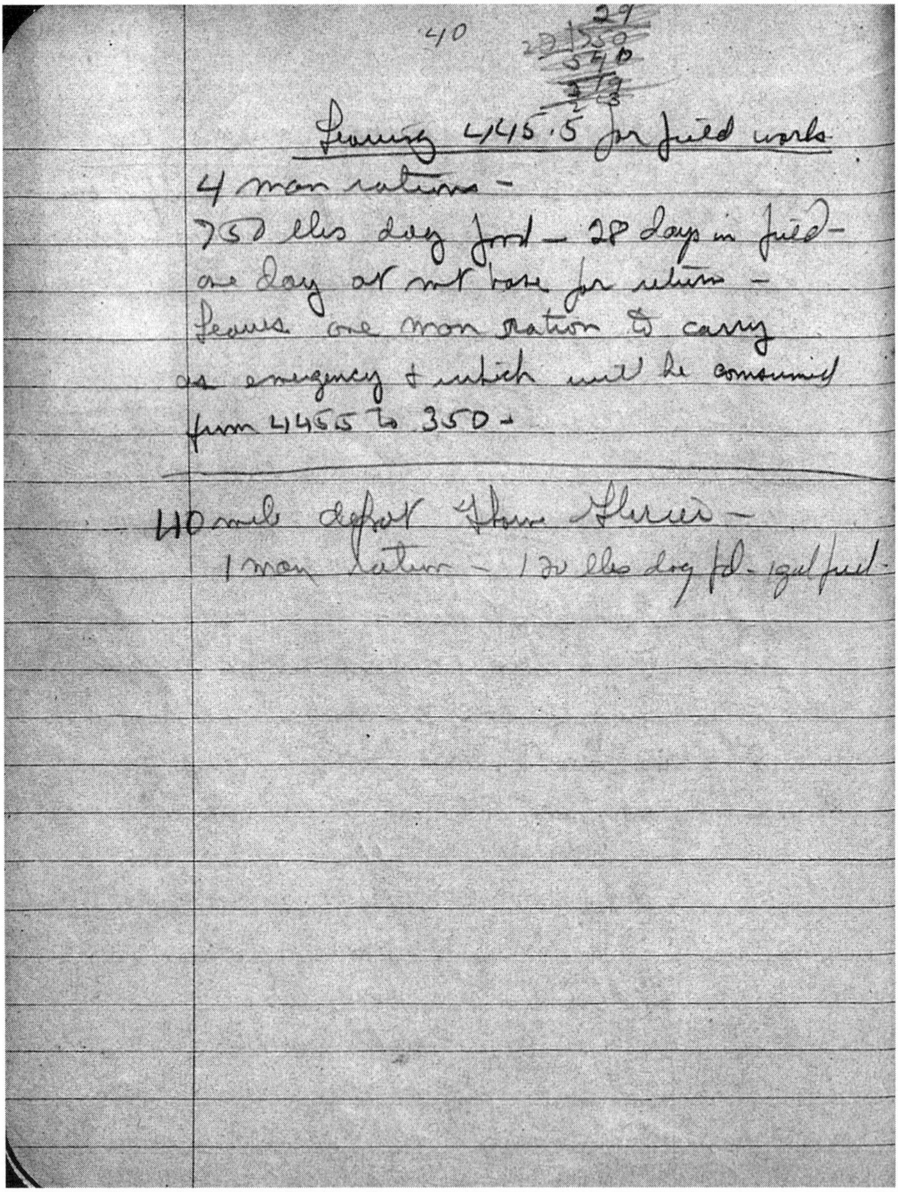

40   20) 550

Leaving 445.5 for field work

4 man rations –
750 lbs dog food – 28 days in field –
one day at met base for return –
Leaves one man ration to carry
as emergency & which will be consumed
from 445.5 to 350 –

110 mile depot from Glacier –
1 man ration – 130 lbs dog fd – 1 gal fuel –

Appendix 6

Navigation and Triangulation Reports:
Summer Journey to the Queen Maud Range

Stuart Paine, the navigator for the Geological Party, compiled his observations and notes into a memorandum to Admiral Byrd: "Navigation Report of the Queen Maud Geological Party," dated July 6, 1935. This report includes routes and positions to the Queen Maud Range as well as the positions of points on the previously unexplored Thorne Glacier. The three-page report includes positions, a description of procedures used, and sources for adjusting observations so that correct positions could be calculated. Paine mentions tables from A. A. Ageton, Nathaniel Bowditch, and Daniel L. Hazard. Paine also noted that the party's schedule was rushed because of the predicted arrival of the ships at the Bay of Whales. Paine's notes on the triangulated positions on Thorne Glacier were typed into a thirty-page memorandum and submitted to Byrd with his July 1935 memorandum. The fourth page in this appendix illustrates one page from the field notes recorded as Paine and Quin Blackburn developed data with which to derive the initial map of Thorne Glacier, now known as Scott Glacier. This map covers the previously unexplored area between Supporting Party Mountain and their discovery of Mount Howe, the southernmost geographic feature. In the subsequent document, the cartographer for Byrd's first and second Antarctic expeditions, Commander Harold E. Saunders, USN (Ret.), asked Paine, in a May 1937 letter, questions regarding his memorandum to Admiral Byrd and the related field notes (Paine Antarctic Collection).

The difficulty of assessing distance and position, especially under pressure of time, distortion of compass readings and light that interfered with accurate line of sight, and of course frequent poor weather, are illustrated by this account: Byrd had a whole chapter at the end of *Discovery* discussing accuracy problems in obtaining mapping data under the conditions experienced by the three field parties. After the expedition, potential field data errors were examined, resolved, and recorded by the navigators, surveyors, and cartographers into useable data. With twenty-first-century technology, slightly different positions and distances may be known.

Additional confusion in tracing the history of this period is caused by the various authors and historians neglecting to identify whether statute or nautical miles are being discussed. This factor accounts for numerous inconsistencies in historical accounts.

Memo to R.E.Byrd

July 6,1935
Durham,N.H.

NAVIGATION REPORT
OF
QUEEN MAUD GEOLOGICAL PARTY
Oct.16,1934-Jan.11,1935

Charts, routes and positions south to 150 miles south as
the trail was laid by the Fall Depot-Laying Southern Party
were submitted to Rawson and Black during the winter. I assume
they are in your hands.
Position of Advance base as determined by Ad. Byrd was
Lat. 80* 07'S Long 163* 52'W
Running DR South from this known position;

125 mile depot-- Lat. 80* 32.5'S Long 163* 43'W

150 mile depot-- Lat 80* 50'S Long 161* 52'W

Bramhall obtained Fix for 152 miles. I do not have
it with me.

Course 152 miles to 155 miles------150* True
  "   155 miles to 159½ miles------ 158* True
  "   159½ miles to 167.3 miles---- 180* True
  "   167.3 miles to 182.4 Miles-- 180* True

From our southing of 182.4 miles we were forced to return
to assist the tractors and we returned to about 168 miles.
Tractors returned to 159.5 miles beacon and steered true
course from there 135* for 12.5 miles to 173 miles depot.

Position of 173 miles depot (Bramhall) 161* 05'W 81* 09.6'S

173 miles to 175.5 miles True course---135*
175.5 miles to 180 miles True course-- 180*

D.R. 180 miles beacon-- Lat 81* 15.8'S Long 160* 53'W

  "   200 miles depot-- Lat 81* 34.6'S Long 160' 08'W

  "   225 miles Depot-- Lat 81* 56.4'S Long 159* 15'W

Fix 250 mile depot   Lat 82* 22.6'S Long 158* 39'W

D.R. 275 Mile Depot   Lat 82* 46.3'S Long 157* 32'W

  DR 293 mile beacon (Supporting Party turned back)
                              Lat 83*02.8'S
                              Long 156* 30'W

D.R.300 mile depot Lat 83*09'S Long 157* 06'W

2

D.R. 325 Mile Depot-- Lat 83* 32.8' Long I54* 55'W

" 350 Mile Depot Lat 83* 56.5'S Long I53* 40'W
   A distinct rise in the Shelf Ice occured about one
   mile to the east of 350 mile depot and was undoubtedly
   the cause of the severe crevassed area between 350miles
   and 357 miles.

Course(true) through crevasses- Around 225

Ob.Lat. at 354.7 miles(in center of crevasses area) 83* 56.8'S

Course 357 miles to 366.8 miles-- I80 true

Obs. Position 366.8 miles Lat 84* IO.5'S Long I54* 50'W

D.R. 375 mile depot-- Lat 84* I9.2S Long I54* 50'W

" 400 mile Depot-- Lat 84*40'S Long I52* 4I8W

Obs. Position 4I2.5 mile beacon-- Lat 84* 46'S Long I50* 45'W

Obs. Position Mountain Base Lat. 85* I6.2¦S Long I48* 46'W

Obs. Position Camp at Supporting Party Mountain   40
                        Lat 85* 27'S Long I47* ₿₿'W

            Gould's Position of his camp as given in his note
          recovered from the summit of Supporting Party Mt.
                     Lat 85* 25' I7" Long I47* 55'W
          Summit of Sup.Party Mt. was about one mile south
            of our camp.
                        Leverett
       Turning to the Wa/stward we ascended the Thorne Glacier
     after crossing the mouth of the ##### and established
     triangulation Station# I at Mt. Weaver. No triangulation
     was done on the way up. Route followed on the ascent the
     same as on the descent. Calculation of positions and
     azmuths of marks enclosed with this report.

Ob. Position Camp at Mt. Weaver--- Lat 86* 57.5'S Long I52* 20'W
            True Azmuth of Mark 34* 30.5'

##. Position Station #2 --- Lat 86* 52.8'S Long I5I* 05'W
            Easterly variation I22* 33.3'

Ob. Position Station #3 Lat 86* 38.2'S Long I50* 20'W
            True Azmuth of Mark-- 352* 40.3'

D.R. Position Sta. #4 86* 29'S Long I48* 40'W
            True Azmuth of Mark-- 328* 38.5'

Ob. Position Sta. #5 Lat 86* 24.5' Long I48* 30'W
            True Azmuth of Mark 336* I9'

3

D.R. Position #6 Lat 86* 12.2'S Long 150* 18'W
   True Azmuth of Mark 344* 57'

Ob. ⌀⌀⌀⌀ Position #7-- Lat 86* 10S Long 150* 35'W
   True Azmuth of Mark 326* 44.3'

Ob. Position Sta. #8 -- Lat 86* 08'S Long 150* 50'W
   True Azmuth of Mark 23* 52' (transit set to this)
   All bearings at this station are true

Ob. Position Sta.# 9 Lat 86* 05'S Long 150* 55'W
   True Azmuth of Mark 259* 02.8'

Best Position Station #10-- Lat 86* 01.8' Long 152* 52'
   True Azmuth of Mark 346* 11.2'

D.R. Sta.#11-- Lat 86*00 Long 153* 10'
   True Azmuth of Mark 359* 48.8'

Ob. Position Sta.# 12--Lat 85* 49.5' Long 150* 55'
   True Azmuth of Mark 343* 45.3'

Ob. Position Sta. #13-- Lat 85* 38.8'S Long 152* 05'W
   True Azmuth of Mark 185* 04'

Ob. Position Sta.#14-Durham Point-- Lat 85* 30.5'S Long 151*15½W
   True Azmuth of Mark 278* 32.6'

These positions were worked out by the tables of Ageton.
For the correction of the observed altitudes tables in Bowditch
were used. The factors for the correction to mean refraction
for height above sea level were taken from Table 2 in" Directions
for Magnetic Measurements" by Daniel L. Hazard. This is published
by the U.S.Department of Commerce, Coast and Geodetic Survey.
     Several of the Stations may have an error in their pos-
itions. Several of the Azmuth calculations for the same
station have a considerable discrepancy. We were rushed for
time, and we must make the best of the data on hand.
     Observations for all stations were made by Quin Black-
burn with myself recording. Our watch times were accurated to
within a second. We checked our watch once a day and sometimes
twice from radio time signals sent out in the United States.
     The map I enclose was made by R.B.Black and is a replotting
of Positions worked out in the field.

     Following out the wishes of Ad. Byrd, all names of
mountains and glaciers are ommitted except those we named in the
field and left notes in cairns upon them(Mt. Weaver, Durham ##
Point,) and those Admiral Byrd has consented to let us
retain. For purposes of the triangulation work we named
everything. In copying the survey notes we took only the first
three letters of the names except in the above cases.
     Any additional data needed please do not hesitate to
call upon me.

                         Respectfully,

                              Stuart D. Paine

(20)

along escarpment spur ridges to NE   southeast of highest point escarpment face
falls off to and merges with glacier

Beyond Mt Com black nunatak	53° 37'	
vert ang	0° 55'	
Adjacent another nunatak	53° 56'	
vert ang	0° 39'	
On escarpment Mt Ril ?	83° 46'	
vert ang	0° 53'	
Between Com and Mai most westerly of group	59° 21'	
vert ang	1° 10'	
westerly end Depot Mt 3 miles off	57° 11'	
summit	85° 13'	
vert ang	10° 46'	

Peaks connected by ridge enclosing Franklin ampitheatre Depot Mt east to west
trending ridge notch in ridge continuing to east   106° 23'

Mt Com sharply rounded summit vertically jointed 3 miles off	125° 25'	
vert ang	12° 36'	
to east notch	135° 30'	
	6° 14'	
Mt Col Broad peak triangular shaped sharp spine on summit	142° 52'	
4 miles away vert ang	9° 32'	

On flanks of last several ridges with minor peaks To NE long ridge bearing
several minor peaks

At head of this ampitheater are visible 3 roughly triangular peaks mostly snow
covered the they show bare rock near summits

Mt Bob 5 miles off 1st peak to SW	171° 11'	
vert ang	4° 40'	
Mt Mon 6 miles away most northerly	179° 01'	
vert ang	4° 19'	
Mt Fly 5.5 miles middle one	176° 20'	
vert ang	4° 11'	

Continuing to NW coming around basin long ridge high point on south almost all
snow covered except rock on south 6 miles Mt Hen   184° 21'
           vert ang   5° 27'

Mt Rose Main organ pipe huge double peak on NE side of ampitheatre 4 miles

East summit	203° 00'	
	8° 58'	
West summit	206° 45'	
	10° 52'	
southeast base	195° 14'	
SW end of Bruce Harkness right	29° 57'	
summit right	47° 10'	
vert angle	11° 18'	angles to right
Double peak to north sharp spine on rounded top	66° 20'	
Mt Ver	vert ang 9° 16'	
Mt Scu sharp double peak west peak	71° 16'	
vert ang	12° 57'	
east peak	75° 58'	
vert ang	13° 31'	
Mt Abe in front of Scu summit	77° 40'	
vert angle	12° 10'	
west base	52° 16'	
east base	90° 25'	

Between Scu and organ pipes a pass leading to Thorne

Mt Per summit 96° 00'		Mt Cor	102° 22'	
vert ang 6° 00			8° 41'	Mt Mur 105° 52'
Mt Sipm 99° 40'		Mt Sta	108° 58'	11° 42'
7° 20'			11° 23'	

U.S. EXPERIMENTAL MODEL BASIN

NAVY YARD, WASHINGTON, D.C.

11 May 1937.

Mr. Stuart D. Paine,
Durham, New Hampshire.

Dear Paine:-

I have completed the task of converting all the bearing angles in your triangulation notes to true bearings, measured to the right from north, all the way up to 360° (navy style). I find a number of items, however, upon which I would like additional information, as follows:-

(1) In your memo of 6 July 1935 to Admiral Byrd, page 1, the position of Advance Base was changed by Rawson (when he was here in 1935) to 80° 07.5 S. and 163° 55' W. This is only a slight change but it is, I assume, in agreement with the best known position. Please check me on this.

(2) On page 1 of the same memo, the longitude of the 173-Mile depot (from Bramhall) is somewhat blurred. Is it 161° 05' W. or 161° 15' W?

(3) On page 2, the longitude of the 400-Mile depot is given as 152° 41' W. Is this correct?

(4) I assume that the true azimuths of the marks for the various triangulation stations on pages 2 and 3 of your memo of 6 July supersede those given subsequently in the triangulation notes, where differences occur. Is this correct?

(5) On page 3 of your memo, I cannot be sure whether the observed position of Sta. 7 is in Lat. 86° 10' S. or 86° 10.8 S. Which is correct?

(6) On the first page of the triangulation notes (not numbered) headed by the entry "December 8, 1934, Camp Innes-Taylor, Mt. Weaver," it states that the index error (on the vertical scale, I assume) was minus 2 minutes, and that the

-3-

(10) On page (10), Station 5, the azimuth of the
south summit of Mt. Content Morse is given as 25° 20',
whereas I think it should be 45° 20', since the azimuth of
the north summit is given as 42° 38', measured to the right
of the mark. Please look this up.

(11) On page (29), Station 14, middle of the page,
there is an entry "Northeast summit Durham mountain R 243° 52',
(and under it) angle mile to summit 12° 24'." Does the latter
mean <u>vertical</u> angle, and that it was a mile to the summit
from the point where the observations were made?

(12) On page (29), extreme bottom of the page, under
"OBSERVATIONS FROM SUMMIT OF MT. DURHAM," you have added
the magnetic variation in pencil. I make it out as
117° 39.5 E.; is this correct?

(13) Am I correct in assuming that your sledge meter
registered nautical miles, and that all the "miles" in your
triangulation notes are nautical miles?

(14) I assume that the various Zeiss and Leica photographs were taken from various places on the ridge at the
top of Mt. Weaver. Can you tell me approximately how large
an area would cover all the positions from which you took
photographs at the <u>top</u> (not on the way up or down)? If you
took them from one <u>spot</u>, was it at the NE or SW end of the
ridge?

          To save yourself time and trouble, you may, if
you like, simply add your comments to the attached white
copy of this letter and return the copy to me.

                              Thanks,

                              H. E. Saunders.

Bibliography

Notes on Archival Sources

Stuart Paine's Antarctic diaries, photographs, letters, memorandums, and other papers form the backbone of this volume. These unique materials are held in the Paine Antarctic Collection, currently in possession of the Paine family. Other materials in the Paine Antarctic Collection and referenced in this volume include Paine's 1935 writings "The Ascent of Mt. Weaver" and "Daily Decrease of Weight on 90 Day Journey"; a memo from Stuart Paine to R. E. Byrd, dated July 6, 1935, entitled "Navigation Report of Queen Maud Geological Party"; and a thirty-page report beginning December 8, 1934, at Camp Innes-Taylor, Mount Weaver, that details the triangulation readings and plotted positions of features seen from Mount Weaver or located on the Thorne Glacier; a May 11, 1937, letter from H. E. Saunders, USN, to Stuart D. Paine; and other materials. Also held are the eight issues of the *Barrier Bull*, the 1934 periodical that was coedited by Stuart D. Paine and Richard Russell; as of 2006, one noncirculating set is available at the University of New Hampshire.

In addition, background for the narrative in the present volume was supplemented through the courtesy of other entities. Ohio State University's Byrd Polar Research Center Archival Program (BPRCAP) provided access to many valuable sources. Among these materials are Olin Stancliff's memoir, written in 1982, "My Life and Good Times," and the eighteen issues of the *Little America Times*, written by August Howard and covering the period between December 27, 1933, and May 31, 1935. The latter, a U.S.-based periodical, was a monthly report on the activities of the Second Byrd Expedition and also the Lincoln Ellsworth Expedition of the same period. Also held in the BPRCAP collection are important photographs and critical maps that were reproduced here or provided a basis for new maps developed for this work. They include the map of the summer field operations, the map of Thorne Glacier, the map of the ships' movements, and the General Foods map. Acknowledgment also goes to the National Geographic Society and General Foods, now Kraft Foods, for their research assistance regarding these maps. Another helpful resource held by the Ohio State University's Goldthwait Polar Library, "The Byrd Book," compiled by Marylouise Burandt (Ethington). It is a collection of fragile scrapbooks created in Barrington, Illinois, and presented to Admiral Byrd upon his return. They contain news clippings, transcribed radio broadcasts, and pictures of Admiral Byrd's adventures.

Additionally, the 1935 film *Discovery,* by Richard E. Byrd, is housed in the National Archives in its Moving Images: Admiral Richard E. Byrd Collection, 1926–1935, and located in the Motion Picture, Sound and Video Records LICON, Special Media Archives Services Division (NWCS-M) at the National Archives at College Park (ARC id. 89109, 200.382, reels 1–5 and 6–10.

Scholars wishing more information about these collections may contact the Paine family through the publisher, the Ohio State University (Goldthwait Polar Library and the Byrd Polar Research Collection), and the National Archives.

Published Sources

Amundsen, Roald. *The South Pole.* 1912. Trans. A. G. Chater. New York: Barnes and Noble, 1976.

Behrendt, John C. *Innocents on the Ice: A Memoir of Antarctic Exploration, 1957.* Niwot: University Press of Colorado, 1998.

Byrd, Richard Evelyn. *Alone.* New York: G. P. Putnam's Sons, 1938.

———. *Discovery: The Story of the Second Byrd Antarctic Expedition.* New York: G. P. Putnam's Sons, 1935.

———. "Exploring the Ice Age in Antarctica." *National Geographic Magazine* 58, no. 4 (October 1935): 399–475.

———. *Little America: Aerial Exploration in the Antarctic, the Flight to the South Pole.* New York: G. P. Putnam's Sons, 1930.

Goerler, Raimund E., ed. *To the Pole: The Diary and Notebook of Richard E. Byrd, 1925–1927.* Columbus: Ohio State University Press, 1998.

Gould, Laurence McKinley. *Cold: The Record of an Antarctic Sledge Journey.* New York: Brewer, Warren & Putnam, 1931.

Hill, Joe, Jr., and Ola Davis Hill. *In Little America with Byrd: Based upon Experiences of the Fifty-six Men of the Second Antarctic Expedition.* Boston: Ginn, 1937.

Hoyt, Edwin P. *The Last Explorer: The Adventures of Admiral Byrd.* New York: John Day, 1968.

Owen, Russell. *South of the Sun.* New York: John Day, 1934.

Passel, Charles F. *Ice: The Antarctic Diary of Charles F. Passel.* Ed. T. H. Baughman. Lubbock: Texas Tech University Press, 1995.

Poulter, Thomas C. *The Winter Night Trip to Advance Base: Byrd Antarctic Expedition II, 1933–35.* [Menlo Park, Calif.]: Thomas C. Poulter, 1973.

Ronne, Captain Finn. *Antarctica, My Destiny: A Personal History by the Last of the Great Polar Explorers.* New York: Hastings House Publishers, 1979.

"The Society Honors Byrd Antarctic Expedition." *National Geographic Magazine* 68, no. 1 (July 1935): 107–16.

Walden, Jane Brevoort, and Stuart D. L. Paine. *The Long Whip: The Story of a Great Husky.* New York: G. P. Putnam's Sons, 1936.

Index

Whitie (dog), 190
Wilcox (dog), 124
Wildlife: Byrd's policy toward, 38*n18*
Winches, 45, 46*n14*
Wind chill, 94*n21*
Wind speed, 84*n6*
Winter (dog), 62*n2*, 65, *71*, 175, 177, 178
Winter Party. *See* "Ice Party"
With Byrd at the South Pole (film of the
    First Expedition), xv
Wolf (dog), 73

Wolverine fur, 288
Wonalancet, New Hampshire, 7, 10
World War II, 280
Wyatt Earp (ship), 56*n34*, 61

Yeoman. *See* Wade, F. Alton
Young, H. R. ("Bob" or "Hal"), 94*n22*, 128,
    129, 137, 139, 161

Zuhn, Arthur A., 94*n22*, 270